THE JAM

THE DAY I WAS THERE

Neil Cossar & Richard Houghton

THIS DAY IN MUSIC BOOKS

www.thisdayinmusic.com

A catalogue record for this book is available from the British Library.

ISBN: 978-1-9161156-7-5

Front and back cover concept by Liz Sanchez
Cover design by Oliver Keen
Book design by Gary Bishop

Printed in the UK by Sound Performance

THIS DAY IN MUSIC BOOKS

This Day In Music Books
2B Vantage Park
Washingley Road
Huntingdon
PE29 6SR

www.thisdayinmusic.com

Exclusive Distributors:
Music Sales Limited
14/15 Berners St
London
W1T 3JL

The JAM

polydor

'There are loads of people who I've met over the course of time who have told me tales of when they were 12, 13 coming to see The Jam and meeting us backstage, or outside a gig or talking to my old man and telling little stories. I think it's really brilliant, it doesn't swell my head it just makes me feel privileged and proud to be part of this thing'

Paul Weller

13 year old Jam fan Neil Crud meets his idol Paul Weller at Deeside Leisure Centre, North Wales on 29 November 1979 (photo by Chris Birchall)

Contents

FOREWORD

Rick Buckler with his treasured MG

Unlike many other bands we had a very close connection with our fans. We did not like a 'them and us' scenario. This parallel came about when we first moved out from the club gigs around Woking and the surrounding area to concentrate on the London scene, hoping to attract our own audience with our own songs and break away from playing covers in venues that had become less and less inspiring for us. The clubs had served us well for five years, with work every Friday, Saturday and Sunday night. We had grown in confidence and skill in our playing, drawing from our influences and experiences, in what was at times a challenging audience to please. We yearned to play to people of our own age and persuasion, so it was time to move on. The London scene beckoned, the pay was less and at times nothing all, so John Weller, who had been successful in securing our shows around Woking, was not altogether convinced that this was the right thing to do. Some of the venues would book two bands, hedging their bets just in case they were let down. Joe Strummer's 101'ers were the preferred act over us at one venue. Disappointing for us, as we had to just turn round and come home without a gig that night.

The move to London proved to be good for us creatively, Paul finding his feet as one of the greatest songwriters of that era. Our set was made up from more of our own material now with only a few choice rock and roll covers thrown in. The *In The City* album reflects exactly what we were like in those days, finished in less than a fortnight shortly after being signed to Polydor Records and recorded mostly 'live' in the studio. Our fast pace and energy soon gained us a reputation and growing fan base in the very lively London pub rock scene and emerging punk culture that was quickly to spread throughout the country and the world.

I suppose that an unsigned band attracting fans in the afternoon, watching us set up and then listening to a few songs seems unremarkable. But as we gained our own following in such places as The Red Cow, The Nashville Rooms, The Hope and Anchor, Upstairs at Ronnie Scott's and the 100 Club, to mention just a few, the word soon got out that at around four or five o'clock was a good time to arrive at the venue as we would always meet and chat with anyone that was into what we were doing. We soon got to know many of our fans, as they started to venture to more and more of our shows further out of London, with the habit of being let in at the sound check becoming very much the norm, very much to the annoyance of some of the larger venues and promoters. If you did not have a ticket for the night, many would work their way in during the afternoon and find somewhere to hide until the doors were officially opened in the evening. A lot of venues soon had to search their venues for stowaways after sound checks. A constant game of hide and seek which I suspect the fans were more successful at.

Each show for me flew past in a blink. Once the nerves from the first number were shaken off it seemed to accelerate furiously and I was absolutely immersed in the noise. Although we did release live albums and they capture the sound from the first song to the last encore, hinting at the atmosphere, they do not give much of an insight into the whole experience fans speak of - travelling to the show, the anticipation and the people met. Each has a different story to tell.

After the shows we would continue to come out and meet anyone who stayed behind, sign single covers or anything the fans had with them. Pound notes became a favourite, especially after the release of *Sound Affects* with 'Pretty Green'. So a strong bond was formed between us - they were ours and we were theirs. At that time we were aware that the band was nothing without the support of the fans, coming to the shows and buying the records. We loved to play live to people who I feel loved us. On one occasion, at the Brighton Conference Centre, I was dawdling around when we were making our way from the Grand Hotel next door for the sound check. There was a secret exit from the hotel into the venue and as I fell behind I found myself shut out of the venue by some fire doors. I banged on the doors for a short while but soon realised there was nothing to do but go back the way I came into the hotel and round to the front entrance of the Conference Centre. As I emerged from the hotel, a few people recognised me and at first just followed behind but by the time I was standing outside the main entrance the crowd had grown quite large. I managed to get the attention of someone inside the foyer but they kept saying through the glass doors that the venue was not open yet. The shouting from the crowd grew louder. They soon opened the door a little and I tried to explain that I was in the band that was playing that night. 'Do you have a ticket? And in any case I can't let you in until show time.' The crowd of fans behind me, almost with one voice, shouted, 'There won't be a show if you don't let him in.' This was persuasion enough to gain my entrance and certainly an occasion when I was glad to be amongst friends.

A lot of fans would travel far from their hometown and follow us around on tour, some as far away as America. Where a few guys had followed us across the States, only to run out of funds and could not pay for hotels or even raise the means to get back home from Los Angeles, we let them stay in our hotel and simply had to buy them tickets home. Whenever I get the chance to speak to any of the fans from those days, the story is always of great memories. 'Soundtrack of my life' is often said. Playing live was a big part of what we were, and if you never saw us play I hope these stories will give you an idea of the friendships that were formed amongst band and fans alike and which have, along with the music, lasted the test of time. Some fans met their future wives or husbands at the shows. We were lucky in many ways signing with Polydor. They had some very good people with them, understanding the band's needs despite, at times, a differing agenda. With a welcome but constant workload, they guided and directed us.

Maybe it was this overwhelming schedule of shows and recordings that led to our early burn out after only five years, but the music is still with us and The Jam meant so much to us long before we split up and continues to this day, something that we are very proud of. I certainly have some great memories and an appreciation that absolutely everything that came after in our lives, for all of us, was as a result of what The Jam achieved.

Rick Buckler September 2019

1972 - 1975

I WAS THERE: NICKY WELLER

In the early days it was all about Paul and Steve Brookes up in Paul's bedroom with the pair of them going through tunes and stuff. It was like a youth club up there. My mum would pass cups of tea round the door because she couldn't even get in there. They would come out with a new tune and play it to Dad. I have a photo of Paul in our garden - he's sitting there with his guitar, him and Steve, it's all he ever used to do is walk around with his guitar strap round his neck - it was constant.

One day we were sat round the kitchen table at our home on Stanley Road with Mum, Dad, Paul and Steve Brookes talking about names for groups and I said, 'We've had Bread and Cream... what about Jam?'

The rest as they say is history.

Nicky Weller with her brother Paul in the back yard of Stanley Road

Paul Weller and Steve Brookes would meet at lunchtime in their classroom at Sheerwater Comprehensive School and learn and play songs. They played their first ever gig in The Albion pub next to Woking train station on a lunchtime. Later in the year the line up expanded with Neil Harris on drums, Dave Waller on guitar, Steve and Paul on bass and guitar. Around this period they became known as The Jam. Bruce Foxton joined the group at the end of May 1974.

For the following three years The Jam would gig in and around the area. One of these early gigs saw them supporting Thin Lizzy at The Greyhound in Fulham and another gig at HM Coldingley Prison just outside Woking. Songs played during this period included: 'Eight Days A Week', 'Walking The Dog', 'World Without Love', 'Oh Carol', 'Roll Over Beethoven', 'Jailhouse Rock', 'I Saw Her Standing There', 'Little Queenie' 'Dimples'and 'Twist And Shout'.

SHEERWATER SECONDARY SCHOOL

1972, WOKING, UK

I WAS THERE: RICK BUCKLER

I was already playing drums with my brother Peter on bass and another schoolmate Howard on guitar, and depping now and again with the school band, when I first heard about Paul and how he was also in a band. Anybody who was interested in music would hang out in the school music room during the lunch hour, listen to records, swap albums that sort of thing. There were a few other drummers, the odd bass player and a lot of budding guitar players. I do remember a really good guitarist, Richard Flitny, who to me seemed very cool. Most wanted to be in a rock band like Led Zeppelin and were looking down on Paul as he was into The Beatles. So when Paul approached me to stand in for a real gig, it was a better proposition than just 'being cool'. The guy that usually played with Paul was going to be on holiday and I could not resist the opportunity. I was soon spending a lot of time round Paul's house, borrowing Chuck Berry albums and rehearsing like mad as there was only about a week before the show. I found the 'twelve bar' format very easy and it was fantastic to have a real goal to aim for. We all got on well and that led to me becoming a permanent fixture in this new group.

Paul Weller: We used to have a knackered old piano under the stairs of our house in Woking, and I used to bash away on that. That's basically what I've done ever since then. I bash away on an instrument.

SHEERWATER ESTATE

WOKING, UK

I WAS THERE: BOB GRAY

I grew up with Bruce Foxton and played in a couple of bands with him when we both lived on the Sheerwater Estate in Woking. We both went to Sheerwater Secondary School. I first came to Canada in 1974 and over the next few years travelled back and forth between Canada and the UK whilst attempting to get my immigration papers. During one trip back to Woking in 1976, I met up with Bruce who told me he was playing in a band called The Jam, and was I interested in playing keyboards? I agreed to a couple of rehearsals at Sheerwater Youth Club and that was where I first met Paul Weller.

I remember being impressed with the amp he was using and he told me, with a wink, it was on loan from Rick Parfitt of Status Quo, who also grew up on the Sheerwater estate. After a couple of weeks rehearsals we went into an 8 track studio to record three songs: 'Soul Dance', 'Back In My Arms Again' and 'I Got By In Time', which I still have on an old Emitape X1000 60 minute cassette tape. I recall playing live on three occasions before I left England and returned to Canada. On one memorable occasion we played together in Dunstable, at the Queensway Hall (21 October 1976), opening for the original Sex Pistols with Glenn Matlock on bass, followed by the 100 Club in London opening for The Vibrators (November '76) and finally Upstairs at Ronnie Scott's. About a month after I left the band I was in the Birch and Pines, the local Sheerwater pub, when I heard Radio Luxembourg playing from behind the bar a very familiar song. When it finished the DJ said it was the new single 'In The City' from a band called The Jam who had just signed with Polydor. The following day I read about it in *Melody Maker*. By the end of the next week I was back in Canada, where I remain to this day.

So why did I leave? To be honest having been involved in music whilst in Canada (just a few years behind the music scene in the UK), I didn't really appreciate what was going on music-wise in the UK, and by then my heart was set on living in Canada anyway. However I went to see The Jam and met up with them again in April 1979 when they played in Toronto at the Rex Theatre. By then, like everybody else, I could fully appreciate the music they were playing then.

As a footnote, I was in LA in 2001 with my 8 year old daughter when I drove past a little club just around the corner to the hotel we were staying at. I saw on the marquee the name Paul Weller who was playing there the following Friday. As I read his name out loud my daughter asked 'Who's he, Daddy?' I told her he is a great musician and that I was fortunate to play with him for a few months back in my hometown in England, many years ago. She asked if we could go and see him but unfortunately I had a commitment in Toronto and we were due to leave town the day before the gig. She then asked me what I would say to him if we did meet him. I told her that I'd ask him if Rick Parfitt ever got his amp back.

AUGUST 1975 - 1976

Paul Weller's school sweetheart Jennifer Harvey wrote to TV talent show *Opportunity Knocks* in an attempt to get the group an audition. After first being turned down, the group, then consisting of Weller and school friends Steve Brookes and Rick Buckler, went to audition at Surbiton Town Hall, 20 miles from their home town of Woking, Surrey.

Paul Weller (*Jamming*): Everybody thought I was fucking mad in Woking. At the time, I really wanted something like the punk movement to come along with everyone playing to kids your own age. Up until then we were just playing to 40-year-old hippies, but I needed something to relate to.

HOPE AND ANCHOR

8 MAY 1976, ISLINGTON, LONDON, UK

I WAS THERE: TONY GAUNT

It was back in the early Seventies when people first started to talk about pub rock. We had Dr. Feelgood, Kilburn and the High Roads and Ducks Deluxe. The Hope and Anchor soon picked up a reputation as a venue where you could turn up and hear some good music. The upstairs bar even had an interesting jukebox where you could drop in a coin and hear Professor Longhair, The Doors, Van Morrison, The Kinks, The Flamin' Groovies and the latest punk rock singles.

Downstairs lurked a tiny black smoke-filled cellar where one could regularly catch great bands. It had a tiny stage and I think the room held around 100 to 150 but the owners crammed as many in as possible - fire regulations weren't as strict in those days. Later, as 1976 dawned, we had a thriving combination of punk and new wave as well as the pub rock regulars and the venue became part of the established gig circuit. Many acts played there. Joy Division played to a sparse attendance for their London debut. U2 were another for the proverbial one man and his dog attendance. (U2 were misnamed as 'The U2's' in promotional material). A significant number of media and record company people showed up along with only nine paying customers.

For The Jam's gig it was no different, maybe a dozen or so people turned up. I remember they looked different and younger than a lot of the groups I'd seen. I didn't know them from Adam but was impressed.

100 CLUB SPRING

1976, LONDON, UK

I WAS THERE: PETE HAWKINS

A promoter call Ron Watts who used to put bands on at the Nag's Head in High Wycombe and the 100 Club in London told me about The Jam when I was trying to get him to book The Stranglers. I went to see them at the 100 Club, thought they were great and got talking to John Weller and it was agreed that I could act as their agent.

I started with a residency at the Red Cow in Hammersmith, then the Nashville, more 100 Club gigs and some colleges. I also got them their first ever foreign gig in Paris which didn't go too well as the French promoter didn't provide the gear he said he would and what he did provide didn't work very well. Needless to say Paul Weller wasn't very happy the next time I saw him.

The band continued building and soon got a record deal with Chris Parry at Fiction (Polydor). The record company thought they should be with one of the bigger agencies so it wasn't long before I lost them to Cowbell who in all fairness did a good job in the UK.

I did go and see them at the odd gig after that. Guildford Civic comes to mind but that was about it with me and The Jam!

I WAS THERE: CHRIS PARRY

Paul Weller had his own way. You can so obviously see where it came from and people know his influences. Small Faces and The Kinks clearly had a big impact on him. Later, so did the whole Stax, soul and Motown thing but he was listening to that lot back then as well. But he also had his voice as a writer very early in his career.

He had written 'In The City' before I met him and that's a great song for a young person - for any person - to have written. He would tell anyone who would listen, 'I know I'm going to be successful' and he had that drive from day one.

Paul Weller: I was waiting for the signal for when it would be our time. When I saw the Pistols in 1976 it was the flare that had been shot up into the sky to tell us all it was our time.

THE WINDSOR CASTLE

6 JUNE 1976, LONDON, UK

I WAS THERE: BOB LITTLE

The Windsor Castle in Harrow Road was near where I lived at the time. My elder brother Clive's claim to fame is that he saw The Who play there in the early Sixties. I was under age but when it was busy I could sneak in without being noticed. I remember seeing The Members and I did see The Jam there once. I recall the sticky, beer-soaked carpet more than seeing The Jam. I recently read that The Clash song 'Protex Blue' was inspired by the condom vending machine in the pub's toilets.

THE GREYHOUND

17 JUNE 1976, LONDON, UK

I WAS THERE: SIMON WRIGHT

I saw The Jam for the first time at the much-missed Greyhound pub on Fulham Palace Road sometime in 1976. We piled into my mother's Morris 1000 Traveller, which later would become band transportation for our band Trash. Definitely present were my co-vocalist Jane Wimble, guitarist Mick Brophy and roadie John Parry. We broke down en route from Weybridge where we were at college but John replaced a broken throttle cable with a wire clothes hanger and we made it to the gig. I remember the suits as much as the music, and that it was free to get in. Seeing their obvious allegiance to the Sixties in general and The Who in particular encouraged us to work up versions of 'I Can't Explain' and 'Anyway, Anyhow, Anywhere' as well as an uber-Mod version of Fontella Bass' 'Rescue Me', which much later would be our audition number for the film *Quadrophenia*.

UPSTAIRS AT RONNIE SCOTT'S

8 SEPTEMBER 1976, LONDON, UK

I WAS THERE: SHANE MACGOWAN

I first saw The Jam Upstairs at Ronnie Scott's. They did a soul disco and played the best soul imports and every now and then they'd throw in something by Patti Smith or Television. I thought The Jam were great. I loved the suits! After that I saw them at The Roxy, The Vortex and The Red Cow in Hammersmith.

QUEENSWAY HALL

21 OCTOBER 1976, DUNSTABLE, UK

I WAS THERE: KRIS NEEDS

Pete Frame, Kris Needs and the late Magenta De Vine

The Sex Pistols are playing one of their first gigs away from their London comfort zone. They are still only a major buzz in the music papers, haven't released a record and Bill Grundy is over a month away, so the cavernous, circular Queensway Hall is sparsely-populated by barely more than a hundred early punks and curious rock fans.

The support band are on when we arrive. Sporting black suits and white shirts, they're playing 'Little Queenie' and also take a spirited stab at Martha and the Vandellas' 'Heat Wave' and Wilson Pickett's 'In The Midnight Hour'. There's four of them, including a rather ill-fitting piano player and bassist with long hair. The drummer is solidly metronomic, but it's the energetic, charismatic singer with a Rickenbacker who stands out.

Two weeks earlier I'd seen The Clash devastate a similar suburban space in Leighton Buzzard, changing my life with their attitude, white-hot onslaught and startlingly-fresh image. I remember thinking in Dunstable that, if this bunch had appeared even a year earlier, their Dr. Feelgood-style economy, young energy and astutely-picked retro set would have cleaned up on the pub rock circuit. But punk rock has arrived to edge it out and changes are happening fast on the back-to-basics turf those bands staked. I had already started writing for *Zigzag*, the original music monthly that set the template for *MOJO* and all the others. Editor Pete Frame knew something was going on, declaring 'Punk Rock' is coming to town when he stuck Eddie and the Hot Rods on the cover. The Jam sounded promising but I didn't know if I'd encounter them again or care if I did.

The Sex Pistols came on and, after the initial impact of Rotten's red glare, their SEX clobber and safety pins had subsided, were lost in the booming acoustics of the near-empty hall, reinforcing my already-formed belief that the coming revolution would be led by The Clash.

100 CLUB

11 JANUARY 1977, LONDON, UK

I WAS THERE: ALLAN JONES

I saw The Jam for the first time at the 100 Club in January 1977. They were bottom of a three-band bill, opening for Clayson and the Argonauts and headliners Stripjack.

John Tobler reviewed the 100 Club performance for the *NME*: I wasn't sure whether to stay for The Jam, but it soon became obvious that I would regret it if I left... in comparison to the much vaunted Clash, The Jam are totally superior, not least because they have sufficient respect for their material to want it to be heard as music rather than felt as noise.

THE NASHVILLE

7 FEBRUARY 1977, LONDON, UK

I WAS THERE: CHAS DE WHALLEY

It's Monday February 7 1977, round about seven in the evening and yours truly, a hardened 23 year old rock writer for the now sadly defunct *Sounds* rock weekly – credited with penning the first talent-spotting features ever on the likes of Graham Parker and the Rumour, Eddie and the Hot Rods and The Stranglers – is sitting at home enjoying an early evening spliff when my mate Pete Hawkins, booker at the Albion Agency which controls West London's premier pub rock venue the Nashville Rooms, calls to urge me to get on down there immediately.

'The headliners have pulled out and the support band will be doing both sets,' he says. 'You'll love them, they're fantastic.'

(18 months earlier the same Pete, then social sec at a college in Surrey, tipped me off about a local band he'd seen playing a Sunday lunchtime pub gig called The Chiddingfold Stranglers. So his recommendations were not to be sniffed at!)

The Nashville was about a 15 minute drive from where I was living. Yeah, I know. Spliffed up, driving *and* with the prospect of a couple of pints before heading home? But it was the Seventies. Things were different then.

The band were well stuck in when I arrived, playing the theme from the *Batman TV Show*, no less. You know the one: 'Dada dada dada dada/Dada dada dada dada/ Batmaaan!'

Except that it took a moment or two to pick out the tune because the sound was – ahem - not of the best. In fact, PA problems were to plague The Jam for at least the next eight or nine months even as they rocketed through the ranks and embarked on their first national tour of town halls and ballrooms in the early summer. But that's another story for another day….

Right now, what they might have lacked in finesse, the three kids up on that stage made up for in energy, dogged determination and an astonishing work rate. I say 'kids' because they were not only younger than me but younger than the majority of musicians working the pub circuit at the time and didn't act like they'd already read the book and seen the movie.

Instead the guitarist and the bass player were balls of fire, bouncing across the stage, crashing into one another and thrashing their instruments nearly to death while the drummer behind them sat cool and collected as he nailed the beat to the floor.

I didn't realise it at the time but this was a band which, in one form or another, had been gigging regularly for some years and had evolved into a six-legged music monster which already knew that the one sure way of winning a crowd was to play like its life depended on it.

Tonight The Jam were giving it their all and they most certainly won me over. As you can tell from the review I bashed out the next morning and took up to the weekly editorial meeting at the *Sounds* Holloway Road offices the following day.

It was printed in the issue dated 19 February 1977 and was the first proper piece on The Jam to appear in any of the music papers. And as I morphed into one of their biggest fans, it was followed by at least a dozen gig reports, features and album reviews, all carrying my byline, with which *Sounds* charted The Jam's rapid rise over the next 12 months.

In retrospect this debut article may be a little short on detail and even shorter on insight. But I can guarantee it's as raw and fresh as it could possibly be!

THANGYEWverymushwheelseeyewaginn!

Exit The Jam

The who? No, The Jam. Three young guys from Woking way who are going to be huge before the year is out.

And by huge I mean, dare I say it, even bigger than Eddie and the Hot Rods!

I walked into the Nashville to find The Jam already strutting their stuff in front of a sparse audience, but an interested one. Dressed in black Burton's suits, white shirts and ties, sporting haircuts like Pete Townshend wore at the Marquee or Clapton affected before they changed his name to God, The Jam

The Jam made Chas De Whally drool

jumped straight into a song of their own called 'Changing My Address'.

It stopped me dead.

Everything about it was solid gold. Pure Sixties from the tune and the aggressive chording, the off-key harmonies and the loud but fuzzy PA to the classic key change one chorus from the end and then the short sharp staccato figures which polished it all off.

I began to drool immediately.

Thereafter The Jam continued as they'd begun through two whole sets – and the Nashville became the Star Club in Hamburg much like the Roundhouse was magically transformed into Wallington Public Hall by the Flamin' Groovies last summer. Paul Weller (lead guitar and vocals), Bruce Foxton (bass and vocals) and Rick Buckler (drums) pounded out the Big Beat and tore the audience apart with spirited and zestful renditions of all your favourite jukebox selections from The Who's 'So Sad About Us' to Lee Dorsey's 'Ride Your Pony'. They slipped in a couple more of their own and then made a real scorcher of Martha And The Vandellas' 'Heatwave'.

High on period perhaps but surprisingly low on cheap nostalgia, The Jam easily transcended the Groovies' lookalike criticism which will be leveled at them from some quarters. They came across as a pure rock pop band with youth and vigour. One of the finest young acts to come along since Lew Lewis left the Rods.

And you should make extra-sure you see them.

Reading it now I am struck by what I left out of that review. Barely a couple of months after the infamous Bill Grundy TV show, punk bands were now creating a big noise on the fringes of the national music scene. Yet the closest I came to connecting The Jam with the Sex Pistols, The Clash, The Damned, Generation X *et al* was to compare them to veteran San Francisco powerpop pranksters The Flamin' Groovies, who had very nearly stolen the show when they supported the Ramones at the Roundhouse in July the previous year.

Instead I saw Messrs Weller, Foxton and Buckler as lining up behind Eddie and the Hot Rods – those teenage pretenders to Dr. Feelgood's R&B crown – who had been the big noise on the street throughout 1976 and were in the Top 10 with their signature single 'Do Anything You Wanna Do' around the time this review was written.

Of course, that could have meant being nothing more than one hit wonders. Who was to know that The Jam would rapidly develop into one of the new wave's tastemaking giants and Paul Weller would be hailed as both the Modfather, a fashion icon and one of UK rock's most revered songwriters?

I must also confess to thinking immediately that Bruce Foxton was (a) the best-looking member of the band (b) the better singer and so (c) would obviously emerge as the front man, even if he only played the bass and not the lead guitar.

Naturally sometimes the greatest notions don't stand up to scrutiny. Before the evening was over it became clear that Paul was a top talent. Not only was he an extremely accomplished musician – able to play lead and rhythm all at the same time like his lookalike idol from The Who – but he had real charisma where others only have charm. Furthermore he exhibited enough strength of character to command a crowd and stop it in its tracks.

At this point I'll let you into a personal secret, if I may. In between penning pieces for the music press, I too was fronting a band in London with fond illusions of becoming a rock star myself. Indeed, over previous months, my outfit had already played a number of support shows at the Nashville. So technically it could have been said that we were ahead of The Jam.

But I came away from that early February 1977 gig recognising that this three piece from Woking hadn't merely materialised from nowhere, powering up on the inside rail to leave us (and a whole load of other young hopefuls) standing in the dust, but - to mix the sporting metaphors still further - their 19 year-old leader Paul Weller had set the bar so high I knew I would never ever be able to match it.

So what was the point of trying? For me then, the dream was over!

For The Jam, on the other hand, it was only just beginning.

THE HUNT HOTEL

19 FEBRUARY 1977, LEIGHTON BUZZARD, UK

I WAS THERE: KRIS NEEDS

A school friend of mine, Chris France, had built up a circuit of local pub gigs in the Aylesbury area (and promoted that Clash gig). Every week, he put on bands in the small but oddly perfect back room of the Hunt Hotel, near Leighton Buzzard railway station.

We'd already had Eddie and the Hot Rods, who were now big enough to headline the legendary Friars Aylesbury club. Tonight it's this band The Jam we'd seen in Dunstable.

Only five months had passed but there'd been major changes. The pianist was gone and so had bassist Bruce Foxton's hair. They sounded sharp, speedy and explosive, like the early Who. Like all good bands, they already had their signature song, 'In The City', screaming to be a single amidst the Sixties soul and Motown covers. Paul Weller also had the arrogant attitude that would often work against him but I now know was sheer self-belief. In the bar before their set, The Jam were sitting in the corner when I walked in. By now, I was firmly in The Clash's orbit, so sported a painted shirt and their name scrawled in black felt-tip on a Union Jack badge I'd bought in Carnaby Street ten years earlier. The Jam were into their adoption of Who imagery, including the British flag; Weller's dirty looks and grumblings displayed his offence that I'd defaced it with one of his band's main rivals. We'd got off on the wrong foot and it was only the blonde presence of my gorgeous first wife that defused any ugliness (although Weller's ever watchful dad would probably have stepped in).

The Jam are great, even if the covers (including Larry Williams' 'Slow Down', the Who's 'So Sad About Us' and the 'Batman' theme) and beat boom uniform place them against what's happening on the streets - actually the whole point (and they should never have been thrown onto the Roxy bill I witnessed around then). The Pistols and Clash camps were closer than the press would have you believe; they saw The Jam as bowing to a major record label's idea of palatable punk, especially as they were signing to Polydor. Joe Strummer referred to them in '(White Man) In Hammersmith Palais').

THE GREYHOUND

25 FEBRUARY 1977, LONDON, UK

I WAS THERE: PHIL WATKINS

I have so many memories of nights at the Croydon Greyhound. I went to my first gig there in 1977, when the Ramones headlined. They were supported by Talking Heads. I saw the Buzzcocks, The Jam, Generation X, Siouxsie and the Banshees to name but a few.

For a while it was very exciting. I used to go to the Marquee during the week and The Greyhound most Sunday nights. But after a while it changed. They tried to stop pogoing because of safety fears and more and more skinheads started to turn up.

I remember one night The Jam getting very pissed off about being spat at. Bruce Foxton threatened to wrap his Rickenbacker over some skinhead's head. Needless

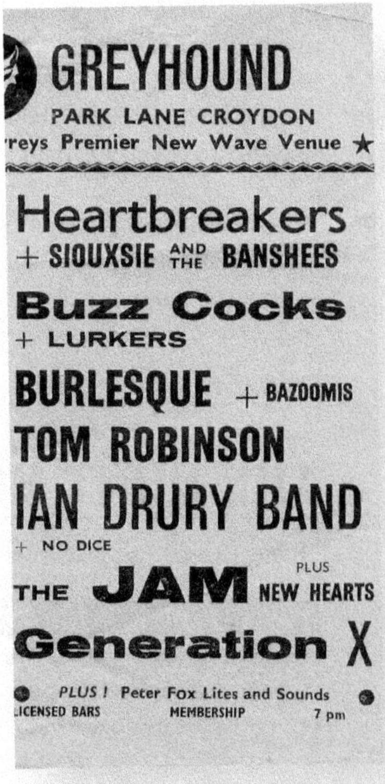

to say that encouraged people to spit all the more. They stopped playing and Weller and Foxton stood right at the front of the stage staring this one bloke out, pointing him out to the bouncers. The guy was taken out of the gig.

THE RED COW

9 MARCH 1977, LONDON, UK

I WAS THERE: PERRY RICHARDS

I saw The Jam 16 times between March 1977 including at the Hammersmith Odeon, all the Nashville and Red Cow gigs, and on the *White Riot* tour with The Clash, Slits, Buzzcocks and Subway Sect. I'm on the *All Mods Cons* album down the front at the Red Cow, next to my school mate John Toovey.

Perry Richards at The Red Cow, 1977

ROCHESTER CASTLE

24 MARCH 1977, STOKE NEWINGTON, UK

I WAS THERE: RICHARD SCHALLER, AGE 23

'Saw this brilliant band at The Greyhound last night called The Jam!' So said a mate to me at Stamford Bridge back in early 1977. I lived in Stoke Newington at the time and at the ripe old age of 23 with around ten years experience of following a host of bands including a period of being into prog rock. Dr. Feelgood woke me up again to good R&B a couple of years earlier at the Kursaal in Southend and put me in good stead for what was about to explode onto the music scene a year later in '76. Although not a practising punk, I felt excited about the impact it made on a tired music industry. Having said that I saw a couple of punk bands in the Hope and Anchor Islington and my head nearly blew up with the noise and energy. Didn't quite do it for me.

When I heard The Jam would play at The Rochester in Stoke Newington at the end of March in '77 I thought I'd take on board what my mate said back at the Chelsea game. The Rochester was a great rough house and I remember a couple of punk bands (Screemer I think was one of them) doing the usual punk thing and getting punks to pogo and what have you. Then when The Jam came on in their slightly ill-fitting Hepworth suits the crowd for the first time pretty much stood there perplexed and some, I remember, told them to fuck off. This was the first time I'd seen or heard of them but when they started it only took a couple of minutes to realise that this was something different and special. Fine rock singing and playing but fused with punk. And it didn't take long for the crowd to get back to feeling energised again with appreciation.

They were obviously playing their set list for their up and coming first studio album *In The City*. I was hooked like I was when I saw Dr. Feelgood. This was loud but the messages were also loud and clear about the times we were living in. I never saw myself a true devoted fan of The Jam and only saw them a further three occasions at The Hope and Anchor, The 100 Club and Hammersmith Odeon a couple of years later. But then I was older than many of The Jam fans and just got into work and travelling, etc. But The Jam were a band who got it right and whereever I went I would play the albums and take the cassettes with me. When asked by author Ian Snowball and Rick Buckler to illustrate for the graphic novel *From The Start to 77* it was great to do something close to my heart.

ROUNDHOUSE

17 APRIL 1977, LONDON, UK

I WAS THERE: JEREMY SMITH

They were supporting The Stranglers. They had been much touted in the music press but I found them very one dimensional and quite boring. I never thought they would become the band that sang 'Town Called Malice' and similar wonderful songs.

THE ROUNDABOUT CLUB

20 APRIL 1977, NEWPORT, UK

I WAS THERE: DEX STUART

I was there sorting the lighting out for the support band and the guys were chatting with three girls who'd turned up really early. They did the sound check, and the snooty roadies said we couldn't move anything. Five minuets later, looking a bit lost, Bruce Foxton came out and asked what the problem was, so we told him what the roadies had said and he kicked their own stuff off the stage. 'Put what you want wherever you want - fuck 'em.'

At the end of the night, all the crew were celebrating how great they were (not the band) and someone walked off with the small mixer that had been near the door. The CID turn up, do the usual plod stuff then ask to speak to the band. The manager sends them to the tour bus and the plod open the back door to see three lads receiving an appreciation from the three girls who were there earlier and unable to speak due to their mouths being otherwise engaged.

On 26 April 1977 The Jam recorded their first of three Radio 1 John Peel Sessions at Maida Vale, recording four songs: 'In The City', 'Art School', 'I've Changed My Address' and 'Modern World'.

Later that week on 29 April, Polydor released The Jam's debut single, 'In The City', which reached number 40 on the UK singles chart and became the beginning of their streak of 18 consecutive Top 40 UK singles. 'In The City' borrowed its title from an obscure Who song of the same name, which was released in 1966 as the B-side of 'I'm a Boy'.

THE PLAYHOUSE

7 MAY 1977, EDINBURGH, UK

I WAS THERE: STEVE DIGGLE

On the *White Riot* tour, with us and The Clash, the first gig The Jam played was at the Edinburgh Playhouse Theatre. I remember it was one of those lovely old theatres with the long curtains and the first thing I heard when I arrived backstage was 'The Modern World'. It was a new song and hearing that intro from behind these old velvet curtains was pretty mind-blowing.

I thought the Pistols, The Jam, Buzzcocks and The Clash complemented each other. That was the nucleus of punk. Weller was very intense. There was a bricks-and-mortar mentality about him. You could see he was searching for that voice. After those initial frantic songs, The Jam defined their own path, but 'The Modern World' was part of that explosion, the punk-rock atom splitting.

RAINBOW THEATRE

9 MAY 1977: LONDON, UK

I WAS THERE: KRIS NEEDS

The Jam are booked onto The Clash's *White Riot* tour for bums-on-seats reasons but don't fit in. While The Clash, Slits, Buzzcocks and Subway Sect do the tour on a mad coach, The Jam travel separately and don't hang out with the rest, who are probably quite hostile anyway. The Rainbow is the big one and they acquit themselves well, the set now weighted with songs that will grace their recently-recorded debut album and In The City going down a storm. They don't last much further on the *White Riot* tour though. This was a genuine new revolution and many consider them old-fashioned and normal in the way The Beatles were nice enough to take and meet your parents when the society-threatening danger was happening in the Stones. Yet there's no denying Weller's talent and 18-year-old promise.

ELECTRIC CIRCUS

15 MAY 1977, MANCHESTER, UK

I WAS THERE: PHIL BRENNAN

As a regular at the Electric Circus I often saw bands that I hadn't heard of or hadn't fancied seeing. On this occasion a pal of mine had said that we should go and see The Jam as he thought they were really good, and even though I hadn't been convinced by his description of the band, I tagged along.

It was unusual to see a band that looked like they had made an effort to dress well and to be honest I was expecting that they would struggle to win over the Circus crowd. Not knowing any of their songs beforehand I instantly loved the rawness of 'In The City' and their brilliant cover version 'Slow Down', which was like a punk version of a 45 single my mum played all the time.

Phil Brennan was a regular at The Electric Circus

Despite my prior reservations I couldn't help but be impressed by Paul Weller's stage presence and the sheer power of the band, and by the end of the evening I came away in awe of the great sound that three men could make.

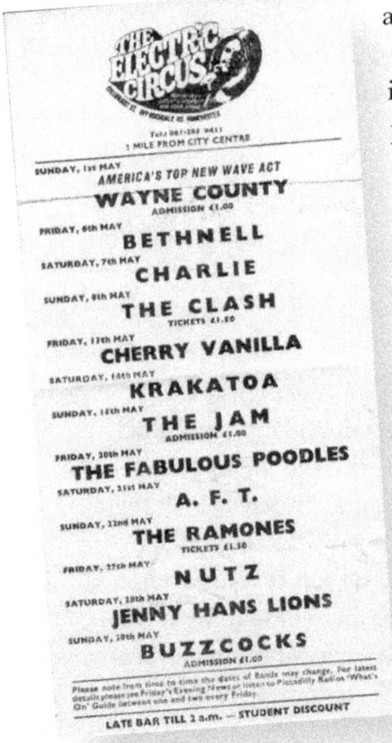

On 19 May 1977, The Jam made their first appearance on *Top of the Pops* performing their new single, 'In The City'. The song resembled the frantic, fast-paced and angry tone of the current punks the Sex Pistols and The Clash, yet The Jam had a different look with their tailored suits.

Despite being seen for the first time by over 15 million viewers the single peaked just outside the Top 40 at No.41. The Jam would go on to appear on *Top of the Pops* over 25 times during the next five years.

Rick Buckler: We didn't like *Top of the Pops*, plastic cymbals and rubber bits on the pedals. We hated it but you had to do it - it was the only show on the TV.

The Jam released their debut album *In The City* on 20 May 1977. Reviewing the album for *Record Mirror* Barry Cain said: 'Armed and extremely dangerous The Jam stalk the decrepit grooves. If you don't like them, hard luck they're gonna be around for a long time. It's been a long time since albums actually reflected pre-20 delusions and this one does.'

TOP RANK

13 JUNE 1977, READING, UK

I WAS THERE: ROBERT BOWIE

I listened to *In the City* all afternoon at home whilst skiving college. My best mate rang me later to ask what I thought of it. Telling him it was mind blowing, he informed me they were playing in Reading that very evening.

Next door to the venue we went for a beer, where the three guys playing pool were Rick Buckler, Bruce Foxton and Dave Waller. Paul Weller wasn't in the pub. We spoke briefly and I congratulated them on a brilliant album.

My first punk gig (though obviously The Jam were far from a punk band), and I was agog at the spiky hair, mohair and leather. The night was life changing. The band were stunning. The following day the long hair and flares were ditched. I've a lot to thank The Jam for.

QUEEN'S HALL

16 JUNE 1977, LEEDS, UK

I WAS THERE: GRAHAM WALKER

Saw them several times but the stand out one was Queen's Hall Leeds. I managed to get in for the sound check - approached Paul and asked to shake his hand. I'd heard he wasn't very friendly and didn't do autographs so was a bit nervous. No need to be as he shook my hand and said 'pleased to meet you'. I then went on to meet Bruce and Rick who were just as pleasant and signed all my merchandise. Thanks for the memories fellas.

SEABURN HALL

17 JUNE 1977, SUNDERLAND, UK

I WAS THERE: KEVIN GERAGHTY-SHEWAN

Two days after seeing The Stranglers at Newcastle City Hall we had our second punk experience much closer to home at Seaburn Hall, about a mile from where we lived. Looking back of course The Jam weren't really a punk band but like a lot of other bands they were caught up in that whole punk/new wave tag. They had just released their first single 'In The City' and the gig in Sunderland came less than a month after their debut *Top of the Pops* appearance.

I don't know if they were selling advance tickets or not but I think it was a case of turning up and paying £1 on the door. There was no support band and I seem to recall that The Jam came on quite late which meant there were a lot of very drunk people in the audience by the time they took to the stage. Most people had got their ideas of how to act at a punk gig from the press so when the band did come on there was a lot of spitting and at one point a beer glass flew through the air and smashed on the stage bringing the gig to an abrupt halt while the band said if it happened again they would just go off.

The band were all dressed in identical suits and the light show consisted of about half a dozen white lights around the band. The set was fast and furious and didn't last much more than 45 minutes and I seem to recall they played 'In The City' twice. This turned out to be the only time I saw The Jam.

The following week the same venue had the Vibrators and local punk band Penetration playing and again we went down to see them. I seem to recall that my mum had got wind of the whole punk thing by then and tried to discourage us but we went anyway. Unfortunately when we got there they wouldn't let us in. I think there had been too many underage people at The Jam gig the week before and they had been told to tighten things up. Disappointed we wandered round the side of the hall and as we did the side door opened and out came Pauline Murray from Penetration. We chatted to her and told her how we couldn't get in so she indicated that the door was open! About six of us piled down the corridor but unfortunately it came out right next to the DJ booth and we were all soon rounded up and chucked out again!

WINTER GARDENS

9 JUNE 1977, EASTBOURNE, UK

I WAS THERE: ELAINE HUGGETT

I was lucky enough to see them in Eastbourne at their gig at the Winter Gardens. It's hard to believe that was 42 years ago now! The Jam (along with a few other bands from that time) were new, young and exciting and a real breath of fresh air on the music scene, which had become a bit staid and boring. I could not believe they were coming to Eastbourne and rushed out to get tickets the day they became available.

The Winter Gardens was not even the biggest venue in Eastbourne, so I was very fortunate to get those tickets.

They looked sharp, sounded great and powered through the set list at a rapid pace. The audience were jumping up and down and cheering them on, as they treated us to songs such as 'All Around the World', 'So Sad About Us' and, of course, the mighty 'In The City', which stills sounds fresh and relevant today. I cannot recall all the songs now, but I do remember them playing the 'Batman' theme!

The Jam went on to produce many other great songs before Paul Weller called it a day, and I am grateful I got to see them in those early days. I'm pleased to say I still have my treasured ticket too!

THE OUTLOOK

20 JUNE 1977, DONCASTER, UK

I WAS THERE: GARY HOLLAND

I first heard 'In The City' on Radio Luxembourg late one night in April 1977 whilst supposedly doing some homework in my bedroom. I was getting into the punk scene at the time but this sound was instantly different from the other music around then - angrier and sharper - with fire and skill in abundance.

I bought The Jam's debut album (£2.99 from Virgin, in Sheffield) on release and played it non stop. To this day tracks like 'Away From The Numbers', 'Art School' and 'Bricks and Mortar' often reverberate round my brain and I am constantly astounded by their pure power, passion and poetry.

My first Jam gig was at the claustrophobic Outlook club in Doncaster in June 1977. The place was so small that Foxton kept putting his machine heads through the ceiling every time he and Weller did their trademark 'Jam jumps' on stage. I wish I had some photos from the night.

I was disappointed by some parts of the *This is the Modern World* album and the infamous 'we're voting Conservative' quote haunted me for a while, but then, as I was becoming cynical towards the trio, I heard 'Down In The Tubestation at Midnight' for the first time. Again I was stopped in my tracks. What stunning musicianship, song writing and production; perfect pop music. To this day *All Mod Cons* remains my favourite album, not just by The Jam, but by any artist - stunning. The artwork on the vinyl LP was simply beautiful.

I saw From The Jam in December 2008 at the Academy in Newcastle with both Buckler and Foxton in the line up. It wasn't, as Weller stated in *Uncut*; 'cabaret'. No, it was a very valid chapter in The Jam's biography. The pair got a standing ovation at the end of the night, which was a response to a fine gig but also a kind of valediction on the one hand and a celebration on the other. It was also a fitting acknowledgement, I think, of Foxton and Buckler's contribution to The Jam - a band which meant and continues to mean so much to so many people.

TOP RANK

21 JUNE 1977, CARDIFF, UK

I WAS THERE: TOM BEECH

I think I was at both Cardiff gigs, and certainly at the Top Rank, but after so many years and thousands of gigs I'm a bit loathe to rely on my memory!

The stage was only a couple of feet higher than the crowd - which wasn't huge. I remember Paul and Bruce pogoing throughout the show. It may have been the first time we'd seen that although we went to pretty well every punk concert in the area. I had a year off between university and law school and my friend Tony and I just went to gig after gig. I particularly remember following the Flamin' Groovies around the country on tour.

THE POLYTECHNIC

23 JUNE 1977, HUDDDERSFIELD, UK

I WAS THERE: STEVEN DORRIL

I was the social secretary for Huddersfield Poly students union from 1976 to '79. I was one of the original punks and went to all the early gigs in Manchester and saw all the punk bands in the summer and autumn of '76. There were a group of us doing Behavioural Sciences which was a new course and there were three of us who were into punk. Mark Nelson saw the Ramones in London when they came over and he'd been to see Patti Smith and the Pistols. It was very clear what was happening.

So I imposed punk on the students. The space in the students union was great. The Stranglers played there. The Skids. I put on The Cure for £50. Students at that time very much still liked rock music and John Martyn and that kind of thing, and some of the best gigs I put on were people like Can.

In the September of '76 I started putting on things like Eddie and the Hot Rods and the Vibrators.

We knew what was in the wind. I knew what bands were coming up. In retrospect I did very well at spotting who was going to do well. At that time you could book bands for fifty quid. I booked The Jam for £150 for the first gig, which was in a small hall in the students union. It was an old church. The little hall officially held about 120 people but we used to pack everybody in and there were about 300 for The Jam.

Paul Weller came with his girlfriend. I remember talking to him and he was just kind of surly and not very interesting. We used to take the bands out to get something to eat and we used to go to a local coffee bar. He said very, very little. The other two were great and were really nice guys. They were talkative.

The actual gig was brilliant. They were very, very good. It sold out very quickly because it just so happened that I had booked them a couple of months before and the single, *In The City*, came out and was just starting to chart. By then they'd become nationally known. When I'd originally booked them, they were still semi-underground.

We sold out 300 tickets and there must have been about 150 people outside trying to get in. Some of them were climbing up the drainpipes to get in, trying to get through the windows upstairs. There was an incident where somebody put their arm through the glass and cut an artery and blood just spurted up. It didn't look too good.

The stage was very low. It was only about two feet high so everybody was very close. It was one of those real sweaty high volume everybody having a good time gigs - the band were great so it was a really good night. And they seemed to enjoy it as well. I immediately booked them back for the bigger hall.

I WAS THERE: GRAHAM CARR

This was at the Student Union, which was known as 'The Black Hole' with all the walls painted black. With no more than 100 people in the room I remember it was very loud as you were very close to the band and the stage was low. I recall Bruce Foxton signing a girl fan's thigh and John Weller counting pound notes on the venue floor.

THE CAT'S WHISKERS

29 JUNE 1977, YORK, UK

I WAS THERE: NIGEL HOGARTH, AGE 17

I was 17 when The Jam came to York. They were the biggest band from the new wave/ punk era to play in the city at the time and our local punk heroes Cyanide were the support, which made it more exciting. I remember walking across Scarcroft Green in the afternoon and bumping into Bob De Vries, who was lead singer in Cyanide. He was a couple of years older than me but we were from the same school. We went down to the Trafalgar Bay pub where I had a few underage pints. I was dressed in a white lab coat from school and green plastic sunglasses!

Gig time at the Cats Whiskers, and we pogoed through the Cyanide set and waited for The Jam. I stood next to Dave Sollitt, another lad from our school, and remember him saying, 'Let's be indifferent', in a gesture of support for our mates in Cyanide.

On came Weller, Foxton and Buckler and burst into life. I don't remember the first song, just the power and anger. Dave just turned to me and mouthed an expletive and our legs and arms burst into action.

I can't remember any songs apart from 'In The City' and, at the end, the 'Batman Theme'. I clambered up on to stage saying that I was with the band at the end as the gig emptied. Rick Buckler was packing up his drums and I mouthed some congratulations. He passed me a bottle of Pils lager and I sat for a minute on the drum riser drinking before disappearing into the York night.

I WAS THERE: WAYNE BRANNAN

What I remember is watching the York band Cyanide, who I had seen a few times. When they finished their set, lots of people were still shouting for them when The Jam came on stage.

I WAS THERE: IAN WARD, AGE 19

I went in a group of four. I had some of their singles at the time. They had released the *In The City* and *Modern World* albums. They were wearing their distinctive suits on the night and there was evidence of the gobbing trend amongst the audience! It was a long time ago so I don't have a specific list of the songs they played. The admission seems a bargain at £1.25. The venue eventually became a nightclub then a bingo hall and was eventually demolished in 2001.

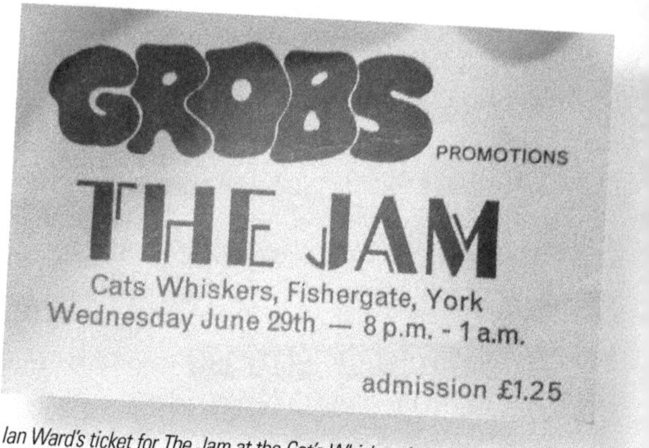

Ian Ward's ticket for The Jam at the Cat's Whiskers in York

I WAS THERE: DAVE PARKER

I was one of the fortunate ones who witnessed the concert. Some things stay with you. Wayne County and the Electric Chairs played the week before, but I remember little of their concert.

I was an apprentice at the York Carriage works and I remember quite a few of us going to Cat's that night, although the only lads I definitely remember were Gary Wroe and Wayne Anderson. Gary had his head in the PA speaker on the left hand side of the stage all the way through the concert. He was deaf for days. Wayne had some plastic sandals on and whilst pogoing he landed on a pint glass and cut the sole of his foot quite badly. He stayed.

A lot of the lads who went were scooter boys but not Mods. The film of *Quadrophenia* had not yet come out.

They covered all the first album. I clearly recall 'Art School', the 'Batman Theme' and obviously 'In The City'. I am sure for the encore they had to do 'In The City' again as they had run out of songs.

After the concert, we ran out to the rear of the club and had a brief conversation with all three of the band, before they got into a red Mark 3 Cortina and drove away. Over the next months, I saw all the main punk and new wave bands, including the Pistols, the Clash and the Adverts. The Jam were the band that stayed with me, seeing them all over the North of England including the Leeds University gig, when afterwards there were arrests at a Leeds hotel where the Australian rugby league squad were also staying.

John Hamlet, *NME 1977*: Rick Buckler hangs tough behind his kit, cool as a spring breeze, snapping out a viciously precise beat with contemptuous ease. If Jimmy Dean had been a drummer he would've played like Rick Buckler. Paul Weller plays his guitar real neat, his right hand coming down over the strings in a tense, clipped fluttering motion like a moth caught in a strobe beam, the chords chasing each other out into the hall, fighting for dancing room. Bruce Foxton is so close to me I could play his bass for him, he hops and pogos around as though acutely aware of each limb as he moves.

THE MAYFAIR

1 JULY 1977, NEWCASTLE UPON TYNE, UK

I WAS THERE: FRANK WEBSTER

I first got to hear The Jam while at college and 'In The City' was on the jukebox. I didn't know who they were or what they looked like. Later I saw pictures of them in their suits and suddenly it was cool to wear suits again. I would make trips down to London from Cumbria where I lived to the same clothes shop as The Jam went - The Carnaby Cavern - and get my clothes made there. It used to cost me a fortune. I had a Union Jack jacket made which cost me about three weeks wages!

I got to see The Jam about nine times in total. The first time was at the Mayfair in Newcastle upon Tyne in 1977. Although it was the opposite side of the country from where I lived, it's only about an hour and a half's drive. The final time I saw them was at Carlisle Market Hall, in 1981. The covered Victorian building became a regular venue for a while with people like The Who, Thin Lizzy and Status Quo all playing gigs there.

I remember seeing them in Lancaster University in 1979 and they were playing 'Girl on the Phone' when a fight broke out. They all stopped playing and Paul Weller told the guys to 'stop fucking fighting' which they eventually did. Then instead of starting the song from the start they counted in and started exactly where they had left off. Another time, at the Reading Festival, Weller thought the sound was so bad he smashed his Rickenbacker up and walked off stage. They came back on and finished the set though.

Probably my favourite albums would be *All Mods Cons* and *Setting Sons* but the first two albums have some great songs on which featured in their live sets.

I WAS THERE: KRIS NEEDS

Polydor's press office fly a bunch of journalists up to Newcastle to catch The Jam's tour. I'm invited as I've just taken over as editor of *Zigzag*; an early taste of promotional budgets stretching to nice hotels and free booze. I've already given *In The City*, The Jam's debut album a good review, describing them as 'original, exciting and quite different from the rest of the new wave groups...loaded with intensity, with enough Seventies awareness and technique injected to save (the album) from the nostalgia wallow that it could have been.' I liken their Sixties flavours to the Flamin' Groovies, and not just the suits. I'm impressed by Weller writing ten of the 12 songs, including 'Art School', 'Away From The Numbers', blistering tear-up 'Change My Address' and, of course, the title track. I love Weller's feedback onslaught in 'Bricks and Mortar'.

That night in Newcastle we hit the bar then the venue; an old school run-down dance hall on a violent weekend night in a square, primitive world. I'm sporting my Lewis Leathers black leather jacket, spikey black hair and Clash t-shirt. The combination of something the beer-and-football throwbacks had only seen in the Sunday papers slurring with a southern accent was enough to provoke one Neanderthal to smash a bottle in my face, breaking my nose. Blood everywhere. Led by a worried press officer, our party cart me into the dressing room and dump me on the floor. Although Bruce and Rick are sympathetic, I'll always remember Weller moaning I was bleeding on the dressing room's beige carpet and demanding my removal. Cunt, I thought.

Obviously, the gash on my throbbing hooter colours my enjoyment of what's obviously a good Jam gig and afterwards a local punkette takes me to A&E then back to the hotel. When it's time to write the piece, I can't avoid mentioning how my judgement was impaired by local meatheads or resist printing my blood-stained tour pass (under the headline 'Blood On The Pass'). Still carry the scars.

MR DIGBY'S

7 JULY 1977, BIRKENHEAD, UK

I WAS THERE: KEV LIONS

Mr Digby's was a nightclub on Thomas Street that had some good bands pass through its doors. Siouxsie and the Banshees, Tom Robinson Band, Wire, Deaf School, Eddie and the Hot Rods and Motorhead all played Digby's. There's an urban myth that the Sex Pistols made an appearance at the club as well. I didn't live too far away from Digby's, the number 10 bus took me there and back so for a while it was a good place to hang out.

Opening for The Jam were The Mutants, and that's all I remember about them. I know they used to play around Liverpool a lot and had a good local following. This was the first time I ever saw The Jam and they were everything I thought they would be and more. They looked like the album cover and the sound was really clear. In fact so clear I wondered for a moment if they were miming, that is how good the sound was.

I seem to remember they played most the tracks from *In The City*, and I remember them playing 'London Girl'. The crowd went mad, loads of pogoing. Between songs Bruce Foxton had a go at some of the punks at the front who were spitting at the band.

I wonder what ever happened to the club? I moved away years ago.

CALIFORNIA BALLROOM

9 JULY 1977, DUNSTABLE, UK

I WAS THERE: STEVE MADDOX

My best friend from college had heard about the band and bought the album *In The City*. To us it was revolutionary, just the music we wanted at that time. Not long after this we bought tickets to see them live at the California in Dunstable.

Travelling from Stevenage in my Ford Prefect we were expectant and excited. The album was playing on the cassette player and singing along we knew most of the words. Outside it was raining and the vacuum powered windscreen wipers were working overtime – going slower uphill and speeding up as we went downhill.

As we drove down Stockingstone Hill, in Luton, the wipers were going hell for leather. All of a sudden one came loose and flew off onto the grass verge. I stopped and my friend Steve jumped out of the car and retrieved it. I got the hammer out and we tapped it back on. Ten minutes later and very wet we got to the gig which was just about to start.

The support was Chelsea. The atmosphere was electric – a cliché but totally true. A couple of fights broke out but they were dispersed. Then out came The Jam. Standing room only, from what I could see, the whole floor was jumping to the music. This was the music we had listened to but now it was raw, not recorded. This was live! It was the best gig I had been to. What a brilliant night! It didn't matter that the other wiper came off on the way home. I just tapped it back on and drove home, listening to The Jam again of course.

TOP RANK

10 JULY 1977, SHEFFIELD, UK

I WAS THERE: PAUL SANDHAM, AGE 14

I'd got some birthday money and I was going to the local record shop to buy an album, my older brother asked me what album I was going to buy and embarrassingly I told him an album by Adam and the Ants. My brother said 'Why don't you give *In The City* by The Jam a try? So I bought that and played it to death. Listened to the words and learnt the lyrics.

A couple of months later they were playing at Sheffield Top Rank - my brother bought me a ticket - £4.50 and two car loads of us went. It was my first experience of seeing anybody live. I'd never seen anybody live except at the working men's club.

We were stood up on the balcony - cracking atmosphere - absolutely electric. It was fantastic for my first gig.

After the gig I went and bought the whole back catalogue - every single, album and any imports, bootlegs anything I could lay my hands on.

I then saw them at the Queens Hall in Leeds in 1982. About six or seven of us went from school. We took the day off school - took the train from Selby in North Yorkshire. The Queens Hall was a little tram shed so it wasn't a very salubrious place by any stretch of the imagination. Concrete floors and concrete pillars blocking your view. When the doors opened we went right up to the front of the stage.

We didn't get back home until gone midnight so we all decided to take the day off school the next day. We hadn't got permission from our parents so on the next day we all got called in front of the head and asked to give an explanation as to why we'd missed a day off school from going to see this pop band. The headmaster asked one of my friends 'How many people would have been inside the venue?' and he looked at me and I said 'I dunno, 3,000, something like that'. It turned out that this boy had never been in a school assembly because he was frightened of being in enclosed spaces, but he'd managed to go and see The Jam with 3,000 people.

I should have had a ticket for the farewell tour - a friend of mine let us down. But my geography teacher at the time, a lady called Jane Wye, had a ticket and she knew how much I was into The Jam so she sold me her ticket at face value. But I felt guilty that my brother didn't have a ticket so I actually gave it to him and I missed the final tour. I've seen The Jam probably about a dozen times and I've seen Weller on his own maybe in excess of twenty times.

MANIQUI HALL

14 JULY 1977, FALKIRK, UK

I WAS THERE: JOHN MACDONALD, AGE 15

I saw The Jam play at the Maniqui in Falkirk in early '77 (also saw The Adverts, Gen X, Doctors of Madness, Johnny & The Self Abusers and a whole load more at that club) - tickets for The Jam cost a princely £1.29 - they were amazing! The energy, the sound and the look combined into a knockout show. I'm 58 now and still remember how good it was.

After the gig my friends and I had to try and get back to Cumbernauld, 11 miles away (I was still 15 and had school the next day). Anyway taxi ranks were mobbed so we walked to a local hotel to call a cab but the desk concierge wouldn't let us in the door. As we sat on the wall outside cursing the 'wee prick' behind the desk, this big orange Cortina drew up and we actually commented how lucky those 'bastards' were, they'd get in no bother driving that car. As the doors opened we were stunned to see Bruce Foxton exit the car with the others and Paul's dad following on. Running over we told them we'd been at the show and had loved it so they took us into the hotel, hung out with us a bit and then - pure class - Paul turns to the concierge and says, 'phone a taxi for these lads', gave us their autographs (lost a long time ago) and said goodnight.

Released between the debut album, *In The City*, and the band's second album, *This Is The Modern World*, The Jam's second single 'All Around the World' was released on 15 July 1977 - backed by the B-side, 'Carnaby Street', becoming their first UK Top 20 hit.

I WAS THERE: NICKY WELLER

We'd left Stanley Road because it was being knocked down and we'd moved to Bramwell Drive. Post just started to turn up with, 'Paul Weller, Woking' or 'The Jam, Woking', and the post office obviously knew who they were talking about so these big sacks of mail just start turning up, so we decided to do a fan club.

My mum decked out what was a coal shed on the side of the house, boarded it all out and we started it from there. It was all hand-written and then we progressed to a typewriter and then it was photocopies. My dad would sneak up to Polydor's offices and he'd say to me, 'Come up and do all the fan club printing up there for nothing.' We weren't supposed to be in there but that's what used to happen. I was about 14, 15, still at school and I was doing the fan club which kind of just grew. They gave me £5 a week to run it.

There were hundreds of big bags, literally bags of it coming in and, me in my infinite wisdom, I put our address in *Melody Maker* and said something like, 'If you want join The Jam fan club please write to 44 Bramwell Drive.' I think at one time I even put the phone number in the paper. So then we would have fans calling all the time - people turning up, it was quite funny.

As well as sending our newsletters with tour dates and news on recordings, singles and albums we had badges made: 'The Jam at the Nashville', 'The Jam at the Hope and Anchor', 'The Jam at The 100 Club'. We had them made specifically for whichever gig they were playing. They became quite popular and we began selling them in the fan club along with t-shirts, so it kind of progressed quite well actually. We hand-wrote everything - all the labels were hand-written, envelopes, letters. We had so many to do that my mum used to get all the neighbours in to write them when had to send out a newsletter. We'd have them all sitting there in the house, having tea and writing the addresses out.

The fan club just grew and grew. We ended up with proper 'The Jam' headed note paper and then the boys would sign things and we would come out with a couple of flexi-discs at Christmas and competitions to win items of clothing or gig tickets. The fan club newsletter was a quarterly thing. I think they joined for a fiver for the year.

ERIC'S

16 JULY 1977, LIVERPOOL, UK

I WAS THERE: JON DAVIES

Eric's was in a basement on Mathew Street opposite the Cavern Club. The list of groups who played Eric's reads like a Who's Who of punk/rock music, from Blondie and The Clash to The Jam and Siouxsie and the Banshees. Little known groups like The Police, XTC and Elvis Costello all played Eric's on their way to stardom, with The Stranglers featuring on Eric's opening night. And of course we had local and Manchester bands Joy Division, Dead or Alive, Echo and the Bunnymen, The Teardrop Explodes. OMD played their debut at Eric's and so did lots of others. The Saturday Matinees at Eric's were legendary, and I do mean legendary. I have great memories from those days.

The gang I hung around with were all under age but we had fake student IDs when we first started going. I saw so many bands there. Skids were fantastic as were Stiff Little Fingers. I also remember a great night with Alberto Y Los Trios Paranoias. I was later told that Courtney Love was a groupie and used to hang around Eric's with Julian Cope!

Many fond memories, but they are all fading fast. I didn't know who The Jam were, but you didn't with loads of bands you went to see at the club. It was the place to go regardless of who was on. I remember they were fast and furious, but not punk. They had a Sixties edge to them, aided by the way they dressed, which made them look different from a lot of the bands around that time. And it was £1 to get in.

I WAS THERE: PETER GRANT

I saw The Jam at Eric's during the punk period. And later in my role as a local music correspondent in Liverpool I met up with them when they had their number one single 'Start!' Not only did they give up their time to chat openly but they took me to the local pub for a pint or two.

The Jam recorded the second of three Radio 1 John Peel Sessions on 19 July 1977 at Maida Vale, recording four songs: 'All Around The World', 'London Girl', 'Bricks And Mortar' and 'Carnaby Street'.

On 24 August 1977 The Jam appeared on the first episode of the Granada TV series *Marc* performing 'All Around The World'. The short-lived show gave T. Rex star Marc Bolan a chance to showcase new bands such as Generation X, The Jam, Radio Stars and Eddie and the Hot Rods.

The Jam started recording sessions for their second album, *This Is The Modern World* on 25 August 1977 at Basing Street Studios, London.

Vic Coppersmith-Heaven, Jam producer: It was very much a three-piece, with a real fiery energy coming from all of them. They had unique arrangements and a unique sound, and it was an engineer's dream, trying to capture their raw excitement on vinyl. Vinyl was lovely stuff because you could make it bleed, you could force it to its limits and make the sound really leap out.

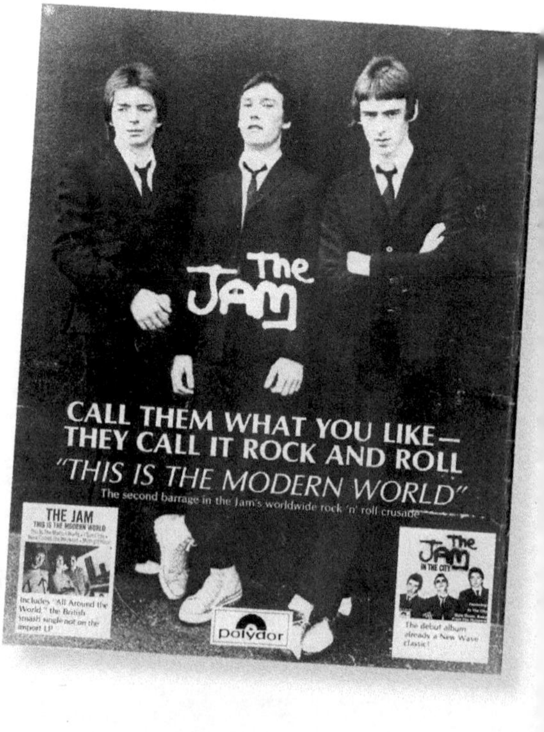

100 CLUB

11 SEPTEMBER 1977, LONDON, UK

I WAS THERE: NICKY WELLER, AGE 15

It was my 15th birthday. It wasn't like it is today. You're not allowed to have hardly anybody in there, are you? There was only room for 300 people and there must have been about 1,000 people in there, it was bonkers. They had no air conditioning at the 100 Club, there was nothing like that then. It was just wall-to-wall people hanging off of everything and I remember sweat dripping down the walls - absolutely disgusting. It must have been a warm night as well in September. I've since seen some pictures. I remember the people in the front who used to follow the band everywhere - it was carnage.

I remember people spitting. The band never liked it. Bruce would shout to the crowd, 'If you gob at me again, I'm going off'. It was disgusting. The Jam's image was more clean-cut and Mod – they weren't into the whole gobbing thing at all. After the gig, it was my job to sell these big blue Jam badges for 10p a time.

I WAS THERE: SIMON WRIGHT

The second time I saw The Jam was September 11th 1977, the night they recorded live versions of 'Back In My Arms Again' and 'Sweet Soul Music' at the 100 Club in Oxford Street. These tracks would later feature on the B-side of the single 'This Is The Modern World'. Once again I got in for free, this time on the guest list thanks to an agent who wanted me to book the support band. By now there were a lot of suits in the crowd.

I WAS THERE: PETER WILSON

When I left Surrey University I got a job straight away as an engineer at Polydor Studios, which didn't have tape ops. Polydor Studio was used for recording demos for the A&R department, and it was really boring. Most of the time it was awful groups, and if it was good groups and the demos went really well, the group got a deal and then they'd go off somewhere and do their album with somebody else, with the result that I never got a look in.

I worked with Sham 69. They had several top ten singles. I think the first one was 'Angels With Dirty Faces'. I recorded four albums with them, and made a bit of money, which was quite handy. Then I did three albums with the Comsat Angels for Polydor and I did a couple of singles with The Passions.

The Jam were signed to Polydor. I was engineering for sessions with Paul Weller when he used the in-house studio to demo new songs. They would then go off to record, mostly at the Townhouse Studio with Vic Coppersmith.

Paul would book two or three days at a time and come in with a bunch of song ideas. 'That's Entertainment' was one such song. We also recorded 'Pop Art Poem'. If Paul was out of songs we would record old covers just for fun – for example The Beatles 'And Your Bird Can Sing' and 'Rain'. The only musicians there were me, Paul and Dave Liddle, his guitar roadie. So we had a lot of fun – I remember hitting record and running out to play the drum kit, hoping the levels were all set up right!

So when they wanted to move on they asked me to engineer and produce with them. It proved to be for a few singles and their last studio album. I took them to AIR studios to do most of that.

The Gift was a bit stressful for all concerned. Like a lot of successful bands The Jam had tied themselves into an album - tour - album - tour treadmill. The strain on Paul of having to come up with an album of great songs was very substantial. Release dates and promotional tours were being planned even before some of the songs had been written. The strain was beginning to tell within the band. They had been hard at it for four or more years and their success had come with a price – the stress of keeping it up.

I think Paul was feeling his way in looking for a wider sound palette and more various styles, and beginning to move away from the guitar dominated style that they had used so successfully. Keyboards and horns were being used and even a string section on 'Bitterest Pill', which I arranged.

Paul had always said he did not want to run The Jam just for the money, and that when it had served its musical purpose he would want to move on. He has got to be respected for that.

OLD WALDORF

9 OCTOBER 1977, SAN FRANCISCO, CALIFORNIA

Photo of Bobby Asea taken by Joey Ramone backstage at the Mabuhay Gardens in San Francisco

I WAS THERE: BOBBY ASEA

The year was 1977 and I happened to have a friend who worked at a local radio station that had carte blanche access to the music venue in San Francisco called the Old Waldorf. He would generously let me accompany him on many occasions and, even when he couldn't make a show, he would always make sure my name was on the guest list so that I could still get in and skip the cost of the ticket. This made it easier for me to see more shows there than I would have if I had to pay and I was all the more fortunate because of it. A million thanks to my dear friend!

At the time, there were many new up and coming bands showcasing their music that was considered punk and/or new wave which I was totally in to. Some of the new bands that performed there that I was able to see were The Damned, Blondie, Dead Boys, Iggy Pop, 999, Mink DeVille, Go-Go's and The Jam. As it turned out, my radio friend was also in a punk band called Nuclear Valdez, and they were the opening act the night that I saw The Jam. *In The City*, The Jam's debut album, had just been released earlier in the year and this was their first American tour supporting that album. When I first heard the album, I immediately loved it. The raw sound of the three-piece band with similarities to The Who was a winning combination for me. Their live show did not disappoint. It was loud and raw but sounded very polished and professional. Compared to some of the new acts that I saw in concert, I could tell The Jam were superior with talent. One thing that sticks out in my mind about that night was that Paul Weller's father was in attendance. I figured the lads were young and it was their first visit abroad and maybe Pop was there to oversee the operations and safety of the band. Not really sure, just a wild guess!

On 15 October 1977 The Jam appeared at CBGB in New York City, the famed venue of punk rock and new wave bands like the Ramones, Television, Patti Smith Group, Blondie, and Talking Heads. The Jam played two nights with DMZ from Boston as the opening band.

CBGB

15 OCTOBER 1977, NEW YORK CITY, NEW YORK

I WAS THERE: MIKE BODAYLE

I never much liked going to CBGB. It was fitting that this dump was in the Bowery, which back in the late Seventies was far from what it looks like today. But not only was CBGBs dirty and overcrowded, it wasn't a friendly vibe. Patrons were more intent on looking and acting cool and being part of the scene rather than being a community of music fans.

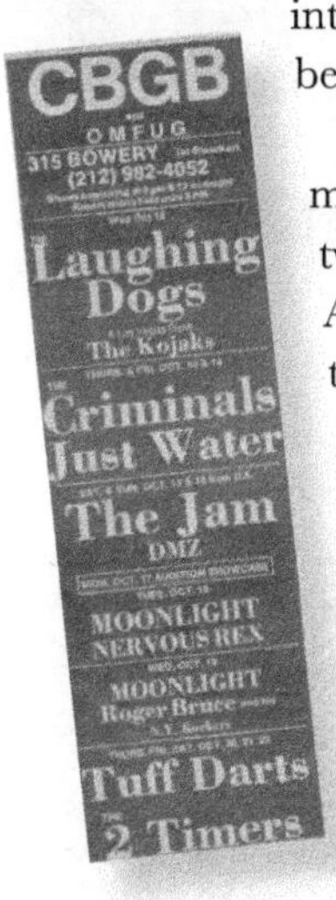

Putting my apprehensions aside, I chose to go see England's The Jam make their New York City debut. This would be the first of a two set, two-night Saturday-Sunday stand and was the close of their short maiden American tour. Short it was, it consisted of only two Los Angeles shows at the Whiskey and two at The Rat in Boston. (In between, they did make a brief appearance on Tom Snyder's *The Tomorrow Show* for a couple of songs and a brief interview.)

The band had released their first LP, *In The City*, back in May, and in just a few weeks, would follow-up with *This Is The Modern World*. Not all that familiar with their music, I was intrigued to see this hot new band play. I was also attracted to the show when I read a tidbit in the *New York Post* that my current fave, Bruce Springsteen, was a Jam fan and was possibly going to be at CBGB for the show.

There were no advance ticket sales for the club, so this meant getting there early to wait on line to get in. A friend and I got there early enough to be near the front of the line and for show time managed to get fairly close to the stage.

Bursting on stage in tight dark suits, white shirts and skinny ties, the three members of The Jam played faster than any band I had ever before seen in my life. Unfortunately, this wasn't a good thing, and the music was not much more than a blur of noise. While the excitement level was high, it sure wasn't a night to sing-along to your favourite songs.

Over the years, The Jam tamed their act a bit, and of course went on to huge success in their native land, while never really making much of a mark in the USA. I still wonder what that stranger I went up to thinking he was the recently-shaven Bruce Springsteen thought I was up to!

SETLIST:
I've Changed My Address
Carnaby Streets
The Modern World
Time for Truth
London Girl
All Around the World
Sounds from the Street
London Traffic
Bricks and Mortar
In The City
Takin' My Love
In the Midnight Hour

28 October 1977 saw the release of 'The Modern World', the first and only single from the band's second album, *This Is The Modern World which peaked just outside the UK Top 20.*

Paul Weller: That song was about school (Sheerwater Secondary in Woking). I found the whole process painful. The hate was directed against the teachers. I'm a bit less cynical now because there's been some relief in writing songs and having the chance to communicate with thousands of people I'd never have met otherwise. Some of the kids who went to school with me are like little old men already, like Toby jugs. But now there's less opportunities than there was for us. A kid leaving school now knows he's straight down the dole office, so his ambition drive is probably zero.

The Jam kicked off a 25-date UK tour at Huddersfield Polytechnic on 17 November 1977.

GREAT HALL, POLYTECHNIC

17 NOVEMBER 1977, HUDDDERSFIELD, UK

I WAS THERE: STEVEN DORRIL

Officially, you could get 700 people into the Great Hall and I think we got about 1,000 in. It wasn't the most popular gig we put on. That was Magazine, where they got about 1,200 people. The Jam were again very good. I think the support band was a local punk band as that's what we tended to do.

Paul's father came as manager. He was really nice. I'd met him before because I'd seen The Jam at other places. They were on a percentage of £500 against 70% of the door. In those days it was only £1 or £1.50 to get in as students didn't want to pay very much. After the gig I remember sorting out the money with John Weller. He wanted it all in cash, which we were willing to do. Upstairs was the staff bar, which we were using. It had the North's biggest collection of malt whiskies outside of Scotland.

We started on one end. I remember sitting down in the corridor and counting out the pound notes with him – 'this is one for you, this is one for us' - and we were drinking whiskies. I talked to him quite a lot. It was strange to find such a nice guy given other bands and their managers and what they got up to. He seemed a very straightforward person. I think we paid them about £1,000. It was a really great night. Financially we did well out of them and they did well too.

The first gig was the better, in that punk in lots of ways was finished by the summer of '77. By the time of the second gig there was a much wider audience and it wasn't quite the same as the early one because of that.

THE EMPIRE

20 NOVEMBER 1977, LIVERPOOL, UK

I WAS THERE: SIMON MURPHY, AGE 13

I went straight from school still my in uniform - I had no tickets. Paul Weller was outside having a smoke and opened the fire escape door at the back when he saw the four of us and let us in! When on stage he said, 'This is for my little mates in the front row'.

KINGS HALL

25 NOVEMBER 1977, DERBY, UK

I WAS THERE: BRUNO GALLONE

I first saw The Jam back in 1977 at the Kings Hall in Derby. An incredible time for a young Jam fan back then which set me in a life long journey. From then on I saw them a fair number of times over the years in place like Coventry, Hanley, Leicester and Birmingham, attending both the sound checks and the gigs (sometimes managing to blag being on one of the bands' guest lists).

On December 15th 1981, I achieve the ultimate fan experience, in actually fronting one of the support acts - my band Reaction at the Hammersmith Palais. I still can't believe we achieved this, a memory which will live with me forever.

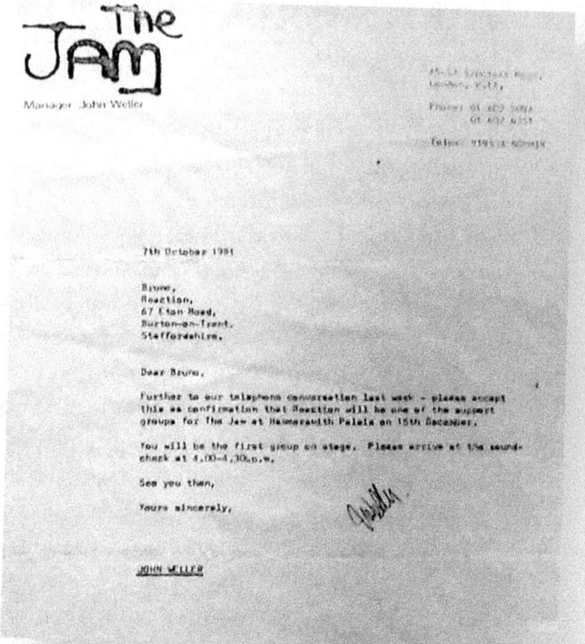

The Jam

Manager John Weller

7th October 1981

Bruno,
Reaction,
67 Eton Road,
Burton-on-Trent,
Staffordshire.

Dear Bruno,

Further to our telephone conversation last week - please accept this as confirmation that Reaction will be one of the support groups for The Jam at Hammersmith Palais on 15th December.

You will be the first group on stage. Please arrive at the sound-check at 4.00-4.30p.m.

See you then,

Yours sincerely,

JOHN WELLER

Bruno Gallone still has the letter from John Weller confirming his band Reaction as supporting The Jam

FRIARS

26 NOVEMBER 1977,
AYLESBURY, UK

I WAS THERE: MICK FAGG

I had fantastic times at Friars from 1976 to 1982 when I saw some great bands. I was a Mod from Dr Challoners in Amersham, converted when I saw The Jam for the first time in 1977 at Friars, but I loved all live music. Stand out gigs were The Ramones, Ian Dury, Radio Stars, Dennis Brown, Stiff Little Fingers and Secret Affair.

I remember getting into my Morris Minor with four or five other people jammed in for the half hour ride to Aylesbury to see some band or other. One time I towed a friend all the way back because his motorbike had broken down and it taking over two hours. I got a thank you from him but I was grounded from seeing my girlfriend at the time because I failed to get her home at the appointed hour.

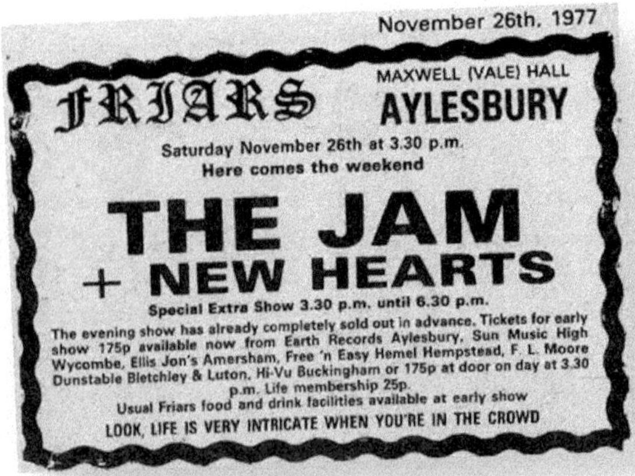

I remember catching Ian Dury's sweaty towel and the idiot next to me biting my arm until I let go and also getting Bruce Foxton's plectrum at the *Setting Sons* gig.

I WAS THERE: SHANE CARLSON

I took a leap of faith into the world of punk at Friars by attending The Jam gig on 26th November. Although this wasn't really my 'thing' it was, nonetheless, an amazing night full of raw energy and buckets of spit. My only regret is that I didn't have an umbrella!

I WAS THERE: KRIS NEEDS

For the first and only time in the venerable club's history, The Jam play a Saturday afternoon matinee show for the kids and an evening one for the grown-ups, although most fans go to both. Weller's obnoxious, uncaring attitude after the Newcastle incident is compounded when he sees me and moans, 'Why did you write about your nose and not The Jam in your article?' Although I'll happily put the band in *Zigzag* for the rest of their duration, I don't go near them again. Apparently, this superior attitude cost him The Jam breaking through in the US too.

Kris Needs on stage with his band The Vice Creems

Happily we make up in 1983 at a launch bash for the new CD format. The Jam's gone, Weller's grown up and acknowledges that I had, in fact been quite seriously clobbered so mentioning my hooter in the review was unavoidable. I've since run into him over the years and it's always a pleasure, including when he brushed Primal Scream's orbit in the Ninties and DJing for him in 2010 when he returned to that same Friars venue to play its closing night. These days, he's an older, wiser soul, some say Britain's greatest living songwriter, and still boasts that restless, questing muse.

Anyway, my nose was a better shape once the swelling had gone down so I owe him one.

BARBARELLA'S

28 NOVEMBER 1977, BIRMINGHAM, UK

I WAS THERE: CRAIG HARPER, AGE 15

My first experience of The Jam, like so many others, was *Top of the Pops* and 'In The City'. At 15 I was totally blown away by the look, the song and of course the energy and from that day no other group came close and probably never has.

Living in the Midlands meant the early London gigs were not possible. However a trip to Birmingham with some older mates, took me to Barbarella's, on 28 November 1977 - my first gig.

My first memory was how small the stage was and how close you were. It was a mixture of fans, punks, etc. but it was also the first time I saw Mods. My older friends had a similar look. They looked so cool and I suddenly realised my baggy jeans and tank top (the ones with the stars on) had to go.

The memory of them coming onto the stage will always be with me. The songs were fast and within minutes the small crowd were jumping up and down, dripping in sweat.

Bingley Hall, Stafford in December 1982 was my final gig. I hadn't missed a tour and travelled up and down the country to see them, never being disappointed. My favourite years were 1979 and 1980, because the playlists were growing and Weller's songwriting was getting stronger. Venues got bigger and of course the fan base grew into almost an army, which made the atmosphere legendary.

One concert that does stick with me was 3 November 1980 at the Queens Exhibition Hall in Leeds. Three of us set off in a knackered old Datsun at 8am, hoping to catch the sound check and also meet the band. Well thanks to the knackered old Datsun, whose driver's door decided to fly off on the M62, we didn't make. However, several hours later enjoying a well earned cuppa in a café, we were joined by Mr John Weller. We couldn't believe it - he had just collected their suits from the dry cleaners. He treated us to another cuppa and loved our story about the door. He had seen the car on the street and all the tape holding it together. He said he would tell the lads how far we had travelled and took a picture of the car.

Like all the concerts, from John's legendary introduction, the walk on stage from the band and the first chord, the atmosphere was electric. There were no fancy lights or screens. You didn't need them. Even the new songs they would put in went down well. I do think that they could have sung 'Chitty Chitty Bang Bang' and we would have all jumped and down.

Did that first *Top of the Pops* appearance change my life? Well, the answer is yes. I'm so glad I had The Jam and their lyrics to help me and of course the concert memories will stay with me forever.

LANCASTER UNIVERSITY

30 NOVEMBER 1977, LANCASTER, UK

I WAS THERE: MARK O'DONNELL, AGE 17

Support was The New Hearts. It was an amazing experience in the heart of the punk explosion. One lad had some toast with jam on it stuck to his leather jacket. Music was fast and powerful for a 17 year old. Amazing memories.

SPORTS CENTRE

2 DECEMBER 1977, BRACKNELL, UK

I WAS THERE: MICK BROPHY

Surrey in 76/77 was a hotbed of punk talent! It seemed like each stop on the train line from London to Woking was home to a band: Walton-on-Thames (The Lurkers), Hersham (Sham 69), Weybridge (Trash; I was the guitarist) and, at the end of the line, The Jam. Chertsey was arguably the most important musical stop, home to Watkins Electric Music (WEM), manufacturers of affordable amps, speakers and guitars – like the

Weybridge group Trash take a break from looking for old coins down the back of sofas at the local tip

Rapier Paul Weller used in the early days. Charlie Watkins invented the modern concert PA system.

The Jam had been gigging locally for a couple of years before punk - I first heard of them from Geoff Horne, Sham's rhythm guitarist, who really rated them as players – but the first time I saw them was at The Greyhound, a down-and-dirty pub in Fulham in summer '76. Having already had my world changed by the Pistols at their warm-up gig in Weybridge late '75, I loved The Jam for the same reasons. Not because they were punk but because, like the Pistols, the early Who and Small Faces were among their influences. Where the Pistols mixed in Iggy and The Dolls, The Jam sprinkled on Sixties soul. Unlike the Pistols, who were more about the attitude than the notes (and nothing wrong with that), The Jam had paid their dues and were really tight. Sweat-wrinkled suits delivering singles-length mini-classics. Bam. Bam. Bam.

Fast-forward 18 months and the second LP is about to be released and the venue is an echoey sports-hall in Berkshire. The band are now Big-Time! Big Stage! Big PA! And - the thing I remember most - Big Lights! Bright White Lights! Everything looked shiny. Shiny sports floor. Shiny white shirts. Shiny brand-spanking-new Rickenbackers. The contrast with the drab-but-fab Greyhound was gob-smacking.

Impossibly, the band seemed even tighter. I can't remember any gaps between numbers. There may have been some technical hitches – there usually was back in the day – but if so, they didn't register. The performance, which may have been an hour but felt like 15 minutes was bam-bam-bam. Faultless.

But as I left the gig I realised something else had changed. Something fundamental. Drawn by the band's commercial success, the audience looked richer, smarter, cleaner. The Jam had a shiny new set of pop fans. For this was The Modern World.

VICTORIA HALL

15 DECEMBER 1977, STOKE ON TRENT, UK

Peter Bowers sleeps with his Jam badge

I WAS THERE: PETER BOWERS

Sunday afternoons in 1977 were mainly spent at my cousin's house in Stoke, listening to punk records and playing football. At 19, I was a few years older than Mark. We both dug the *In The City* LP but it was the follow up release, *This Is The Modern World* which I really adored. I bought it the week it was released and listened to it incessantly, digging the songs, the great live photo on the back cover and scrutinising the inner sleeve words and colourful sketches. When I heard about the Stoke gig, I made sure I bought a ticket well in advance. I didn't want to miss this one.

I drove from Keele University to the venue and with the anticipation building, took a place in the standing area near the front. When John Weller's introduction was over, the lights dimmed and the band appeared with Paul and Bruce in black and white Sixties style clothing, matching red Rickenbacker's and Rick in dark glasses. The Jam launched into their set.

I was transfixed. The pogoing at the front meant being knocked around to various vantage points but the excitement was unrelenting. It wouldn't let go. The songs I loved came alive, hammered out with energy and urgency. I was absorbed in every moment, every leap, every cymbal crash, every sung word, every Rickenbacker chord. The Jam played an encore, maybe two, before the lights went up and the gig was over.

And here's the crux of the story.

I turned towards the side exit doors, along with the rest of the sweaty young punks and felt as if I'd returned from a different place. I was likewise sweating but unexpected tingles were rushing up and down my body and my mind felt like it was glowing. Surges of excitement overwhelmed me as I walked towards to winter air outside.

I had never experienced anything like it and drove back to Keele reliving the thrills I'd just witnessed. I hadn't the words to describe the emotions of the night when I got back and was asked how the gig had been. 'Yeah…really good' I think I muttered to a couple of friends before taking myself away to sit down to try to make sense of the excitement. I'd probably have been too embarrassed to try to explain anyway.

It's been a long time since that night in December 1977. I must have attended hundreds of gigs over the years, including a dozen or so Jam gigs at various places - Stafford, Deeside Leisure Centre and The Rainbow amongst others – but the sheer excitement and joy of that night tops all of them.

The Victoria Hall is still there. It's been modernised a bit but whenever I'm passing, I'll often stop, drift away in thought and relive the late teenage thrills of seeing The Jam that night in December 1977.

1978

MARQUEE CLUB

25 FEBRUARY 1978, LONDON, UK

I WAS THERE: ED SILVESTER

Ed Silvester (left) with brother John at Brighton coach station

On a bitterly cold Saturday back in February 1978, our little group of Epping punks excitedly set off on a 40-minute tube journey to the West End of London. This time, we were to see another of the rising stars of the new wave, those Woking wonders The Jam, at the famous Marquee Club in Soho - as part of their London Blitz tour to promote their forthcoming single, 'News of the World'.

What was it about these 'smart punks' that interested us so much? For sure, they still had the energy and manic sound typical of most punk bands of that time, but they wore smart black suits, and black and white shoes! What was that all about? We'd been attending punk gigs in our paint-splattered and ripped and torn shirts, leather jackets, and bondage or Sta-Prest trousers. This began to feel a bit passé, after occasionally seeing and hearing The Jam on the box and radio, or reading about them in the *NME* or *Sounds*. We had to copy our heroes and discard our usual clobber, so after a quick visit to a charity shop and mixed with white shirts and old school jackets (adorning them with loads of punk badges), and with the same DIY punk ethos, we thought we now looked the part. The first rush of excitement that we'd felt for the punk explosion was now slowly beginning to wear off. The Pistols had gone to the States where they had imploded and broken up a few weeks earlier, so it really did feel like the end of something special for us, and was the demise of the Sex Pistols to be the final nail in the punk coffin?

Maybe The Jam could push this energetic new wave sound along a new path. The Jam's second album - *This Is The Modern World* - hadn't been well received by the music press bigwigs and the band were now being written off by many pundits. But, along with thousands of other like-minded kids, we loved the album and I believe the band's difficult second album has certainly stood the test of time. The last track was an old Sixties soul cover by Wilson Pickett, 'In the Midnight Hour'. Along with their suits, this was yet another sign that the band's Mod roots were breaking through and we had now started to take note of Weller's modernist influences.

Most people had considered that the new wave baton had been passed to The Clash and that they were now the number one punk band. But hadn't they been singing that there'd be no more Elvis, Beatles or The Rolling Stones the previous year and that the old rock order had to be swept away? Their philosophy now began to feel a bit like a contradiction, as we'd always kinda liked bands like The Beatles and The Who. The Jam reeked of Mod and they did stand out against their contemporaries, even though the music press were pushing power-pop bands as the next big thing.

We had jumped off the tube train at Oxford Street underground station and quickly walked down Oxford Street until we reached the turning into Wardour Street. We'd arrived early to buy tickets and after first making our way to a little local pub The Ship for some refreshments - and giving ourselves plenty of time - we then queued up near the entrance of the venue in Wardour Street with loads of other eager teenage punters, nervously chatting and keeping our fingers crossed that the tickets wouldn't sell out by the time we got to the ticket office, which would only cost a couple of quid at the time. Even with inflation the tickets were peanuts compared to today's extortionate prices and, with hindsight, certainly fantastic value for money. Finally, after what felt like ages, we were in.

You could cut the atmosphere with a knife. It certainly was a smoky, shady and dimly lit club. After walking down the short hallway, we headed straight to the small bar on the left hand side for a beer. We'd try and make this pint last for a long as possible, as most of us weren't exactly flush with cash, and start chatting with some new found friends. We would listen to all the exciting tunes that were blasting out of the DJ's speakers, realising that this old stuff was kind of exciting. Tapping our toes to a smattering of Motown hits and intently listening to the occasional classic by The Who or The Kinks. This really was a journey of discovery for us.

After half an hour there was a buzz of excitement as the support band - in snappy blue suits with darks lapels - hit the stage. It was those Scottish punksters The Jolt. They played a fast and furious set that was clearly influenced by punk and The Jam. We weren't expecting much from the support band but they were terrific. There really was a buzz about the place now as the level of excitement and expectation had increased.

Just after nine o'clock The Jam crashed onto the stage - no longer wearing their black suits, but sporting blue three button jackets and white trousers, but still wearing the standard issue, black and white Jam shoes. Through the constant pogoing we worked our way to the front of the stage. We could now feel the sweat of the band and the full energy of the audience. We could now see the future - and it was definitely not going to be jam tomorrow! This band were going to be huge and would later lay the foundations of the Mod revival.

We managed to see The Jam on numerous occasions over the years, and with my brother John we saw them in Brighton a few times. We've also still got all of our old Jam tickets, which we now have framed. My brother and I both met Rick Buckler at a Camber Sands scooter rally a few years ago. We managed to get him to sign his autobiography and have a few photos taken with him. A memorable day.

Ed Silvester has his mates would make their pints last for as long as possible

In March 1978 The Jam found themselves Stateside opening for Blue Öyster Cult. The tour did not go well, with fans booing the be-suited neo-Mod three-piece off the stage on more than one occasion. The Jam returned to the UK dispirited and to make matters worse, they had a third album to deliver and Paul Weller was suffering from writer's block. The demos that they recorded were rejected by their A&R man and producer, Chris Parry, who suggested they retreated to their home town of Woking and write a new set of songs.

TOWER THEATRE

18 MARCH 1978, PHILADELPHIA, PENNSYLVANIA

I WAS THERE: CHRIS O'BRIEN, AGE 16

The Ramones opened, followed by The Jam, and the Runaways closed. Ramones were awesome, Runaways only so-so. They were not really punk at the time. The Jam? I just fell in love with the rawness of the music, the starkness of the show. Just music and musicians: no flash, no glitter. It reminded me of clips I had seen of early Who shows.

RICHFIELD COLISEUM

25 MARCH 1978, RICHFIELD, OHIO

I WAS THERE: GUY TURNER, AGE 17

They were the opening act, followed by Be Bop Deluxe and headliner Blue Oyster Cult. A very eclectic bill. I owned a copy of *This is the Modern World* (still do) and was pumped to see an English band perform. It was maybe my fourth concert. It was a great show. My best friend was very into Be Bop Deluxe - I ended up buying *Drastic Plastic* thanks to him and the band's performance. BOC's third song was 'E.T.I.', which is still my Cult favorite track. Eric Bloom had a wrist-mounted green laser, which he moved in an arc across the ceiling during that song. My 17 year old self was absolutely knocked on my ass. Simpler, younger, happier times and good memories.

I WAS THERE: DENNIS MUNDAY

I was first generation Mod in the Sixties, although I wouldn't ride a scooter as they were too dangerous in the wet and, as you know, it rains a lot in the UK. Since the Sixties, every generation of teenagers thinks of themselves as being elite, and they're the first to find sex, drugs and rock 'n' roll. All this goes with territory of being a teenager. However, we were the first generation of teenagers to be educated. We also had a freedom that no

other generation had and we had no problem finding employment. It was much easier for my generation than the generations that followed.

For me the Mod look, which was based on American Ivy League with a hint of Italian and French thrown in for good measure, was a classic look and it will never go out of fashion. However, the most important part of being a Mod was the music. Yes, the clothes, the haircuts, and the shoes were important, but the music we listened to transcended all of this and still does to this day. Paul Weller was inspired by my generation's music and style, and now he's gone on to inspire other bands and by doing this he's passed on the Mod baton; as they say, once a Mod always a Mod.

During the late Seventies, Polydor was downsizing and my position was being phased out. I was promoted to become a Senior Product Manager, looking after the acts that were signed by the American arm of Polydor. I can't say I enjoyed this promotion, as I wasn't into American rock music. After about nine months, a colleague left to work for United Artists records, and I saw the chance to take over his position. This was around June 1978, and it bought me into contact with Polydor's punk bands - Sham 69, Siouxsie and the Banshees and, of course, The Jam. Chris Parry had signed them to Polydor in 1977 and, along with Vic Smith, produced their first two albums.

I should say at this point that Polydor had failed to sign The Clash and the Sex Pistols, and only signed The Jam to a contract for two singles, with an option for an album. They were given an advance of £6,000 and it's possible that as The Jam were not a pure punk band, Polydor thought they might not last. If my memory is correct, The Clash signed to CBS for £30,000, an album, and the Pistols for even more money.

I took over The Jam when they were about to release 'David Watts' and were recording their third album, which turned out to be *All Mods Cons*. During the recording of this album, Chris Parry fell out with John Weller and The Jam so, as well as being their product manager, I was now their A&R man. This lasted for a couple of years but the workload was too heavy and the hours too long (60 to 70 hours a week) so I decided to concentrate on A&R on all my bands, which by now included The Chords, a second-generation Mod band.

The Jam's first single and album were hits, and the one tune that stood out on the album *In The City*, was 'Away From The Numbers'. I was genuinely amazed that a teenager was capable of writing such an accomplished tune. The structure of the song is far superior to the rest of the album, with lyrics that belie Paul's relative lack of maturity.

However, early success is always difficult to follow and many people were disappointed with their second album, *This Is The Modern World*. For me, it was recorded too quickly, and rushed out the same year as their debut album. It would have made no difference to Polydor when the second album came out, and they should have realised that the band would have been better served if it had been released later. They should have released a new single and postponed the album until mid-1978. This would have given Paul the time to write more songs and the band to play them in before recording a second album. By doing this, Polydor could have ended The Jam's career before it had started.

If you ask what the defining moment in The Jam's career was, it was the album *All Mods Cons*. With the release of this LP, Paul and the band came of age. Whenever I am asked what my favourite Jam song is I reply, 'It's Too Bad', and no matter how many times I hear this tune I never get bored and often play it repeatedly. It's a nod to The Who's 'So Sad About Us' and The Beatles' 'yeah yeah' guitar riff.

Following *All Mods Cons* and the relative failure of the next two singles, the company lost interest and saw the album as the apex of The Jam's career. I didn't and was very angry. I wrote to my bosses with regard to the company's attitude towards The Jam, and I bluntly pointed out that, unlike the other bands on the label, The Jam had a long-term future. I suggested comparisons with artists from the past, listing the two or three that went on to have careers that lasted three decades or more. I was lucky not to be fired, but fortunately 'The Eton Rifles' saved the day. *All Mods Cons* laid the foundation to the greater success that The Jam later achieved in their career.

Featuring Bruce Foxton on lead vocals The Jam released 'News of the World' on 3 March 1978, which peaked at number 27 on the UK charts. The video for the single was filmed on the roof of Battersea Power Station in Battersea, London.

LYCEUM

18 JUNE 1978, LONDON, UK

I WAS THERE: ROBIN QUARTERMAIN, AGE 16

My first Jam gig was at the Lyceum in the summer of 1978. I had just turned 16, and me and three buddies trooped up to London on this Sunday night for a life changing experience! Supported by Jab Jab and the brilliant Scottish Mod band The Jolt, during

Robin Quartermain (former President of The Vespa Club of Britain) on his 1978 Vespa 150 Super

the show The Jam previewed a few new songs that would later appear on *All Mods Cons*.

We stood behind Billy Idol then of Generation X who loved it. Paul Weller stopped a song because as always a fight broke out on the dance floor and offered the offenders to see him outside afterwards, as if!

In later years I deejayed at From The Jam shows with Rick and Bruce and one night as I finished my set walked off and waited backstage. I thought I had whispered to my mate Paul, 'Bet you didn't think you would be stood here 30 years ago?' Rick heard me and said, 'I didn't think I'd be doing it either!'

Great times from 1977 until 1982 - if you missed it you missed out life changing times indeed. I still ride a Vespa and wear Fred Perry, etc. and up until recently was President of The Vespa Club of Britain. I blame The Jam!

I WAS THERE: MARK ANDREWS

Potentially the first ever concert I would attend - The Jam at the Lyceum Ballroom, London but it took some sorting out. First off my friend Matt and I had school the next day, so we had to get both sets of parents to agree. Job done. Next my dad agreed to buy the tickets from the box office as he was working in London and I was panicking for days as I waited for him to come home with them. As always he delivered.

What to wear was the next problem. I finally went with a military style shirt, tie and assorted badges to show my allegiance.

The day finally arrived and I had my tea at Matt's mum and dads. We set off on a blistering hot day for London - excited, nervous and not at all sure what to expect.

Outside Charing Cross station we bumped into a group of lads who were dressed to impress and they put us both to shame. They pointed out the venue and we both knew from that day on we would need to work harder on 'the look'. Once inside the venue we tried to work out where to stand for the first support band, Jab Jab. We were on the stairs.

For the second, The Jolt, I think we were in the middle and as we prepared for The Jam we had a good spot left of centre, closest to Paul.

The rest of the gig is a blur - I started bouncing from the moment they hit the stage. Matt did not believe I would be able to keep it up for all the gig and he was right. It was loud,

I was sweating and it passed in a flash. Time for a cliché but it really changed my life.

We wandered wide-eyed outside with our ears ringing and there was my dad in his Ford Capri waiting to take us home - proper rock and roll.

I WAS THERE: EUGENE MCCAFFREY, AGE 16

I was 16 and doing my O Levels. I was living with my parents in Brixton. My dad was a lorry driver and my mum a cleaner. I had been a fan of the group since seeing them do 'All Around the World' on the Marc Bolan show. I was walking out of the room and caught sight of these three guys in suits.

A friend bought the single and on about the second play it just hit me – it was difficult to describe but it was like a rush. His older brother was an apprentice electrician and we all got into them. I obsessed about the band. When the Lyceum gig came around, we just went down there to get tickets on the door. There was a long queue, snaking around the pub on the corner (the Lyceum Arms) and into the Strand. I can remember worrying we would not get in and ended up buying a ticket from a tout who was going along the line. My mates kept telling me I had bought a counterfeit but when we got to the door we all got in.

The support were The Jolt. All we knew was they were Scots. Now I'd have paid more attention to 'See Saw', but I was unaware Weller had written it. It seemed an age before The Jam came on. John Weller came on to announce them and the next thing the band came on in pale blue suits, I think, that looked grey under the lights. I was transfixed by Weller: he was so slim and radiated charisma. They were very loud. I remember that on 'Modern World' a strobe light came on. I'd never seen one before and the sight of Weller moving across the stage in the stuttering light during his lead solo has never left me. I thought they were awesome.

We all became Mods and followed other bands like the Chords, Merton Parkas (who gigged in Clapham regularly) and the Purple Hearts. I was desolate when the band split and have followed all the twists and turns of Paul's career, through the Style Council to his solo career, seeing him live in all his guises.

The double A-side "'A' Bomb in Wardour Street" / 'David Watts' was released on 18 August 1978 as the first single from their third studio album, *All Mods Cons.* Once again Bruce Foxton was given a turn to sing lead vocals, featuring on The Jam's cover of The Kinks 1967 hit 'David Watts'.

18TH NATIONAL JAZZ, BLUES AND ROCK FESTIVAL

25 AUGUST 1978, READING, UK

I WAS THERE: DAVID BIRCH

Headliners were The Jam (who moaned about the sound system throughout) - ultimately with Weller declaring that '..someone had stitched them up!' Other acts were a strange mix – a brilliant Patti Smith, Sham 69 with a bizarre Steve Hillage taking the stage with them and John Otway, as eccentric as ever.

I WAS THERE: PHIL BRENNAN

I travelled to Reading with a pal of mine who had convinced me to go as he was driving down for the opening night as the festival was putting a few punk bands on for the first time, including Radio Stars, Sham 69, Ultravox and The Jam. Barney's plan was that we would drive there, watch the Friday night gig, sleep in his car and then drive over to Newport the following day to watch our team Stockport County. How could I resist?

The two of us set off from Stockport very early on the Friday morning, arriving in Reading just after dinner and parked the car in a pub car park not too far from where the festival was being held. Having enjoyed a couple of pints with our dinner we bought a few cans of beer from the local shop and made our way to the festival. Once we had made our way into the main field, we noticed that there had obviously been some fighting as there were a couple of lads being treated by the St John's people.

We made our way towards the front where there were two stages. There was a band already playing on the one of them, although neither of us recognised the band or their music. They were obviously not going down well as we could see that there were cans of beer being thrown towards the stage. They didn't last much longer before giving in to the constant barrage.

The first couple of bands that we saw were The Automatics and The New Hearts. Neither were particularly to our taste and both also were subject to a few cans thrown from the crowd, The Automatics cutting short their set to save their bodies from further punishment whilst the singer of The New Hearts stopped their set after their guitarist was struck on the head by a can.

Next up were Radio Stars who we were both looking forward to, as we had seen them together in Manchester earlier in the year. Having witnessed singer Andy Ellison climbing up into the rafters above the crowd in Manchester whilst singing, it came as no surprise to us to see him climb up the stage rigging during their set. He was pelted with cans whilst climbing but then when he reached the top the cans stopped and he was roundly applauded for his efforts.

Radio Stars set was great and their song 'No Russians in Russia' certainly got the crowd on their side. It was a warm day and apart from the odd skirmish between a few skinheads and some bikers, it was enjoyable and trouble free.

Penetration were next on and they were very good. Singer Pauline Murray played the crowd well and there was no sign of beer being thrown whilst she was on stage. However, the atmosphere certainly changed when Sham 69 took to the stage. When we had arrived earlier in the day, we had seen a large number of skinheads being escorted into the venue, as the band came on stage the 'Sham Army' suddenly made their presence felt.

There were fights breaking out sporadically during the set but when the band kicked into their hit song, 'Borstal Breakout', it was as if the blue touch paper had been lit on a firework. There was mayhem for a while and singer Jimmy Pursey appeared to collapse before being helped off the stage in tears. The fighting continued between rival factions for a while until The Pirates took to the stage.

The Pirates were the original backing band for late Fifties and early Sixties singer Johnny Kidd and so by my reckoning were already far too old to be playing on the same bill as Sham 69 - how wrong could I have been? From the minute they plugged in, the threesome absolutely blew the crowd away. Storming through a great set of great songs, some that I recognised from my younger days along with several new ones, never before had I witnessed a band change the mood so positively.

Skins, punks, bikers and hippies were all up dancing and singing along to the likes of 'Please Don't Touch', 'Don't Munchen it!' and 'Shakin' All Over'. With peace restored, and in truth with the majority of the skinheads gone, Ultravox came on stage gaining the advantage of the fading light to use their superb lighting show, the opening song 'Slow Motion' setting the trend for a great show and highlighting what a strong front man John Foxx was.

Headliners The Jam suffered in comparison. Singer Paul Weller appeared to be in a bad mood from the off, although to be fair he did well to avoid a beer can that was launched at him as he walked on to the stage. Their white backlighting looked great with the three band members dressed in their sharp grey suits.

I didn't actually recognise any of the first few songs that the band played. I thought they were decent enough but based on my previous experience I was actually expecting more. The thing that stuck in my mind was the fact that from the first song, Weller kept complaining about the sound system. Despite his moaning, the band carried on and once they launched into the old Kinks song 'David Watts', the crowd around us warmed to them.

The set concluded with more songs that I recognised - 'Down in the Tube Station at Midnight', "A' Bomb in Wardour Street' and finally 'News of the World'. As good as their end of set had been, as the band trudged off stage I got the feeling that they were just glad to get to the end of their set.

As we were preparing to leave, Jimmy Pursey came back on to the stage and led a sing along version of 'You'll Never Walk Alone' but by then Barney and I were making our way through the discarded Party Sevens, Courage Jackpot cans and leftover burgers back to the comfort of his Hillman Imp in readiness for our trip to South Wales the next day.

I WAS THERE: STEVE SWIFT

I remember Weller getting stroppy about the sound, but I thought they were awesome - one of the best gigs I ever saw. They were plugging their upcoming album *All Mods Cons* and it was the first time I heard 'Down in the Tube Station at Midnight'. It was phenomenal - probably one of the top musical highlights of my life.

I WAS THERE: DIZZY SKINT

Penetration were great, with a tight set (I always prefer Pauline to Siouxsie). I also remember seeing The Tourists but thought better of it and Sham 69 through the cans, gob and fighting. And then The Jam - well, it was the first year they had the huge screens put up and so from any distance you could see the group looking sharp in grey mohair suits. I do remember the sound being fucked around a bit but what an experience. A set list of performers playing to our generation! The days of love and peace had come to an end and things would never be the same.

I WAS THERE: PETER STITT, AGE 15

It was my first proper gig. Me and a mate camping, aged 15, miles away from parental control. It was magical. I had already fallen in love with Sham 69 and found it amazing that Jimmy Pursey would spend most of the day hanging around with us idiots. He was, and remains, a really genuine bloke, always accessible. The Jam didn't get a fair deal on the sound front but they just drove straight past their supporters into the back-stage enclosure, no talking, no autographs. Good socialism, comrade Paul. They were always better suited to small halls anyway, that type of band.

I WAS THERE: JAMES WINDSOR

When The Jam played, there wasn't a single can thrown. I think the crowd would have pelted the royal family before ever tossing a can at The Jam. I attempted once or twice to get close to the stage, but each time was repelled by the crushing masses and ear-splitting volume, so retreated to a safer and more comfortable distance. Considering the rough activities at the front of the stage, I probably was lucky I couldn't reach them.

I WAS THERE: TIM JONES, AGE 15

I attended Reading Festival in 1978, but for just one day - the Friday. I was only interested in the punk bands. It was a real experience for a 15 year old.

There were can battles between sections of the crowd and cans being thrown at the stage from early on in the day. The first band on - I do not remember the name - on the right hand stage (where Penetration, The New Hearts, The Pirates and The Jam performed) had an open piano. The can throwers were trying to get the cans into the piano. Every now and then - or it might have been only once - one hit a string and would get a cheer from the crowd.

I was at the front for all the right hand stage acts and at the front for Sham 69 who were on the left stage. For the Radio Stars, the Automatics and Ultravox, I was on the right hand stage front looking across.

John Peel tried to stop the can battles by threatening to play Burt Bacharach, Bee Gees and Andy Gibb records. I remember him playing some of these and the can throwing would die down for a while. He also got the crowd to chant if things went wrong. The chant was – 'John Peel's a cunt'. This rang out many times from the festival site by the Thames in Caversham through the town of Reading from the afternoon to the night. The locals and the organisers were not too impressed and I think he got banned from the festival for a number of years as a result.

The Jam were the headliners and good, but the sound was a little ragged and Weller was getting really upset as girls kept being pulled out of the crowd past him and the sound did not improve. I remember him smashing a guitar at one point, but I am not sure how damaged it was.

I WAS THERE: SIMON WRIGHT

The third time I saw The Jam was dispiriting. I was working backstage at Reading Festival in August 1978, which meant that once again I saw The Jam for free, but it was not a happy weekend. The bill was a queasy mix of new wave and old wave - 'Punk's Altamont' was a fanciful headline. The punks didn't like the hippies and the skinheads didn't like the mods. On the Friday night there was a lot of fighting during Sham 69's set. Jimmy Pursey bringing on Steve Hillage to guest did little to help. The throwing of mud and Watney's Party Sevens full of liquid (probably not beer) brought a real edge to aggressive songs like ''A' Bomb in Wardour Street'. Weller trashed his gear at the end, maybe in frustration at the poor sound or maybe just totally fed up with the goons in the audience.

The Jam released 'Down in the Tube Station at Midnight', the second single from *All Mods Cons*, on 13 October 1978. Originally Paul Weller had wanted to exclude the song from the album on the grounds that the arrangement had not sufficiently developed during the recording sessions. He was persuaded to include it by the record's producer, Vic Coppersmith-Heaven. The front cover photograph was taken at Bond Street tube station, on the westbound Central line. On the back cover was a portrait photograph of Keith Moon who had died a month prior to the single's release.
Nick Hayward: 'Down in the Tube Station at Midnight' is definitely alongside Paul McCartney's 'Silly Love Songs' as the greatest pop bass line of all time. It's the first thing I play when I pick up a bass in a music shop.'

EMPIRE

1 NOVEMBER 1978, LIVERPOOL, UK

I WAS THERE: IAN PROWSE, AGE 14

It was a Wednesday night in Liverpool, November 1st 1978 and I was 14 years old. Paul Weller walked out onto the Liverpool Empire stage, pencil thin, sharp all-black suit, black shirt, bright green tie and Jam shoes. He plugged in his bright red flashing Rickenbacker blade, slashed at it a few times and bellowed into the microphone: 'Seen you before, I know your sort, you think the world awaits your every breath…'

And that was that. All was changed utterly in that instant. It's never been unchanged either – whatever alchemy took place within my teenage self at that very moment, it hit so hard, so deeply and with such force, that it's still the artistic fuel I'm running on 38 years later. My first ever gig was The Jam and, just like your first match when you emerge from within the stands and see the green pitch for the first time, your first concert never leaves you – it's outside of all your previous experiences. The noise, the lights, the massive PA (Muscle Music!) and the theatre of it all - punk poet Patrik Fitzgerald and cartoon act The Dickies were the supports.

It wasn't just The Jam's gigs that affected me so profoundly – I attended another five Jam concerts, including the infamous blood bath that was the first Deeside Leisure

Centre show – it was the songs and, in particular, Paul Weller's words. Ya' see, he was singing about me and my world: working class, council estate kid, parochial, resentful, in awe of the nearby big city… but, most of all, teenage. My overriding memory of the gigs was how teenage they were: I don't recall any old people (by old, I mean over 23). It really was all about the kids.

This Is The Modern World was my first album, the lyrics at the top of this piece were my Road to Damascus moment and, listening to it on my terrible little cassette recorder, by the time he sings the expletives with such rage and venom, I was a goner. If the Liverpool Empire gig had made me want to be in a band months earlier in 1978, the songs themselves were like missives from the one who understood us… our leader. I was too young and uncool to realise that much of this era Jam had been appropriated from The Clash and that all became irrelevant two days after the Empire gig, when they released *All Mods Cons*, a masterpiece. The backwards guitar coda to 'In The Crowd' can still reduce me to tears, 'Down in the Tube Station at Midnight' is still the bench mark for all lyric writers and 'Mr Clean' still does punk anger better than punk did – and it's the best song ever written by anybody about the class war. They still copied The Clash, but this time brilliantly, on ''A' Bomb in Wardour Street' and Weller also did the unthinkable and put acoustic love songs on the record: 'English Rose' and 'Fly'… good god, he knew our working class angst was complicated by our feelings for girls, too!

He was 20… the bastard. Then they had a genuine hit single on the next album, 'Eton Rifles', and became massive. I kinda got off the bus at that point, as I couldn't stand all the nerds getting into my band. Privately, of course, I loved them as much as ever and bought every single thing they put out: 'Liza Radley', 'Funeral Pyre', 'Ghosts', 'Scrape Away' (come on, they were better than ever, I was just being a divvy!).

I love that they will never get back together. I love that Weller split them up when he did: at the very height of their fame and power. I love the righteousness of it all, his clear reasoning, brimming still with conviction. So brave. They were our Beatles… thank god, then, they never became our Rolling Stones.

While out on tour last year, I made the pilgrimage to Somerset House to see the exhibition. It brought it all back and I'm thrilled and proud that it came to Liverpool – a true honour for all involved. If it wasn't for The Jam, I doubt I'd have picked up the guitar and I definitely wouldn't sing like my life depends upon it. Thank you Paul, Bruce and Rick.

Gary Shelley once saw Ken Dodd in panto

I WAS THERE: GARY SHELLEY, AGE 16

My next door neighbour and good mate Robby knocked on the door of our family house in Birkenhead to say he had a spare ticket to see a band called The Jam. My mum and dad had concerns about this trip to Liverpool and were more than justified as at this point I had only

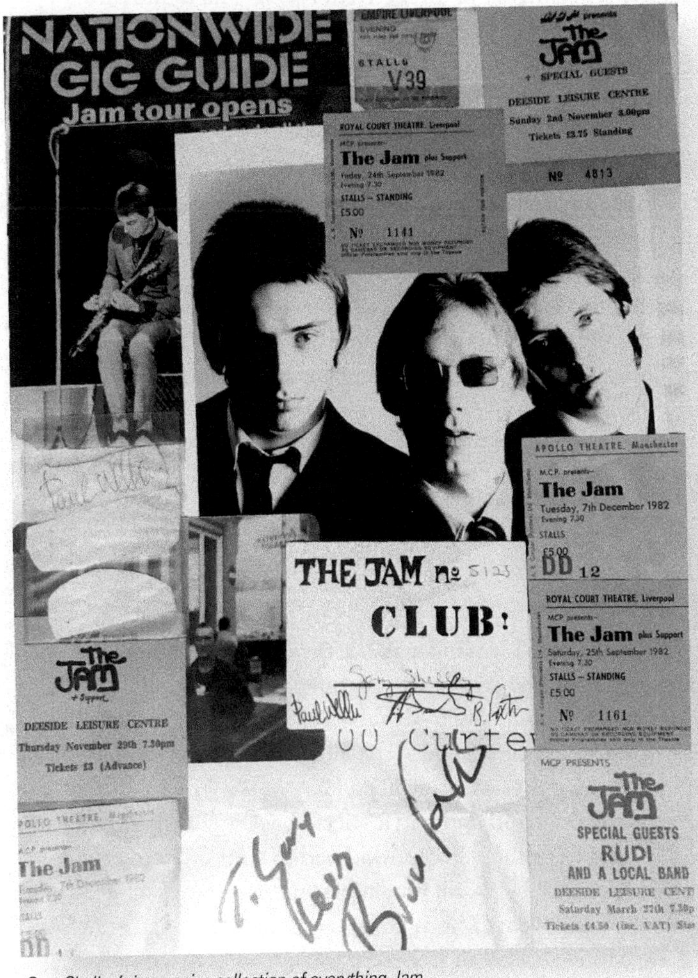

Gary Shelley's impressive collection of everything Jam

seen Ken Dodd in panto and musically I had only travelled as far as the school disco. I was playing ABBA records and my dad's Fifties and Sixties 45s collection which, in hindsight, included many a Mod anthem!

But I did get permission and thankfully had the 'bottle' to go to the Liverpool Empire in November 1978. Suddenly the world changed!

The Empire was and is a traditional all-seated theatre. On the night support acts were a punk poet called Patrik Fitzgerald, who was booed off, and then the Dickies, who were fast and loud – superb! The perfect preparation.

Then The Jam appeared in their suits with a backdrop of a burning building. This was the *Apocalypse* tour. I could not believe the attitude, anger, power and energy that three people could produce. They meant it. As soon as they started some of the crowd stood up from their seats. How could anyone expect you to sit still? But the bouncers/stewards would not let anyone stand up. One of them punched a lad on my row. Weller stopped mid-song, screaming at the bouncers to leave us all alone. Then World War Three kicked off and - the crowd won! We all stood up and there was nothing anyone could do.... it was a riot. Seats were being smashed up and thrown into the orchestra pit and set alight and The Jam played on. I stood up like everyone else and in my innocence waited for the police to arrive!

It was The Jam and us against the world together... I was Paul Weller! Or, at least, I suddenly wanted to be. To be someone, ''A' Bomb', 'Tube Station' and 'David Watts' having been on *Top of the Pops*. It was life changing, the intimidating atmosphere and feeling part of something very, very special. This meant something and I wanted more..... That spotlight constantly reflecting off of Bruce Foxton's bass, high into the ceiling of the Empire. Again, superb!

Then it was over. We entered the dark wet night and headed home. I wrote 'The Jam' on the misty bus window. I remember just staring at it as it started to run. What the hell had just happened?

The next day 'THE JAM' was etched in black gloss paint and took pride of place on my school haversack. They changed my life. I felt part of something very special and it turned out to be exactly that. Clothes from Carnaby Street and a lime green Lambretta with Pretty Green painted on the panels. Scooter rallies, waiting for Rox Records in Birkenhead to open the box with 'Strange Town' in it. I'm happy to say I managed to see The Jam on 10 occasions and nothing compares to a Jam gig. It was a coming together, great support acts… a happening! A Jam gig felt like home. Fantastic memories, all thanks to The Jam and a spare ticket.

DE MONTFORT HALL

2 NOVEMBER 1978, LEICESTER, UK

I WAS THERE: TIM FILOR

The Jam will always be my favourite band. I was lucky to see them live four times. My mate Steve Bizley had introduced me to The Jam about the time of 'All Around The World'. That was the first Jam single I bought along with the Sex Pistols' 'Pretty Vacant' and the Stranglers' 'Peaches'. I purchased the *Modern World* album not long after that and, despite the slagging off in the music press, I really liked it.

Steve was the bass player in our school band and had a Rickenbacker copy bass like Bruce's. He only lived down the road from the school so we used to go down and listen to records in our sixth form study periods. I can still remember one session when he plonked 'Strange Town' on the deck and said, 'This is amazing', I agreed.

My first Jam gig was at the De Montfort Hall in Leicester. I'd only seen two bands prior to this, 10cc sometime in1976 (I think) and The Stranglers in 1977. I'm pretty sure I went with Steve as I remember him buying a 'Tube Station' t-shirt at the end. The third person with us may have been Chris Lazzari who was a punk at the time, but I can't remember.

The Vapors were the support band and I remember thinking they were pretty good, plus a punk poet who was mildly amusing. His party piece was getting an umbrella out to protect himself from a potential barrage of gob from the audience. I can't remember a torrent of phlegm falling down on him. That sort of thing was a bit old hat by then.

The Jam came on framed by a painting of a big tower block in the background. I'd heard nothing like it before and they just blew me away. I remember the stuff from *All Mods Cons* just leaving me breathless. I hadn't heard the album prior to the gig as it hadn't been released but storming versions of 'To Be Someone' and 'Mr Clean' left a lasting impression on me. We were standing about halfway back from the stage. People

were leaping about in front of us. I was just standing there stunned by the power of the music.

Some choice cuts from the *Modern World* and *In The City* albums followed plus most of the current singles leading up to the final number "A' Bomb In Wardour Street'. The backdrop lit up as the song crashed to the end. We screamed for more and got it, though I can't remember exactly what the encore was.

A few days after *All Mods Cons* was released I went Christmas shopping with my mum and dad in Peterborough. I rushed into Boots and got the album. It was straight on my music centre when I got home and it didn't disappoint. The secret track on the album, 'English Rose', is the only one I don't really like. Mike Reid used to play it a lot on Radio 1 and I know a lot of fans love it so I'm probably in the minority when I say it's the one thing that stops it being the perfect album for me. I remember a critic in one of the music rags reckoning that this album was Weller's rewrite of *Revolver*. What I want to know is what track did he think was the new 'Yellow Submarine'?

The third and probably the most memorable gig for me was again at De Montfort Hall in Leicester in 1980. Originally I'd purchased a ticket for me, and my mate Chris Lazzari to go.

We, plus a lot of the audience, were now living the Mod lifestyle. Chris and I both had scooters and lived in parkas and Mod suits, etc. It had all become clear to me now why at Loughborough the parka clad boy had taken a beating as I'd had a few close calls myself.

The popularity of The Jam was now on an upward surge and they usually did a two-nighter at Leicester. I hadn't left getting the tickets that late as I worked near the ticket office but I was disappointed as the only tickets left were in the balcony sitting down for both nights. I always liked being in the stalls.

The night before the gig Chris was taken ill and he didn't think he would be well enough to go so I offered the ticket to another mate, Pete Barratt. He was well pleased because it was close to his birthday. He'd been at my school but we actually got friendly after we'd left due to a mutual interest in Mod. It was good that he came because the night wouldn't have been anything like as good if he hadn't.

We started off in the balcony but we could see that it was more fun in the stalls. The Jam came on and it was crazy at the front part of the stalls. Pete had also been a punk and liked leaping about so we decided we wanted a piece of the action. We went downstairs and sneaked into the back of the stalls.

We gradually weaved nearer the front and new songs from the *Sound Affects* album rang out as we slowly edged forward. We were getting pretty close to our objective when the opening riff of 'In The City' rang out. It was like a catalyst for us (bearing in mind our previous love of punk) and we started leaping about like madmen. I don't think it went down too well with those around us but we didn't care. This was what we had come for. I can't remember how much more of the gig was left but we bounced around till the final chords of the encore faded out.

I think we were both pretty knackered at the end and I started to make my way out with the rest of the crowd. Pete grabbed me and suggested we hang around. We wandered around the hall while it emptied, avoiding the stewards. I was a getting a bit nervy but Pete persuaded me to hang on. The other people in the hall had permits of one sort or another.

What happened next left me gobsmacked, Bruce and Rick came out and stood very close to us and a small crowd gathered round them. We had to get an autograph but all we had was our ticket stubs so that's what we handed over. They kindly took them out of our sweaty hands and somehow managed to get both signatures on them. We needed the full set but where was Paul?

We had a little wander and found him in another part of the hall leaning up against a pillar. He looked a bit sullen and a fan was speaking in his ear, something about 'prima donna'.

Pete very politely asked Paul if he'd sign our stubs and a few seconds later we'd got the full set. It was a magical end to a brilliant night. It just showed how well the lads treated the fans. How many bands at that same level of fame would have come out like that after the gig? Not many I suspect!

I was pinching myself on the way home I just couldn't believe it. When I told Chris about it the next day he was well naffed off. It's still one of my most treasured possessions and it's a brilliant reminder of a great night all those years ago.

It was a little while till I saw the lads for the final time. I kept track of the vinyl output but I was madly in love with a girl at the time whose taste in music was somewhat different to mine so I missed out on the gig scene for a while. I'd lost contact with Chris as he'd met a nice Modette at a Chords gig and that was basically the last I saw of him socially ('thick as thieves' comes to mind). I hadn't been much better with Pete and Steve but didn't completely lose contact with them and I actually went to see Slade with Pete at De Mont (well, I was a big fan in the Seventies). My image had changed a bit as I was now a bit of a biker but thankfully that phase didn't last long.

It was now March 1982. I wasn't quite so young but I was free and single and a live Jam fix was needed again ASAP. I didn't have to wait long as they visited De Mont on the 23rd. My old mate Steve kept me company for the second time. I could only get balcony seats again which was a bit of a bummer but we were near the stage so it wasn't too bad. There was no chance of getting in the stalls this time as security had been tightened and you had to show your ticket to get in.

As we looked down we could see the Mods sweltering in their parkas. They seemed so young - probably only fourteen or fifteen. The support act may have been the Piranhas as they did 'Tom Hark' but that could have been at an earlier gig.

The Jam came on and the room yet again erupted. They were huge now, we didn't know at the time that it was close to ending, we just sat back and enjoyed the ride. A constant stream of little Mods were getting pulled out of the front as the crowd surged forward. They had a brief moment with their heroes on stage before being hauled off by the bouncers.

The band had lots of material to choose from now and a new album to promote. I'd like to say I can remember what they did but my memory is coloured by a video I have of virtually the same set at Bingley Hall that had been recorded the previous night. The backdrop was a banner saying *Transglobal Unity Express.* I can remember them doing that song and also 'Scrape Away', which seemed to be extra long, 'Pretty Green', 'Man in the Corner Shop' and finally 'Happy Together'.

We left the gig elated and made a quick dash to the Old White Horse on London Road to catch last orders. It was a real spit and sawdust pub in those days but was later refurbished. I must have been full of adrenalin as I never rush anywhere normally.

As we supped our beers we never really thought that would be the last time we would see the band live but sadly it was. I didn't get to see any of the final gigs and had to be content with the final outing on *The Tube*. I have to admit that once the boys had unofficially expanded to five it wasn't quite the same for me but with hindsight you can now see where Paul wanted to go.

I did quite like the Style Council but it wasn't quite the same experience when I saw them live.

Bruce's solo stuff was pretty good and I bought 'Freak'. My future wife had the album and, again, it was as good as Paul's output at the time. There was a brief moment of excitement when Rick and Bruce almost got a band called Sharp together with a guy from The Chords (I think) but it was sadly not to be.

All I can say is a massive thanks to The Jam, it was good while it lasted. The legacy for me is that it inspired me to get in a band with three other Jam fans mourning the demise of the best trio in the world. I was literally about to sell all my gear when I saw an advert in the local rag placed by a student at Leicester Uni called Rob Snape quoting The Jam, among others, as the musical direction that the band would take. I had actually bumped into him a few years back at an Elvis Costello gig and it was good to see him again. When I first joined the band in 1983 I was talking to Martin the drummer as we'd pretty much been to the same gigs. At De Mont, Paul Weller had suddenly left the stage for no apparent reason and then came back a bit later with a smirk on his face - unusual for him at the time! Martin explained that he had split his trousers and had to go off and change them.

I obviously never found fame and fortune but I did carry on playing in various line ups till 1997. Over that period of time I met my wife and a lot of my friends and I now have two great kids and a lot of memories.

My regrets are few but I wished I'd seen The Jam live more, particularly in 1977 when they played at the Poly (now De Montford Uni) and later in the Eighties at Granby Halls. I never got the chance to hear 'All Around The World' live as it was never played at any of the gigs I went to. They broadcast a gig on the radio and it was the last track but it faded out halfway through, much to my frustration. The same gig is on *The Jam at the BBC* CD, which I thoroughly recommend.

My final note is it's a terrible thing getting old. It's taken a while for me to compile this as I had to consult diaries, memorabilia, etc. to get my facts straight. I have to admit that I thought I'd only seen the lads three times and got some events muddled up. I think it's pretty accurate now.

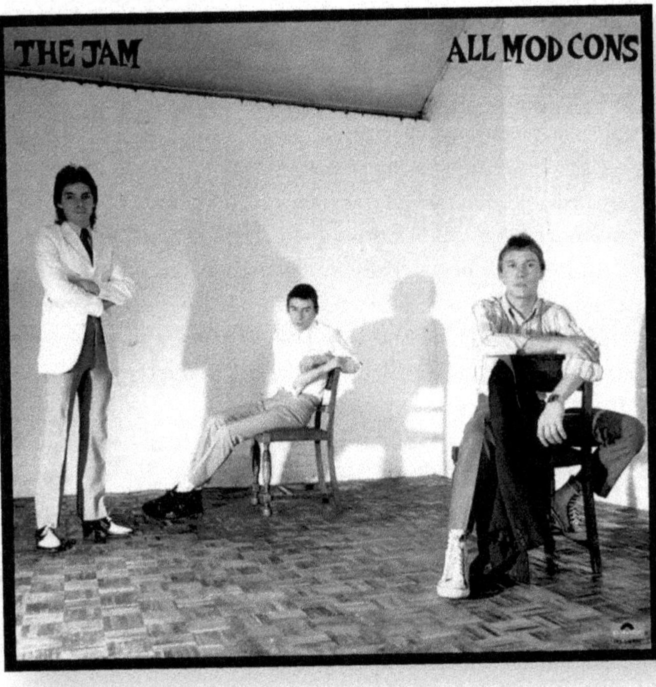

I hope this revives some memories of what it was like to be at a live Jam gig because I've not seen a band since who can even come close to it.

3 November 1978 saw The Jam's *All Mods Cons* released which became their first UK top 10 album. In his review for *NME*, Charles Shaar Murray said that the album was 'not only several light years ahead of anything they've done before but also the album that's going to catapult The Jam right into the front rank of international rock and roll; one of the handful of truly essential rock albums of the last few years. Weller is – like Bruce Springsteen – tough enough not to feel he needs to prove it any more, strong enough to break down his own defences, secure enough to make himself vulnerable. The consciousness of *All Mods Cons* is the most admirable in all of British rock and roll, and one that most of his one-time peers could do well to study'.

CITY HALL

4 NOVEMBER 1978,
NEWCASTLE-UPON-TYNE, UK

CITY HALL
Northumberland Road, Newcastle upon Tyne 1
Saturday, 4th November, 1978, at 8.00 p.m.
MEL BUSH
presents
THE JAM
plus support
BALCONY £2.80 SEAT E 60
Booking Agents: City Hall Box Office
Northumberland Road, Newcastle upon Tyne (Tel 20007)
This Portion to be retained.
SMITH PRINT GROUP

I WAS THERE: FRANK WEBSTER

Coming from Cumbria we went to Newcastle mainly to see live bands. The first time was at the Mayfair ballroom in November 1977 and it cost £1.50. All the other Newcastle gigs were at the City Hall. At Newcastle I remember once or twice the last song before the encores was "A' Bomb in Wardour Street' and at the build up at the end of the song the sound of a bomb went off and the sound was deafening. It made your hair stand on end. 'The Butterfly Collector' was another standout song. I remember songs like 'Billy Hunt', 'News Of The World' and 'Strange Town' always got the crowd going. We used to go in a friend's car or sometimes a minibus if there was a few of us. I got to see The Jam nine times between 1977 and 1981, but sadly never got to see them on the last tour in 1982.

I WAS THERE: CHRIS HUNT

I'd been a big Bowie fan, I'd listened to Bowie since I was eight - I had a massive love for music, my dad was really into music and Bowie was everything, but then that waned a little in the Seventies at the end of *Diamond Dogs*. Bowie was probably getting cleverer and I was not old enough to understand it.

Chris Hunt still has his Jam parka with 'The Jam The Modern World' painted on the back

Then The Jam came along. I remember buying *All Mod Cons* from Woolworths. Listening to the lyrics in 'To Be Someone' - '…to be one of the bastard sons' I was horrified 'Jesus, what's my mum and dad gonna think when they hear me play this on the radiogram in the living room?' But my dad was good with it, he liked the music, it passed the test. I would turn the volume down when those lyrics would play. And then also 'Mr Clean' - 'if I get the chance I'll fuck up your life', they were both off *All Mod Cons*.

The first time I saw them was in 1978. I went with my brother. I was in the Mod clothes - I've still got my old Jam parka in the garage with 'The Jam The Modern World' painted on the back. I've still got my Jam shoes up in the attic, posters on the wall.

When I was at school they weren't the biggest band in the world, everybody's favourite band in the North-East of England was The Clash, or the Sex Pistols, or X-Ray Spex, and The Jam were almost a bit of a joke because they were posh boys who got dressed up and wore a shirt and a tie - they were almost a little bit dismissed by a lot of people in the north of England.

I went to college in Gateshead, and there was a big record shop, which I think was called Windows. I remember queuing outside - going up early because I was going to college that day and was waiting for the release of *The Gift*, which came in the paper bag. I loved the lyrics on the album - they were almost like he was talking to the young people, whereas Bowie, which was my original, was always a little bit too surreal. The Jam was real, it was about going to school, it was about going to work, it was about friends, people you didn't like, people you really like. They were just honest songs, and probably as much as anything I just loved the coolness and the style and the suits and the ties.

I remember going to see them - it was a real event - you were were with like-minded people. Even by the end of the night, people were sweating - a sweaty mess, literally bedraggled. Whereas when you went in the room, you knew you were sharp, or at least you thought you were. It was the whole package, it wasn't just the music - it was about being a bit different - it was important to feel a bit of elitism about that.

APOLLO

5 NOVEMBER 1978, GLASGOW, UK

I WAS THERE: TOM LUSK

There were two support acts for a change. There was The Dickies, whose singer entered from the back running down the aisle carrying a suitcase. But that wasn't the most memorable moment. Nor was The Jam. It was getting my precious fatigue jacket stolen. What was more, I had my driving licence in the pocket!

The best was yet to come. About a week later I got a letter from a female fan from Bellshill who sent me my driving licence along with a wee sweet note saying she found it, and wasn't it a great gig. It saved ma blushes a bit. As many people commented at the time, 'Whit wis a dain kerryin a drivin licence tae a concert fur?'

UNIVERSITY OF ST ANDREWS

7 NOVEMBER 1978, FIFE, UK

I WAS THERE: JOCK DUNCAN

It was day five of the Rock Festival put on by the Students Union. First on was

Patrik Fitzgerald who came on with his acoustic guitar and sat on a stool throughout his performance. He was good but not everybody's cup of tea, but 'Safety Pin Stuck in My Heart' went down well. Next on was The Dickies - they were great, they used all the stage to their benefit, great fun and they went down a storm.

Then The Jam. Well, what can I say - they were amazing, very professional, sound excellent, very tight. The two previous acts just put you in the mood for them. I remember Paul Weller saying something about the price of the tickets and about students, can't remember exactly what it was.

SHEFFIELD POLYTECHNIC

10 NOVEMBER 1978, SHEFFIELD UK

I WAS THERE: PAUL BREEZE

I'm unsure if we had tickets or we paid on the door, but I remember you had to be signed in as we weren't students. We somehow one by one managed to sneak in through the main door as other people were arriving. We then worked our way down to the front as The Dickies took to the stage.

This was the first time I'd seen The Jam and as time has passed it's all become a bit blurry but one thing I do know is that the night changed everything in my life. Over the next four years I went on to see The Jam over 20 times, and along the way had some truly great times, made some great friends and watched a truly great band just get better and better.

I WAS THERE: GREG SIMPSON, AGE 14

This event is 39 years old and obviously the few memories I have of this are jaded to say the least! I'm not quite sure if we had tickets or it was pay on the door, but one thing is you had to be signed in. This was of course back in the days when the 'students' were all a bit elitist, ie. you had to be one to drink cheap cider in the students union bar even though you had put fuck all in to the system, keeping the riff raff out type of thing - all that shit. It was a nightmare and as a 14 year old you can only stand being told to fuck off so many times. The thing with the students around that time was it was their kind of music circuit, which was basically for them and nobody else.

So there we were, me and Jimmy, and I'm not sure who else was with us, standing around trying our hardest when the man himself Paul Weller came walking down the steps in a parka. We managed to grab him and have a word about getting us in, but no chance as there was loads on the guest list, but somehow one by one we managed to get in, and assemble at the bottom of the steps that went up to the concert hall. I remember on getting to the door that led into the concert hall there being a table selling t-shirts and stuff but not purchasing anything at all. I can clearly remember the sound of Patrik Fitzgerald banging away on his guitar playing the song 'Safety Pin Stuck in My Heart'.

I think we worked our way down to the front as all 14 year olds would do at the time. Next up where The Dickies, a great band from America who played everything at

100mph. I already knew both artists from the John Peel radio show, so they were another two added to my slowly growing list of bands I had seen.

So show time came for The Jam and to this day I can hardly remember anything about them playing this night. It was the first time I had ever seen The Jam. One thing is, I went in as a 14 year big Jam fan but came out a massive Jam fan. This gig along with a few others put me on to a lifetime of listening to this great band and later all the Paul Weller solo stuff, The Style Council and the future recordings of Bruce Foxton and Rick Buckler.

Why mention this you may ask? Well it's 39 years to the day that I saw this band, which changed everything in my life after coming out of the now demolished Sheffield Polytechnic building. Things were different, these events in life may not really be important to a lot of us, however over the next four years I went on to see The Jam 25 times, and along that way I had some truly great times, met some great lads and lasses, and of course watched a truly great band just get better and better. Would I swap this event for anything? No! In fact I won't swap any of the times I saw The Jam, probably not even to see the Sex Pistols who are the only one of my favourite bands I never got to see.

Paul Weller: I was on a mission and I was trying to keep the band on course, which was difficult sometimes. There were lots of things the record company suggested we should be doing that I thought, 'No fucking way.' I had a lot to fight against.

LEEDS UNIVERSITY

12 NOVEMBER 1978, LEEDS, UK

I WAS THERE: REVEREND ANDREW GRIFFIN

1978 was an amazing year. I left school, spent a summer just mucking around with my mates, met my wife who I have been happily married to for 31 years, loved the punk rock scene which was in full flow, and came across a band that totally blew me away. A band called The Jam who I still have an amazing passion for to this day.

There are many times I sit down to decide which of their eloquently written albums I will listen to. I still go see Paul Weller live. Most of the time he still rocks although there has been the odd occasion where I have thought, 'Come on Paul, liven it up a bit'. And I still go see From The Jam, who still make the hairs on the back of my neck stand up with excitement.

1978 and one of my favourite bands, The Dickies, were supporting The Jam on a UK tour (the *Apocalypse* tour). I honestly had never heard of The Jam. A few of my mates said, 'Come on, it'll be great.' When I heard who was supporting I decided to go along. The Dickies came and played their set. Actually, they sounded dreadful.

Then The Jam came on. It was like someone had flicked a switch of excitement and adrenalin on. Sharp suits, sharp set - they blew my mind. The passion in Paul Weller's lyrics, not the greatest guitarist in the world, but the rhythm section from Bruce Foxton and Rick Buckler just glued it all together. This band I could never describe as being cool were vibrant, exciting, new, fresh, energetic… I could go on, but I'm sure you get the picture.

In 1979, *Quadrophenia* was released at the pictures, based on The Who's 1973 rock opera album and I believe one of their best. The streets of Britain, which had seen young figures with slashed pants, bum bags, coloured hair in the style of the Mohicans that looked like circular saws, safety pins and zips galore, now started to see young smart dressed men in sharp suits, smart haircuts and fishtail parkas, some riding on Lambrettas and Vespas. The women had bobbed hair cuts and black and white dresses with everyone trying to outdo each other. The Mods were back, and The Jam were right at the centre of it all.

As a young guy who loved all this it was an exciting time. There were many more Mod bands around - The Lambrettas, Secret Affair, The Purple Hearts, Squire, The Chords and more. But The Jam were the top band for anyone like myself. They immediately become iconic and my bedroom wall was covered in posters of The Jam with a big Union Jack hanging from the corner of the walls. I had scrap books with every newspaper clip I could find, from the *New Musical Express, Melody Maker, Smash Hits, Record Collector* and more. I had a fishtail parka with around 100 badges going down the front in nice neat lines. I still have all the badges in a box in my office at home. I am now a priest working for the Church of England, but at the time The Jam were sacred to myself, my mates and many others. In the church I give talks about not worshiping idols, but this is what I did. I worshipped this band, and to be honest they still and always will have a place in my heart, and a passion that has always fuelled me and continues to do so even though I am now in my mid fifties.

In my last year at school in 1978, we had a school uniform but I decided to wear a two tone purple and gold mohair suit, my school tie and hush puppies. I felt amazing strutting to school but it was short lived, as I was escorted to the headmaster's office and sent home. The day after, my mum made sure I was back in my school uniform. I loved the very short moment of feeling rebellious, but I wasn't going to go against mum.

In 1979 The Jam played Queens Hall in Leeds, an old tram shed. I saw many bands there and the sound was never great but the atmosphere always more than made up for it. The Vapors supported The Jam. Ironically this year (2019) The Vapors are supporting From The Jam on a UK tour and I can't wait. It has taken me right back 40 years. I am as excited now as I was then - my wife says, 'Calm down and grow up!'

Back in 1979, I turned up in a smart suit, fishtail parka and some red suede shoes. I went to pay a visit to the urinals and who should come and stand next to me whilst doing what we do but Bruce Foxton? I have told this story many times, but Bruce unintentionally splashed on my red shoes. With anyone else I would have been cheesed off, but I was chuffed to bits. I wasn't about to go and frame them, but I have always told people about the day Bruce Foxton pissed on my shoes!

That same tour was the *Setting Sons*, an album that has sort of been my favourite. I love the harsh tough production to the LP with amazing melodies. When I listen to it now, I get a sense of how ambitious it was. At the time it was on my turntable constantly. I still love to sit and listen to *Setting Sons*. Some people may find this hard to believe, but there is not a Jam song or album that I didn't like, or even feel was weak.

When you think Paul Weller was only 19 when he wrote *All Mods Cons*, it's crazy, but life was a different culture to what we have now. It was a time before computers, laptops, mobile phones, Apple. The technology was buying a large black disc, placing it on the turntable and listening to music with a faint crackle in the background. I have all my music - around 6,000 LPs - now on iPods. None of it sounds as good. I got rid of my record collection eight years ago. But I still have my Jam collection - all my vinyl singles, LPs, promos, bootlegs, flexi discs, box sets, tribute albums. I have bootlegs which I have seen sell for hundreds of pounds. I estimate my collection to be worth thousands of pounds, yet I still can't part with them. My most prized album is a 12 inch vinyl of *The Gift*, which came with a paper bag stating 'The Jam... A Gift'. I still have one and unless my kids got to it, it should still have the seal on.

Waiting for the next record to come out again was something in itself. I would be waiting outside Pearson Record shop in Bradford Market for a new release, and I wouldn't be on my own. There would be a few of us patiently waiting. We would discuss previous releases and what we were hoping for the new release, which would never be what we thought it would be. There was a great sense of unity, loyalty and friendship amongst Jam fans. Once I purchased the vinyl I couldn't wait to get home, put it on, set the volume to loud, lie on my bed and enjoy - great moments and surprises. The Jam had a knack of producing something new and which always sounded fresh yet retained that Jam rhythm. I can still tell Bruce Foxton's playing to other bands, even when he was in Stiff Little Fingers or Casbah Club. His sound is unique and distinct. Listen to Weller's 'Fast Car, Slow Traffic' featuring Bruce. It stands out a mile.

I saw the band live many times over five years. I once went to see them at Bridlington Spa during a really hot summer. I think it was called *The Bucket and Spade Tour*. It was great. Me and my mates had made a weekend of it, not booking anywhere to stay. The gig was amazing and the band were really on form. We then went on to have a few beers after the show. I remember waking up in a field full of cows, just outside Bridlington. I had a digital watch that played *Yankee Doodle Dandy*. It had got wet and wouldn't stop playing it. When I woke up all these cows were looking at me, munching grass. I don't know how I got there. I had to walk back to Bridlington and get the train back to Bradford, much to the laughter of my so-called mates once we got together. It was all part of the camaraderie of growing up together.

Another time we went to see The Jam in Amsterdam. It cost £19.99 to get the coach, ferry and tickets to the gig. I was only 18 at the time, and again me and my mates went and it was such a great sense of adventure. During the concert someone told us The Jam were playing in Paris a few days later, so me and two of my mates decided to hitch hike to Paris. We didn't think we would make it or we wouldn't get tickets when we got there, but we did. It was a great time. I can't even remember how we got the tickets, probably from touts. Although my French is not that great - we managed to see The Jam in Paris! We then got the train and ferry back home. The whole experience cost us around £60 each which doesn't seem a lot now but my first wage when I started working was £29 per week so it was equivalent to two weeks' wages. But the memories, the adventure and the sense of achievement have always been there. I have had a good life, and continue to have a good life, but that moment in my life really was the best times.

The Jam in concert was something special, I have many images in my mind. I remember in Leeds once them playing 'Butterfly Collector', with simple rigging and lighting, and Paul Weller had a yellow light shining on him, singing 'And I don't care about morals cause the worlds insane and we're all to blame anyway.' I still have that image in my head of him singing that line as though it was yesterday. The jumping up and down on stage by these young energetic guys, not that much older than myself, was electric.

We once got in at one of the sound checks, met the guys and they were all great. It was like 'being with the boys', they had a real heart for the fans and that really came across. I got my parka signed and later when it started to fade I got my girlfriend to embroider the signatures. We did what at the time seemed silly things, but at the time it meant so much. It created a culture of loyalty that I still believe is with any hardened Jam fan today. How many of us go into HMV, look in the CD section for The Jam, with a hope there will be something new? I know I still do it. There was a mutual respect between the fans and the group, and today when I hear Paul, Bruce or Rick in any interview, if The Jam is mentioned they still talk about the fans with a passion. The loyalty still exists to this day – it is quite amazing.

When The Jam announced the split, there were a lot of mixed emotions, it was almost like the end of an era. Paul Weller said he didn't want to be like the Rolling Stones, who actually I still follow and are still incredible live.

At the time it became really hard. I don't remember if I shed tears, but it wouldn't surprise me if I did. The was a lot of bitterness towards Paul, but I have continued to follow him through everything else he has ever done, and still find him an incredibly talented musician. For me he will always be an all time great. I even enjoyed his more melodic CD *Other Aspects, Live at the Royal Festival Hall* although I can understand why it may not be to some people's taste. I find him so versatile. Maybe it's my age that I can appreciate something less subdue. But as the years have gone by, I actually take my hat off to him that he had the courage and balls to stop what he was doing at the top of his game. What it created was a moment in time that has remained as fresh today as it was then. I think if The Jam had gone on there was always a chance they could have gone stale, a little like Oasis and many other bands who continued to try and capture what they initially created.

As a Jam fan I will always have the memories of an exciting vibrant adventurous time. It may have been cut short, but it never had the chance to go stale.

The Jam – still the best fucking band in the world.

HMV RECORDS

13 NOVEMBER 1978, MANCHESTER, UK

I WAS THERE: NEIL COSSAR

Leaving secondary school in 1974 I didn't want a proper job. All I wanted to do was be a pop star and appear on *Top of the Pops*. I was already playing guitar in bands in and around Manchester and was convinced that one day my parents would proudly watch me on TV performing my latest number one hit on the TV. It didn't happen. My band The Cheaters did sign to Parlophone in the early Eighties and we released one single for the label which disappeared without trace, but we did later make three albums, made a living out of it for around 10 years and played over 1,000 gigs. Our manager was a lovely guy called Pete Hawkins, who had previously worked as The Jam's first London agent, and like The Jam we played all the venues in and around London, The Greyhound, Rock Garden, Dingwalls, Hope and Anchor, etc. Pete believed in the work ethic of get out there and play everywhere, get in front of people and play. The Cheaters were a power pop group and funnily enough it wasn't until years later looking at old photos I realised we looked a bit like Mods with the jackets, shirts and skinny ties. Happy days.

Back to the summer of 1974 and my mum announced this group business was going nowhere and I needed a proper job. She spotted a vacancy going at HMV in Manchester and before I knew it I was stood behind the counter selling records. I loved it. We had a great team of people and to be paid to work listening to music all day with like-minded people made for an easy working day. At the time, HMV Manchester was the second largest record store in the UK with a huge floor space on the first floor reached by some narrow stairs from Market Street. We were a chart return shop, which made us a prime target for not only all the record company reps but an ideal location for personal appearances and signing sessions. We had a real mixed bag of stars who came to the store to meet their fans, sign their latest albums and singles, which all helped towards sales for that weeks chart.

We had Andy Williams who at the time had his American prime time TV show high in the ratings. Over 2,000 middle aged women turned up to meet him, so many in fact that we had them file up the stairs at the front of the shop and leave by a dirty old fire exit into an alleyway full of bins at the back of the shop. Other stars who made appearances included Cliff Richard (smaller than he looks), Judas Priest, Marc Bolan, Kate Bush, Motorhead, Rolf Harris, Deep Purple and The Clash, who almost did cause a riot. The punk/new wave scene brought quite a few acts in including Sham 69, Buzzcocks and others.

During this period one of my jobs was to change the front window display, which was on street level. Nothing too fancy, just a selection of all the latest singles and albums laid out on the floor, with a few featured albums hanging down from the ceiling in plastic wallets. Shortly after the release of the Sex Pistols' *Never Mind The Bollocks* album, a Virgin Records shop manager in Nottingham was arrested for displaying the record. HMV Nottingham were taken to court for displaying the aforementioned album cover under the 1899 Indecent Advertisements Act. When our shop manager heard this news, I was instructed not to remove the ten Pistols albums hanging in the window but instead cover up the offensive word 'Bollocks' with brown packing tape, which I did.

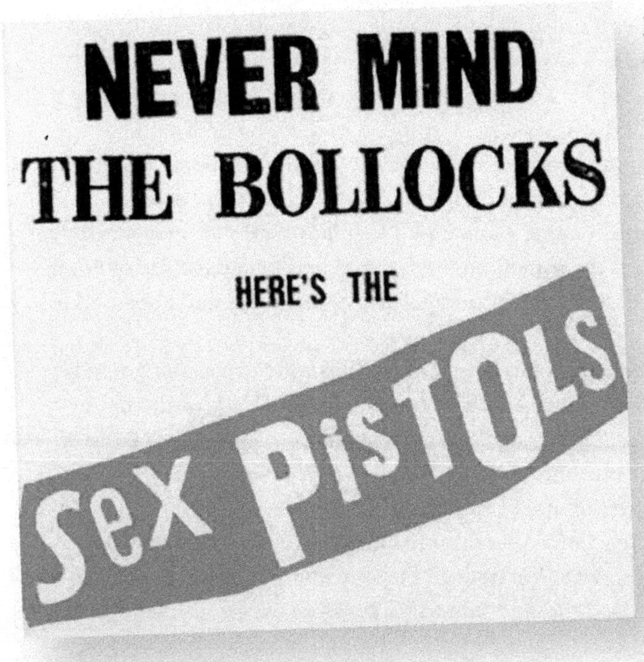

On Monday lunchtime 13 November, Jam fans started to arrive carrying singles, posters and copies of *Smash Hits* for their idols to sign. It was amazing how the news of these events would spread. We would simply advertise the news of appearances with a single poster in the shop window, 'The Jam appearing here for the launch of their new album on ….' This of course was in the days before CDs. All we sold were albums, shrink-wrapped with the record inside, cassettes and 8-tracks. Thousands of albums were on display in the racks. By 2pm there must have been at least 500 punters waiting for the band to arrive, which was a nightmare for our two plain-clothes security guards.

The shop was heaving, so they couldn't move around to see what was going on or help to get people in some sort of lines ready for the signing session. It was madness. I remember we had a phone call saying Rick and Bruce were outside in a car and ready to come in, but no Paul. We were told he was suffering from a heavy cold and was resting for that night's gig at the Apollo. The store manager Pete Waddington was very distraught on hearing this news, thinking we might have a riot on our hands when the fans realised that only two of the group were here. Pete decided he would make an announcement to let everybody know and the reason Paul couldn't make it. He took a chair from the office, turned off the music that was playing (*All Mods Cons* on repeat), placed the chair behind the long counter, stood on it and shouted, 'Can I have your attention please? Hello, hello. I'm very sorry to say that Paul Weller can't be here this afternoon....' which was met with very loud boos. 'Paul is unwell... but Bruce and Rick are here and will start signing their new album for you when you start to form a queue from the back of the store and line up along the counter.' Well, this was met with loads of pushing and a scramble to get as near to the counter as possible for 500 fans. No one formed a queue! At the same point Rick and Bruce appeared amongst the crowd at the top of the stairs, surrounded by hundreds of fans, and with the help of their driver pushed their way through to the safety of a position behind the counter. The next two hours were fairly chaotic, with the two of them signing anything that was thrust in front of them and of course once a fan had his or her turn they didn't leave the store but hung around to be in the same room as their heroes.

After a couple of hours the pair were whisked away to their awaiting car outside and the fans started to drift off. What I do remember was the state of the shop afterwards. Whole sections of albums had been stolen. The Kinks section was empty, Small Faces albums all gone, Motown, punk, new wave albums – we must have lost at least a thousand pounds worth of records! Ken and Jim the two security guards were fuming, but there was nothing they could do. They'd been trapped in the masses of fans.

Many years later, and running my own music PR company, I was fortunate enough to work with Rick Buckler arranging promotion for his *That's Entertainment* book. Rick worked so hard over a few months, visiting radio and TV stations around the country, and never complained once about the sometimes early starts and long days. He did over 80 radio interviews, six TV appearances and countless press interviews and appeared to enjoy every minute of it.

Almost everywhere we went people would come up to Rick and have a chat and talk about The Jam days - train stations, pubs, hotels, you name it - and Rick would be so happy to talk to them. We had a standing joke where we would see someone looking at Rick, do a double check to see it was him and then come over. We would clock this and under our breath say, 'Here we are, another Jam fan....'

One day we were in Media City, Salford sat outside having an early lunch after Rick had been a guest on *BBC Breakfast News*. We noticed this guy in a suit looking over and he started to head our way. I noticed this and said to Rick, 'Here we go' as the guy approached. He stopped and stood in front of us and I noticed he was looking at me and not Rick. 'Bloody hell' he said. 'Neil Cossar from The Cheaters. I used to follow you everywhere!' I was gobsmacked to say the least. Rick was pissing himself laughing. Fame at last.

APOLLO

13 NOVEMBER 1978, MANCHESTER, UK

I WAS THERE: DEN DAVIS

I lived in the suburbs of Manchester in a little place called Bredbury Green near Stockport. My brother is five years older than me and he and his mates got into The Jam from the start. We shared a bedroom; I was only 10 at the start of '77 and still had posters of Man United and The Smurfs on my bedroom wall!

By the summer of '78 I was moving up to senior school and had been playing the records every time my brother was out. By the time *All Mod Cons* came out I was totally hooked.

I was pretty big for my age and not far off my 13th birthday. I held my own at football with the older lads and much to my brother's annoyance I was welcomed into The Jam fans clan (shortly after he became a David Bowie fan to avoid me tagging along).

I remember my first Jam gig really well, November 1978 Manchester Apollo and that black and white suit of Paul's, who could forget. Crushed against the stage - the energy,

Above and previous page Jam fans enjoy a visit to the About The Young Idea exhibition in Liverpool

the sweat, exhausting for a kid but I couldn't get enough after that. I joined The Jam fan club and got to as many gigs as I could, blagging the older lads to get me there by whatever means of transport was available. I saw them 37 times - I spent 1982 bunking off school to get to the gigs and record the shows for The Jam tapes collection.

I've collected everything to do with The Jam obsessively since my first visit to the Manchester record fair at the end of '79. Most people know about me losing the vinyl side of the collection in the Manchester bomb in '96. Thankfully the memorabilia was safe at home. In 2000 I rebuilt the vinyl and thanks to the Internet I soon amassed a huge collection. I'd kept diaries of my adventures during '82 and decided to write a film script. I took it to Universal and pitched ideas for the film accompanied by box set releases, documentaries and an exhibition, About The Young Idea.

I always did things via the proper channels and it was great to be able to partner up with Nicky Weller and her partner Russ to make all this a reality with the full support of the band and the record label.

I'm still working on the feature film and we are about to announce a new exhibition for summer 2020.

COVENTRY THEATRE

15 NOVEMBER 1978, COVENTRY, UK

I WAS THERE: MAX MCCONNELL, AGE 17

It was my 17th birthday and me and a couple of mates went to Coventry Theatre - a great venue no longer there like many others. It was also a place we could easily sneak into but we did pay this time. Being young punks from Wyken, Coventry, we all used to sit in each other's bedroom and listen to each other's records on cheap record players from that time. I got mine from the Co-op on HP from my £25 per week wages. I loved the earlier punky sounding Jam and as great bands do they progressed into something truly wonderful. The hardest question to answer - favourite track? Right now I would say 'Butterfly Collector' but tomorrow I may say something else!

THE DOME

21 NOVEMBER 1978, BRIGHTON, UK

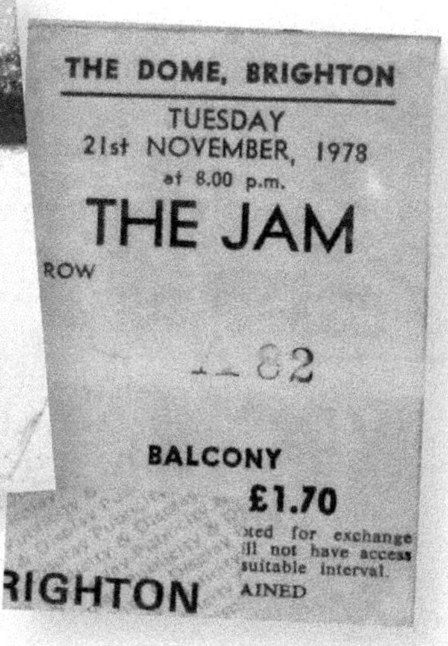

I WAS THERE: SIMON TOURLE

Sporting a new pair of Monk Buckle Gibson shoes that I had finally saved enough dough to get from Streetwalkers along Western Road. There were four of us making our way to the gig on a bus. One of the group had freshly sprayed his jacket with a Jam logo in gloss enamel which duly stuck to the bus seat. Plonker.

We were all revved up for this one - *All Mods Cons* was a masterpiece and we all had it on permanent rotation as we sat in our bedrooms examining the inner sleeve's every detail. I loved that montage of memorabilia, so cool.

The support was Patrik Fitzgerald, who I have very little memory of unfortunately, and then The Dickies - who were great! So fast and animated. Bruce Foxton was enjoying them from the side of the stage - we could see him from where we were in the front row of the balcony nodding away in approval. He was wearing a Levi's grey hoodie which was a relatively new addition to the brand - hair immaculate of course.

Simon Torle thrashing his 330

The Jam hit the stage and the place rocked! I was mesmerised by the Rickenbacker 330 Weller was thrashing away at and promised myself I would get one of those, which I did on the never-never from Broadway Music in Worthing, which I found out recently whilst chatting to Russell Hastings was where he got his (same model, same year! I love recounting the story!) It sounded amazing! Weller was sporting the exact same pair of shoes as me. The clothes were always an important part of the gigs and the buckled version of the Gibson was a rare version at the time - most were laced so I was well chuffed. Some great leaps from Bruce pounding out those amazing bass lines and Rick was just the coolest drummer I had ever seen. He made the drumming look effortless. The 'James Dean' of drummers!

A great set and an even greater encore with suits changed as they finished with "A' Bomb' in a massive explosion of pyrotechnics - awesome!

I walked out of there with a new perspective. I wanted to do what they were doing! I wanted to thrash one of those gorgeous 330s and sing my lungs out in every venue in the country! That feeling never left me and it spurred me on to learn to play guitar, start a band and relive that moment I had just witnessed.

Since that gig I have played The Marquee, The 100 Club, Dingwalls, Europe and even a 50k Festival in New York. I have wrung every second out of every minute out of my life armed with that Burgundyglo Ric 330.

I would not change a single second of those great days and I owe it all to The Jam - and to my lovely wife who taught me my first three chords and accompanied me on the 18 plus Jam gigs that were to follow.

God bless 'em!

COLSTON HALL

26 NOVEMBER 1978, BRISTOL, UK

I WAS THERE: PAUL HIRIART

I was 15 when I first saw them at Bristol Colston Hall. They had the 'Bomb in Wardour Street' big explosion at the end of the gig. The were backed up by Secret Affair. Then I saw them about 10 times afterwards in various venues and they never once got any less amazing. Weller with his angry riffs and vocals and the boys keeping rhythm in the background. Just the best thing ever, never quite got over it.

GREAT BRITISH MUSIC FESTIVAL

29 NOVEMBER 1978, WEMBLEY, LONDON, UK

I WAS THERE: LORAINE WALSH, AGE 14

This was a strange one. I went down to the first of the three days on the Wednesday with some mates from school. Slade also played on the Wednesday as well as Generation X and The Pirates. Only a few rows from the stage there was a stabbing during the Slade set or that's the rumour that went around and loads of police came in.

The Jam came on late, very late, and played a great set. I remember Paul Weller saying something like, 'We're gonna do a love song now, and if any of you are laughing, someone was stabbed tonight…' before launching into 'I Need You' and the audience went into a deathly ironic hush.

MUSIC MACHINE

21 DECEMBER 1978, LONDON, UK

I WAS THERE: SIMON WRIGHT

The fourth and last time I saw The Jam I actually bought a ticket, after seeing them for free three times, although at £2.50 (advance) it was a steal even then. It was a nice Christmas present to myself. I went with my friend, the minimally dressed Marie-Claire, which was always enough to generate plenty of attention (for her, not me). By now the *All Mods Cons* songs had settled nicely into the set and this was the best time I saw The Jam with 'David Watts' and 'It's Too Bad' being particularly memorable. No violence, no trouble, just a sold out partisan crowd totally into the songs.

Trash singer Simon Wright (third from left) sat next to Marie-Claire

1979

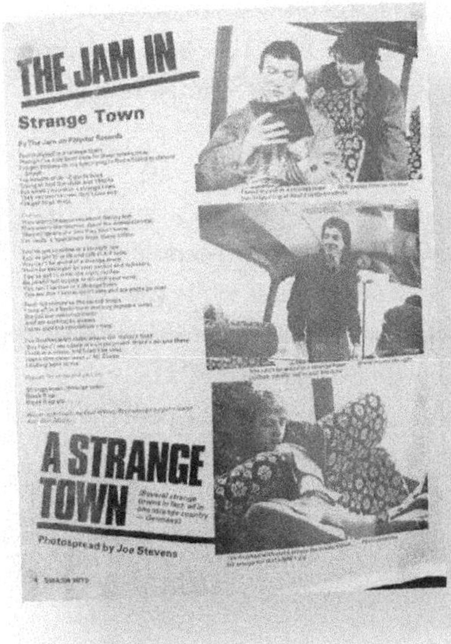

'Strange Town' was released on 9 March 1979 and reached number 15 in the UK singles chart on 8 April. Backed by the Paul Weller-penned 'The Butterfly Collector', it only appeared on one of the band's studio albums, the Canadian Polydor pressing of *Setting Sons*.

REX DANFORTH THEATRE

10 APRIL 1979, TORONTO, CANADA

I WAS THERE: GLEN NICHOLSON

That feeling - that something I had hoped to find at the Elvis Costello concert - well , I found it here. This was a killer show. The Jam were burning with passion and, with sharp rapidity, they delivered one of the tightest sets I've seen. I think Paul Weller hit one bum note the whole night – and, boy, did he look pissed when he did it! He, Bruce Foxton and Rick Buckler seemed to be energy incarnate, never flagging for a moment.

The Jam's *In The City* was the first punk rock album that I bought, during a trip to the UK in the late summer of 1977. Only a few of the British punk bands had released their debut albums at that point, with an onslaught arriving that autumn including the classic *Never the Mind Bollocks, Here's the Sex Pistols* in November.

Given the choices available that August, I selected *In The City* based on the great press it had gotten but probably also because it had an old school element as well, 'old school' in this instance meaning mid-Sixties UK Britpop, especially The Who and The Kinks. Both were and remain big touchstones for me. That period not only influenced this trio's sound but their style as well as they adopted a Sixties UK Mod look.

I immediately liked the short and speedy, yet catchy and tuneful retro-ish songs that made up the album. I instigated repeat-playing it at home, often alternating it with my other very different obsession du jour, David Bowie's *Low*. The Jam's LP was joined in my library in quick succession with albums by The Stranglers, Sex Pistols, Elvis Costello, The Vibrators, Ramones, The Boomtown Rats, Patti Smith, The Clash, Buzzcocks and Nick Lowe.

Shortly after I had left the UK, The Jam issued a quickie follow-up, *This Is The Modern World*: a clever title with one foot in each of their key reference camps, alluding to both the 'It's happening NOW' ethos of punk as well as a play on 'Mod'. Unfortunately, it was a typical case of the second record being a rush job and suffering for it. Not horrible, but not a record that moved forward on its predecessor's promise. But, hey, they were still churning them out at least annually in those days. It's incredible to think that it was not only normal for artists to release albums every year but sometimes twice a year. And 1977 had a run of superb-to-good double dippers such as Bowie, Iggy Pop, Ramones, The Stranglers and The Jam.

They'd had minor UK success with their first discs but needed to come up with something special to take it all to the next level. And they delivered with their autumn 1978 LP, *All Mods Cons*. Weller's songwriting and the band's scope developed substantially with this third disc, refining what they had started with their previous releases while veering off in a variety of new directions that would diversify their sound and subject matter. The Kinks and Who influences were made explicit via the album's two hit singles: a cover of the former's 'David Watts' while the Down in the Tube Station at Midnight 45 boasted a cover of the latter's 'So Sad About Us' as one of the B-side tracks, with a youthful picture of the then-recently deceased Keith Moon on the reverse of the sleeve.

All Mods Cons and 'Tube Station,' a topical, anti-racist UK Top 20 hit, made The Jam full blown stars in their native Great Britain. As for my own personal *Top of the Pops*, from this point until their dissolution at the end of 1982, they arm wrestled with The Clash for the title of My Favourite Band, with Joy Division making it a three-way at some point in the middle of that period.

They may have been a big deal in their native land but over here in North America they never really made much of an inroad, particularly in the US. In Canada, they finally broke through near the end of their career, with *The Gift* going Top 30 as well as having a bona fide Top 20 single with the Motown-ish 'Town Called Malice'- but that was all several years in the future.

When I saw them in April of '79, they were touring *All Mods Cons* on this side of the Atlantic and had just released a brand new single, 'Strange Town,' back in the UK. Once again, a sibling had returned from England brandishing a copy of Weller & co's latest release, only this time it was my brother (my sister had brought *All Mods Cons* back from the UK in October '78 - I guess I started a family tradition of bring Jam records back from there).

My ramped-up obsession with The Jam meant that this was going to be a particularly exciting show for me, not to mention my first concert in Toronto. Growing up just two hours away, I have pretty much been in and out of that city regularly throughout my life. Toronto had hosted many of the new punk groups from both New York and England and, then as now, there are a lot of acts that tour who will play the Ontario capital but nowhere else in the region.

A bunch of us went down in a couple of cars on a grey, early spring day. It was held at the Rex Danforth Theatre, an old converted movie house. This was the first show that I had attended at a smaller venue (holding just over a thousand people) and I loved the intimacy and immediacy of the Rex. It was great to be comparatively much closer to the stage and the heat of the activity than I had been at previous shows.

There was a thrill in being there that was reminiscent of going to see Roxy Music four years earlier in that it was a new experience of sorts - a different city with a different vibe and crowd. And, unlike with the Costello show I had seen, it didn't have the Biff-n'Buffy rent-a-cops nor many 'tourists' (the name given to those who would show up at punk gigs and clubs more to gawk or to say they had been there, rather than genuinely going for the music). It was the real deal fans, and this gig by one of the reigning acts from the UK who had just released an acclaimed album had a genuine sense of occasion.

The retro-mod look was oft-reflected in the crowd. I stylishly made the scene in my black leather winkle pickers and leather jacket with a growing collection of badges announcing my preferred punk and new wave bands of the day.

As for the main attraction, The Jam did not let the sense of occasion go unheeded as they raced onto the stage, launched into their opening number, and delivered a high-energy show that never lost its intensity, even when playing some of the slower numbers such as 'The Butterfly Collector.'

They spat out taut renditions of 'In The City,' 'All Around the World,' 'Away From the Numbers' and more, frequently leaping into the air and playing like they meant it. The highlight for me was the performance of 'Strange Town' and 'Down in the Tube Station at Midnight,' the latter particularly receiving thunderous applause.

Following encores, the house lights came up on a drained and exhilarated audience. As with the Roxy show, I knew I'd seen something special this time. It really did feel like this was the modern world I'd been waiting for, happening for us in this little venue, while the shag-haired universe plundered on around us.

This show was also an end of an era of sorts for me. Starting that upcoming summer, I would begin going to the punk bars and seeing bands playing in tiny venues, making live music-going a continuing activity in my life: much less precious, but more varied in terms of venues, genres, and overall experiences. And certainly no less engaging and celebratory.

PALLADIUM

14 APRIL 1979, NEW YORK CITY, NEW YORK

I WAS THERE: SUZANNA LAMBIAS

I saw them just the once. I went with my guitar teacher, it was before they turned it into a dance club. They were great. John Weller introduced them of course. They never said they were breaking up, someone said see you next year.

SHEFFIELD UNIVERSITY

4 MAY 1979, SHEFFIELD, UK

I WAS THERE: ROY HAYWOOD

Every time The Jam played Sheffield I would be waiting for the doors to open to enjoy the sound check and occasionally get to speak to one if not all of the group. After their second of two nights at the University - they played there two nights back to back - when the gig had finished I hung around watching the roadies take the gear down. To my amazement someone jumped on stage and ran off with Paul's sweat towel. A second later someone else jumped up and nicked Bruce's. I was a coward so I asked one of the roadies very nicely for Rick's. He said he couldn't give it

to me, as he'd get in trouble. I was too shy or scared to climb on and steal it so I kept on asking him. Eventually he picked it up, threw it at me and told me to fuck off!

Fast forward to 1988: newly married, mortgage, lovely house needs decorating. By this time the towel had been my prized possession for nine years. Yes, I know now that was very sad but I didn't realise it back then. I came home from work one day and my ex-wife proudly informed me, 'I've just finished wallpapering the back bedroom. I cut that dirty old towel in your wardrobe up and used it to wipe the paste off the paper. I hope you don't mind.' Laugh? I was totally devastated. Incidentally, that isn't why I divorced her.

RAINBOW THEATRE

10 MAY 1979, LONDON

I WAS THERE: NICK KEMP

Nick Kemp reviewed this gig in *Pop Star Weekly* on 14th May 1979.

One sentence. 'Ullo, this is the Modern World'. The audience went berserk and The Jam had taken 20 seconds to consolidate their position at the top of the new wave hierarchy.

The Jam have progressed considerably in the last year or two. The first time I saw them they were supporting Squeeze at the Marquee and on a free night at that. In those heady days they'd play 'In The City' about five times and they were the only support band I ever saw that always got at least two encores. Nowadays they don't play 'In The City' at all, but with songs like 'A Place I Love' and 'Mr Clean' in the set, you don't really miss it.

The first highlight had to be 'Strange Town', which didn't retract from the single version except perhaps the live sound was beefier and even easier to relate to. 'News of the World' and 'London Girl' served as a prelude to the big one and over the PA the tapes played of that well known sound of an underground train pulling onto the station. The Rainbow went bananas, and we were taken away from Finsbury Park Astoria to Finsbury Park Station, and the incredible 'Down in the Tube Station at Midnight'.

'They smelt of pubs and wormwood scrubs and too many right wing meetings' Weller muttering the lyrics and Foxton soaring above him on backing vocals. 'Here Comes the Weekend' was taken at a faster pace than usual and following that Weller took the time to emotionally thank the appreciative crowd, who were mostly decked out in Sta-prest pants and parka's decorated with Lambretta badges and The Who insignia!

With the final crash of Rick Buckler's almost desperate drumming a bomb exploded on the stage heralding 'A' Bomb in Wardour Street' and terminating a magnificent set from a magnificent band. Encore one comprised of two cover songs, first an old Motown classic 'Love is like a Heatwave', and then another Jam biggie, 'David Watts' which had everybody either pogoing or dancing.

Off to thunderous applause, finally back to play a medley of standards, 'Bricks & Mortar' and winding up with the silliest number on their first album, 'The Batman Theme'. We would have stayed there all night had we been allowed, but the sight of the safety curtain being lowered put the majority off. Simply the best gig I have seen in ages.

I WAS THERE: DEREK WILSON

We grew up in Darlington. My mother took me and a brother to London for a weekend and reading the *NME* on the train on the way down I noticed that The Jam were playing at the Rainbow. I managed to talk my mum into letting me go over to the venue in the hope of maybe seeing the band and sneak into the sound check. When I arrived I got talking to this girl and it turned out she had a spare ticket for the night. So I got to see them when I least expected it. I remember thinking that the crowd and atmosphere was really lacklustre compared to when I'd seen them in Newcastle and I seem to recall Weller saying back then that the best audience response was always from 'up north'.

I WAS THERE: TREVOR GLYNN

They were superb. I was only young and coming out of glam and pop music with punk and mod. I remember getting in through the fire escape doors round the sideway that someone had opened.

My favourite Jam songs are 'Strange Town' and 'Down in the Tube Station at Midnight'. Because I was so young and small I kept falling over the seats, I remember they had the rawest sound I had ever heard. I go to see Jam tribute bands now – I've seen both The Gift and From The Jam.

I WAS THERE: HELEN WORTHING, AGE 15

I saw them at the Rainbow. In the row behind us were a bunch of skinheads chanting, 'We hate Mods, we hate Mods' and outside after the gig it kicked off.

I WAS THERE: PAUL THOMAS, AGE 16

It's September 1978 and it's the first day of my new school. I'm already into the new wave music that is sweeping the country. Punk was too radical - mum would never have let me dye my hair or wear safety pins on my clothes - perish the thought! But I did like some of the bands and their music.

Paul Thomas got a copy of All Mods Cons for Christmas

I quickly settle in at the new school and make new friends. Ian Dury is popular as he sings about 'Billericay Dickie', a town barely 10 miles away. We talk about bands and borrow each other's records. One lad lends me a single, 'All Around The World' by a band called The Jam, that was released the previous year. The tunes are good but I'm more struck by the cover - these lads look cool in their suits and black and white shoes! Around the same time I hear the 'David Watts' single on Radio 1 and upon hearing it's The Jam I make plans to record it on my little tape recorder when the top 20 count down is played on Radio 1 on Sunday night. I play this track continuously for weeks!

By now I'm hungry for more and in November I hear 'Down in the Tube Station at Midnight' for the first time. I'm blown away and rush out to buy it and again play it to death. The lyrics, the tune - awesome!

Christmas is fast approaching and my mum asked what I want for Christmas. I've seen The Jam's new album out called *All Mods Cons* in Our Price records and ask for that. Christmas Day comes and I'm straight up to my bedroom at the earliest opportunity and the LP is on. Immediately I love it. The tunes impress and I'm hooked. This is the band for me.

1979 dawns and by now I've got the band's two previous albums and all three are played constantly, but I still want more. I buy the music papers every Thursday on the way to school. The *NME* is my favourite. I scour the pages in the playground - The Jam are in the paper most weeks. Then one week I see the news that The Jam are touring in May and playing London – for me just an hour away by train. A plan is hatched - I have to see this band play live.

Excitedly I obtain the telephone number of the Rainbow Theatre and ask mum's permission to go. She's not keen as its London and I'm only 16 but she relents and I ask to use the phone mounted on the kitchen wall -no mobiles in them days! I excitedly dial. The lady answers the phone and tells me the tickets are on sale this coming week from the box office - no internet sales sites in them days!

A few days later I venture up to London, get the tube and arrive at Finsbury Park. Seeing the theatre the excitement ramps up. There's a small queue outside and now I'm excited as well as nervous. The tickets have been on sale a few days. Would there be any left? Visions of the box office closing as I approach the window loom large. Thankfully that doesn't happen and I get to the window and thank god there are tickets left. I've got two of my friends' money with me and buy thee tickets. Row K - that's only 11 rows from the front - not bad!

The weeks drag waiting for the gig. Then the day arrives but first I have to go to school. After school I rush home and change and then rush out the door to catch the bus to town and the railway station. I jump off the bus and see my friends Siggy and Debbie waiting. I'd got their tickets for them at the box office.

We purchase tickets and get on the train. It's an old fashioned carriage with small compartments and a door at each side which we have to ourselves. By now we know a lot of the words to the songs of The Jam and the journey passes quickly as we sing and chat excitedly about tonight's gig.

We arrive at the Rainbow Theatre and there is a large crowd all excited too. We get inside and head straight to the merchandise stall. There's t-shirts and badges but my pocket money will only stretch to a tour programme!

We enter the auditorium and get to our seats. We are much closer than I thought we would be - I can almost touch the stage. I'd seen from live gig photos of The Jam that Paul Weller always stood on the left of the stage as you look at it and would you believe it we were seated right in front of the mic stand - result!

The support band come and go (no, I can't remember who they were) and their equipment is cleared away by the roadies. You can feel the excitement and the air of expectation as we wait as The Jam's equipment is set up. The minutes pass agonisingly slowly and then at last the lights dim. I can hear and feel my heart beating. Suddenly a spotlight illuminates a man with a silver hair and I know it's Paul's dad John who announces the band. He thanks us for coming and then says the immortal words... 'Put your hands together for the best fucking band in the world.... THE JAMMMMMMMM.'

The lights go up and then the band walk onstage and I feel the hairs on the back of my neck go up and feel the tears well up in my eyes as Paul Weller is there for real, right in front of me. He's wearing a sharp grey suit and he looks the business. I think to myself, 'I'm going to spontaneously combust with excitement' as he plugs in his guitar and the music erupts as the band launch into 'All Mods Cons', the title track of the new album.

They sound amazing and play so sharp and tight. Euphoria washes over me and I catch Siggy's eye. No words are needed, her eyes are welling up too and we hug and jump and scream together. The audience laps up each song and we all sing along, knowing every word. Weller has such stage presence and I'm instantly in awe of him - he's the man!

Now I've been to a few gigs and had seen The Boomtown Rats a few months before and they are really good but The Jam? Well, they were different gravy!

They sound was amazing. How can three guys make such a sound? Their stage presence, the suits, the hair cuts, the Rickenbacker guitars - everything is just right.

All too soon the gig is over but we want more. We clap, cheer and whistle for what seems an age and then the band are back for an encore finishing with ''A' Bomb in Wardour Street' and the lights go up and there is the sound of an explosion as the song ends. Then it's all over. WOW! I'm blown away.

We spill out into the night and the journey home is a blur of excited chatter and reliving the gig. I've never experienced a gig like it and I can honestly say it was the best gig I had ever been too and my life was changed forever that day. I was left wanting more and I didn't have to wait long as another tour was soon announced for November that year and of course I was there! I feel privileged to have seen The Jam at their peak and on almost a dozens occasions. There music still means so much to me 40 years later. 'Fire and Skill' indeed!

I WAS THERE: NICKY SAUNTER

My friend Tony got tickets for him and Ginger, his mate. The night before the gig, Ginger lost his wallet and didn't have the money for the ticket. Tony asked me if I wanted to go and I jumped at the chance.

We used to listen to The Jam together when his dad was down the pub - they had a high rise flat on the Waterloo Road council estate, round the back of Romford station. I fancied Tony, but he fancied my sister, so we were just mates.

That's how I got into The Jam. Tony was a Mod, we listened to The Jam and the *Quadrophenia* album. I loved *All Mod Cons*. I still do.

I love 'To Be Someone', 'Mr Clean' (which resonated when I got my first job in the city), and 'Tube Station' of course! When 'Down in the Tube Station' went straight to number one, I was crouched over a transistor radio in school, on my lunch break waiting for it to be played - I was on the edge of my seat as they counted down the new charts. The last song was number one and it was The Jam! I was ecstatic!

Nicky Sanunter loved All Mod Cons

I WAS THERE: SHAR DAWS

I first heard 'In The City' on the radio aged 14 in 1977. I bought the album by the same name, and then *All Mod Cons*, From there on in I was hooked! Money was pretty tight back then, but when I met my boyfriend when I was fifteen, we both shared a passion for The Jam!

My boyfriend was older than me, and working so he would buy tickets for us to travel to London to see them. We both lived in Newport Pagnell at the time, but I was a London girl and born in Chelsea. I distinctly remember the clothes we wore and have a pic taken before we set off to see them at The Rainbow.

We'd go to see them whenever we possibly could. I hate to admit this, but it was true, I always took cotton wool with me, stuffing it into my ears as I found the music was way too loud!

We bought every record they made, and 'Butterfly Collector' was a favourite B side. Obviously, we couldn't access them on the internet as there wasn't such a thing in the Seventies and Eighties. We relied on radio, music mags, TV appearances and off we went to gigs whenever we could.

All Mod Cons has always been my favourite album but *Setting Sons* and in particular 'Little Boy Soldiers' had a profound effect on me, though in truth all their lyrics did, and 'Private Hell' scared the life out of me at the time too!

I remember the news on the radio that they were splitting up. I cried, we were on our way to work, it was pretty early in the morning, and we were still living in Newport Pagnell, but by this time we were both working in Finchley. We were married, and I was pregnant with our first daughter - but was still doing the commute by car, we'd just come off of the motorway when it was announced on the radio. I was so upset and felt pretty angry and betrayed - I thought there was still so much more to come!

I never really took to Style Council and to be absolutely truthful when I went to see From The Jam I just left feeling miserable it was a bit sad too - the old blokes in their Fred Perry Polo shirts and their pints of whatever - and then I realised possibly why Paul Weller had taken the decision to end The Jam - by this time they could no longer legitimately express themselves with such powerful lyrics when they had moved to the other side of the track so to speak - it was apparent that we'd all moved on from those days (apart from a few of the Fred Perry's of course) the Seventies were poverty-stricken times for many of us - but we'd all come out of the Eighties knowing we were never going to be Smithers Jones, we no longer had to live a private hell and David Watts didn't matter anymore or in some cases had died young and was no longer the figure of the politics of envy - and of course Paul Weller now has more money than a fifteen-year-old could have dreamed of at any time!

STUDENTS UNION BUILDING

12 MAY 1979, LOUGHBOROUGH, UK

I WAS THERE: MARTIN BLENCO

It's nearly 40 years ago now since I saw The Jam live. Distant echoes.

I was never a Mod, but The Jam's music cut through all the crap that emanated out of the post punk era. I bought *In The City* and several of the singles. There was a Jam single every three months, and they were releasing stuff that wasn't always on albums, making the announcement of each 45 and the launch of the accompanying video a real event.

In 1978 I went to university in Loughborough, a not very much place in northern Leicestershire. The university was large but the town didn't punch its weight as a stop off for touring bands, that would more likely play Nottingham or Leicester if they were coming to that part of the world. If we were lucky, we got bands like The Undertones (I remember being 15 feet from Feargal Sharkey and studying his parka and his acne up close) and Buzzcocks, who did three encores despite the crowd not calling for that many. Pete Shelley was speeding to high heaven, his eyeballs whizzing round in his head like a character in a *Tom & Jerry* cartoon.

The Jam were something different. They were at the height of their powers, an A list band playing a B-list town. They probably played a lot of B-list towns, setting fire to provincial Britain everywhere they went. That night they were fast and furious. I don't remember Weller saying a word to the audience, just that pinched angry face as he spat out the lyrics to classic after classic. They had a stage lit only with green and white lights, an effect that worked brilliantly. They finished with ''A' Bomb on Wardour Street', and whoever was doing the pyrotechnics had overstuffed the explosives because the blast on which they finished nearly brought down the lighting rig.

When the smoke cleared, they had gone. It was an explosive, fabulously angry set. Another provincial town brought briefly to life.

I WAS THERE: TIM FILOR, AGE 18

The lads were playing at Loughborough University student union as part of The Jam *Pact* tour. My mate Jim Grainger was on a course there and he'd got a ticket for me as a present. It was the day before my nineteenth birthday.

Jim didn't know much about The Jam. He had been a Tom Robinson Band fan. It just took a few plays of 'Strange Town' on the common room record player, after removing 'Sultans of Swing' by Dire Straits on repeat play, to convince him it may not be a bad night after all.

As we arrived at the venue we were heckled by some punks, who hadn't been able to get in. Once inside we went straight to the bar and I saw a lad in a parka getting a beating from some long-haired rocker biker types and I wondered why.

The support band was called the Rockets and they were okay. We were too busy getting the beers in to pay that much attention. Beers in hand we moved down into the stalls and the entertainment continued courtesy of some lesbians having a good snog in front of us. I'd led a sheltered life up to this point and it was all new to me.

Paul's father came on and did his usual introduction (I wondered who he was at the time) then the place erupted and the lads stormed into a brilliant set, similar to the previous gig at Leicester. I remember that they did 'Away from the Numbers', 'Tonight at Noon', which I really love and wasn't played at the previous gig, and 'Strange Town/ Butterfly Collector' which was the single at the time. They obviously did more classic single and album tracks but they were the ones that stuck in my mind.

It was the last song of the main set which proved explosive in more ways than one. The backdrop was a tower block again and at the end of a scorching 'A' Bomb' an explosion went off. It seemed strange, as the smoke was so bad you could only just see the band. I remember just being able to see Bruce through the gloom and the smoke seemed to hang around for ages. The band soldiered on despite this and after the encores we headed back to the halls of residence full of beer and adrenalin. We carried on the party till about five in the morning.

I woke up the next day thinking this was the best birthday ever and wishing I hadn't messed my exams up as student life seemed pretty damn good. I was now pretty disappointed that I was off to work the following July.

The write up in the local rag the next day mentioned that the pyrotechnics had been faulty and gone off early. One of the technical guys had been slightly injured. I went to see *The Kids Are Alright* about a year later at the pictures and often wondered if Rick had done a 'Keith Moon' and bribed the technical guys to pack more explosive in.

The third and probably the most memorable gig for me was again at De Montfort Hall Leicester in 1980. Originally I'd purchased a ticket for me and my mate Chris Lazzari to go.

We, plus a lot of the audience, were now living the Mod lifestyle. Chris and I both had scooters and lived in parkas and Mod suits, etc. It had all become clear to me now why at Loughborough the parka-clad boy had taken a beating as I'd had a few close calls myself.

The popularity of The Jam was now on an upwards surge and they usually did a two nighter at Leicester. I hadn't left getting the tickets that late as I worked near the ticket office but I was disappointed as the only tickets left were in the balcony sitting down for both nights. I always liked being in the stalls.

The night before the gig Chris was taken ill and he didn't think he would be well enough to go so I offered the ticket to another mate, Pete Barratt. He was well pleased because it was close to his birthday. He'd been at my school but we actually got friendly after we'd left due to a mutual interest in Mod. It was good that he came because the night wouldn't have been anything like as good if he hadn't.

We started off in the balcony but we could see that it was more fun in the stalls. The Jam came on and it was crazy at the front part of the stalls. Pete had also been a punk and liked leaping about so we decided we wanted a piece of the action. We went downstairs and sneaked into the back of the stalls.

We gradually weaved nearer the front as new songs from the *Sound Affects* album rang out as we slowly edged forward. We were getting pretty close to our objective when the opening riff of 'In The City' rang out. It was like a catalyst for us, bearing in mind our previous love of punk, and we started leaping about like madmen. I don't think it went down too well with those around us but we didn't care, this was what we had come for. I can't remember how much more of the gig was left but we bounced around till the final chords of the encore faded out.

I think we were both pretty knackered at the end and I started to make my way out with the rest of the crowd. Pete grabbed me and suggested we hang around. We wandered around the hall while it emptied avoiding the stewards. I was a getting a bit nervy but Pete persuaded me to hang on. The other people in the hall had permits of one sort or another.

What happened next left me gobsmacked. Bruce and Rick came out and stood very close to us and a small crowd gathered round them. We had to get an autograph but all we had was our ticket stubs so that's what we handed over. They kindly took them out of our sweaty hands and somehow managed to get both signatures on them. We needed the full set but where was Paul?

We had a little wander and found him in another part of the hall leaning up against a pillar. He looked a bit sullen and a fan was speaking in his ear, something about 'primadonna'.

Pete very politely asked Paul if he'd sign our ticket stubs and a few seconds later we'd got the full set. It was a magical end to a brilliant night. It just showed how well the lads treated the fans. How many bands at that same level of fame would have come out like that after the gig? Not many I suspect!

I was pinching myself on the way home. I just couldn't believe it. When I told Chris about it the next day he was well naffed off. It's still one of my most treasured possessions and it's a brilliant reminder of a great night from all those years ago.

It was a little while until I saw the lads for the final time. I kept track of the vinyl output but I was madly in love with a girl at the time whose taste in music was somewhat different to mine, so I missed out on the gig scene for a while. I'd lost contact with Chris as he'd met a nice Modette at a Chords gig and that was basically the last I saw of him socially - thick as thieves comes to mind! I hadn't been much better with Pete and Steve but didn't completely lose contact with them and I actually went to see Slade with Pete at De Mont – well, I was a big fan in the Seventies. My image had changed a bit as I was now a bit of a biker but thankfully that phase didn't last long.

It was now March 1982. I wasn't quite so young but I was free and single and a live Jam fix was needed again ASAP. I didn't have to wait long as they visited De Mont on the 23rd. My old mate Steve kept me company for the second time. I could only get balcony seats again which was a bit of a bummer but we were near the stage so it wasn't too bad. There was no chance of getting in the stalls this time as security had been tightened and you had to show your ticket to get in.

As we looked down we could see the Mods sweltering in their parkas. They seemed so young - probably only 14 or 15. The support act may have been the Piranhas as they did 'Tom Hark'. The Jam came on and the room yet again erupted. They were huge now. We didn't know at the time that it was close to ending. We just sat back and enjoyed the ride. A constant stream of little Mods were getting pulled out of the front as the crowd surged forward. They had a brief moment with their heroes on stage before being hauled off by the bouncers.

The band had lots of material to choose from now and a new album to promote. I'd like to say I can remember what they did but my memory is coloured by a video I have of virtually the same set at Bingley Hall that had been recorded the previous night. The backdrop was a banner saying Transglobal Unity Express. I can remember them doing that song and also 'Scrape Away', which seemed to be extra long, 'Pretty Green', 'Man at the Corner Shop' and finally 'Happy Together'.

We left the gig elated and made a quick dash to the Old White Horse on London Road to catch last orders, a real spit-and-sawdust pub. I must have been full of adrenalin as I never rush anywhere normally.

As we supped our beers, we never really thought that would be the last time we would see the band live but sadly it was. I didn't get to see any of the final gigs and had to be content with the final outing on *The Tube*. I have to admit that once the boys had unofficially expanded to five it wasn't quite the same for me but with hindsight you can now see where Paul wanted to go.

I did quite like the Style Council but it wasn't quite the same experience when I saw them live.

Bruce's solo stuff was pretty good and I bought 'Freak'. My future wife had the album and, again, it was as good as Paul's output at the time. There was a brief moment of excitement when Rick and Bruce almost got a band called Sharp together with a guy from The Chords but it was sadly not to be.

All I can say is a massive thanks to The Jam. It was good while it lasted. The legacy for me is that it inspired me to get in a band with three other Jam fans mourning the demise of the best trio in the world. I was literally about to sell all my gear when I saw an advert in the local rag placed by a student at Leicester Uni called Rob Snape quoting The Jam, among others, as the musical direction that the band would take. I actually bumped into him again a few years back at an Elvis Costello gig and it was good to see him.

When I first joined the band in 1983 I was talking to Martin, the drummer, as we'd pretty much been to the same gigs. At De Mont, Paul Weller had suddenly left the stage for no apparent reason and then come back a bit later with a smirk on his face, which was unusual for him at the time. Martin explained that he had split his trousers and had to go off and change them.

I obviously never found fame and fortune but I did carry on playing in various line-ups till 1997. Over that period of time I met my wife and a lot of my friends and I now have two great kids and a lot of memories.

My regrets are few but I wished I'd seen The Jam live more, particularly in 1977 when they played at the Poly (now De Montford Uni) and later in the Eighties at Granby Halls. I never got the chance to hear 'All Around the World' live as it was never played at any of the gigs I went to. They broadcast a gig on the radio and it was the last track but it faded out halfway through much to my frustration. The same gig is on *The Jam at the BBC* CD, which I thoroughly recommend.

My final note is it's a terrible thing getting old. It's taken a while for me to compile this as I had to consult diaries, memorabilia, etc. to get my facts straight. I have to admit that I thought I'd only seen the lads three times and got some events muddled up. I think it's pretty accurate now.

I hope this revives some memories of what it was like to be at a live Jam gig because I've not seen a band since who can even come close to it.

GUILDHALL

24 MAY 1979, PORTSMOUTH, UK

I WAS THERE: JULIE JOHNSON, AGE 16

I saw them for the first time in Portsmouth Guildhall in May 1979. I was 16 years old. My mum thought I had taken drugs the next day because I was so high!

I lived and breathed The Jam for the next three years and saw them 27 times across the whole country. I met them many times and travelled with them on the tour bus, thanks to Mike their driver and Malc who smuggled us on the bus and into the gigs.

Julie Johnson (on the left) with John Weller and best friend Ange at Balmoral Drive (Paul's family home) in Woking

Julie Johnson's collection of Jam tickets

My friend Ange Glover and I spent every penny of our wages travelling the country, sometimes hitchhiking and sleeping rough. We also bunked in to other fans' hotel rooms for the night, as we didn't always have money or accommodation.

We socialised with the band in various hotel bars when we were lucky enough to get past security. On one occasion we actually broke in to a theatre through a downstairs window to gain entry because we didn't have a ticket. Often when we didn't have a ticket, Mike or Malc would get us guest passes - thanks guys!

We were proud as punch at one gig when Paul personally requested that we take care of his grandmother in the gig. She sat with us in the balcony and we felt like family having her with us. One time we met John and Ann at Balmoral Drive (Paul's family home) in Woking and they welcomed us in, where we were given tea and cake and chatted about the band.

I was also mentioned in the *NME* by the journalist describing the dedicated fans waiting outside Finsbury Park. He made a comment about the girl in the red Harrington. We were always invited into every sound check where Paul often came out and sat and chatted with fans.

Julie Johnson once looked after Paul Weller's grandmother at a gig

We made friends with fans across the whole country

The originals and still the best: The Jam, who are currently recording an album at Virgin's Town House Studio in West London and have a single 'When You're Young' / 'Smithers-Jones' out on Polydor on August 17. The album is likely to appear in October coinciding with a tour by Weller & Co.

RECORD NEWS

and although we didn't have Facebook in those days or any social media platforms, we managed to connect with them all when tours were happening and stayed at some homes and returned the favour when the band were in Portsmouth.

I remember at 16 my indignation when I was informed I would 'grow out' of it. I still haven't.

The Jam released the stand alone single 'When You're Young' on 17 August 1979 which peaked at number 17 on the UK chart.

By the end of 1979 The Jam released *Setting Sons*, their second of four Top Ten albums on the UK charts. 'The Eton Rifles' became the group's first top 10 UK hit, peaking at number three, followed by a double-sided non-album single, 'Going Underground' and 'Dreams of Children', which became their first chart topper in the UK.

Inspired by a news article that Weller read about unemployed demonstrators on a socialist 'Right to Work' march being heckled by what he later described as 'a bunch of tossers' from the prestigious Eton College, 'The Eton Rifles' encapsulated all that was best about The Jam: Foxton's pumping bass, Buckler's powerful drumming, a catchy refrain and Weller's hard-edged vocal delivery of sardonic lyrics - in this case, dealing with class war and opening with the typically colloquial 'Sup up your beer and collect your fags, There's a row going on down near Slough'.

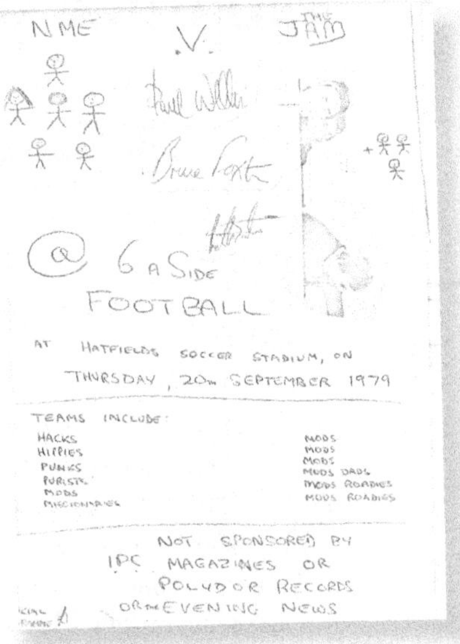

On 29 Sept 1979 the three members of The Jam took part in a 6-a side football match at Hatfields stadium playing against staff from the *NME*.

Paul Weller: I don't know how David Cameron could have misread the words to 'The Eton Rifles' so much. It's pretty simple. They're just fucking stupid, I think.

I played the bass part on my Rickenbacker as usual, but Vic came up with this idea of a distorted chord to go over the top, which starts the song off. I liked it because it was a darker tune Bruce Foxton

I WAS THERE: VIC COPPERSMITH-HEAVEN, JAM PRODUCER

We tried recording 'The Eton Rifles' once during the *All Mods Cons* period and it just didn't work, and then we kept going back to record it. This was at the Townhouse during the time we were finishing off *All Mods Cons* at RAK. I was working on some other records at the Townhouse and really liked the recording environment there, so I introduced The Jam to that studio. I thought we could achieve a much more exciting sound there.

In all, we recorded 'The Eton Rifles' three times. The first time it just didn't have the power, it just didn't have the excitement - either the arrangement or the sound wasn't right, so we left it and worked on some other tracks before coming back to it. I don't recall having that problem with the other songs on the album, and that's probably because 'The Eton Rifles' hadn't been played in. A lot of potentially exciting live tracks would suffer from that if they hadn't been exploited onstage, whereas if they had been played onstage for six months or more you'd be able to capture the performance easily in one day.

The second version of 'The Eton Rifles' was pretty much the same story. There were a lot of exciting tracks on *Setting Sons*, like 'Burning Sky', 'Thick as Thieves' and 'Private Hell' - they had loads of energy, and in the early stages of recording, 'The Eton Rifles' just didn't have that kind of bite. The overall band sound developed during the course of recording *Setting Sons* - the drums improved, the bass sound would get better, and when that happened we'd often drop a new bass part, for instance, into a track that we'd been working on days before.

MAIDA VALE STUDIOS

29 OCTOBER 1979, LONDON, UK

The Jam made their third and final Radio 1 John Peel Session at Maida Vale, recording 'Thick As Thieves', 'The Eton Rifles', 'Saturday's Kids' and 'When You're Young'.

MARQUEE CLUB

2 NOVEMBER 1979, LONDON, UK

I WAS THERE: KAREN WHITING

I saw quite a lot of The Jam live as I was the right sort of age. They were my band and I was living in London. The shows never sounded great live to me although the energy and commitment from the three was staggering. Weller's voice and the sound of the band was a bit one dimensional, and the crowd (like The Clash) were hard work and were made up of obnoxious yobs.

The Marquee was one of my favourite clubs from that period. Going in, walking down the corridor into the bar, never knowing who you were going to see in there - friends, famous faces from other groups. The hot steamy main room, the tacky floor, getting crushed up against the thigh-high stage; sweat rising as steam and condensing on the ceiling before dropping back down in cold drops. Happy days!

Weller's lot had become huge when they performed at this tiny London venue under the pseudonym John's Boys. When word got out, queues for a glimpse of the band snaked right round the block. As for the gig itself - the place was packed, and a huge fight famously broke out in the crowd between the Mods and the skins.

FRIARS

17 NOVEMBER 1979, AYLESBURY, UK

I WAS THERE: MIKE SEARLE

I took a collection of shots at Aylesbury Friars in Buckinghamshire in November 1979 on a Russian made Zenith SLR using Kodak Ektachrome slide film. I was experimenting with a rainbow starburst filter, hence the strange coloured rays emanating from the lights on the photos.

In those days of course mobile phones didn't exist and very few people, if anyone, took photos at gigs, so these are almost certainly the only images existing of this gig or even this tour. It was a fantastic gig - even the support act were good, The Vapors, who had just had a hit with 'Turning Japanese'.

It was an exciting time. Punk was breaking down barriers between bands and their fans and I remember walking into the bar and seeing Jam drummer Rick Buckler standing there, having a pint before the gig. My mate went over and had a chat with him. Those were the days!

ARTS CENTRE

18 NOVEMBER 1979, POOLE, UK

I WAS THERE: SIMON DONLON, AGE 16

My first ever gig – I ran straight to the front of the stage. I survived the support band, The Piranhas. They had one hit, 'Tom Hark'. Fans had no time for them. When they played the chorus 'de dah de dah dah' the fans finished each line with 'Fuck off! The Jam came on and I survived about two minuets at the front. The floor was literally swaying beneath my feet. Great memories.

CIVIC HALL

22 NOVEMBER 1979, WOLVERHAMPTON, UK

I WAS THERE: IVAN CLOWSLEY, AGE 15

I went to see the Jam in 1979 when they were at the height of their powers and one of the biggest bands around at the time. The gig was at the Civic Hall Wolverhampton. I went with my mates but the tickets sold that quickly we only managed to get seats on the balcony. We'd much rather have been in the stalls.

Ivan Clowsley hard at work shortly after leaving school

We really looked forward to the gig and played our Jam records constantly. The big night was a Thursday - a school night. We lived in a small village about five miles away so we queued in the dark about 6pm with our excitement growing at the bus stop. All we could talk about was what songs would be on the set list that night.

We got to the Civic and the fans where standing outside chatting waiting for their mates - a mixture of Punky types and mods. We were only 15 so no visit to the pub for a pre gig pint. The fans were friendly enough but you could feel an air of anticipation building.

We made our way inside through security and up the stairs to the balcony. We had good seats over looking the stage near to the front. When The Jam came on the crowd went wild and the mosh pit was in full flow - it looked great down there as we looked on enviously. We got all the hits that night. 'In the City', 'Down in the Tube Station at Midnight', 'Eton Rifles', 'David Watts' - a great sweaty gig and we were sitting down, well most of the time! God knows what it was like down below in a heaving mass of humanity.

So out we reluctantly went into the cold Wolverhampton night off to catch the last bus home with grins on our faces. What a night we couldn't wait to tell our classmates on Friday morning what a brilliant night we'd had.

I can't believe that was nearly 40 years ago now but although the years have dimmed the memory I still remember the night I saw the Jam!

GAUMONT THEATRE

23 NOVEMBER 1979, SOUTHAMPTON, UK

I WAS THERE: PAT JOINERS MULDOWNEY, AGE 14

I saw The Jam 20 odd times. I first discovered them in 1978. I was 13 years old and I saw two of their singles in a 50p box at the local newsagent. I brought them home and was hooked.

The first time I saw them was at the Southampton Gaumont in 1979. They were the first band I adored. They could do no wrong. I also saw them at the Rainbow Theatre on the same tour. I also saw them in Cambridge in early 1980. I was now 14 years old and told my mum I was at a sleepover. I'm sure she never found out.

When John Weller used to come out and say 'the best fucking band in the world' they really were and still are. Nothing has ever come close. I loved The Smiths, I loved Oasis, The Libertines and today I love Idles. None of these touch the first time seeing The Jam live or queuing up to buy *Setting Sons* on the day of release and sitting in the park gazing at the sleeve.

I'm nearly 54 now and remember it like it was yesterday. I got sacked from my first job because of The Jam. I'd told my boss weeks in advance I was going to see them. On the day the prick asked me to make 300 lasagnes to freeze, an impossible task. At 3pm I'd done about 90. I unplugged my radio and he rushed into the kitchen. 'Where do you think you're going?' 'I'm going to see The Jam' I said. 'Don't come back tomorrow then'. 'I fucking won't' I replied.

The Jam were more important than any job. That was June 23rd 1981. Portsmouth Guildhall. The only time I saw them and wasn't up for it. I blame Mr Bennett, the restaurant owner, and I still hold a grudge nearly 40 years later.

I saw them many times after that but couldn't bring myself to go to any of the final gigs. I was devastated. I still get choked thinking about Paul Weller telling the world it was over. I've stuck by Weller over the years, packed him up a few times, but always asked him out again.

BINGLEY HALL

25 NOVEMBER 1979, BIRMINGHAM, UK

I WAS THERE: TOM RUSHWORTH

I turned up to see The Jam at Bingley Hall in November 1979 only to find that it was sold out. I hung around to see if there were any ticket touts, but they were too expensive. I was about to leave when one of the roadies walked by with a groupie on each arm. He said, 'Need one of these?' Thinking he meant one of the ladies I was about to politely refuse, but he was actually waving a ticket. When I asked how much he said, 'Nothing, just enjoy the gig.' I took it out of his hand, showed it at the entrance and walked in as Paul, Bruce (in a glistening powder blue suit) and Rick came on stage. Now that was worth waiting for.

I WAS THERE: STEVE DOWNING

I saw The Jam at Bingley Hall three times including the gig that was recorded for the live video in December 1982.

I WAS THERE: JANE PENDROUS, AGE 12

I told my parents I was going on a school trip and spent my bus fare for a week buying my ticket. I walked to school and back three miles each way just so I could see them. It was my first ever gig - I was right at the front singing my heart out. After the gig I got back to the station and found my mom waiting for me - I was grounded for a month but it was worth every day. Still the best one of my life!

DEESIDE LEISURE CENTRE

29 NOVEMBER 1979, QUEENSFERRY, UK

I WAS THERE: NEIL CRUD, AGE 13

I had just turned 13: my dad worked as a photographer for the local paper (the *Evening Leader*) so I tagged along on his 'plus one' press pass. This was my first gig, having been introduced to the world of punk rock a year earlier at Denbigh High School.

Neil Crud meets his idol Paul Weller at Deeside Leisure Centre (photo by Chris Birchall)

The Mod revival was well under way and The Jam were one of those bands who straddled both punk and Mod. The music had the punk energy but the fashion was most definitely Mod-orientated. With half the ice rink being filled by punks and the other half being filled by last year's punks who are now Mods, there was always going to be friction, and it didn't take long to spill over. The whole evening was smattered with skirmishes as fist fights broke out. At one point Paul Weller stopped the show and called someone in the crowd a 'cunt' and offered him out.

I watched all this from the safety of the balcony, although I had to tell Huw Spew and Susan Forber (two of the school Mods) I was in the thick of it, otherwise they'd be calling me a coward.

The Vapors were up first, so they were the first of the thousands of live bands I've seen. I of course remember them playing their one hit wonder, 'Turning Japanese', and its B-side, 'Here Comes The Judge'.

As for The Jam, I again have very little to recall: I don't even remember the songs, just the fighting. One advantage of having a press pass was meeting the bands! Bruce Foxton legged it onto the bus but Rick Buckler was happy to autograph my book, as was Mr Weller. I did ask him what he thought of the show, but he just passed my book back and walked off.

My dad took some great photos at the gig, but unfortunately had to surrender all the negatives to the newspaper, which of course will be long gone. He did print an ace full stage pic of the band, which has been swallowed up by a teenage bedroom wall many, many, years ago.

I do recall that The Jam went to a club in Chester after this show and a band was playing and invited Weller, Foxton and Buckler to play a couple of songs, which they did.

Russ enjoys a few pre gig drinks with his girlfriend

I WAS THERE: RUSS AMOS

I was 17 when I first saw The Jam at Deeside Leisure Centre in 1979. They were supported by the Vapors. A lad I worked with got me into them. I had been into the punk and new wave thing but not heard The Jam but as soon as I did I was smitten. They were great, the music was different and it related to the way of life we lived then.

I remember buying the *Setting Sons* album and thought 'wow'. Every song was brilliant and, as we did back then, I learnt all the words to every song. Loads of new acts were appearing such as the Specials, Madness, etc. and I thought the music was great but The Jam were top of the list and I couldn't wait to see them live.

When they announced they were going to play Deeside we were all chuffed to bits and queued for hours to make sure we all got tickets. The gig itself was fantastic. Our heroes were right there in front of us and I couldn't have been happier.

As new albums were released I was down the local record shop and snapped a copy up. I bought all the singles and even got some imports from Japan and America.

They played again in 1982 and again we all got tickets to see them play all their new material. They were supported by The Alarm, who were a local band at the time from down the road in North Wales and this added to the excitement. The gig was great - apart from the trouble. There was quite a bit of it both inside and out of the venue between rival groups of locals and people from Merseyside. I remember Weller's dad coming on stage and telling the crowd that unless the fighting stopped the band wouldn't play. After this, things settled down very quickly and the gig went ahead. Again they were excellent and we all went home happy - a bit bruised and battered but happy!

I went to a lot of the gigs at Deeside Leisure Centre and saw some big bands, but the two Jam gigs were at the top of the pile. I still listen to their songs and sing along and dance at weddings, etc. although the pogoing has slowed down a bit. I've still got all their records tucked away safely at home and have been to see From The Jam several times to get my Jam fix.

The sad thing is all these Seventies and Eighties bands are all making a come back (I just went to see Madness) but we will never get to see The Jam one more time as Mr Weller feels their time came and went and he needs to move on. Tell Bruce that! In his Sixties and still giving it some on stage!

I WAS THERE: SUSIE WYNNE, AGE 13

I went to this gig with a school friend. They were supported by The Vapors. I remember at one point Paul Weller stopped singing and had a go at someone in the crowd!

I WAS THERE: MITCHELL GREGORY, AGE 14

The Jam had arrived. It was the *Setting Sons* tour and 'The Eton Rifles' was shooting up the charts. The Vapours were 'Turning Japanese' as they supported. The North Wales Mods were battling the Merseyside Mods. Bottles were flying, fighting everywhere. But we were just young 14 year olds and didn't care. We were too young to get hurt, right at the front, against the barrier. Bruce Foxton stopped the show and bollocked the crowd for crushing the fans at the front. We were all soaked in sweat and loving it all.

I WAS THERE: MIKE EDWARDS, AGE 15

I was a 15 year old kid and shitting myself – there was fighting everywhere. In the end the bouncers piled in and started swinging what looked like iron bats around to disperse the trouble. It certainly worked.

I WAS THERE: MARK RUSSELL, AGE 13

The Vapors were the first band I'd seen live but I only wanted to see The Jam. Unfortunately the attendant took my ticket and never gave it back. I was really pissed off at this but I was only interested in getting in to the area to see the band. I managed to get to Deeside Leisure Centre for the gig the following year on 2nd November. I couldn't get a ticket but my dad phoned John Weller and the great man had two guest tickets left at the desk for us.

I WAS THERE: ROB TAYLOR, AGE 15

March 1982 and my dream had come true. I was 15 years old and finally I had my first Jam ticket for Deeside leisure centre in North Wales. My older brother was also going with all his mates on a local coach company. I had my ticket and couldn't wait to tell everyone. When I broke the news to my brother and his mates, my brother turned to me and said, 'No way are you going to that concert with me. You're too young and I'm not looking after you. The Deeside venue is renowned for trouble with the Welsh and English clashing and so you're not going'.

I begged and begged to go but he was adamant I wasn't getting a seat on the coach and that I'd have to sell my ticket. He said to me that I could go to the next year's tour as I would have left school by then, but little did we all know that this would be the final year of The Jam and that I'd never get the chance to see them again.

I sold my ticket and that was my opportunity to ever see them gone. When the news broke they were splitting up I found it so hard to take and I had a lot of bitterness towards my brother who denied me the chance of ever seeing the band that shaped my future. The next best thing I had was eventually seeing Paul Weller in the Nineties. Then, when they held the *About The Young Idea* exhibition in Liverpool, I attended both questions and answer nights with Bruce and Rick. I got the opportunity to have a photo taken with Rick at the venue when I slipped past security just before he went on stage. I explained to Rick that when I was growing up and all my mates wanted to be Paul Weller, but I wanted to be Rick Buckler. Rick said I had sense!

The day after Bruce had done his Q&A, I was shopping with my wife in Liverpool city centre and I bumped right into Bruce who was going to HMV. I had a chat and got a few photos. It sort of made up for never seeing The Jam. The same lads who saw them at Deeside when I didn't get to go never said they were jealous of me meeting Rick and Bruce and it sort of made me feel a bit better. The only way I see them live now is YouTube but it still hurts 37 years on that I never saw the best band in the fucking world.

I WAS THERE: LESLEY ALLEN, AGE 14

They were our gods for years. As a young girl I was very much influenced by their music and I still love them today. It's like a club that means you were a cool kid, when I was such a misfit. They were our life. I fancied a lad at school and he had The Jam written on his backpack so I got into them thinking it may attract him to me. I was very much a Saturday kid.

I loved the lyrics and it taught me the politics of the day. I saw them live three times, including at Deeside Leisure Centre and in Liverpool. We were only 14 and I had to have my friend's big brother tagging along to keep us safe. We soon lost him though!

I WAS THERE: PAUL BERRY, AGE 14

My first Jam album was *All Mods Cons*. It must've been early summer 1979 when I was 14 years old. I recollect being sat on my bed after school watching Wimbledon, probably waiting for it to kick off between McEnroe and Connors!

There was a knock on the front door and my mum shouted up the stairs, 'Paul, Mark's here to see you!' Bona (Mark's nickname) bounced into my room waving this LP at me, 'Fuckin' hell Fez! (my nickname) I just bought this LP for 50p and it's fuckin' brilliant - have a listen!'

We got my little record player out, opened the lid and put the needle on the first track. 'One, two, three, four…' and out blasted a Rickenbacker 330 - the rest is history. It literally just blew me away. I remember saying to myself, 'Fuckin' 'ell. Weller writes about my life!'

Six months earlier I'd been listening to *Grease* and drooling over Olivia Newton-John. Now I was jumping around the room to ''A' Bomb in Wardour Street' and getting all emotional over 'Fly' and 'English Rose'. Life changing moments. (I still drooled over Olivia Neutron-Bomb - I was a teenage lad after all).

To this day I tell my mates that if they outlive me they must place my original copy of *All Mods Cons* on my coffin at my funeral. 40 years on, that circular piece of black plastic still means that much to me.

I thought my first listen to *All Mods Cons* would be my best life-changing moment until 29 November 1979, two days after my 15th birthday. I used to read the *NME* word by word and the only way you usually found out about a tour was in the music or local press. There it was, The Jam at Deeside Leisure Centre, about 45 minutes drive from where I lived. That was it. Word got around the classrooms and me, Mark Jones (Bona), Andy Burton, Dave Brown, Helen Jones and Lesley Parker were all mad for it. We got our tickets - £3.00 each - and luckily Helen's dad had a mini bus. Sorted!

We queued up and walked into the Leisure Centre. The ice rink had been covered with carpet where the fans stood. The atmosphere was electric - the ice underneath failed to cool it. There was a bit of a kick off between Scousers and Taffs and gaps appeared in the crowd and it got a bit lively. Security jumped in and the adrenalin was certainly pumping. It was my first gig - what a baptism of fire!

The Vapors, who were support, came on stage and rattled out 'Prisoners', 'Turning Japanese' and some tracks from their forthcoming album, *New Clear Days* - a great set and well received by the crowd (Bruce Foxton was their manager). Then John Weller came on stage and gave his legendary introduction and it went ballistic. 'The Eton Rifles' was in the charts, *Setting Sons* was just released and the band launched into the most blistering delivery of fire and skill I'd ever encountered. Weller's Rickenbacker screaming out feedback on 'Strange Town' and 'The Eton Rifles', Bruce's bass making the floor bounce and Rick's sticks beating out with military precision.

Minor scuffles continued in the crowd and Weller threatened to stop the gig at one point. Needless to say relative peace then ensued until we all walked out - ears ringing, soaking wet through with sweat, the happiest kids on the planet.

Next day in school I remember sitting in Maths class, ears still blaring, and Andy Burton looked over to me, shook his head and said, 'That was the best two hours of my fuckin' life.' I didn't have to reply. My face said it all.

I WAS THERE: JOHN TIERNEY, AGE 15

I was a 15 year old Mod and me and three mates from Walton, North Liverpool had made it to Deeside Leisure Centre, North Wales to see 'the best fucking band the world'. This is how John Weller, Paul's dad, introduced them. The noise of the crowd was deafening when he announced the band and we had all bullied our way to the front, right opposite Paul. The strobe lighting added to the band's 'god like' presence and we had come to worship them. The testosterone in the room was flammable. You could feel it was about to explode at any second - it always did - and for some reason we loved it.

I sang along to every word of every song like hundreds of others but Paul sang directly to me and my mates, not the 'Wools' who were pushing us in the back. Anyone that wasn't from Liverpool was a 'Woolly back' at the time!

Paul understood us and he sang about things that mattered to young teenage kids, like love, violence, girls, poverty, Saturday's kids, monolith monstrosities councils call homes. 'Down in the Tube Station', 'Mr Clean', 'Smithers-Jones'. It just made sense. We were just four scallies from Liverpool in Thatcher's Britain trying to take on the world.

As each song played I watched how skilfully Bruce Foxton's fingers charged up and down the fret board, nailing every bass note needed. Paul sang with passion, aggression and an intensity that entered my soul. I just didn't want it to end and then a fight broke out behind me and a small circle of space appeared to reveal one of my mates trying to punch someone for pushing him. The song ended and everyone was threatening everyone else for starting the fight. Paul was threatening to walk off stage, but that would have made things ten times worse.

'Found myself in a strange town, though I've only been here for three weeks now' brought the audience back together and everybody settled down.

The Jam were so fucking cool they could not help revving the audience into a frenzy which always turned into a fight. I know Paul Weller never wanted this to happen but it just couldn't be stopped! There was nothing quite like it and I have seen lots of top bands but never experienced anything like a Jam gig - you definitely knew what you were in for.

Other Jam gigs were great also, but we didn't like the fact they were becoming so popular and we didn't want to share them with anyone. We were there from *In The City* the first album then *This Is The Modern World* which no one liked, except me and my mates. They belonged to us!

I realised and understand much later why Paul had to break up the band. He had created a Frankenstein monster of an audience that could barely be controlled.

But didn't we have a nice time?

I WAS THERE: TIM WATSON

The Jam gig was attended by the Merseyside Mods, who spent most of the gig attacking the security with scaffold bars!

RAINBOW THEATRE

4 DECEMBER 1979, LONDON, UK

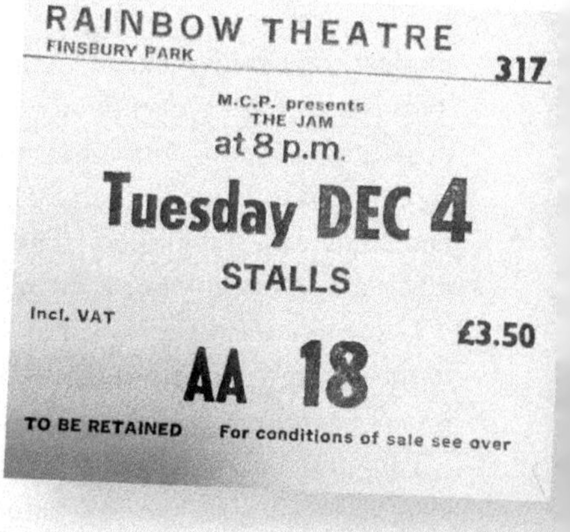

I WAS THERE: MICHAEL FARRAGHER, AGE 15

The first time I saw The Jam live was at The Rainbow Theatre in London. I was fifteen years old. A school friend had a spare ticket that I bought from him. It was 4 December 1979 - the *Settings Sons* tour. I had got into The Jam quite late, despite a string of incredible singles and albums. Tonight was the last of three sold out nights at the Rainbow, a venue The Jam were to play so often that Paul Weller once quipped he should have a bed upstairs!

It was a seated gig and I had a ticket in the front row! I took lots of photos. What I remember most was that I was completely blown away by the raw energy of the gig. For a three-piece The Jam had such a powerful sound, their live shows were intense and exciting and there was a sense of danger because it could get quite rough.

I had only been to a handful of concerts before and seeing The Jam up close was unlike anything I had experienced before. I waited around in the venue after the gig and to my surprise Paul, Bruce and Rick came back into the hall to meet fans and sign autographs. I went home floating on cloud 9.

I was completely hooked from that day on. I've always been obsessive where music is concerned. Over the next few weeks I went out and bought all The Jam's back catalogue and played them over. The lyrics were intelligent, insightful and political. Paul Weller was an incredibly gifted songwriter. I loved the music and the image.

Paul Weller and Michael Farragher bond after a drink

Over the next three years I saw The Jam live 29 times, in London, Loch Lomond, Birmingham, Stafford, Guildford and Brighton. Basically, anywhere I could afford to get to. All but two of those times I was with my younger sister Rita – it was an experience we shared together. There's only 18 months in age between us and we were into a lot of the same music.

The Jam meant everything to me. When The Jam were playing four nights in London, then I had to go to every night. We would arrive at the venues early in the day in the hope of meeting the band and found that very often you would be let in to watch the sound checks which was unbelievable – it was like a sneak preview of the gig. John Weller was always great with 'the kids' as he called The Jam's young fans and we got to know Kenny Wheeler, The Jam's tour manager. As well as meeting The Jam at gigs, me and Rita would go up to the BBC when they or Paul were being interviewed or doing a radio appearance.

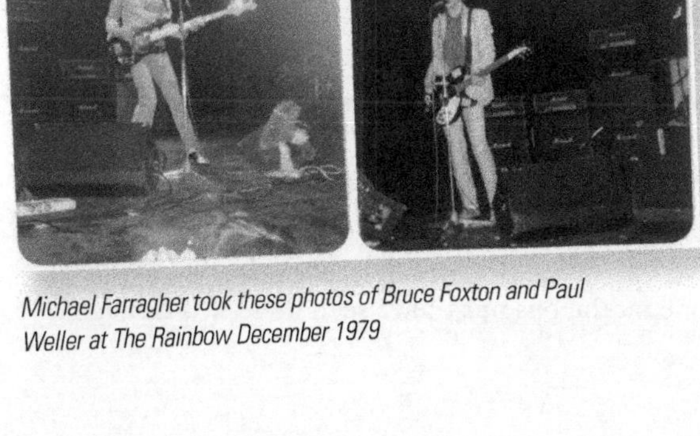

Michael Farragher took these photos of Bruce Foxton and Paul Weller at The Rainbow December 1979

I did part time jobs after school and at weekends to pay for records, gig tickets and travel. I bought every music paper and magazine with The Jam and had posters all over my bedroom walls. I had a big collection of Jam badges and my school blazer always a different Jam badge on it. I slept the night outside venues to get tickets, stayed in coach and train stations and even public toilets because I didn't have the money for a place to stay. The Jam were a band that inspired that kind of devotion and all these years later my love for them hasn't diminished.

I WAS THERE: ANDY PHILLIPS

My first memory of The Jam was hearing 'Strange Town' on the radio and immediately after that I bought *All Mod Cons*. I loved it. That album also got me into The Kinks via 'David Watts'. I was 14 at the time and I think that might have been the crest of the Mod revival. I just loved The Jam and didn't really like the Mod-associated acts like Secret Affair and Squire, etc.

I saw The Jam at the Rainbow in December 1979 with two mates. You had to send a cheque to the box office and my mum did it for me. I remember we were in the stalls, half way back on the left facing forwards. The support act was The Vapors who were actually great. I do remember that it was really hot. I also remember feeling very young compared to everyone else there! The energy was incredible. I have seen hundreds and hundreds of gigs (I was a musician in my twenties so I have seen a lot of bands!) and I will always remember the intensity of that gig. Paul Weller seemed very angry to a 14 year old. I saw them a few times after that – Wembley Arena with Big Country supporting springs to mind – but it wasn't the same. I'm not sure a venue that size suited The Jam.

I haven't followed Rick or Bruce if I'm honest. I quite liked the Style Council but haven't followed Paul's work particularly. I still listen to The Jam. *Setting Sons* is probably my favourite album, which is the album they were touring at The Rainbow. I doubt they would reform and if they did I wouldn't go and see them. I'd like to remember them as they were.

APOLLO

8 DECEMBER 1979, GLASGOW, UK

I WAS THERE: STEPHEN BROWN

My friend and I were standing at the stage door listening to the sound check. After a while somebody shouted that the band are leaving from the front door, we ran round to see them getting on the tour bus. My mate and I just looked at each other and started running down Renfield Street after the bus. Not to far down the road the bus stopped and Rick was about to get off, someone on the bus must have seen these two teenage guy's running, waving and shouting so they told Rick to get back on. We got a thumbs up from Rick and Bruce, which made our day!

The gig that night was amazing. This band got me into playing the drums and after year's of playing I got the chance to play in a tribute band - The Underground Jam. A few years back I met Rick at his book launch, very approachable and he seemed very pleased he had an influence on someone.

As most Jam fan's will testify they were an important part of growing up they are still my band.

The *Modern World* album takes me back to a time which for me the band were brilliant and only getting better. I went to see them again in 1980 and 1982 at the Glasgow Apollo and Loch Lomond festival in 1980.

Stephen Brown met Rick Buckler during his book tour

CAIRD HALL

9 DECEMBER 1979, DUNDEE, UK

I WAS THERE: DITE BURNS, AGE 18

Weller and I are the same age give or take six months. Me and my mate, now sadly passed, were Jam fans before they got huge. We viewed them as 'our' band. We even spray painted the local public toilets because they were tiled white in the same size tiles as the cover of *In The City*. I was old enough to know better but still young and daft enough to think it mattered!

The first and most memorable time I saw them was in Dundee. I went with my young brother and his mate. Inside I met two old mates, totally unplanned. One was in the Black Watch and the other was a Royal Marine, both on leave.

Dite Burns spray painted the local public toilets like the cover of In The City.

I was dressed in my recently made silver grey mohair suit, black Fred Perry with yellow tips, white socks and black Frank Wright loafers. I wasn't a Mod but at the time an ex-skinhead and soon to be a skinhead again once I realised it wasn't the company I used to keep or the style that got me into bother.

The place was jumping. It was mobbed with a real mix of Mods, herberts, straights and punks. The Vapors were the support and went down really well, but I have to admit that 'Turning Japanese' was the only song I really knew.

We pinned ourselves to the front of the stage which seemed like a great idea. The Perth Mods were literally dripping from the balcony and one was mooning or being 'debreeked' by his mates - I thought he was going to drop to the stalls! There were chants of 'We are the Mods' and 'We are the punks' mixed with 'We want The Jam'. The chants were silenced by Paul Weller proclaiming, 'We are the Mods, we are the punks, we are fuck all. We are here for a good time and the rest of ya can fuck off home,' which was met by cheers from just about everyone, even the culprits .

I honestly can't remember the set list but it was a great set, a great night. Even the two suited twats trying to wind Bruce up by singing 'Clash City Rockers' between numbers shut up by Bruce kicking out towards them in a jocular fashion.

I can remember hitting the cool air outside and the steam rising from my soaked suit - my Fred Perry stuck to me like a second skin. My suit didn't fare so well as the lining shrank once it dried. It was dry cleaned and I had to have it relined. Twin vents don't look good when the lining has shrunk.

I was buzzing, very little alcohol and no drugs but I was high as I'd seen 'our band'. I still have the ticket from that night.

QUEENS HALL

11 DECEMBER 1979, LEEDS, UK

I WAS THERE: PETER FLETCHER

Where to begin? I guess late Seventies - I was into Kate Bush, ELO, Queen and ABBA during my last days at school, ABBA are a bit embarrassing but still a guilty pleasure. I worked at an engineering firm and they sent me on day release to Kitson College in Leeds and, like all students at the time, I bought the *NME* to read between lectures. A few of the other engineering students were into punk and they talked about The Clash, Sham 69, etc. and they got excited when The Jam were releasing their new single 'Strange Town' - it got a good review in *NME* so I bought it. I loved the song and the B-side 'Butterfly Collector' but I had a new favourite band - The Police - and *NME* advertised they were coming to Leeds Queens Hall on 10 December 1979. My brother said he wouldn't mind going so I went to Virgin Records to buy some tickets on a Saturday morning. This was going to be great my first time attending a concert.

I looked around Virgin. They had their Christmas free zone promotion going on so I had a good look around as it was a break from all the Christmas songs playing non-stop in all the other shops. Then I went to go buy the Police tickets. 'Sorry, sold out' said the guy serving. He must have seen the disappointment on my face as he followed with, 'We have some Jam tickets left though.' I snapped them up as it was only a day after the Police concert - I think it was about £5 for two tickets. I also then bought The Jam's latest album *Setting Sons* with the intention of playing it to death so that I knew some of their songs. Don't get me wrong - I had heard other songs by The Jam in my mate's car, he played *All Mods Cons* quite often - but I wasn't overly familiar with anything except for 'Strange Town' and 'Butterfly Collector'.

I later explained everything to my brother and he was still up for it and I started to play the *Setting Sons* album and I loved it. I played it everyday as soon as I got home from work and at the local youth club where I met friends regularly. My brother wasn't as keen - he liked The Human League and Lene Lovich who had the hit with 'Lucky Number' - but still wanted to go to the concert.

11th December came and my brother and I set off for the concert, not fully knowing what to expect at our first ever live show. I felt excited and a bit apprehensive as we joined the queue around the side of the Queens Hall. This went down quite quickly and we entered the hall. There were no checks like they have now - the security just looked mostly for cameras or recording equipment. The hall was quite full and I could smell food so I went to see what was available. It was this night that I had my first ever Pot Noodle - curry with a mango sachet. That's nothing to do with The Jam but it sticks in my memory!

I was eating the noodles as the lights went down and The Vapors were coming on stage. They were loud and pretty soon everyone was singing their hit 'Turning Japanese'. I finished the noodles and located a bin to put the pot in. But I lost sight of my brother so I spent rest of The Vapors performance looking for him and eventually found him looking for me.

The Vapors finished their performance and you could feel the atmosphere build - the place was buzzing and electric as the excitement mounted. The lights went down again and The Jam came on dressed in their suits and bowling shoes, Paul chewing gum and singing like he does and Bruce with his fluffy, spiky hair. You could hardly see Rick - just his head and drumsticks over the drum kit.

My brother and I edged closer to the stage, wanting to get a better view, and we ended up next to the speakers. It was loud but brilliant. I couldn't tell you exactly what songs were played but most of the *Setting Sons* and *All Mods Cons* albums plus of course 'Strange Town' and 'Butterfly Collector'. I also remember seeing Bruce do his jump with his guitar and the crowd going wild and cheering, singing and sweating. It felt like it was raining as condensation formed on the ceiling and dripped off the steel girders onto us below. We didn't care. This was brilliant - there was no band better than The Jam - end of. Eventually Paul said goodnight and thanks, etc. after I think their second encore and the lights came on. I hadn't bought a t-shirt or a programme. I just had a ticket and the memories (Pot Noodle included) of what was one of the best events of my life.

That's how I became a fan of the group and from then on they could do no wrong. I decided I was going to complete my collection of Jam recordings buying all their singles and albums. Unfortunately some of their back catalogue was no longer available and I wasn't going to have my collection completed without paying through the nose for it. I managed to get all the albums and then luckily for me, owing to the group becoming more popular, Polydor re-released The Jam's entire back catalogue which I promptly bought over the coming few weeks.

My collection was complete and I was playing the singles at the youth club mixed with all the Police discs I had. I found myself swaying more to The Jam though. I think 'De Do Do Do, De Da Da Da' was to blame for the Police to fall out of favour. The Jam's singles brought me and my friend Mark closer together - he was a Boomtown Rats fan but he loved all The Jam songs I was playing and I talked non-stop about the concert. We decided to go to the next one together and we even bought some bowling shoes which we never took off our feet.

I WAS THERE: IAN DAVID ROBERTSON

I was at that gig and remember the sound quality was bloody awful! Nothing to so with the band, rather the Queen was built for trams, not music. Still digging holes today from the raw energy and excitement of that night.

I WAS THERE: PAULA FOTHERBY COATES

Almost passed out by being squashed at the front then a burly security guy picked me up and took me to the back! Gutted.

KING GEORGE'S HALL

12 DECEMBER 1979, BLACKBURN, UK

I WAS THERE: ANDY YOUNG, AGE 14

Wednesday 12th December 1979. John Lennon still had about a year to live. Margaret Thatcher was just starting to get into her stride as Prime Minister, and Blackburn Rovers were a Third Division football club, in every respect.

On this day, while a coup d'être was being carried out in South Korea by General Chun Doo-hwan three young men from Woking, Surrey were in the latter stages of a nationwide tour to promote their fourth album, the sublime *Setting Sons*. King Georges Hall, Blackburn was their latest port of call.

I was about to turn 15 and despite my relatively tender years and the fact that I lived in a fairly small provincial northern town that sits about 25 miles from Manchester and 35 from Liverpool, both obvious stopping off points for major bands on UK tours and not places easily accessible to one so young, this was not the first time I had seen The Jam in action. They were in fact regular visitors to Blackburn, and had played King George's Hall some 18 months previously, just before *All Mods Cons* was recorded. That night Weller had introduced 'Billy Hunt' as 'our next single'.

Anyway, that was then. Last time out, the 4,000 capacity hall had been about two-thirds full, mainly consisting of punks. Generally speaking, if it happened in London, it took about two years to reach Blackburn. At least it had always seemed that way. However what happened on 12th December 1979 was part of a national phenomenon that captured a generation of British kids from all four corners of the land.

This time around, The Jam had started to attract attention and some decent chart placings and the gig was a sell out despite the fact that the tour also took in Lancaster, Manchester (two nights), Deeside Leisure Centre and Leeds; all within the reach of the north west youth.

We decided to get to the gig in plenty of time to watch the support band, The Vapors. We arrived soon after the doors opened and quickly spent a small fortune (probably about a fiver each – I know, I know!) on tour t-shirts and badges. The two that seemed to shift the most were the *Setting Sons Tour* shirt with the bulldog and rising sun graphic, and the 'Eton Rifles' shirt with the army cadets marching. They were truly iconic and as cool as fuck. They still are. We had no money left for either a beer or our bus home, so made our way straight into the hall and got down the front.

The Vapors were excellent, and they played just about the whole of the then unreleased *New Clear Days* album. I particularly remember 'Turning Japanese' (obviously) and also 'Spring Collection'. The hall was beginning to fill up now and you could feel the atmosphere getting more and more tense. It was a heady mixture of genuine fear at what could kick off at any moment, given some of the chants that were being sung, and real excitement at who was about to enter stage right. Who needed booze on a night like this? These were tough, violent times. While I don't recall there being much of a gang culture as such, there were certainly parochial battles aplenty, with many small towns making up the East Lancashire conurbation, and a gig such as this was a tinderbox.

Speaking of which, you could still smoke everywhere in those days - most of us did - and once the house lights went down (always the signal that emptied the bars and caused a crush in the hall) all you could see were the red ends of hundreds of fags and the wispy smoke billowing out of them. No mobile phones in those days. Then the spotlight shone onto the right hand corner of the stage, and a stocky man with white hair sauntered on stage. In his unmistakeable gruff voice, he bellowed 'Alright, put your 'ands together for the best band in the fuckin' world, The Jam!!'

I actually thought the roof was going to come off the place! Apparently the ringing phone effect was played, but I doubt anybody heard it, as the band launched straight into 'Girl on the Phone'. The bit where the word 'cock' is used in the song's lyric signalled a mass punch in the air (later to be repeated on 'Pretty Green' on the following tour!) Bearing in mind I saw The Jam a few times and Weller in his various guises many more since, and my memory isn't what it was, so I'm quite happy to be corrected by anyone else who was at the gig as to what they were wearing that night. My recollection is that Weller – whose hair was longer than when I'd seen them 18 months earlier, had a navy blue and grey polka dot shirt and either grey or slate blue Sta-Prests. I have no idea what he had on his feet, but I seem to recall they weren't the black-and-white 'Jam' shoes that had previously been a trademark. Foxton was wearing a grey tonic suit - he did have Jam shoes on - and he lost the jacket after just a couple of numbers. Rick had a striped button down shirt on. It could have been pale blue, but it soon became dark blue!

As for the crowd, the whole place was a sea of fishtails, Fred Perrys and boating blazers. You could normally tell after a song or two whether Paul was 'up for it' – he generally was – and I have to say (partly with the benefit of hindsight) that I have never seen him strut quite so aggressively around a stage as he did that night. I wonder whether he'd lost at cards or something on the coach on the way in?

''Ow are ya, alright?' He looked at me when he said that! Okay, I'm sure every kid in the hall thought the same thing, but we were as one. They rattled through the set at breakneck speed as usual. I can't remember the exact order of songs but it would have followed a similar set list as the rest of that tour. I do remember they played 'Strange Town', 'When You're Young' and 'The Eton Rifles' one after another in that order. I only remember that because they had been the last three singles, in that order, and I reflected afterwards that it showed how good they were that they didn't feel a need to hold any of them back for the encore. Incredible noise, and there were only three of them! The feedback Paul got during 'Rifles' was ear-splitting.

Another that sticks in my mind was 'Little Boy Soldiers'. My late brother was in the army at the time and it sent shivers down my spine hearing that song played live. It still does!

'And if I get the chance I'll FUCK UP YOUR LIFE, Mister Cleeeeean, Mister Cleeeeean'.

I cannot put into words how loudly the crowd sang the bit in capital letters. Weller didn't even bother singing 'Is that seen?' - we did that for him!

The last song of the main set was '(Love is Like a) Heatwave'. Now, most Jam fans (including me) are of the view that this song had no place on *Setting Sons*. Paul now agrees, and concedes that they had no choice but to use it to close the album as he had no more songs. I think they would have been better using 'The Butterfly Collector' personally. However, '(Love is Like a) Heatwave' definitely had a place on the *Setting Sons* tour. It was the most rousing way to close the set and the crowd went ballistic. It was probably the closest I have come to imagining what Beatlemania must have sounded like. Again, I think it was a brave song to leave the stage on, given the hits they already had under their belt at the time.

Another thing gigs get measured on – well they certainly did then anyway – was on how many encores were performed. The Jam did two that night. The first one was 'David Watts', followed by 'The Modern World.' Off they went again.

'Thank you, goodnight.'

A few people thought that was that and started streaming towards the exits, entirely satisfied that they had just seen one of the biggest - if not THE biggest - bands in Britain performing at the peak of their powers in a smallish venue.

I have no idea why I remembered this, but I realised they hadn't played 'Tube Station'. Also, the house lights hadn't come back on. I said to my mate that they were probably going to do a second encore. Sure enough, a roar greeted Paul, Bruce and Rick as they jogged back on stage, the former and the latter puffing on rather suspicious looking cigarettes!

They ended proceedings with an incredibly intense version of ''A' Bomb' (how many of us would actually be able to spell apocalypse if it hadn't been for this song, be honest?), followed by, of course, 'Tube Station', complete with sound effects (note the 'e').

This time 'Thank you goodnight' echoed around the hall as the band left the stage, and this time the house lights did go up and it was time to step out into the cold December Lancashire air.

The last thing that struck me as I was leaving King George's Hall that night was the steam and sweat literally rolling down the walls of the venue. I have never seen anything like it, except in the sauna at my local Bannatynes.

Normally, after a gig or a football match in that neck of the woods, there would be sporadic battling between the different factions, but I can honestly say that all I saw was a sea of smiling faces, made so by three lads not much older than us.

Little did I know that within six months they would be back, and this time I would get to meet my heroes.

I WAS THERE: MARK CASSIDY

I've still got the poster from my first Blackburn Jam gig. It was one of the first misspelt ones. It says 'Nothgate' when it should spell 'Northgate'. Top gig and it was my second time seeing The Jam. I hand painted the silhouette images on my bedroom wall and also on the side panels of my Vespa scooter.

Mark Cassidy's misspelt Jam poster

I WAS THERE: KEV GRAY

June '78. I'd just left school and was disillusioned with the desperate music scene. Everyone wore huge patch pocket flares and had long hair and the charts was full of shit - Boney M, etc. I remember the feeling of being in the middle of something unbelievably exciting and energised. The thrill of knowing you were smack bang in the middle of a movement where you felt so angry and disenfranchised yet so powerful was immense. That was before I'd seen The Clash at an Anti Nazi League concert in London, so little did I know….

We had a few drinks of Kestrel lager in my mum's back yard - piss would be a compliment in describing it – and me and four mates boarded the Accrington to Blackburn bus. On the bus we met a few people who were older than us, but they must have only been in their early twenties. We jabbered excitedly about seeing The Jam. We couldn't believe it - The Jam! I'd seen them do a song on *Marc*, Marc Bolan's TV show, and 'All Around The World' sounded brilliant. I'd memorised the words, which was, it seemed, a natural process back then. Paul Weller was a cool looking bloke but it was the energy of the music that gripped me.

Entering KGH I remember looking behind me as we walked in - a mix of punks, 'straights' and a few Mods. But mostly there were punks. Burnley, Keighley, Leeds, Accrington, some Blackpool punks and, of course, the 'Blackburn lot'. When The Jam took the stage I got as near to the front as possible.

Kev Gray and friends at a recent Youth Club reunion

Two days later my ears were still ringing. They came out and exploded. That's the only way I can describe it. Sharp looking bastards in black, incredibly tight as a band and, coupled with strobe lighting, looking, sounding and feeling every inch what I'd hoped they would be. Smoke hung like a blanket over the venue. It got hot, then it got really hot. I've never felt so alive. They sounded so raw and yet so polished, I was a big Pistols fan but I couldn't get over how three people could bang out so much energy. The songs were quality too. Not just three chord thrashing and screaming. I will never forget catching myself in the moment and realising I was experiencing music history.

The gig itself was unforgettable. However the bastards that boarded the Accrington bus back with bike chains to do a bit of damage to us, who were really just kids, was a precursor to football violence, using punk and its energy as an excuse to kick someone's head in.

We were punks, naïve to the tribal hatred of Blackburn Rovers fans who assumed that as we came from Accrington, we must support Burnley. This happened after every gig. We'd walk the short journey to the Boulevard bus station, and adults would pour out of pubs and give us a good kicking. But it never stopped me going to gigs in Blackburn. Nothing could stop us.

I WAS THERE: KEITH DAVIES, AGE 17

It was the first real concert I'd been to. Paul Weller didn't say much during the concert, just the obligatory 'thank you' and introducing the songs. But as a 17 year old Jam fan, it was a great experience. The band were promoting *Setting Sons* and played a fantastic gig. I remember being in my parka and sweating like hell the same as everyone around me. I'm still a massive Weller fan and have seen him twice solo in Australia, where I now live. Good memories.

I WAS THERE: CRAIG HOYLES

I'm almost certain it was the band's first visit. At the time, the town of Blackburn had a couple of far right councillors and a fair sized National Front support, although the councillors weren't NF. Because the band were a Mod style band the union flags (Jacks) the band liked to have on stage were wrongly associated with the far right. To make this point Paul Weller had a sticker on his guitar that said 'This machine kills fascists'. It shows you how close to the stage we were as I was able to see and read it, but yes that's stuck in my mind for over 40 years and every time I see or hear the Jam or Paul Weller solo I think of that sticker on his guitar!

I WAS THERE: MARK TAYLOR

Two 16 year old mates and another just 15 years old travel from Chorley on the bus to Blackburn to see The Jam live for the very first time. We find ourselves in the pubs around King George's Hall close to Blackburn Tec where I am about to attend day release from work. My first job as I have just left school in that summer of '79. It blows our young minds. Up until this point the only thing in life is football. The scooters, the drinks, the 'We are the Mods' chants and the jukebox blasting out The Kinks - and that's before the gig. Shortly after watching The Vapors, The Jam hit the stage and we don't really know what's hit us as, we are carried along by the crowd. Our feet don't touch the floor till at least the end of the opening song. We are sold. The Jam are the band for us.

In a flash we are back at the bus stop - have we missed it? We might have to walk about eight miles home. Would it have mattered? No! Because we had just witnessed The Jam live for the first time.

40 years on, now living in Melbourne and 83 Paul Weller gigs later, across not only Europe but the globe, including America, Australia and Asia, I always think back to where it all started for me, on 12 December 1979 at King George's Hall, Blackburn.

I WAS THERE: GAYLE POWELL

I was a massive Jam fan, in fact I still am and I'm heading out tonight to see From The Jam-Bruce Foxton playing here in Brisbane.

Back in '79 I was in fourth year at high school, and went along to King George's Hall with a group of school mates. My stand out memory from that show is that at the end, a group of us went to the loos near the back door of the stage and we saw Rick and Bruce. Bouncers were try to rush us out, but we stuck around and eventually they cam out again and met us, even signing autographs.

That inspired me for the June '80 show, which was the same day as my first O level, to take along all my albums and singles. On that night, I bought a 'Strange town' t-shirt for one pound! How I wish I still had that. At the beginning of the evening we saw them heading to the show in a van, (Rick and Bruce, not Paul) and we waved – and much to our excitement they waved back. Later on, in the venue, we were up on the balcony and could see all three backstage listening to the support- the Expressos.

I've written in my diary that it was obvious they were not happy with the acoustics, but did two encores. Again, at the end of the night, my friend and I hid in the loos near the back stage door for a while. We were fortunate to meet them all again, and I also met Paul's dad, John. They signed all my record covers, which I still have to this day. I remember them as being approachable to us all. I also wrote to Paul as a 16 year old, and he wrote back- I have that letter too!

SOPHIA GARDENS

13 DECEMBER 1979, CARDIFF, UK

I WAS THERE: MARTYN LEWIS

I couldn't get tickets to see The Jam at Cardiff Sophia Gardens in December 1979, so went around the back trying to find ways to nick in, and saw this window slightly open. I climbed onto the wall and tried to open the window when someone approached and to my amazement it was Bruce Foxton. He actually helped me through the window into his dressing room, then got one of the security and said, 'Don't chuck him out and find him a space in the crowd!'

In an extra twist of fate, 25 years later I was a guest at Bruce's niece Nicola Foxton's wedding and finally got to thank Bruce and he said he actually remembered it happening. He also sent me two backstage passes to the next From The Jam gig in Cardiff!

1980

WOKING YMCA

15 FEBRUARY 1980, WOKING, UK

I WAS THERE: DERRICK JOHNSON

We are from Ottershaw, which is just down the road from Woking. In 1977 my mate's older brother asked us to buy a new LP called *In The City* for him when we were in Woking. We brought it back to my parents house, put it on and thought it was on the wrong speed as it was so fast! That was the start of it. We loved The Jam and in all I saw them seven times, including two secret pre tour gigs at Woking YMCA, one in Leicester at the De Montford Hall, one in Guildford at the Civic Hall and three times in London at the Hammersmith Odeon.

We were lucky enough to get tickets for two secret pre-tour gigs at Woking YMCA. It had a capacity of about 100 and so we were able to get very close during the gig and then talk to them afterwards, even getting into their dressing room at one of the gigs to get autographs (which I have since lost).

I have worked out that one was about in 1980 as we wanted to hear 'Going Underground', which was just about to be released, but Bruce Foxton told us after that was too complicated to play it in that venue. Sadly I can't remember when the other one was.

I went with about six mates and I asked one of them, for his memories and he supplied the following:

We went to two gigs - my father took the tickets on the door at the second one and, not knowing who The Jam were, refused them entry as they had no tickets. Paul Weller's father had to insist he speak to Mary who was the YMCA manager to let them in!

Somebody allegedly in the band told the *Woking News and Mail* reporter the drummer's name was Pube Buckler. Paul Weller's mum had a drink thrown over her, and his dad got upset and promised not to return.

My postscript to this story is that 32 years later I met Rick Buckler when he was promoting his book in Waterstones in Woking. I reminded him of the YMCA gigs and he said that after one of them he got in his car to drive home and a head popped up from behind the car. He'd interrupted some scamp trying to steal his number plate!

I spoke to another mate who attended the YMCA gigs and he remembered that at one of the gigs The Jam were supported by a band called Department S who had a hit with a song called 'Is Vic There?' They opened their set with 'Is Vic There?', played another song and then closed their set with 'Is Vic There?', apparently a little short of material.

The turn of the decade saw The Jam sweeping the board in the *NME* Readers Poll. Best Group was awarded to The Jam, *Sound Affects* won Best Album and Best Dressed Sleeve, Paul Weller picked up Best Male Singer and Guitarist, and Songwriter, Rick Buckler won Best Drummer, Bruce Foxton, Best Bass Player and 'Going Underground' won Best Single and the Most Wonderful Human Being award went to Paul Weller.

When 'Going Underground' unexpectedly barged its way into the chart at number one in March 1980, Paul, fearing that the band had sold out by releasing such a popular single, appeared on *Top of the Pops* wearing a Heinz Tomato Soup apron, in reference to The Who's 1967 album *The Who Sell Out*. BBC bosses persuaded Weller to wear the apron backwards fearing a backlash for allowing such flagrant product placement.

I WAS THERE: NICKY WELLER

I went to tons of their *Top of the Pops* appearances. My dad let me bunk off school most Thursdays to go and do that. I remember getting some stick at school because a lot of people were jealous. I had a couple of mates who thought it was cool but no one else from my school was doing anything like that.

I met loads of people at *Top of the Pops* - my heroes David Essex, Marc Bolan, Mud - it was that time. It was the time where there was just wall-to-wall stars. I was really into dancing and I remember meeting Flick Colby and all the Pan's People girls.

The Jam would go and record the track on the Wednesday at the BBC studios and then go back and mime to it on the Thursday for filming. Paul hated it because it was all mimed; everything was mimed on there. No one really liked it but the show was a necessity to sell your records because that was really the only music show at that time.

Afterwards we would all go to the bar upstairs once they'd all finished the recordings. Paul was always adamant about messing up his bits, like not miming properly or wearing something he shouldn't be wearing - he always used to do that. But it was a great time. My dad always used to say 'don't have to go to school today, come watch *Top of the Pops*.'

One time I was in a lift at the studios going between floors - there was just me and Madness who were on the show and it broke down, probably for 15 minutes or something. So I was stuck in a lift with that lot.

AMUSEMENT PARK

7 MARCH 1980, CHICAGO, ILLINOIS

I WAS THERE: JOEL PARKER

Way back in March of '80 (damn I am getting old) south of Chicago there was a mall called Old Chicago, which included a small indoor amusement park of all things. I'd got my tickets for The Jam and, being that it was an odd venue choice to say the least, I wasn't certain what to expect. Would they be able to play loud enough to overcome the noise of the rollercoaster and other rides? A handful of fellow fans waited by the stage then bang! With a volume that made you forget where you were on came The Jam.

To this day this particular show still stands as my favourite concert - the setlist (*Setting Sons* had just come out), the sound, the incredible energy. The capper was after the encore Paul Weller, the Modfather himself, came down and asked, 'Did you like the show?' My friend Mike who hadn't heard them before the show was slack-jawed and told Paul 'you guys sound like The Who' which got Paul laughing and, giving the new fan a smack on the back of his head, told him, 'Don't let that get out!' I still have my signed ticked stub. Loved The Jam, still do.

I WAS THERE: ANDREW ORCHIN, AGE 14

As a 14 year old Mod in America in 1980, nothing was more thrilling than seeing The Jam in College Park. To me, at the time, this was the biggest band in the world. The small group of Mods from Washington, DC would spend hours at Yesterday and Today Records combing through the 45s of the Mod section of the store, buying everything we could from the Chords to the Purple

Hearts to the Lambrettas, but obviously The Jam were the top of the top.

To actually get to see them, live in concert, was a dream come true. As soon as the lights went down, we jumped the barrier to get to the floor of the venue, and in an instant were in the front row. We stayed there for the entire set, as close to the boys as one could get. Over 35 years later this is still one of the best nights of my life.

The Motives circa 1982 with Andrew Orcin on bass

ST PAUL CIVIC CENTER

9 MARCH 1980, ST PAUL, MINNESOTA

I WAS THERE: SCOTT BRADLEY, AGE 10

The Jam were the first band I saw live during Spring 1980. I was 10 going on 11 which now seems so young to be going to a gig. I'd got the LP *In The City* and knew all their songs as my older brother Les had the LPs and singles. I kept a poster I had on my bedroom wall for a long time after they split. I remember my mother letting me have the next day off school because my ears were ringing so much from the gig. They were loud!

The Jam split when I was 13 and I couldn't believe it. I felt cheated with the Style Council. They seemed a long way away from The Jam. I used to listen to them regularly and learnt most of their songs on the bass guitar about 20 years ago.

ARMADILLO WORKS

22 MARCH 1980, AUSTIN, TEXAS

I WAS THERE: HARRY REDMOND

I remember seeing The Jam at Armadillo World Headquarters in Austin, Texas. I was in college and having devoured all print info available at the time on the band, I knew that Paul's father was their manager. I had a Batman t-shirt that I wanted to give Paul, so I searched out John Weller to give it to him for me.

The show was excellent, but I think The Jam's meaning was lost on some of the hippies and bikers that somehow showed up and didn't know what they were in for. In the end, John Weller took me and a bunch of my New Orleans buddies backstage to meet the band. Gibby Hanes of The Butthole Surfers was with us (he was a classmate of mine at Trinity University in San Antonio, and was not yet a rock star). We were totally blown away by an invitation to accompany the band to the bar at their hotel.

One thing I remember was that 'Going Underground' had just been released as a single, and Bruce was disappointed that 'Dreams of Children' was on the B-side (the show opened with that number). Afterwards, Bruce kept shaking his head, saying, 'It was supposed to be a double-A.' And when I requested Paul to perform 'English Rose' on an acoustic guitar at the bar, he did not say no, but he just smiled and we all laughed. I'll never forget that night. What a band. What a show.

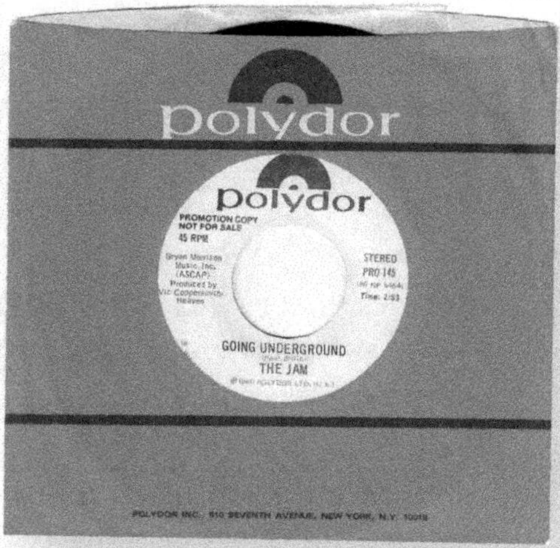

PAVILLION ELTARD

17 MAY 1980, PARIS, FRANCE

I WAS THERE: ANDY SAWYER, AGE 16

I first saw The Jam at the Music Machine in Camden on 21st December 1978. I was 16 and had been obsessed with the band since seeing them do 'All Around the World' on the Marc Bolan kids TV show in August the previous year.

I remember the support bands were Gang of Four and The Nipple Erectors (Shane MacGowan's first band) and they were both great. But The Jam were incredible. Everything I expected and more! Me and my cousin got soaking wet from sweat (we were both right down the front) and having to get two night buses back to South London afterwards in the winter cold, we both caught chills and my cousin spent the whole of Christmas ill in bed.

Over the next four years I was lucky enough to see the band 60 times before they split up and there were many, many memorable gigs. Secret gigs at The Marquee (where I climbed through a toilet window to get in) and Bromley Art College, lots of European gigs including an entire European tour in April 1982, all five nights at Wembley on the farewell tour and of course the last ever show at The Brighton Centre (I've still got the t-shirt!) but one that has always stuck in my mind was a show in Paris in 1980. It's stayed with me for many reasons. It was the first time I'd been abroad, apart from a couple of day trips with the school to Calais and Boulogne, as well as being the first time (of many) that I saw The Jam abroad, and also loads of my mates went as well (at the time I was deeply involved in the Mod revival scene in London).

We first heard about the show when we saw an advert in the *NME* advertising a coach trip to Paris for the gig. Why we chose not to go on the coach trip I can't remember. Maybe we didn't get it together to buy tickets before it sold out or maybe we thought

Andy Sawyer (far right) Dave Hey (second in pic) Steve Bickle (head poking out) plus three of mod-ettes they hung our with in Paris

we were too cool to go on an organised trip, but for whatever reason we decided to do the trip independently. My mate Ray Margetson (editor of the classic Modzine *Patriotic*) rode down to Woking on his scooter the day before and went to Paul Weller's house, spoke to his mum or his sister Nicky and secured places on the guest list for me, himself and my mate Stevie Bickle (Ray didn't know his name so he went on the list as 'Tezel Mehmet', a name that's stuck with us ever since).

On the day itself a sizeable group of us including me, Ray, Stevie, Dave 'The Strawman' Hey and a group of Mod-ettes who we hung around with in the Mod clubs and gigs of London at the time met up at Victoria Station to get the boat train to Paris. Just before we got on the train Ray rung my work, pretending to be my dad, telling them I was ill, as I hadn't been able to get the time off work!

When we arrived in Paris we started doing what Englishmen abroad have been doing for generations – we started drinking! By late afternoon we found ourselves next to the Arc de Triomphe in a severe state of inebriation and for some reason chucking empty beer bottles at this symbol of French imperialism. This was obviously extremely unwise not to say downright dangerous and before long a squad of gendarmes were on the scene. Probably provoked by Ray's decision to wear a Union Jack jacket for the trip, they singled him out as the ringleader. Memories of what happened next are sketchy but I believe they at least attempted to arrest our mate and a scuffle ensued. I really have no memory of the next few hours but certainly by the time The Jam hit the stage we were all (including Ray) inside the venue The Pavillion Eltard.

Although I'd sobered up somewhat by this time, I don't remember too much about the gig itself apart from the venue being very dark and there being lots of aggressive French punks in the crowd. Probably again provoked by Ray's Union Jack jacket, the punks decided towards the end of the show to attack the English Mods. Chaos ensued for the next few minutes. Now, I've always been a lover not a fighter but we had no choice but to defend ourselves against the attack. The first of many times we were attacked by French punks at various gigs over the next couple of years – gig-going could be a dangerous business in those days.

After the gig the atmosphere was toxic but being young and carefree (and extremely naïve) we hadn't given a thought to what we might do after the show. We weren't booked to go home until the following day and certainly had no money for a hotel so we were vulnerable to further attack by the many punks intent on spilling English blood.

Just as things were starting to look like turning particularly nasty an English voice cried out, 'Come with us'. It turned out to be the voice of an English teacher living and working in Paris and his French friend (who turned out to be his boyfriend) who invited loads of us to come and stay at their apartment to get us away from the mayhem!

There must've been at least a dozen of us sleeping curled up all over the couples' apartment that night and they almost certainly saved us all from getting a good kicking! Not one of the most memorable Jam gigs I ever went to, but certainly memorable for the circumstances surrounding it.

KING GEORGE'S HALL

3 JUNE 1980, BLACKBURN, UK

I WAS THERE: DAVID HALL, AGE 12

They say you always remember your first gig. I was a 12 year old, driven with my school friend by his dad from Clitheroe and picked up after the show. I remember queuing up outside with the punks and the Mods and the band staring down on us from the glass walkway from the venue across to the library. They were the biggest band in the UK at the time. I seem to remember that the ticket price was £4 and a few of the locals had baulked at what seemed an expensive price for a ticket. The hall was indeed only half full when the support act The Expressos opened.

The Jam on stage King Georges Hall 1980 (photo by Pete Eastwood)

I went into the bar for a soft drink and came out towards the end of the set. No more punters had arrived and on came The Jam. The set was just like listening to the band on record - tight and flawless. It was mainly a *Setting Sons* set list but they also played 'Going Underground' soon after it had been number one. And I remember when Weller said, 'This is a new song called 'Start!'. I've seen many concerts since but that's not bad for a first one.

I WAS THERE: ANDY YOUNG, AGE 15

I honestly thought this gig had been during the month of May and I would have put my mortgage on it. However, I have just checked the archives and we had actually crept into June. Damn you, Father Time!

Nottingham Forest had recently been crowned Champions of Europe for the second year running, and my own team, Blackburn Rovers, had just been promoted from the third tier to the dizzy heights of the second division after an incredible second half of the season under the leadership of Howard Kendall, who was still playing at that time – and what a player (and manager) he was! In the cinemas were three classic films; *Urban Cowboy*, *The Shining* and *The Empire Strikes Back*, while *The Bourne Identity* was still just a book; and a brand new one at that.

Meanwhile this 15 year old schoolboy was slap bang in the middle of his GCE 'O' Levels, with an exam – Mathematics if I remember correctly - due to be sat the very next morning. Respect to my parents for allowing me to attend the gig under the circumstances. Had they known I had already begun a career in drinking and smoking I'm not sure they would have been quite so accommodating.

The Jam had only played King George's Hall some six months previously so it was a surprise to hear about this gig, as there was no album to plug and no UK tour planned. I had thought they arranged this date and two others (at Wolverhampton and Stoke) as a warm up for a European tour but I can find no trace of such a tour having taken place. Perhaps they originally intended to simply visit the towns and cities of all the founder members of the Football League?

Whatever the motive for the gig, things had really taken off for The Jam in those six months. *Setting Sons* had sold in spades, 'The Eton Rifles' made the top five in the singles charts – their first single to do so – and triumphantly, their most recent single, 'Going Underground', had made The Jam the first artist since Slade almost a decade earlier to enter the singles charts at number one. The Jam was the biggest band in Britain at that time. Officially.

Despite all of the above, the gig was not a sell-out. This fact may surprise people, but the fact that lots of kids were in the middle of exams, the very recent previous gig at the same venue, and the – for that time pricey - £4 cost of tickets (up 25% from the previous gig) meant that there were probably around 3,000 people present in a hall that took 4,000. Anyway, I'm getting ahead of myself.

We had heard many stories about kids getting let into sound checks, etc. from the *Setting Sons* gig, and so me and a handful of mates who were lucky enough not to have had an exam that afternoon (some did – and how they must have regretted that fact later!) went down to the venue early (about 2pm) to see whether we could see any of the band. After hanging around for what seemed like ages, a large chap who we now know to be Kenny Wheeler ushered us in through a side door. 'Fuck me' I said to one of the other kids, 'all those rumours were true!'

We were let into the hall through an entrance I didn't even know existed, and there were a few technicians and roadies floating around the stage, but the kit seemed set up and ready to roll. 'Alright lads, how are you all?'

I had heard that gruff voice before, and turned round to see John Weller, who at that time was probably younger than I am now, striding towards us looking like the cat that got the cream. He'd obviously had a decent hand that afternoon! He had a black leather jacket on and I always thought he looked like an archetypal rocker, ironically. He explained to us that the group would come out and play through a couple of numbers and then have a quick chat with us kids, but that they were a bit pushed for time. He said he would make sure we all got something signed before they were finished. 'What a lovely bloke,' we all agreed.

It was bizarre. There were roughly between 50 and 100 kids – almost exclusively lads, there may have been a couple of girls, at most, there – waiting for our heroes to come on stage and (in our mind's eye anyway) play a mini-gig, just for us.

Rick was first to appear. He also had a leather jacket on (which he took off and threw on top of a speaker). He waved at everyone and went through a few moves. Then Bruce arrived on the scene, wearing a t-shirt and jeans. He plugged in and played a few notes and tested the microphone out. Paul then casually walked through the hall and jumped up onto the stage from our side. I suspect he'd been with Gill, probably in the Ribblesdale pub next door (they were certainly in there in 1978!). Paul got the loudest cheer, and I don't really remember what he was wearing, other than he had scarf on! Paul lit a fag and started testing his microphone. Then he turned round and said something to one of the roadies, then to Bruce and Rick, and plugged in his guitar. He then addressed the kids. 'Thank you for coming, we really appreciate you buying the records and coming to the shows. This is a song I've only just written, hope you like it.' He didn't actually tell us what it was called, but it was 'Start!' For a while afterwards we assumed it was called 'What You Give is What You Get' or something similar. The interesting thing about it is that the bass line was much lower in the mix and the 'Taxman' comparison was much less obvious the way it was played that night. I think he was probably still shaping the song to be honest. I already had *Revolver* and a couple of the other songs that were played that night I spotted similarities to immediately, but not with 'Start!' played that way, and yet it is one of the most obvious nicks of Paul's (or maybe Bruce's?) careers. They didn't play 'Start!' during the actual set, so it obviously was a work in progress.

I can't for certain say what the other two sound check songs we heard were; I think one of them was 'David Watts' and the other could have been one off *Setting Sons* ('Thick as Thieves' or 'Private Hell').

Then the band came down into the hall to speak to us kids and sign things for us. All I had was my ticket, a fag packet and The Jam t-shirt I was wearing – we hadn't even been to the merchandising stall yet – in fact it probably wouldn't even have been open

at that point! I got them signed anyway, and to be honest I was a little bit star struck, and just said 'Thanks'. Not that the band members had much time to speak. Paul seemed quite tense, but Bruce and Rick were smiling away. Once Kenny and John were satisfied that everyone had got something signed we were ushered out the way we had come in and we had to queue up like everybody else.

From memory, the merchandise stall consisted of two new t-shirts – the 'Going Underground' shirt with the bomb and a great 'Dreams of Children' shirt with a flower on the front. Both had matching badges, and as a special bonus they were selling 'Strange Town' t-shirts for a quid. After all, they were SO last year!

The actual gig itself was fairly similar to the one from six months previously, with the added bonus of four new songs – all of which would end up on *Sound Affects* but none of which any of us had heard before. They were 'But I'm Different Now', 'Dream Time', 'That's Entertainment' and 'Set the House Ablaze'. It is possible I may have one of those wrong with the passing of time, but the minute they played 'But I'm Different Now' I recognised the 'Doctor Robert' riff.

There was only one encore this time, which was perhaps a measure that it wasn't quite at the level of the previous Blackburn gig. Not that any of us 'sound check crew' were overly concerned about that – we had been privy to a song that nobody else had heard yet, as well as the four new ones they played to the proles.

The mates that had been sitting an 'O' Level while we were meeting The Jam were desperate for a piece of the action. So we decided to sneak up to the balcony and hide under the seats and wait for the hall to empty, as we had heard that the band sometimes came out into the hall after gigs.

Once we thought the coast was clear, we ventured back downstairs. I held the door open for a bloke behind me, only to discover it was none other than Bruce Foxton! He said 'Blimey mate, you look like you've seen a ghost!' I have no idea what my response was, other than to explain that we'd been lucky enough to have been allowed into the sound check, but that three of our group had been sitting an exam and had missed it, and wouldn't mind getting autographs, etc. He motioned for the lot of us to come over and signed whatever we had in our possessions and posed for photos – one of the 'exam lads' had sneaked a camera into the gig, an absolute no-no in those days. How times have changed!

He also told us he would get the others to do likewise and disappeared back into the dressing room area, while motioning us into the hall. There were probably another 30 or so kids that had the same idea, so by the time all three band members came back, there was a mini-stampede.

Bruce was as good as his word and we all ended up having our photos taken with him and Rick. I vividly remember Rick saying to one kid, 'I'm just a normal bloke, no need to look so petrified.' He also gave me a fag!

Unfortunately, Paul was getting too much attention for comfort, and all he could do was try and sign an autograph for everyone, which he did with good grace, despite being very obviously knackered. My mate did get some photos of a few of us next to Paul. One in particular I loved as it showed me right next to him. I looked like his little brother! Sadly, nobody knows what became of those photos, though we all still have our signed stuff.

So, in summary, this actual gig probably wasn't as good as the one six months earlier, but for me it was the most memorable Jam gig I ever went to.

We all left high school and went in different directions about two weeks after this gig, not a bad place to end things.

Oh yeah, and for the record I passed the maths exam!

I WAS THERE: SAM GARFORTH, AGE 12

I have a signed *Setting Sons* album cover somewhere. I'm sure they played a song which Paul said was called 'Julie wants to fuck me.' I was shocked as he was managed by his dad. I must have been 12.

VICTORIA HALL

3 JUNE 1980, HANLEY, UK

I WAS THERE: GAVIN JONES

I was lucky enough to see The Jam about 20 times, nearly always getting into sound checks, on guest lists and after parties - great times that I still reflect fondly on now.

I was always impressed how the group had time for their fans, and Weller's lyrics still amaze me that he could write with such foresight at such a young age, and watching them being blasted out with a mixture of passion, anger, vitriol as he strangled his Rickenbacker remains fresh in my mind. In later years I ran a high level motor racing team, and always tried to use the same values of The Jam when fans asked for visits/autographs, etc. as they taught me a lot about having time for the people that care.

Back in 1980 my friend Steve told me at Tech College about an unadvertised Jam gig he heard about in Stoke, as a warm up gig for Loch Lomand. This was on 3rd June, the day before the gig! We both bunked off work the next day and picked up our mates Mark, Trev and Cas in my trusty Beetle. Off we went to Stoke on a screaming hot day.

Once we got there we went to the hall and could see the roadies loading stuff in, so parked up and went to a local record store where we heard you could get tickets, and sure enough they had some left and we were in - £4 each! We went back to the hall to see if we could get into the sound check and after about an hour of hanging around their tour coach pulled up.

Paul got off first, and came straight over to us (a group of about 15 kids) and asked if we wanted to come in for the sound check, so we followed him in and chatted to him sat on the floor in the hall while Rick went through his drums, one by one. Eventually they all got on stage and went through about six songs, including trying 'Wasteland' but Paul kept cocking up the recorder, so they threw it away! They also ran through a new song called 'Start!'

After the soundcheck we got some chips and went to a pub with some of the locals we'd met at the venue. Charlie and his mate and were a bit knackered after walking around all day in the sun.

Back to the gig, we all bought a 'Strange Town' shirt for £1 and watched support band Expressos, with a very nice girl lead singer. Eventually John came on and said, 'Put yer 'ands together for three lads, The JAM!' It was a great gig, mostly *Setting Sons* and *All Mods Cons*, with 'Going Underground' and 'Start!' in there and – I think - two encores.

We gave Charlie and his mate a lift to the station (seven up in a Beetle) then drove the hour back home, all completely knackered but elated. I only fell asleep at the wheel once and went straight over a junction - oops!

The Jam headlined the first day of the Loch Lomond Festival. With an audience mix of skinheads, punks and Mods the festival was marred by fighting and violence. As The Jam took to the stage bottles were thrown at the group. Paul Weller unsuccessfully asked for the fighting to stop to no avail, resulting in local police having to restore order. Over 40 arrests were made and more than 30 fans were taken to hospital.

LOCH LOMOND ROCK FESTIVAL

21 JUNE 1980, BALLOCH, DUMBARTONSHIRE, UK

I WAS THERE: RICHARD HUGGINS, AGE 18

I was there only for the Saturday as new wave was my thing. There were four of us up from Lancaster University and we must have been 18. I remember it was a day of extreme emotions: fear, joy, tiredness, fear, anger - and a bit more fear.

Fear - it was war for most of the day: Scottish punks v Scottish skins. Bottles, sticks, fists... at one point a fire raged. The cops and fire brigade arrived to curb the worst aspects, but the fighting ebbed and flowed through much of the day.

Anger - I was the only black guy at the concert. I felt a thump in the back, and thought 'here we go.' As I got up, a big lad stumbled on about five steps, fell flat on his face, vomited, quivered and stayed there for the rest of the day. I thought, 'Let him die!'

Joy - the best sets for me were the Tourists, Stiff Little Fingers and The Jam. Stiff Little Fingers actually stopped the fighting with their rendition of the Specials 'It Doesn't Make It Alright'. It kicked off again immediately afterwards. The Jam were the last act, in time for the setting sun. By then, the gangs had fought themselves into submission, and the boys produced a set that will live in my memory forever.

Tiredness - we all fell asleep in the car going back. All of us. I was driving and woke up on the motorway inches behind a lorry.

I WAS THERE: STUART CARR

The promoters went for a two way split of more new wave bands on the Saturday and a heavier rock mix on the Sunday, (Ian Gillan, Saxon, Wishbone Ash). It also gave a fair few local bands a chance to show off their potential to a large audience. Saturday was a good line-up, The Chords, The Only Ones, The Regents, Punishment of Luxury, Stiff Little Fingers, The Tourists and The Jam.

All was well between the rival tribes strangely united by The Chords - a Mod band with a decidedly 'new wave' sound. The Stiff Little Fingers fans in the crowd seemed happy enough with their music if not their clothes, and a good reception enabled them to nip back onstage to steal an unplanned encore.

Such is festival etiquette that this meant all subsequent bands should also take a bow. Unfortunate, as next up were Bad Manners. In the subsequent 20 years I've never seen a worse performance than the set from Buster and pals - a while before they became a lovably eccentric British institution and Buster became a hotelier. Tuneless and feckless, they were downright awful.

Fortunately, the Tourists took the stage and the fighters lapsed into a coma at Annie Lennox's horribly miscast power-pop. The Jam managed to reunite the crowd as punks and Mods saw their heroes, who, if memory serves, played 'Going Underground' for the first time ever.

I WAS THERE: PAUL BRANNIGAN, AGE 16

My very first festival, at the grand old age of 16. The Saturday was very grey and I can clearly remember watching Bad Manners from through the fence at the back. They were a lot of people watching from the back fence. I could obviously only afford a one day ticket. Sad as it seems I also caught Stiff Little Fingers, The Tourists and The Jam from the same fence.

I WAS THERE: ALISTAIR EMERY

I was at both days and at one of them there was a guy actually inside the roundabout toilet who had dropped his watch inside. He couldn't get out and was covered in excrement. I never found out what happened to him.

Also there was a guy who was feeding the bears raw meat inside the bear enclosure. Those were the days. The security guards were in their towers too, keeping an eye on us. I felt like I was in a concentration camp!

A plane organised by the event flew overhead dropping little parachutes - hundreds of them, with something inside that no one knew what it was. They all ended up in the no go area, the swamp, in the middle of the area inside the ground. This area was covered in really thick mud and bear shit with some kind of caves at the back. Some guys ran into it and quickly sank in the mire. One guy I spoke to who had been there and retrieved one told me inside the parachute was a sweet! Someone was having a laugh, probably the pilot!

I WAS THERE: JAMIE MENZIES

My dad and his friends were into The Jam and they took us. We were all baby Mods - we were into Madness, The Specials and The Jam. My dad took me, my older brother Terry, and his friend's son. I remember the route up to the gig - there were loads of scooters heading towards the venue.

There were people there who were absolutely wasted. And I remember all these skinheads and Nutty Boys and hundreds of Mods. When it came to the fighting, I remember surges of people, all running. We were getting protected. There were bottles and alcohol getting thrown about but it was a fantastic day. The Tourists played that day, as did Bad Manners and Stiff Little Fingers - their lead singer, Jake Burns, came out into the crowd. My dad had given me a Dexy's Midnight Runners poster flyer, and I got Jake to sign it. He was in hysterics at my Mod gear and pork-pie hat. It was on my bedroom walls for years, but sadly I don't know what ever happened to it.

John Campbell covered one of his guitars in Jam photos

I WAS THERE: JOHN CAMPBELL, AGE 13

I attended my first ever gig when I went to see The Skids at the Odeon Theatre in Edinburgh, but Loch Lomond I could not wait to get to as I was going to see The Jam. My early gigs experience has to go as a big thank you to one of my mate's big brothers - he had the most amazing vinyl collection, always getting the newest releases as soon as they came out, and he was a guitarist in a punk band. We would help them with their equipment anytime they played local gigs and as very young kids it was absolutely instrumental in giving us the love for live music that we still have to this day.

It was through him that I got free ticket to Loch Lomond. I still remember the day well, miserable Scottish weather as about a dozen off us piled into a old Bedford van and started the 90 minute journey. It was a mixture of older teenagers and us younger ones - the older ones had a carry out with them and would supply us younger ones with the odd can of lager. We were full of excitement going to something like this - we had all been to gigs before but nothing ever like this as we knew there would be a mixture of Mods, punks, skins and rockers, but we felt safe with the older ones in our group.

The highlights for me were obviously The Jam and Stiff Little Fingers as I'm a big fan off both, but The Jam definitely blew everybody away with a blistering set of about 20 odd songs. The festival was marred with lots of fighting and bottle throwing - fights and mud everywhere. If I remember correctly I even think there was a fire at some point.

I managed to get to see the band another four times - twice in two nights at Edinburgh Playhouse, one at Ingliston, just outside Edinburgh and lastly the Glasgow Apollo.

By this time I was getting heavily into the Mod scene and at the Ingliston gig it was just full of scooters outside. Not long after that I got my first scooter and love them to this day.

I for one wouldn't like to see The Jam reform and I would imagine most fans that saw them live would feel the same. People that want them to reform I guess are the ones that never got the chance to see them live which I totally understand.

I wish for only one thing - for Bruce, Paul and Rick to get together for a photograph all together. Long live the memories of the best band in the fucking world.

I WAS THERE: MICHAEL FARRAGHER, AGE 16

I decided to make the journey on my own from London to Scotland to see The Jam at Loch Lomond. I was 16, had just left school, this was my first festival and my first time away from home by myself. I was nervous but very excited. I had seen The Jam three times so far at the Rainbow and this was a totally new experience. I didn't have a ticket for the festival or anywhere to stay after it and I was banking on being able to buy a ticket on the day outside. I set off on the coach from Victoria to Glasgow and from there on to Bear Park, wherever that was. I remember on the journey seeing a Japanese guy with a Sony Walkman which back then was the very latest in music technology!

I finally got to Bear Park mid-afternoon, managed to buy a ticket and I was in, looking forward to seeing The Jam again. As I remember the weather wasn't all that great, but I wasn't bothered. During the day I saw Bad Manners, The Lookalikes, The Chords, The Tourists and Stiff Little Fingers. There was trouble during the day with beer cans and bottles flying all over the place and fights breaking out between skins and mods and mod and rockers who were there for the next day. I stayed well clear of it!

The Jam were the headliners and they were was amazing. They debuted three new songs – 'Pretty Green', the next single 'Start!' and 'But I'm Different Now' which would all appear on the *Sounds Affects* album later in the year. It was a fantastic day and one I'll never forget.

After the festival I got the bus or train back to Glasgow and arrived in sometime after midnight and had expected the coach station to be open all night so I could wait there until I got my coach back to London the next day. But the coach station was closed and I had nowhere to stay. Two guys in the taxi queue said I could come and stay at their place and in my naivety I saw nothing wrong in that. They let me sleep on their couch and gave me a lift into the coach station the next morning. Nothing untoward happened!

At the start of July 1980 The Jam set out on the first of three Japanese tours, appearing in Osaka, Kyoto and ending with three nights in Tokyo.

MAINICHI HALL

3 JULY 1980, OSAKA, JAPAN

I WAS THERE: TAKUJI NAMBU

I was a Japanese high school boy when I first watched The Jam playing 'In The City' on TV in 1977. Though being a big fan of The Who, frankly I was not much impressed with them then. A year later, charmed with the *Modern World* Mod-style sleeve, I bought the LP then instantly fell in love with them, particularly 'Life From The Window' which assured me that we'd got The new Who for our generation!

Takuji Nambu stands in front of Jam posters in London

The next year I formed a cover band of The Jam and The Who. Maybe we were the very first band in Japan to copy 'The Eton Rifles' late in 1979.

The first Jam gig for me was the one in Osaka in July 1980. They kicked off with 'Thick as Thieves'. I remember they played the then-unreleased 'Start!', 'Pretty Green' and 'But I'm Different Now'. They left the stage with 'Turning Japanese' by The Vapors playing in the background.

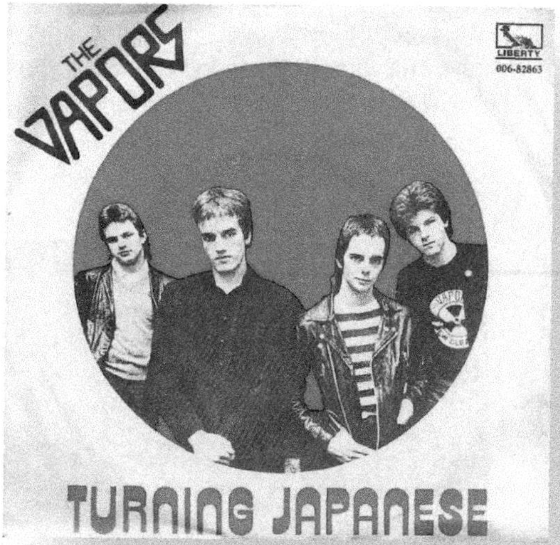

I WAS THERE: DAVE FENTON

We were discovered by Bruce Foxton. We were playing a pub called the White Lion just outside Godalming, near Guildford, and he just happened to be there with a mate. I didn't even know he was there until afterwards.

Bruce offered us a couple of dates on the next Jam tour – it was just a matter of luck! We did those dates, and John Weller saw us, liked us and he went on to co-manage us with Bruce. We weren't Mods, we didn't want to dress up as Mods, and we regarded ourselves as a clever punk band. We then got tagged as new wave but we didn't invent that term either.

Supporting The Jam was our first real dabble into life on the road, going from playing to 20 people or one man and his dog in a pub to 2,000 seaters. We each had our own minibus and every time we got to a service station we had water pistol fights in the car park. They'd tape our clothes to the ceiling while we were on stage, that sort of thing, while we'd put talcum powder on the snare drum. I've got really happy memories of all that.

We knew 'Turning Japanese' had potential, I'd loaded it with lots of hooks, but nobody can say what's going to be successful. It took a long time to be a hit, it crept up a few places every week. It could just as easily have been turning Portuguese, but 'Turning Japanese' just seemed to sound right. There was a week when we were at No.3 in the charts and The Jam were at No.1 with 'Going Underground'.

United Artists got bought up by EMI. Prior to that, the label only had about twelve acts, bands like Buzzcocks, Fischer-Z, The Stranglers and Dr. Feelgood. It was a good atmosphere. The front door was always open, and everybody was on first name terms.

After the buy-out, most of the staff were made redundant and we found ourselves signed to EMI imprint Liberty. All the A&R staff who'd signed us and helped develop us had disappeared. To add to that Bruce and John were on a long European tour with The Jam so couldn't be on an American tour with us. It got too awkward, John held his hand up and said, 'Sorry, it doesn't work anymore'. So within a few weeks of that hit we'd lost our record company and management.

The eleventh UK single 'Start!' backed by 'Liza Radley' released on 15 August 1980 gave The Jam their second UK number one. It is said that Paul Weller got the idea for this song from reading George Orwell's book *Homage To Catatonia*, which is set in the Spanish Civil War.

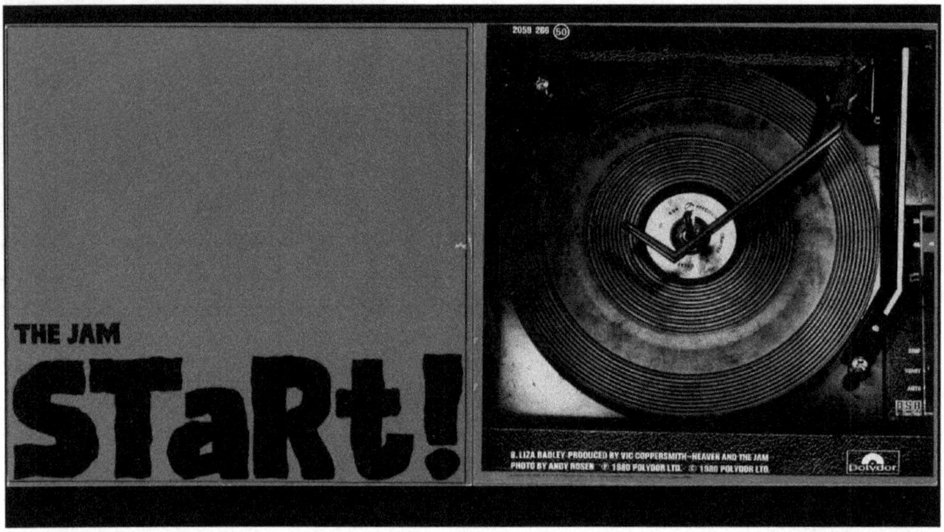

TOP RANK

26 OCTOBER 1980, SHEFFIELD, UK

I WAS THERE: ALISON LAVERICK

I saw The Jam when I was 16. It was my first gig and I had no idea what to expect. We were in row O, about halfway back in the stalls but when they came onstage everyone surged forward and we ended up about five rows further forward!

It was a fantastic gig. They'd just released their *Sound Affects* album and the first track they played was 'Dream Time'. I couldn't believe how loud it was - I was deaf for three days afterwards. They played 'Down in The Tube Station' and the whole place went mad.

I remember a TV crew was there and Chris Cowey the presenter from the show *Check It Out* was bopping away at the end of our row.

After the gig we hung around the stage door. The door opened and there was a bit of a scuffle. Somehow I ended up in the dressing room and I got to meet all three band members. They were lovely and they signed my ticket. I wish I still had it.

For a first gig it certainly didn't disappoint.

CITY HALL

27 & 28 OCTOBER 1980, NEWCASTLE UPON TYNE, UK

I WAS THERE: COLIN BARLOW, AGE 15

I was there on the second night, (the first show was recorded for Tyne Tees TV). This was one of my very first gigs and it was just one hit song after hit song. I felt like I was part of a proper music movement, like being part of some sort of collective. It was a fantastic experience as a 15 year old to be sweating down the front in the middle of that mass of bodies and bouncing along. It was also the first time I really appreciated a bass player enjoying his craft.

I remember the PA broke down and left the band without vocals or drums. After a few minutes the band carried on and played and instrumental version of 'In The City' with the crowd singing every word.

Once the roadies had fixed the problem the set continued full steam ahead with a version of 'Going Underground'.

SETLIST:
Thick As Thieves
Boy About Town
Monday
Going Underground
Pretty Green
Man In The Corner Shop
Set The House Ablaze
Private Hell
This Is The Modern World
Little Boy Soldiers
But I'm Different Now
Start!
Scrape Away
When You're Young
The Eton Rifles

I WAS THERE: MICHAEL DUNN

I lived in a small town called Bedlington, about 14 miles north of Newcastle. I picked up on the band round about the release of ''A' Bomb on Wardour Street'. I bought all the usual music magazines to follow them - *NME* and *Sounds* - and went to my local record shop to buy every single and album from then onwards on the day of release. I would listen to Radio Luxembourg and John Peel and I remember sitting in front of the radio to hear the first play of 'Beat Surrender' (I think it was Dave Lee Travis on Radio 1) and trying to get my mum to understand the significance of the record and break up of the band. I'd persuaded a couple of mates to come to gigs, but none followed them in the way that I did. I absorbed all the material I could. It all seems like a lifetime ago!

Reading about Paul Weller and his reference to his influences meant I bought The Beatles back catalogue and also found The Kinks. I remember one interview where Paul talked about 'Waterloo Sunset' and in another the Small Faces so I then also got into them. I think at the time The Jam introduced a lot of their young fans into other music.

Then there was my school bag was a haversack. Every new single or album logo with The Jam written in a new style font was faithfully replicated in enamel and gloss paint onto the bag. Simple pleasures but I had to show my devotion and stay one step ahead at school!

I went to see The Jam in 1978, 1979, 1980, 1981 and in '82. To get to Newcastle I would travel on the bus and I'm pretty sure that I and just one or two others were the only Mods in my town. I went to every gig at Newcastle City Hall as well as shows at Whitley Bay Ice Rink on the *Bucket and Spade* tour. The City Hall gigs were always special - the balcony moved and it was always as hot as hell in the venue and smoky. Everyone would be singing all the words. We all did. We lived and breathed The Jam and devotion was total.

Standouts at the shows were the all the big singles and anthems. I loved all albums, but *Setting Sons* is a constant and played regularly to this day. My favourite track - all the singles from 'Down at the Tube Station at Midnight' to 'Going Underground' - the greatest run of singles ever. My all time fave track has to be 'Strange Town'. The Jam, their songs, the gigs and all my memories – the best days of my life!

I WAS THERE: IAN TURPIN

Somehow, Sunderland went from being a musical Mecca in the Sixties and early Seventies to becoming a musical wasteland. Stories abound of all the talent that would play in various venues around the town, in particular at the Bay Hotel at Seaburn and the Mecca, known as 'The Fillmore North' just across the bridge from the town centre. Geoff Docherty's book *A Promoter's Tale* gives an excellent insight into those golden days.

Despite the Sunderland Empire Theatre being the biggest theatre between Leeds and Edinburgh, which had played host to The Beatles in the Sixties (as well as being the venue where comedy actor Sid James gave his last breath, as his ghost continues to haunt the place), the story goes that due to the damage done by fans during a gig by The Boomtown Rats, the nearest to contemporary acts they would book thereafter was Showaddywaddy. This meant that my generation had to travel through to Newcastle to see any worthwhile musical entertainment. Being the days before the Internet and Ticketmaster, the only way to score tickets was to go to the City Hall box office in person.

I would call their number on a weekly basis in the hope that along with 'Northern Symphonia and the wrestling' I would hear the name of a band I wanted to see on their recorded message. In autumn of 1979 I finally heard 'The Jam' amongst the usual list of American rock bands. I could barely believe my ears, and nicked off school the next day to get the train through and be there as soon as they opened ('box office hours are 10:30 to 5:30') to get three tickets.

The date was for December. Soon after it was announced that the school trip to Derwent Hill Outdoor Centre in the Lake District was going to be the same week, so the other two lads I'd bought tickets for dropped out and sold their tickets on. In my 'To Do' list, seeing The Jam came higher than rock climbing and canoeing, as I'd recently done that anyway on a trip to a similar place named Langdale, so I stuck with the original plan.

On the night we got the train through and walked up to the City Hall. This was my first ever gig. The stage was already set up, with a backdrop logo of The Vapors. They duly played their set and seemed to me to do a decent job but I'd never heard of them and wasn't familiar with their songs so viewed with vague interest. I did end up buying 'Turning Japanese' later, and thought the album *New Clear Days* had some great tracks on it ('America', 'Trains', 'Bunkers'), all with that signature chugging rhythm guitar, but their career was short-lived.

Finally The Jam took the stage. My seat was towards the front centre of the balcony so was in a decent spot but at some remove from the stage. Gig reviews are often boring to read and my memory is getting fuzzy for details anyway, but I do remember it was one of the most exciting nights of my young life, to see my heroes in person. I know they played with loads of energy and I heard most of the songs I was hoping for. This was the *Setting Sons* tour, among their strongest albums in my opinion, and most of the tracks were played along with other songs from *All Mods Cons* which were already becoming anthems in the soundtrack to my youth.

I returned to the City Hall in April and again in September of 1980 to see Secret Affair, scoring tickets near the front both times and meeting the band afterwards. At one of these gigs the support band was The Step. They had a brass section and did a great version of Smokey Robinson's 'Get Ready', but unfortunately not much more was heard of them.

In October of 1980 The Jam came back to Newcastle City Hall and this time I scored tickets for a bunch of my Mod mates. We all managed to swoop down to the gap about eight rows back from the stage, and were able to take turns squeezing into the front row for a few songs before having to withdraw due to heat exhaustion. This gig, with Weller wearing a yellow polka dot shirt and grey strides, was recorded and shown on TV. If you look closely there's a glimpse of me, drenched in sweat, leaning over a seat with arm raised, wearing a red Fred Perry v-neck and parka. I wasn't even sure it was me when I first saw it on TV (we didn't have a VCR so didn't have the luxury to record and review in slow-mo!) but the next day at school one of the lads verified that he'd seen me, and with future viewing of the *Complete Jam* DVD he was right! Anyway a good time was had by all. Witnessing so much power and energy, so close to the front of the stage, for a 15 year old on the threshold of breaking out into the world, it really was a great time to be alive. Well, apart from things like parental-imposed curfews, lack of funds and approaching O levels!

A few weeks later, in November 1980, I went for a long weekend trip to London with my mam. We stayed in a small hotel right next to the Bond Street tube. As soon as we got settled I nipped across the street for a snoop around in the HMV shop and as I walked in they started playing 'Burning Sky'. I thought I was leading a charmed life, but there was more to come. I pulled out my tour t-shirt and saw on the list of venues that The Jam were playing at the Rainbow that weekend. On the Saturday afternoon I took the tube over to Finsbury Park. There was a queue of Mods round the side of the building, hoping to get in to see the sound check so I joined in. I got on talking to a girl and asked her if she knew of any tickets going. She told me she had one spare and wanted to give it to me for free. I made her take five quid and sacked off the sound check as I now had to get back to the hotel to get changed for the night and tell my mam what was up, this of course being before the age of mobile phones.

So back I went to the Rainbow that night and got to see The Jam all over again. It was strange seeing them in such a large venue, with the atmosphere much more subdued than at the City Hall. I had heard that Weller had mentioned in an interview that they got the best reception from fans when they played in the North East. Maybe seeing The Jam wasn't such a huge event to Londoners, maybe they got to see their heroes more frequently, or maybe they were just less effusive down south, but as happy as I was for the windfall opportunity, the event wasn't as good as gigs at the City Hall. Still, I scored a few Mod credibility points at school the next week, and was lucky enough to see The Jam several more times after this.

I WAS THERE: HILARY FALL

We went down to Newcastle in hope of seeing them (as we did not have a ticket) as they were playing City Hall. As we were standing about, Paul's dad John Weller let us into their sound check. We were very chuffed and he was such a nice bloke to do that.
I also saw them play Edinburgh Playhouse on two consecutive nights. Good memories - loved them.

PLAYHOUSE

29 OCTOBER 1980, EDINBURGH, UK

I WAS THERE: COLIN LEVY

At the time of the Dundee concert I was living in a place called Forres in the North of Scotland and on the day of the concert it was nearly a three hour drive each way for me and my best mate Dean. At the time I was 18 and I first heard The Jam on late night radio in 1977 (might have been John Peel show) and as a result bought the album *In The City* and followed that up by buying all their album releases which involved queuing at the record shop in Elgin on the day of the releases.

The Dundee concert was a bit wild with many punks in attendance being out shouted by regular choruses of 'we are the Mods' by Mods in what was a young audience.

In 1980 I moved to Penicuik (near Edinburgh) as my partner at the time had moved due to her parents splitting up - but this gave me the opportunity to see The Jam at The Playhouse in Edinburgh.

I remember going to buy tickets at the venue and had to queue around the back of the building. I thought there were too many fans in front of me that I would never get tickets but thankfully I did - three, which were also for my girlfriend (soon to be wife) and her brother.

This was another great concert but slightly different as it included brass instruments. I remember one of the support acts was a poet who whilst trying to read out poetry was continually booed. When Paul Weller came on stage he was not happy about this and made his feelings clear.

To this day I still say that both the concerts were the best I have ever been to and I've been to a lot and have continued to follow Paul Weller.

My favourite Jam song is 'That's Entertainment' as the words like many of Paul's songs have a meaning which I can refer to.

APOLLO

30 OCTOBER 1980, GLASGOW, UK

I WAS THERE: MALCOLM MCPHEE

I'm from Paisley originally, now living in Glasgow. I heard of The Jam via friends and radio and music magazines at the time. I saw them twice at Glasgow Apollo, once at the Magnum Centre in Irvine and again at Ingleston near Edinburgh. I just remember the energy and vibrancy from the gigs – it seemed as if they really believed in what they were doing and singing about. My favourite Jam song is 'Tube Station' closely followed by 'Butterfly Collector'. Fave album is *Setting Sons*. I think the evolution from album to album is very evident.

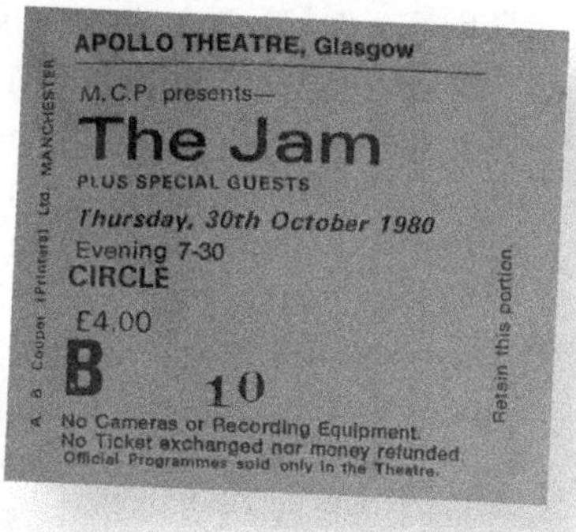

I WAS THERE: WILLIAM MOORE

Seen them a few times but the best was in 1980 at the Glasgow Apollo – I was in the upstairs circle and could feel the whole place vibrating! Thought it was going to collapse - brilliant gig!

I WAS THERE: GRAEME BOYD, AGE 13

I saw The Jam just once, my age being a factor preventing me seeing them elsewhere or before, at the Glasgow Apollo in 1980. I was 13. Thanks to having an older brother, it was he who bought the tickets and we toddled along with a couple of his mates. I'd been in the Apollo before and was tremendously excited by actually seeing The Jam as I'm sure many others felt.

The Piranhas were the support that night and although popular enough at that point due to their 'Tom Hark' single, they weren't going down that well with the impatient Glasgow crowd! If I remember correctly, announcing 'alright we'll do one more and then piss off OK?' Massive cheer.

When the lights went out there was a thunderous noise and it continued through every song. Singing along and the place was just bouncing. The band looked like they were really enjoying it as well. I was in the second row on the circle seats - it was a great view and even better when the two guys in front of me turned round, saw how small I was, grabbed me and lifted me over their seats to stand beside them for an even better view!

The *Sound Affects* album had been out for a while by then and obviously they were still promoting it. I particularly remember 'Dream Time' and 'Pretty Green' and of course I was already familiar with the rest of the set list. In fact - I'm sure they started with 'Dream Time'.

It was such a privilege to see them. They were just one of those bands that I knew even then that in the future I would say to people - and I do - I saw The Jam. It felt important if you know what I mean. Three guys who could stand there and totally blow you away is special and I'll never forget it. Their final tour sold out so quickly I never got the chance to see them again. I have seen Paul many times live but it's not the same. How could it be?

Another nice memory from that night was leaving the venue and the crowd swarming over Renfield Street grinding the traffic to a halt as we all walked towards our bus or train home. The Apollo crowd high on The Jam singing – 'we are the Mods, we are the Mods, we are - we are - we are the Mods!' Fantastic!

APOLLO

31 OCTOBER 1980, MANCHESTER, UK

I WAS THERE: GAVIN JONES

The fourth gig of the *Sound Affects* tour, and we had no tickets! I booked the time off work and went with my girlfriend Helen to this one, who wasn't sure about the 'no ticket' situation, but this was The Jam.

I picked Helen up at ten in the morning, and two hours later we were in Manchester outside the Apollo and parked in a nearby car park. There was a big sign saying 'Tonight The Jam – Sold Out', which didn't do our confidence much good, but we found the stage door down the side where roadies were beavering away, asked them when the sound check was, and they said about 4pm, so we went to a nearby pub for refreshments.

Once the pub closed at 3.30pm we went back to the stage door and I was asking the other kids there if they had spare tickets but none of them had tickets either! I started talking to a group of Scousers, especially one nice lad Ray Finch who was a good laugh and had stayed at Paul's house once when he went down to London for a gig!

The group turned up and we got in, We sat and talked to Paul as Rick and Bruce went through their sound check. Then we were treated to our first hearing of 'Pretty Green', 'Dreamtime', 'Man in the Corner Shop' and 'Boy About Town', as well as a couple of older songs. It was a good sound check. We had a quick chat with the group after and then Big Kenny kicked us out.

I hooked up with Ray again and he said he had got us all on the guest list, so we had to stay close to him. To kill time we went to the train station to hang around, and finally went back to the Apollo about 7.45pm. Unfortunately we got split up in the crush, and Ray got in and we didn't, so now I was desperate for tickets. Suddenly an old boy jumped out of a taxi and asked if we wanted two tickets for £9, only £1 more than face value, so I snapped his hand off and we pushed our way in.

Not long after we got in, support band The Piranhas came on who were OK. I only knew their song 'Tom Hark'. After a long break The Jam came on and ripped into 'Dreamtime', all in all doing about eight new songs and old favourites, with two encores. They did a brilliant version of 'Down at the Tube Station at Midnight', 'To Be Someone', 'David Watts' and finished with a booming version of ''A' Bomb in Wardour Street'.

A great gig, difficult drive into the night on the way home, but I had to laugh on Saturday morning when I reflected on the gig and looked at the ticket. It was for that night, the 1st October the day after the show we went to. I hadn't noticed and we got in no problem. Good job I didn't notice or I would have been shitting myself that we wouldn't get in!

DEESIDE LEISURE CENTRE

2 NOVEMBER 1980, DEESIDE, UK

I WAS THERE: ANDY JONES

'Don't Stand So Close to Me' by The Police was somewhere near the top of the charts when The Jam arrived at Deeside Leisure Centre in north Wales for the latest leg of their 1980 tour to promote arguably their best album, *Sound Affects*, which incidentally hadn't even been released at this point! I only mention this, because the police were called to that venue on more than one occasion that night, and you definitely didn't want to be standing too close to a certain faction in the crowd, believe me!

Little did we know it, but we were just five weeks away from the shocking murder of The Beatles' John Lennon on the pavement outside his New York apartment building, shot dead by a deranged fan whose newly released *Double Fantasy* album Lennon had signed on the same spot some six hours earlier. The irony of roughly half of *Sound Affects* being influenced by a Beatles album – *Revolver* - was not lost on me. (As an aside, my dear mum died on the same date as Lennon, 8th December, some 24 years later, RIP to both of them). It was also exactly two years before the launch of *Channel 4*, on which The Jam would bid farewell to those not lucky enough to have tickets for the final few gigs, by appearing on the debut airing of *The Tube*. The Beat Surrendered.

I had left high school at the tender age of 15 some five months earlier. However, I wasn't technically old enough to leave school and get a job (a long story, relating to the 11-plus test), and in any event I had a career lined up, but wasn't due to start that until 1981, so I was forced to attend a Catholic sixth form college in Blackburn, Lancashire (also immortalised by that same doomed Beatle). I say 'attend'. I had about as much motivation to actually go to a lesson as I would have had to drink my own piss. Instead, I would register every morning, go and play some music in the common room, while waiting for the pub next door, The Sportsman's Arms, to open so that I could drink somebody else's piss and practice my pool technique!

A few lads from my high school also attended the College – St Mary's College for anyone familiar with Blackburn - and a handful of them were into The Jam.

The Jam had only recently played Blackburn King Georges Hall twice in the space of six months, so we were not expecting them to announce that the next UK tour would call into this small provincial town, and sure enough it didn't!

A few of us got our heads together and decided that we should make a trip to one of the northwest gigs. However, the demand for tickets was likely to be intense, so in our wisdom we thought it would be easier to get tickets for Deeside Leisure Centre – a cavernous venue – than the relatively small Manchester Apollo. We managed to get 10 tickets. We didn't even try for Manchester, though I have to say I never personally had a difficulty getting a ticket for a Jam gig there.

The one thing we hadn't worked out was how the fuck we were actually going to get to Deeside. We didn't even really know where it was - my mate said 'somewhere near Chester, I think'. There was a fairly regular train service to Manchester, even on a Sunday, and we were that keen on getting tickets for all of us, we hadn't really given that much thought.

In those days there were still priests teaching in the Catholic schools, among other things, and I have no idea how the subject was broached – given that I barely attended lessons – but an old priest called Father Tulloch (affectionately known as Pop Tulloch, and when I say 'old', I mean about 50....) offered to drive us all over there in the school minibus. IN THE FUCKING SCHOOL MINIBUS! Apparently they had raised thousands of pounds to buy this thing – a Ford transit type bus – and here was this priest offering to take ten teenagers who would be smoking, drinking and - if we were lucky – much more besides, on a 130 mile round trip. All we had to do was cough up the petrol money. It wouldn't be the only thing getting coughed up that night, believe me.

We toyed with the idea of trying to get into the sound check, etc. but figured it wouldn't really be fair on the old priest to have him hanging around any longer than was necessary. With the benefit of hindsight it also wouldn't be very fair on the young boys of the Chester area. So we set off at about 4pm, figuring that it would take the old boy at least two hours to drive the 65 miles from Blackburn to the venue, despite the vast majority of it being motorway, even in those days.

The first thing that struck me when we got into the minibus was the strong smell of alcohol. It so happened that most of the teenagers present, including me, had been playing in a football match at the school and therefore had little or no time for a beer before boarding the minibus (which was probably just as well, given the lack of alcohol tolerance of most of them). One or two of the lads had been in the Sportsman's Arms, but they looked okay and had probably only had one or two.

Anyway I thought no more about it, and settled back. Someone had the foresight to bring along a cassette player so we rotated *All Mods Cons* and *Setting Sons* and got in gig mood.

Fuck me, Pop Tulloch obviously didn't get out much. Either that, or he fancied himself as Nigel fucking Mansell! We got to Deeside Leisure Centre in a little over an hour. He must have floored it all the way there, and it is one of only three occasions I've actually been scared by someone's driving – the second time was on the return journey, but more on that later. He parked in a car park near the venue and told us he'd meet us in the same spot at 11pm, he was going to visit the local parish priest. Yes, of course you fucking are, Pop! Lying is a sin, didn't you know?

As we turned the corner to get to the venue, we saw the longest queue imaginable to get in! It was just like a conga of fishtails, boating blazers and Paul Weller look-a-likes. Except this conga wasn't fucking moving. This was at 5.45pm with the doors due to open at 6pm. Even when the clock struck six, there was absolutely no movement and we seemed as far away from the doors as we had ever been. Every now and again, an irate Mod – on the assumption that we weren't moving because someone ahead was trying to push in – would say 'Typical Scousers', whereupon some Scouser further up the queue would come back with 'What was that soft lad?', or 'Come 'ere, you fucking woollyback dickhead' and all hell would break loose.

'Come on lads, we're all here to see The Jam, we're all part of the same family aren't we?' 'You can fuck off an' all.' Then you would get a similar exchange involving the Mancs and the Welsh....

So we saved our breath, kept out of it as much as we could, and plodded our way eventually to the front of the queue, where we could see why it was taking so long for everyone to get in. Everybody was going through a fairly extensive body search. Apparently there had been a couple of incidents at this venue on the *Setting Sons* tour, and they weren't taking any chances this time.

While we were queuing up we could hear the support band, The Piranhas, playing their set. They had recently been in the charts with a cover of Elias and His Zig Zag Jive Flutes' 'Tom Hark', and I remarked that they were either going down like a lead balloon or they didn't have much of a set as they had already played Tom Hark twice by the time we eventually got to the door.

A big Scouser in front of me didn't have a ticket. We had watched him cut a newspaper up into note-sized rectangles and wrap a pound note around the outside and hold the bundle together with an elastic band. As he got to the front of the queue he nodded to the doorman and handed him the cylindrical bundle. The doorman nodded, accepted his 'expenses', went through the motions of patting the lad down and let him in. I got in at the same time as the fellas they were frisking in a two-man team, and I congratulated him on his entrepreneurial skills. His response? 'I hope he reads the fucking Echo'.

Anyway, once inside we found the bar surprisingly quiet – probably because there were still loads of folk outside – and while we were ordering our pints we heard The Piranhas play 'Tom Hark' twice more!

I bought a very decent *Sound Affects* tour t-shirt at the merchandise stall – and remember the album wasn't yet released so it was good to see the artwork, and they were also selling the 'Start!' 'picture sleeve' shirts, similar to the one Bruce Foxton had taken to wearing on a regular basis. However, the star of the show for me was the 'WHAAM' shirts. Truly iconic.

We ventured into the cavernous hall, which was normally an ice rink and was fucking freezing. The atmosphere was equally frosty, especially down the front. Normally, we would have headed there straight away, but most of these were older and bigger lads, mainly from the northwest's two biggest cities, so we decided that discretion was the better part of valour. It was very clearly a powder keg and easily the worst atmosphere I've ever experienced at a Jam gig (though Ocean Colour Scene at the Barrowlands in Glasgow a few years later came close).

It was also the furthest back I've ever stood at any gig, including festivals! Eventually John Weller came on stage and I think, even at that stage, he issued a warning to the idiots that the band would come off if there was any trouble.

I don't remember an awful lot about the set that night, other than they played about eight off the then-unreleased *Sound Affects*, some of which I recognised from the Blackburn gig a few months earlier. I think they played 'Pretty Green', 'Boy About Town', 'Scrapeaway', 'Set The House Ablaze', 'Man in the Corner Shop', 'But I'm Different Now', 'Monday', and of course 'Start!', which had already been released as a single at that point. No 'That's Entertainment' that I can remember, although they did play that at Blackburn.

I can't remember whether the band actually went off stage at any point, but they certainly had to stop playing at least once because of all the fighting and they couldn't get off quick enough.

There was no waiting around, hoping they would come out into the hall for us, not this time. Like the band, we couldn't scarper quickly enough.

There were fights aplenty on the car parks and streets around Deeside Leisure Centre that night, and I reflected on how different the atmosphere had been from a year earlier, when 4,000 happy Lancastrians had piled out into the December night grinning from ear to ear at what they had just witnessed on the *Setting Sons* tour.

Jam gigs were always a fine line in that sense, always a brooding shadow of violence lurking. On this night, the coin had fallen the wrong way.

We got back to the minibus to find Pop Tulloch absolutely wankered and asleep in the driver's seat. He had been in the pub since just after 5pm and was in no fit state to drive ten young lads back to Blackburn.

As it happened, one of the other lads had a driving licence, and had only had one pint. However, he'd never driven a minibus before in his life. We bundled the priest into the back and the kid drove us back at approximately half the speed we had maintained during the outward journey, with the priest emptying the contents of his stomach every two or three miles all the way back along the M61.

Not my favourite Jam gig by any means, but it was exciting hearing new songs live before you'd heard the recorded version. I don't think I've ever looked forward to an album coming out as much as I did with *Sound Affects*, and it sure as hell didn't disappoint!

I WAS THERE: DAWNIE GUEST

I had used a blue spray in my hair. As we all pushed forward and jumped up and down to the music the guy behind me ended up with a blue face... he looked like a Smurf!

I WAS THERE: TRACY OXTON

The one and only time I saw The Jam. Got to the front and chipped my front tooth on the barrier. Had a crown ever since. Worth it though.

I WAS THERE: MARK JONES

I was about 15. I went with two friends from Holywell High School. I can remember wearing a red Harrington jacket, black Fred Perry, stonewashed Levi's and black 10 hole Docs that I purchased from my mam's Kays catalogue and I thought I was the dog's bollocks. It was my first ever concert and I was so excited. They didn't disappoint – a brilliant act. I can also remember the North Wales' lads fighting like mad with gangs from Merseyside which is only about 12 miles away from the leisure centre. The Scouse lot were calling us sheep shaggers and woollybacks. Great days! I live in Workington, Cumbria now. I saw From The Jam a few years back in Whitehaven. Rick was still playing drums then - they were brilliant. I also saw Weller in Carlisle but he never played any Jam stuff which was a bit disappointing. I still live in hope before I die that we will get a reunion. We all live in hope. Every time I hear their music it takes me back to the late Seventies and early Eighties when we were leaving school with no jobs. Their music kept us going.

RAINBOW THEATRE

15 NOVEMBER 1980, LONDON, UK

I WAS THERE: DAVE LEWIS

Dave Lewis saw The Jam at The Rainbow

This was a great show at the old Finsbury Park Theatre – a compact venue with its sloping floor. It made for a great atmosphere on what was something of a celebratory gig for Weller and co. At the time, The Jam were riding high off the back of two number one UK singles in 'Going Underground' and 'Start!'

Both of those gems were included in a set list that had plenty of previews from their imminent new album *Sound Affects*. 'Dream Time', 'Boy About Town', 'Monday', 'Man in the Corner Shop' and 'Pretty Green' were vivid examples of the growing maturity of Weller's song writing and the band as a whole. The performance of 'Dreams of Children' – the B side to 'Going Underground' - was another highlight on the night.

The big hitters were also all present and correct with 'Strange Town', 'The Eton Rifles', 'Down in the Tube Station at Midnight', 'A' Bomb In Wardour Street' and 'David Watts' sending the crowd into a frenzy.

The Eighties had arrived and The Jam were leading the pack as this memorable gig demonstrated.

HAMMERSMITH ODEON

18 NOVEMBER 1980, LONDON, UK

I WAS THERE: ANNIE O'ROURKE, AGE 15

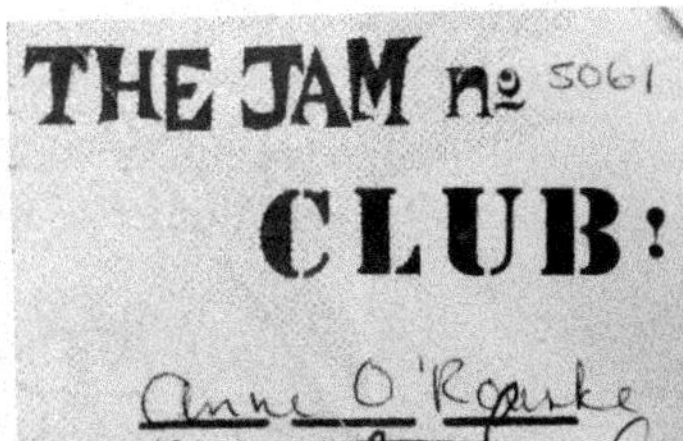

Annie O'Rourke was member 5061 of The Jam Fan Club

Born in 1965, I grew up in Hammersmith and Fulham in West London. I loved music and bought my first single in 1975/76 but with the introduction of pocket money into my life in 1978 I started buying singles on a more regular basis and really getting into music.

I loved a wide range of artists and genres, but The Jam were the band that would become my teenage passion and as a result a huge influence on my music and cultural tastes. There were always eclectic support bands at Jam gigs that would awaken interest in different types of music and DJs playing between sets. I learned so much from these gigs and my love of Sixties bands and soul music was definitely helped by this exposure. Also, references to literature, film and poetry were used in lyrics, sleeve notes and interviews. These were things I was into too, so as result I would try to find out more about the things The Jam, and Paul in particular, were in to. Being a Jam fan was like being in a really cool gang. To be fair there were more boys than girls in this gang, but it was an inclusive and interesting gang to be in. I had such a good time listening to and seeing The Jam, and even though I was just 17 when they split up my lifelong love of both recorded and live music started there.

The first Jam single I bought was 'Strange Town' in March 1979. I was 14 and really getting into buying records. I was aware of The Jam before and liked them as I was always listening to the radio and watching *Top of the Pops.* All the cool boys at school liked The Jam too and at that stage I was in a minority of girls who were into them. I think they were, even then, considered to be a bit of a lad's band.

I loved 'Strange Town' and the very unusual B-side, 'The Butterfly Collector', so was waiting in anticipation for the next single. With only my meagre pocket money to fund my growing vinyl collection, singles were the thing!

Then one night when listening to the radio in bed (with my tape recorder poised to record any music that piqued my interest) I heard a song that would come to be known as 'the record that changed my life'. The show was Nicky Horne's 6 of the Best on Capital Radio and the song was 'Down in the Tubestation At Midnight'. On hearing the opening bars, I was hooked and immediately pressed record on my tape recorder. Then, as was my habit at the time, I played the song over and over. Sometimes that was enough for me, but this song was different, I hadn't been aware of it and that annoyed me and furthermore I needed to have a copy of my own. I just had to have it.

So as soon as I could I went to Virgin Records in Kensington High Street and found a copy of the single. There was only one copy and without a picture sleeve, but I bought it anyway and rushed home to play it. But when I played it the record was scratched and jumped. So, I was straight back on the tube to Kensington High Street to get a replacement. However, there wasn't one. Seeing my clear disappointment with this one of the staff showed me the album the track was on - *All Mod Cons.* I decided to buy the album, a big financial commitment for me. I would have to spend all of my money on it and not do anything else for a week, but I felt the sacrifice would be worth it. How right I was...

Once I got the record home and listened to it, I was hooked and so began my obsession with The Jam.

From then on, I bought each single and album as they were released and sought out their back catalogue even persuading one of the cool boys at school to sell me his copies of the first two albums for £2 - bargain! Soon I was up to date and had a complete collection of their stuff and scoured the *NME* and later *Smash Hits* for any information I could find about my favourite band.

One frustration was this young music fan was that I wasn't allowed to go to see bands live. To be fair to my parents I was only 13/14 but I still felt aggrieved! However in December 1979 there was a breakthrough when my friend got tickets to see The Police and Squeeze at Lewisham Odeon. It was a Capital Radio (again) 'Tickets for Toys' charity gig and as it was for charity and at Christmas my dad relented and drive us to Lewisham and waited in the car whilst I enjoyed my first gig.

But it wasn't until almost a year later that I got to see The Jam for the first time. This was largely because what I'd seen as a breakthrough my parents saw as a one of treat for their 'still-too-young-to-go-to-gigs' 14-year-old daughter.

I didn't give up though and using the geographical proximity of Hammersmith Odeon (minutes away from my school) as a bargaining chip and the fact that I was now 15 and about to go into the fifth year at school I was finally allowed to buy some gig tickets.

Lifelong Jam fan Ann O'Rouke took this photo of Paul and Bruce on stage

So in August 1980 my best friend Margaret and I went along to the Hammersmith Odeon box office with enough money to buy tickets for two gigs (we must have saved up). I immediately noticed that The Jam were playing two nights in November but Margaret also noticed that Gary Numan was playing in September. Much discussion followed and eventually and somewhat inevitably we bought tickets to see both Gary Numan and The Jam.

Then on 18th November 1980 I saw The Jam for the very first time. It was the *Sound Affects* tour and they were supported by The Piranhas (as I recall).

It was everything I hoped it would be and I was intrigued when John Weller came on at the end and said something like 'see you again before Christmas, London'. Was he referring to a gig I didn't know about? Well, I didn't leave it to chance. I scoured the music press but found nothing. I wasn't prepared to give up though, so I started calling music venues and eventually The Music Machine in Camden confirmed that The Jam were booked to play there on 12th December 1980. The following day as soon as school was over, I got the tube up to Mornington Crescent and bought tickers for me and Margaret and for this time only another friend Marion, to see The Jam for what would be the second of many more times – 12 times in total.

The Music Machine gig was amazing. It seemed a bit secret, off the radar in some way. It was also just after John Lennon had been shot and Paul Weller dedicated the song 'Liza Radley' to his memory that night. It was a very emotional moment in an otherwise raucous gig. For example, a very drunk Shane McGowan came on and joined in with a version of 'Heatwave' towards the end of the set, joining Paul on vocals, whilst being helped to stand. The Nips were the support band that night, and I think it was one of their final gigs – Shane was very, very drunk!

After this gig I was totally hooked on The Jam and on going to gigs and I saw them as well as other bands as often as I could.

Here's a list of the ten other Jam gigs I went to:

17 June 1981 – The Rainbow, London. I remember the date because I sat my last 'O' level exam that day (RE) and it marked the beginning of a great summer in between 5th year and 6th form.

December 1981 – Michael Sobell Centre, London – two nights And Hammersmith Palais – two nights.

March 1982 – Fair Deal Brixton and Alexandra Palace

September 1982 – Brighton Centre – a big deal as I hadn't seen The Jam outside London before this. It was a real adventure for me travelling on the train with loads of other Jam fans and on the way back everyone was singing.

December 1982 – Wembley Arena – two nights. I had tickets for every night but in an altruistic moment I gave tickets away to my brother and his friends who were three years younger as otherwise they would never have got the chance to see the band they also now loved.

I had no qualms about buying tickets for every night of a tour that I could get to. This is not something I have done since unless it's a band with someone I know in it. However, Jam gigs were events in their own right, with lots of support bands and DJs, so no two nights were the same. They always were amazing value for money too which as a fan (and a young one with little income) that mattered greatly. The same goes for their records with brilliant B-sides and singles that weren't also on albums you always felt that you weren't being ripped off by The Jam. Something else that I have never done before or since is join a fan club but I did join The Jam Club and loved getting regular updates and letters from Paul.

I recall getting out of school at lunchtime (we weren't allowed out) in March 1980 and going to WH Smiths, in Kings Mall, Hammersmith to listen to the chart and hearing that 'Going Underground' had gone straight in at number one.

In 1981 I started to regularly go and see bands that I knew and liked from the charts but I also wanted to see live bands that I didn't know, so in August 1981 I began to go and see the bands on Jamming and Respond records labels, especially The Questions and Dolly Mixture who I was really into. I met Paul a coupe of times and Bruce once at

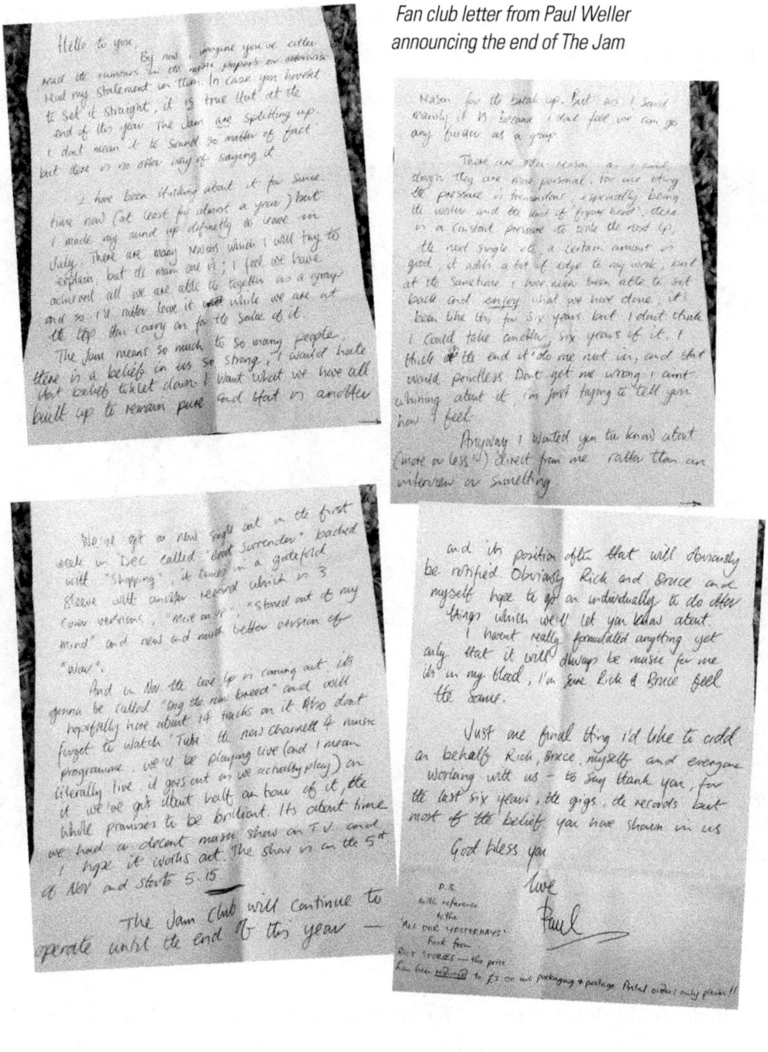

Hello to you,
By now I imagine you've either read the rumours in the music papers or otherwise read my statement in them. In case you haven't to set it straight, it is true that at the end of this year The Jam are splitting up. I don't mean it to sound so matter of fact but there is no other way of saying it.

I have been thinking about it for some time now (at least for almost a year) but I made my mind up definitely to leave in July. There are many reasons which I will try to explain, but the main one is; I feel we have achieved all we are able to together as a group and so I'd rather leave it while we are at the top than carry on for the sake of it.
The Jam means so much to so many people, there is a belief in us so strong, I would hate that belief to be let down. I want what we have all built up to remain pure and that is another →

reason for the break up. But as I said mainly it is because I don't feel we can go any further as a group.

There are other reasons [illegible] though they are more personal. For me [illegible] the pressure is tremendous, especially being the writer and the kind of 'figure head', there is a constant pressure to write the next LP, the next single etc. A certain amount is good, it adds a bit of edge to my work, but at the same time I have never been able to sit back and enjoy what we have done, it's been like this for six years but I don't think I could take another six years of it. I think in the end it'd do me in, and that would be pointless. Don't get me wrong I ain't whining about it, I'm just trying to tell you how I feel.

Anyway I wanted you to know about (more or less!!) direct from me rather than an interview or something. →

We've got a new single out in the first week in Dec called 'Beat Surrender' backed with "Shopping", it comes in a gatefold sleeve with another record which is 3 cover versions, "Move on Up", "Stoned out of my mind" and new and much better version of "War".

And in Nov the live LP is coming out. It's gonna be called "Dig the new breed" and will hopefully have about 14 tracks on it. Also don't forget to watch 'Tube' the new Channell 4 music programme, we'll be playing live (and I mean literally live it goes out as we actually play) on it. We've got about half an hour of it, the whole promises to be brilliant. Its about time we had a decent music show on T.V. and I hope it works out. The show is on the 5th of Nov and starts 5.15

The Jam Club will continue to operate until the end of this year —

and its position after that will obviously be notified. Obviously Rick and Bruce and myself hope to go on individually to do other things which we'll let you know about.
I haven't really formulated anything yet only that it will always be music for me its in my blood, I'm sure Rick & Bruce feel the same.

Just one final thing I'd like to add on behalf Rick, Bruce, myself and everyone working with us – to say thank you, for the last six years, the gigs, the records but most of the belief you have shown in us

God bless you

Love

Paul

P.S. With reference to the 'ALL OUR YESTERDAYS' book from RIOT STORIES — the price has been reduced to £2.00 inc packaging + postage. Postal orders only please!!

Fan club letter from Paul Weller announcing the end of The Jam

these gigs and they were both lovely to me. I also felt they had a lot of time for their fans. At one Respond bands gig at the Venue in Victoria both Paul and Bruce were in the audience. So, I rushed out to a tourist shop at Victoria Station and bought a photo of them both and got it signed. They were totally cool and obliging about it.

By this time I had got to know some of the people in the bands I was seeing and later that night at The Venue, I went backstage at The Venue to meet Paul. However, I lost my nerve and didn't speak to him then. All was not lost though as later he came out into the main auditorium to say goodbye to the bands and bought a round of drinks for everyone. I ordered a lemonade which as a shy-ish 16-year-old I immediately thought was uncool, but I was in such a state of shock that Paul Weller was buying me a drink I just said the first thing that came into my head. He didn't bat an eyelid and duly returned with drink!

Around that time, I started buying the *December Child* Fanzines and poetry books published by Paul on Riot Stories. I was a bit of a completest and was trying to write poetry of my own at the point.

Copies of December Child Fanzines belonging to Anne O'Rourke

I was also lucky enough to go to see *Top of the Pops* being recorded many times but the stand out occasion for me was in (I think) February 1982 when The Jam who were at number one, did both Town Called Malice and Precious. In the bar afterwards Paul said hello to me, and we had a bit of a chat. I fancied that he had remembered me from The Venue 'lemonade incident' of the year before, but it was probably just because I was wearing a Jam badge! Anyway, once more he was lovely and happy to chat to a fan and we discussed what I thought of the other bands on *TOTP* that night. My friend, Margaret, took a photo of me chatting to Paul that night, but although you can see Paul, only the back of my head is visible. It is still a treasured possession though.

QUEENS EXHIBITION HALL

3 NOVEMBER 1980, LEEDS, UK

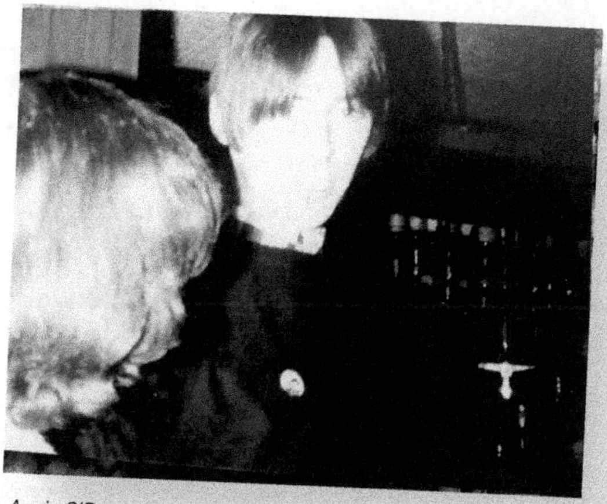

Annie O'Rourke talking to Paul Weller at TOTP

I WAS THERE: COLIN SIMPSON

The Piranhas were the support along with Red Lorry Yellow Lorry. They were in the charts with 'Tom Hark' at the time and I remember all The Jam fans chanting the chorus through their entire set.

I WAS THERE: PETER FLETCHER

My friend Mark and I were at the front of the queue. It was about 9am. We sat on the floor by the entrance, wearing our new bowling shoes. We were top Jam fans - we had all the singles, all the albums, the shoes - we knew all the songs.

Soon enough the fans started to arrive and the dodgy t-shirt vendors started trying to sell us their unofficial merchandise. We noticed some other fans had started queuing at the opposite side of the door to us and we chatted to the guy opposite who had some unusual bowling shoes on - a totally different style. He was betting us that Paul would be wearing similar at the concert. Mark and I weren't too bothered - to us it wasn't about looking exactly like our idols. Shoes were as far as we went and even then Mark had black and red ones while mine were blue and black.

Passing the time, we sat and read newspapers and took turns going to the toilet or fetching bacon butties. We even started a game with the guy across from us, seeing who would have the most people behind in the queue. Time seemed to slow down as it got nearer to the doors opening. The fans started to buzz around - some hovering near the centre of the door. The guy opposite us told them to do one and get to the back of the queue. The guys said something like, 'Who's going to make us?' and we heard a shout of a lot of people from the opposite side shout back in unison, 'We are!'. The guys went up the side of the hall to the back of the queue followed by jeers and cheers.

Soon the doors opened and we were gutted because the right hand side door opened before ours and about 10 people got in before our door opened. We dashed in. No programmes and no t-shirts for us. We had one aim - get to the front of the stage and as near to the centre as we could. We both congratulated each other on achieving our goal. Now we just had to hold onto our prime position. The hall filled up quite quickly. The atmosphere was building and the guys from the opposite side of the doors outside were alongside and we were unmovable. The atmosphere was calm but electrifying, kind of like the feeling you get before a thunderstorm starts. Eventually the lights went off, the fans surged forward and we could feel the weight of the crowd behind us. The Piranhas came on stage and the crowd were singing in unison, 'Ner na ner ner na ner' (start of Tom Hark). The Piranhas were quite good but all I remember was thinking when are they going to finish and get off?

The Jam came on. I couldn't tell you what songs they sang at this particular concert as I saw them a number of times but they played a lot of singles amongst songs from the *Sound Affects* album. I do remember the crowd jumping up and down. I let myself just relax and lo and behold I was bouncing up and down without actually jumping. Paul was wearing the shoes the fan outside was wearing - Bruce was jumping more than usual and the band seemed slicker and more active than when I first saw them. My friend Mark's face was a picture as I guess mine was too as we were shouting out the words to every song they played. We could almost touch the band we were that close.

Soon, like all good things, the concert ended. We had been there a whole day and it was still too short. The crowd was leaving the venue, the condensation dripping from the roof again. I looked at Mark. His hair was wet and stuck to his face and his t-shirt was dripping wet and stuck to him. I realised I was the same. We stepped out into the night - it was cold but we were glad of it. We were still buzzing and on a high so we didn't feel the cold anyway.

We were already talking about the next tour and what we would do different. Programmes and t-shirts definitely next time.

BRACKNELL SPORTS CENTRE

7 NOVEMBER 1980, BRACKNELL, UK

I WAS THERE: JO BARTLETT, AGE 14

The first time I saw The Jam, and to be honest, from this point forward, there was no looking back for me! I saw The Jam a few times - seven I think in total.

Like every right-minded youth in the early Eighties, The Jam were my favourite band. I was too young to have been there in their early or even middle years, joining in the fun for the *Sound Affects* tour in November 1980.

I went with a boyfriend who was a couple of years older than me and could drive. We also took a friend from Scotland, Alastair Baird.

My god, what a gig. I returned sweaty and elated. Jumping up and down for the whole gig, elbows in my face - using other peoples' shoulders to propel myself upwards. My older brother Tom was having his 18th birthday party at our house that night. We came back from the gig and played records by The Jam to pogo to and tell everyone what an amazing concert we had just witnessed. If I hadn't been hooked by gigs and music before that night, I sure was after it. I was 14 years old and my life had just been mapped out for me.

The support band were from Brighton. The Piranhas, and had one hit –'Tom Hark'. I had the seven inch single and knew all the words to all three tracks. Dancing in an Eighties style either in my room or at parties, singing along at the top of my voice.

The gig was brilliant, getting right to the front and having to get the hell out before I died and freezing to death outside soaked with sweat. Oh and the Piranhas getting booed if they played anything other than 'Tom Hark' or whatever it was called.

I used to write down the gigs I went to on a scrawly hand written sheet – which includes quite a few of The Jam gigs.

I had a ticket to see them at the Michael Sobell Sports Centre in December 1981. It snowed very heavily and my local train station, Farnborough, closed. I couldn't get to London and was heartbroken. I still have the unused ticket!

Jo Bartlett's unused ticket after being snowed in

I WAS THERE: ALASTAIR BAIRD

I came down on the train from Aberdeen to go to the gig with my friend Jo. The gig was brilliant. I remember talking to the guy at the door who turned out to be Paul Weller's dad, getting right to the front and having to get the hell out before I died and, after the gig, freezing to death outside soaked with sweat.

Sound Affects, The Jam's fifth album in four years, was released on 28 November 1980, going on to spend 19 weeks on the UK chart and peaking at number two.

SOPHIA GARDENS

10 NOVEMBER 1980, CARDIFF, UK

I WAS THERE: GREG ARCHER

I was 13 when I first became aware of The Jam. It was late 1978 when a school friend got hold of a copy of *All Mods Cons*. We listened to it over and over for about a week and then copied it to cassette so we could keep it. I think that the imagery of the sleeve and cover had as big an impact on me as much as the music did. I immediately thought, 'This is for me' and from then on I have been a Mod.

Into 1979, and the band's golden period of each single release improving on the one before. I started to try to copy Weller's look as best I could, saving up my meagre pocket money, especially at Christmas and birthday with money I would get. My proudest moment was when I finally bought a pair of the black and white 'Jam' shoes.

I lived in a small village in South Wales where all the young people around my age were into heavy metal, so myself and my friend and his sister stood out like sore thumbs in our parkas and boating blazers.

Concerts were still something that I hadn't experienced yet but that all changed in November 1980 and the *Sound Affects* tour. I went to Cardiff to Spillers Records and bought three tickets at £3.50 each for myself and two school friends. The excitement as the date neared was incredible, but on the day of the concert my two mates told me they couldn't go.

I was really pissed off but I had to go - it may have been my only chance to see The Jam. My mother wasn't happy at the thought of me going to Cardiff on my own, but I told her there would be about 2,000 people dressed the same as me, so safety in numbers!

I can't remember much about the show but I managed to get down to the front, right in front of Paul. The atmosphere was electric. The support band the Piranhas didn't get a very warm welcome but as soon as they finished it was just a short while until John Weller came on to introduce the band. I do remember the bass line intro to 'Pretty Green' and it all went mental.

I was walking on air the next day in school, boring everyone with my stories from the night before. It was an incredible occasion for me. The Jam were such a massive part of my life then and I've remained a Paul Weller fan to this day.

I WAS THERE: CRAIG BROWN

I remember buying a pair of Jam Shoes from *Smash Hits* in the early Eighties. I was a UK size seven at the time and they sent me a six. They crippled me every time I wore them and spent more money on sticking plasters on my feet than the shoes themselves (£14.99) but I didn't care one bit. I made them fit.

I WAS THERE: TONY PAYNE, AGE 15

In 1980 I was 15 and about five foot tall. I was in year four at Radyr Comp and had just bought my first parka second hand from Army and Navy. I'd never been to a gig but knew I had to see The Jam. I didn't have a ticket for the gig but my mate Simon Roberts who lived in the next street was going and offered me a lift with his mum who was dropping him off and picking him up.

When we got there my chances of getting a ticket looked about zero, but that night I got lucky. There was a huge crowd milling around outside the front when we arrived. My plan was to see if I could buy a ticket from someone who had a spare but didn't rate my chances as I only had £5. Failing that, after Simon went in, I found a group of Mods all a bit older and taller than me who said they were going to listen from outside as they didn't have tickets either.

Half way through the support act - Department S? - while I was standing around with my new mates, a face appeared in a window next to the main entrance. This was a room off to the side where the t-shirt sales were happening. Next thing I knew the guy in the window opened it wide enough for us to pile in. I think about ten off us made it through. I dived in and jumped into the group of people buying t-shirts, but the others dashed about and caught the eye of some bouncers, who grabbed a couple, whilst I melted into the crowd. I spent my £5 on a new *Sound Affects tour* t-shirt, then went to look for Simon.

Both being small we stood about half way back on the left hand side but we got a great view of the band and danced all the way through the gig. What an awe inspiring experience for a first ever gig. I went on to see The Jam at Port Talbot a number of times but that first night was the best. For me this was the best period for Jam singles – 'When You're Young' and 'Strange Town' - and I was totally into *Setting Sons*.

At the end Simon and I wandered up to the stage to get a better look just as Rick threw out a few drum sticks into the crowd. Together we dived onto one and grabbed it together. I've still got it. I promised to share it with Simon six months at his house and six months at mine. A promise I didn't keep.

I'm in my fifties now and the last time I bumped into Simon in Cardiff after years of not seeing him that drum stick was all he could talk about...

BINGLEY HALL

11 NOVEMBER 1980, BIRMINGHAM, UK

I WAS THERE: GAVIN JONES

I started off with a car load for this one, but one by one they dropped out, so I went with my friend Lisa. We found the place OK after about an hour, parked up and went to suss out the hall in the freezing November rain.

Once again, no tickets and Lisa was sceptical about whether we'd get in, but we went to ask the roadies when the sound check was (4pm ish) and went to get some food. We went in a pub and met Charlie Stoke, so stayed and chatted with him until he bit his glass and it shattered so the landlord asked us to leave!

We had a long wait in the cold for the sound check, which happened about five o clock in the end, and we had to stand back from the stage as they were finishing building it. They ran through about five songs, but we were kicked out straight away so didn't get chance to ask to be put on the guest list.

We met Charlie again outside and went for a drink in the Brum Rep Theatre across the road. There was no one in the bar, but Charlie leant over and poured us a couple of free pints, and when we looked outside we saw the queue going all round the hall. We went for something to eat, and I bought a tour t-shirt and then went back to the main door looking for touts. Lisa had lost all hope now of getting in, but I was confident I could blag it!

As we waited I heard the Piranhas come on and do the same set which was a bit boring, and even I was losing hope now, when out of nowhere a tout appears and offered two tickets for £12. We only had £11 between us so I got them for that, £1.75 over face value, and we were in, skint but happy!

The Piranhas had nearly finished, and after a short wait John came on and said, 'If anyone falls over, pick em up, here they are, The Jam'. There was a crowd of mainly skins and Mods which led to a charged atmosphere and some of the Mods were chanting, 'We are the Mods' which Paul didn't seem too keen on. I don't know if it was because of the atmosphere, but this gig was a bit less charged than normal, and fell a bit flat, especially when some twats threw beer cans onto the stage and hit Rick's kit just before the start. A packet of fags was thrown on the stage near Paul and he picked them up and said, 'This is for whoever threw these' and went into 'Set the House Ablaze'.

It was an OK gig, just not stunningly as brilliant as usual, and when we got back to the car some twat had let two of our tyres down. Luckily a guy sitting in his car had a pump, so I got home about midnight, ready for a night's kip and more fun at Leicester over the next two days.

DE MONTFORT HALL

12 NOVEMBER 1980, LEICESTER, UK

I WAS THERE: GAVIN JONES

I'd been to Bingley Hall in Birmingham on the 11th without a ticket, got into the sound check but got rushed out before I could ask to get on the guest list, so bought a ticket off a tout outside at the last minute. They were at De Montford Hall on the 12th, so when I woke up that morning, ears still buzzing from the night before I knew I had to go, ticket or not.

I set off about lunchtime (I lived about an hour from Leicester) and parked up in a side street in my orange Beetle, then went to De Montford. This is a big hall set in grounds with a wall around and locked gates, but I managed to squeeze through and went to the side of the building where the three Renault artics were and roadies were milling about. I walked through a side door to a sort of cafe on the side of the hall and sat in there trying to look like I should be there. About ten other kids turned up and we were all chatting Jam stories when I saw Ray and Mick outside, the Scousers I had met at Manchester Apollo a couple of weeks before. I invited them into the cafe and learned they had bunked the train from Liverpool on a platform ticket, as ever drawn to The Jam like a moth to flame!

We had a couple of hours to kill until the 3.30pm sound check so went for some chips then went back waiting for the sound check with about 40 kids. Then Big Ken came to the door and let us in, where we walked past Paul, resplendent in his long black corduroy coat and paisley scarf, playing an old piano that was in the hallway, with Rick and Bruce stood drinking lager.

During a lull in the sound check while Rick messed with his drums, Paul came to the front of the stage and we asked him if we could get on the guest list. As we'd been to a few sound checks, he recognised us and said he'd put us on the list but couldn't give us a pass as he'd none left. This was great, but also gave you trepidation that he would remember to put you on when you didn't have anything solid.

After a couple of hours in a pub, we went back and there was a queue around the block, but we walked straight to the front and said we were on the list (fingers crossed!) and there were our names and we went straight in - thanks Paul! After watching the Dolly Mixtures and Piranhas, eventually The Jam came on, introduced by John, and it was a barnstorming set. They were really up for it. Most of *Sound Affects* was played, mixed in with older songs, kicking off with 'Monday' with Paul's Steve Marriott hairstyle blowing up as the stage fan kept him cool. They encored with 'Down at the Tube Station at Midnight', 'David Watts', 'When You're Young' and 'Billy Hunt' - all brilliant!

After dodging the security we waited by the backstage door, and the group came out to chat with us and about 20 other kids. After chatting with Paul about *Sound Affects* and of course politics, we went over to see Rick who was on his own, and asked him for a guest pass for the next night. He said he'd give us some at the sound check the next day, so I said Ray and Mick could stay at mine and we went the next day as well.

True to his word, at the sound check the next day we called Rick over and he gave us three guest passes. While talking to Paul afterwards, someone asked him if they had done any older stuff on the tour, and he said they had done 'In The City' a couple of times, so I said cheekily to him that it would be great if they played that tonight as it was always a great one to see them play with loads of energy.

More food, then back to the gig to see supports Kids Next Door

and the Pirahnas again, not my favourite so we went in the foyer watching kids come in, and saw some mates from home - Chillo and Steve who rushed in as they paid a kid a fiver for his name on the guest list and couldn't believe it worked as they rushed into the crowd!

Soon enough The Jam came on with a slightly different set, then encores 'Down at the Tube Station at Midnight', 'David Watts', ''A' Bomb in Wardour Street', 'When You're Young', and yes, 'In The City'.

We had a chat with John Weller afterwards who showed us the European dates in case we could get to any. Sadly we didn't manage to in the end as I lost my job in December!

I dropped Ray and Mick off near the M6 in the freezing rain for them to hitch back to Liverpool, sure we would meet up at another Jam gig somewhere. Life was so different then with no mobile phones, phone camera, etc. to keep in touch, but we seemed to manage.

I WAS THERE: STEVEN CROWDER

I saw them at Leicester De Montfort Hall, Vapors supporting. Many years later while in the army I met Bruce Foxton in a club in Guildford Surrey, it was the night before Spurs played Man City in the F.A. Cup final. When I asked what he was doing in a dive like the club was he replied squaddies don't bother you, they're too busy drinking.

ST AUSTELL COLISEUM

8 DECEMBER 1980, CORNWALL, UK

I WAS THERE: BRIDGET FAIRBROTHER

I remember Rick Butler throwing his drumsticks into the crowd at the end of the concert. Paul Weller not saying much but an amazing experience. Think it was one of the highlights of my life. I was gutted when he announced their split. Remember where I was and what I was doing when I heard it on the radio.

I WAS THERE: RICHARD ALLMAN

This was the first and only time I've been spat on at a concert! Paul's dad, John had to come on stage halfway through and ask the crowd to calm down as people were getting squashed at the front. The concert finished at 10.30pm and the last train back was 10 15pm. We had to decide whether to leave early and miss the encore or stay till the end and spend the night at St. Austell Station waiting for the milk train. We decided to leave early.

I WAS THERE: EVELYN PERRY, AGE 24

Big Country said they were doing the whole thing as The Jam had cancelled - I was gutted. It wasn't true they arrived and played and were amazing! We were all shouting Jam! Jam! I just melted when I saw Paul.

MUSIC MACHINE

12 DECEMBER 1980, LONDON, UK

I WAS THERE: MICHAEL FARRAGHER

This was one of my favourite Jam gigs. I met Paul Weller at an earlier gig and he told me they were doing a 'secret' gig at the Music Machine in London – later called the Camden Palace and KOKO. This was a small venue for a big band like The Jam and I was desperate not to miss it. I went up the night before the tickets went on sale and slept overnight outside the box office to be certain of getting tickets, although I don't remember getting too much sleep. But I got the tickets so it was all worth it. The support was The Nips fronted by Shane MacGowan. The Jam were on fire that night and the atmosphere was electric. This was the smallest venue I would ever see them in and a definite highlight.

1981

Written - so legend has it - in 10 minutes during a lager-fuelled burst of creativity at Weller's Pimlico flat, 'That's Entertainment' was never released as a single in the UK but charted in January 1981 as an import single peaking at number 21 on the chart. 'That's Entertainment' is the group's lone entry, at No.306, on *Rolling Stone's 500 Greatest Songs of All Time* list released in 2004. It consistently makes similar British lists of all-time great songs, such as BBC Radio 2's *Sold on Song* 2004 Top 100, at number 43.

Bruce Foxton: It's such a simple song. Lyrically it's great observation from Paul. He lived in Pimlico at the time, and he wrote it after a bit of a session in a pub. It took 10 minutes. A lot of great songs like that come straight away. It's an opinion on a society that he was part of at the time and felt bored with. He had a sense of frustration, and thought, 'There must be more to life than this'. Bands like The Streets have taken that subject of ordinary life and Saturday-night drinking and turned it into careers.

It was quite experimental and initially my reaction was, well, what do you want me and Rick to do? It was so fantastic and succinct. We crept in with a bit of bass and a snare drum, but it didn't need anything else. The snare drum is like a punch in the gut.

I compare Paul to Ray Davies. He seems to be able to take in everything that's going on around him, and turn it into a great song. I don't think his antennae ever go down, even now.

LEISURE CENTRE

23 FEBRUARY 1981, CRAWLEY, UK

I WAS THERE: KEVIN WATT, AGE 13

I think I was 13 and on my brother's shoulders and it was absolutely rocking.

This was my and my brother's first Jam concert. My brother is six years older and had been following The Jam from the beginning

We are responsible (and this is no bullshit - I'm claiming this for sure) we put the 'oi' in 'Pretty Green'! We did it at Brighton Arena! We were amazed it travelled around the country. I think we found out by listening to a Jam live album.

I WAS THERE: ANDY ROSCOE

I first got into The Jam after hearing 'Tube Station' on Radio 1 when I was 15. I live in Crawley so London, Brighton and Guildford are easy to get to. I saw The Jam 27 times in total, mainly Brighton and London including Brighton Dome and Brighton Centre, including of course the last gig.

They played at Crawley Leisure Centre in 1981 and I got back stage after and enjoyed some beers with the guys. I had a league cup final ticket for West Ham v Liverpool the following month and Paul, Bruce and Rick all signed it. At the final I nearly wasn't allowed in as my ticket had been 'defaced'!

MARKET HALL

6 MARCH 1981, HAMBURG, GERMANY

I WASN'T THERE: RUTH BEUYS

I had a ticket for their gig in Hamburg. I became ill that very day, had a fever so my mum didn't allow me to go! She promised me a ticket for their next gig. Unfortunately it was their last gig ever in Germany. At least I had the ticket framed - but one day someone stole it at a party.

ROYAL COURT THEATRE

27 APRIL 1981, LIVERPOOL, UK

I WAS THERE: DAVID VAUGHAN

I was living in Liverpool at the time and I'd got two tickets and, as this was a one-off gig, they were like gold dust. This was a time of first love for me and my girl friend Julie who was also a Mod, so when I told her we were going, I really was the best boyfriend in the world!

We got to the gig early and got right on the barrier, where Paul Weller would be stood. By the time the boys came on, the atmosphere was pure electricity. At the opening number the crowd went crazy, and it was full-on moshing down the front! By song three

Julie was getting concerned for her ribs on the barrier, such was the crush. The security guys spotted this and suggested she be lifted over and re-enter at the back. A look of relief lit up her face, and with some assistance, she was promptly lifted over to safety.

Well chivalry hadn't yet found me in life, and I was oblivious to the fact that I should then have followed and ensured she was OK. Thing is though, I was front row and The Jam were on fire, and tonight we were getting the world premier of 'Funeral Pyre'. I was going nowhere. And remain I did, wondering if Julie was having as much fun at the back as I was at the front.

Once the gig was over, I thought I best catch up with her, and luckily she was waiting at the bus stop, right over the road from the venue - with a face like thunder. Well of course first love seldom lasts, and we were no different, and eventually went our separate ways. Years later we got back in touch and I'm now forgiven!

I found The Jam via a close pal who had a great ear for music and invited me round to his home. He played me *All Mods Cons*, still my favourite album of all time, and I have an original Japanese copy, complete with fantastic signatures from a sharpie from Paul, Bruce and Rick. It was a wonderful night and later in life I was lucky enough to meet both Rick and Bruce and I told them this story, much to their amusement - that I put The Jam before first love.

THE RITZ

26 MAY 1981, NEW YORK CITY, NEW YORK

I WAS THERE: MARTY FELER

If my memory serves me right, they showcased the brand new 'Funeral Pyre' video right before the band came on. It was an unbelievable show, with many tracks being performed from the new album, and plenty of classic tracks from the past. I even managed to make my way past the bouncers and to the band. Rick was kind enough to chat a bit and spare a few of his Silk Cut cigarettes!

The following tour (*The Gift*), I saw the band twice, once at the Palladium in New York and then at the Orpheum in Boston. At the Palladium gig, I managed to make my way right down to the front. Man these guys were LOUD! Both shows, as I recall, featured the extended band with the horn section and the sets were brilliant. The band came out after the Palladium show was over and hung out with us and a few other audience stragglers.

Being a young drummer and DJ at that time, I was influenced by Rick's playing as I thought he was one of the most interesting of the British punk/new wave drummers of that era. He had power and speed and his own way of throwing cool fills and cymbal accents in just at the right spots. Check out the opening to the 'Batman Theme' on the first album. Great fills and a great groove too. Rick progressed with the band and while the music The Jam created toward the very end of their career became more palatable to main stream audiences, the band never lost its great power and originality thanks to the great rhythm section of Rick and Bruce.

These gigs were priceless and out of the hundreds of concerts I have attended throughout my life, these three definitely rank at the top end of my list.

THE CHANNEL

29 MAY 1981, BOSTON, MASSACHUSETTS

I WAS THERE: DAVID WILNER

We got there early, along with a few dozen other people, and were let in for the sound check. Got to meet the band and have an album signed - they were really good about talking to everyone. I remember when the doors opened I went straight to the front of the stage and remained in place the whole night. The Jam must have come on around 10 or 11.

Paul Weller on stage in Boston 1982

'Funeral Pyre', The Jam's thirteenth single, was released on 29 May 1981 reaching number four on the UK singles chart. The track was the only single co-written by the band and only the second song which has writing credits for all three members, the other being 'Music for the Last Couple' which features on the *Sound Affects* album.

GROAN LUND

10 JUNE 1981, STOCKHOLM, SWEDEN

I WAS THERE: TERO LARSSON

I lived far away from Stockholm and took the train (by myself) to the town, and then took the bus from the central station to the venue. Strangely, I had shaved my head before the gig, but wore a green parka, and in the back of the bus were 30 skinheads staring at me, figuring whether they should beat the hell out of me or not. They decided to go for the first, and I jumped off the bus and was chased a couple of hundred metres until I saw a bus and jumped on it, glad to see 20 Mods cheering at me at the back of the bus, and at the same time chasing away the skinheads.

A rather strange night, which involved a little bit of everything, including a brilliant concert by The Jam as the icing on the cake.

RAINBOW

17 JUNE 1981, LONDON, UK

I WAS THERE: RICHARD NOBLE, AGE 16

My first gig was The Jam at the Rainbow. I was 16. Myself and a similarly mad Jam fan school friend of mine booked tickets, including coach, via a local concert travel agent. I remember being handed my ticket on the coach by the travel agent just before we were getting off and thinking we are actually going to see them, so it wasn't going to be a scam after all! When we were outside the venue, it was just a sea of people dressed just like us. For some obscure reason, I felt very important to be part of all this. I could sense all the passing traffic and passers by were looking at us all in wonder, even though they probably saw concert crowds every week. My mate stood out a bit, as he had a haircut based on Bruce Foxton's, whereas there were heaps of people sporting Weller haircuts.

The first band on were The Exploited (so if you split hairs, they were the first live band I ever saw). John Weller introduced The Jam in his gruff sarf London bark and they kicked off with 'Going Underground' of all songs! We were upstairs standing up in our seats. During the gig, there was also a fan who managed get on stage and looked like he accidently poked Bruce in the eye. They also did one song, which my friend and I didn't recognise, and I cannot even say to this day (even scouring the internet for set lists) what it was. The only thing I was disappointed about was they didn't do 'Tube Station', as I was so looking forward to singing along the chorus, just like on the live ('Going Underground') EP.

A couple of the lads who'd travelled with us somehow managed to get in downstairs in the mosh, even though their tickets were upstairs only. Afterwards, they were absolutely soaked in sweat and they said it was mental as soon they kicked off with 'Going Underground', as no one was expecting that!

I was never one of the cool kids in school but although many in my year were mad on The Jam, none of them had actually seen them live, so in a way my credibility went up a few notches almost overnight.

The days after the gig, I remember just being on a high and I wore my t-shirt bought at the gig for about a week solid. It was at the time in my life, as with millions of other kids my age, when I was discovering music and it set the scene for scores of gigs being attended and records bought, etc. At that time I wanted to start learning to play the drums and that gig gave me more impetus to do so.

All the future Jam gigs my friends and I went to were so exciting for us. Personally, the only way I could describe it was like when you were younger and you couldn't wait for Christmas Day to arrive.

The Jam still resonates with me a lot after all these years. I now live in Melbourne, Australia and I still keep a close eye out for every new release of records/CDs, box sets etc. and I am always scouring fan sites for new unearthed info. I also arranged a trip back to the UK around The Jam exhibition in London. I thought I had a decent collection until I saw Den Davis's and others, which made mine pale into insignificance. Lol! Being a Jam nerd, I'm curious about additional unheard takes/mixes and unseen video footage of the band that was filmed such as at the 100 Club, *The Tube* and *So It Goes* at the Electric Circus, etc.

I met some great friends via From The Jam when they first came to Melbourne. I carried on playing drums and things have come full circle. In September 2019 my band supported From The Jam in Melbourne.

People like Rick Buckler, Shaun Hand, Laurence Prior and Steve Carver have been immense with their stories, writings, collections and insight in keeping the flame alive.

I WAS THERE: ADRIAN STRANIK

Adrian Stranik in his Jam days (photo by Senga McBeth)

As far as The Jam were concerned, I was late to the party. In 1977 I was a teenage rockabilly living in South West London. I was a fervent listener to the two Fifties rock and roll shows that Capital Radio used to broadcast on Friday and Saturday nights. The rest of their playlist would be current fare, and this is where I first heard The Clash, Elvis Costello and… The Jam.

I liked what I heard but, if you chose a tribe in those days your record collection never erred beyond the soundtrack that went with it. Being a rockabilly, I refused to publicly acknowledge anything that was recorded after 1960. Of course, when Matchbox and The Stray Cats hit the scene, the game was up. The underground 'Rockin' scene that had been the perfect antidote to trendy and 'with it' punk became ridiculous almost overnight. While the rest of the country suddenly became rockabillies for the next few months, I left London and started being a bit more open-minded about what I listened to.

I first heard 'Going Underground' blasting from a neighbour's house one night and was blown away by it. I nicked a copy from the local youth club and played it to death and tried to figure out how Weller played those lead-lines and heavy guitar chords at the same time. I was just learning the guitar then and was so naïve, I had no idea about overdubs. By the time the next single, 'Start!'/'Liza Ridley' was released, I was a fan!

Soon I had everything they'd released and realised what a sterling job I'd done of looking at the world through Fifties-tinted shades. I was vaguely aware of 'Tube Station' and 'Eton Rifles', but 'In The City', 'All Around the World', ''A' Bomb', 'Strange Town', 'When You're Young' and the rest had all previously escaped my notice.

The first time I got to see them live was at the Rainbow when 'Funeral Pyre' had just been released. I saw Ray Davies and Chrissie Hynde getting out of a car across the road and entering the venue by a side door - a promising start to the evening. I was in the foyer waiting for the show to start when all of a sudden everyone started charging towards the hall. The Jam were already on stage and had opened with 'Going Underground'. They were the first 'name band' I'd ever seen and could hardly believe I was breathing their air. The power of it was overwhelming and to this day I still rate them as the best live band I've ever seen. And I've seen The Jim Jones Revue!

I was surprised that all those lead harmony parts were absent and that the live experience was a whole different ball game. Having come from a Fifties perspective when the whole performance would be recorded live in the studio and would, presumably, sound exactly the same live (venue acoustics aside) the dark art of overdubs suddenly became clear. But the intensity was a sonic baptism. (I still have one of Weller's guitar picks from this show framed on my wall).

After that, Jam gigs were a regular occurrence – little did any of us realise that they would be no more by the end of the following year. Getting down the front was the main objective – but then that's where the fun started. It became an endurance test to stay down there. The crush was life-threatening and when the 'break it up break it up' bit of 'Strange Town' kicked in it was a miracle no one got seriously hurt. I should imagine they did on some nights. I was just lucky to have survived it. My eardrums, however, were not so lucky. They'd be ringing for days afterwards.

We were all shocked by the split and the mad scramble for tickets for that final tour were made in a state of shock. To my eternal pride I got to see two of the Wembley shows and the final three. Those first couple of weeks in December 1982 are something of a blur now, but the highlights roar across the decades.

Biff! Weller smashing his Rickenbacker on the third night at Wembley!

Bang! Some girl handing me her bra to throw at the stage at the penultimate Guildford show. (Weller spun away to dodge it and it wrapped around his legs!).

Pow! That final chord (G!) of 'In The City' ringing out around the vast expanse of the Brighton Conference Centre on that final night and the slow sombre march of the crowd out of the venue and onto to the streets, when the usual procedure would be the nutters among us trying to incite riots.

Adrian Stranik the Psychedelic years (photo by Gaynor Clem)

The Jam's split seemed to coincide with the demise of British sub-cultures such as the Mods, skinheads, punks, Teds, smoothies, soul boys, rude boys and, of course my old tribe the rockabillies – the only time since the advent of the 'teenager' when they all existed at the same time. The Blitz Kids, psychobillies and the New Romantics were the last gasp before a coming decade that would be dominated by corporate sportswear and synth pop duos. I might have been late to the party, but today I drop the needle on *City, Cons, Sons* or *Affects* - the four horsemen of The Jam Apocalypse - and forty years evaporate and the Trans Global Unity Express thunders on.

I WAS THERE: PINKERTON PUMBLER, AGE 15

I saw The Jam on my own as a fifteen year old Asian girl. They were amazing to say the least and I felt honoured when Paul Weller saw I was surrounded by NF skinheads who he told to 'fuck off' as this wasn't what the Jam were about. Oh the smile on my face.

An ironic twist to my story is that I worked for PR at the BPI. Paul received a Brit Award but wasn't too bothered about collecting it. It sat in my cupboard safely for two years, so I like to think I paid him back!

I WAS THERE: NICKY WELLER

I don't know why but the gigs at The Rainbow always stick in my mind as some of the best shows I ever saw them play.

It might be might be because on one night I got locked out. I got shut out of the venue without a pass and was outside with all these mobs and it was like the Beatles film *Help!*. Someone found me eventually - one of the security guys - and I was let back in. I used to think that was a great venue.

FESTIVAL PAVILION

20 JUNE 1981, SKEGNESS, UK

I WAS THERE: MICHAEL WELTON

I'm originally from Scunthorpe, but we moved to London, then Lagos, Nigeria in the Seventies. My exposure to music was essentially what we took to Lagos with us: *Dark Side of the Moon, Tubular Bells*, the Beatles' *Hard Days' Night* album, Lindisfarne etc. all of which I retain a fondness for. They also had Medicine Head's 'One and One is One', which I certainly do not! For some reason my parents also had an album by the Stylistics, which really jars with everything else they listened to. One artist that we liked was Fela Kuti, and I still have an excellent EP by him.

When we returned to the UK to live in a North Lincolnshire market town called Brigg, punk was all over the radio. I really liked the energy and freshness, but also the fact that song lyrics were aimed at us. Most kids at school identified with bands: you were either into Led Zeppelin, AC/DC etc. or newer bands. When I started buying my own records, my favourite bands were the Skids, XTC and The

Jam. I discovered The Jam through listening to the Radio 1 Sunday evening chart show, which I used to record on my crummy tape recorder. We also watched *Top of the Pops*, which even as a 14 year old recognised was a bit naff. I also think the band featured on the *Old grey Whistle Test* and *Rock Goes to College*, which featured full concerts on TV. The older brothers of some school friends also had copies of albums which we managed to listen to. Me and two of my school friends were so much into The Jam that we joined the fan club, and I still have some of the fan club material. My point of entry was 'Eton Rifles', although when I listened to the band's back catalogue, I realised that I had already heard some of their earlier singles.

We heard from a friend's older brother that The Jam were playing at Skegness Festival Pavilion, and my parents agreed to drive us there. This would have been the *Bucket and Spade* tour 1981. It's about an hour or so drive from Brigg to Skegness. They dropped us off at the venue and (I think) went out for the evening. We were 15 years old. I remember I wore a US Vietnam war era parka. Very heavy, to which I'd sewn a union jack flag to the back. I remember the gig being very intense and energetic. They came onstage and kept the tempo up for the entire gig. It was something I had looked forward to for ages, and they didn't disappoint. From memory, they played 'Strange Town' (a particular favourite as I played bass in a school rock band), a song with a strong bass line which I had managed to learn how to play. Bruce Foxton was (and is) one of my favourite bass players. They also played quite a lot of *Sound Affects*, which I believe they were touring at the time.

Bruce Foxton is one of Michael Welton's favourite bass players

One standout memory was that a woman asked me if she could sit on my shoulders. That was the first (and only) time that anyone has sat on my shoulders at a gig. I was over six feet tall at the time, so have never had a problem seeing the stage when I've been to gigs. She was there for three numbers, clearly enjoying herself, but after the three songs I had to ask her to get off! It was far too warm. They didn't play 'Down in the Tube Station at Midnight' though (another song with a strong bass line). After the gig, a few of us hung around to speak to the band, and security allowed us to stay, which doesn't happen these days. Sure enough Paul, Bruce and Rick came to the front of the stage to speak to fans. I was too awestruck to say anything. One of my friends asked Paul about the poem on the back cover of 'Strange Town' (I don't recall Paul's reply). We did manage to get a pound note signed by the band.

The following year, we all went to see the band at Sheffield City Hall. The Jam were touring *The Gift* at the time, and featured a three piece horn section. The gig was great, but it didn't have the same impact on me personally as the gig at Skegness the year before. Possibly because no-one asked to sit on my shoulders! And they still didn't play 'Down in the Tube Station at Midnight'.

Michael Welton still carries his signed pound note around with him

The band split up shortly thereafter and Paul went on to form the Style Council, which seemed to be a natural trajectory following *The Gift* album. I just couldn't get into them, and instead got into harder edged music after The Jam split up. I already liked The Who, so from that starting point, Seventies rock and metal was an easy step.

I still look out for reissues by The Jam. My favourite albums are *All Mod Cons* and *Setting Sons*, both classic albums. Favourite singles would be their output from 1978 – 1980, but especially 'Tube Station', 'Strange Town', 'When You're Young', 'Eton Rifles' and 'Going Underground'. One aspect of the Jam that we really appreciated was that they would release non-album singles, rather than release an album then release a load of songs from that album as singles. Also, their B-sides were always strong songs. You never felt ripped off by The Jam.

I have seen Bruce Foxton's From The Jam live, which I've thoroughly enjoyed, and have also seen Paul Weller live but, as good as they are, for me neither come close to the excitement, immediacy and energy of The Jam, and especially that great night in Skeggy.

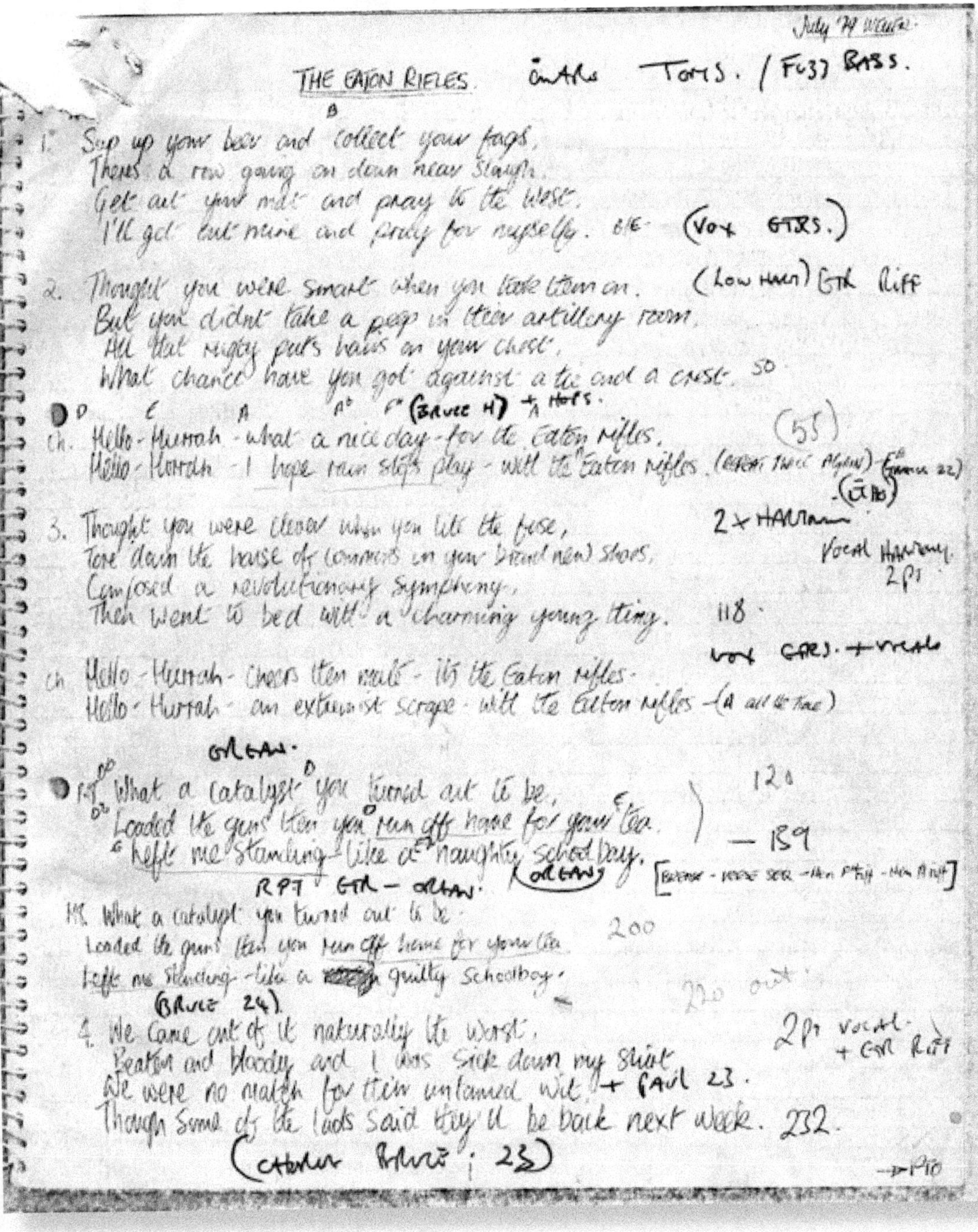

July '79 Woking

THE EATON RIFLES. Guitars Toms. / Fuzz Bass.

1. Sup up your beer and collect your fags,
There's a row going on down near Slough.
Get out your mat and pray to the west,
I'll get out mine and pray for myself. (Vox GTRS.)

2. Thought you were smart when you took them on. (Low Harm) Gtr Riff
But you didn't take a peep in their artillery room.
All that rugby puts hairs on your chest,
What chance have you got against a tie and a crest. 50

Ch. Hello-Hurrah - what a nice day - for the Eaton rifles. (55)
Hello - Hurrah - I hope rain stops play - with the Eaton rifles. (Repeat twice again) - (Gtrs)

3. Thought you were clever when you lit the fuse, 2 x Harm
Tore down the house of commons in your brand new shoes, Vocal Harmony 2 pt
Composed a revolutionary symphony,
Then went to bed with a charming young thing. 118.

Vox Gtrs. + vocals

Ch. Hello - Hurrah - cheers then mate - it's the Eaton rifles.
Hello - Hurrah - an extremist scrape - with the Eaton rifles - (A all the time)

Organ.

M8 What a catalyst you turned out to be, 120
Loaded the guns then you run off home for your tea.
Left me standing - like a naughty school boy. — 139
RPT Gtr - organ. (organ) [Break - verse ...]

M8. What a catalyst you turned out to be
Loaded the guns then you run off home for your tea 200
Left me standing - like a guilty schoolboy.
(Bruce 24) 220 out.

4. We came out of it naturally the worst, 2 pt vocal. + Gtr Riff
Beaten and bloody and I was sick down my shirt
We were no match for their untamed wit, + Paul 23.
Though some of the lads said they'll be back next week. 232.
(Chorus Bruce ; 23)

→ P.T.O.

GRANBY HALLS

22 JUNE 1981, LEICESTER, UK

I WAS THERE: NEAL HALFPENNY, AGE 12

My first Jam gig and my first ever gig. I was two weeks short of my 13th birthday. Long before the birth of the Internet it was word of mouth that bands were touring.

Neal Halfpenny at The Jam Exhibition at Somerset House

I'd fallen in love with The Jam in 1978 when I was just 10 years old. My best mate David Bradley (he still is) had an older brother who had played me 'The Modern World' and 'David Watts' and I instantly connected with them.

The Jam had toured the *Sound Affects* album the year before and had played two nights at De Montfort Hall in Leicester but my mum wouldn't let me go. I suppose at that tender age she was only being a proper mother.

Granby Halls Leicester before it was demolished

Around eight months later I got word that The Jam would be playing at the smaller Granby Halls venue on Welford Road, right next door to the Leicester Tigers Rugby Union ground. My mate's brother, the same one that had played me those records, was going to get tickets.

I have no idea why but back then you couldn't go to the box office in person to get tickets - you had to send a postal order. My mum gave the green light for me to go, as we were going with my mate's older and more responsible and mature brother. The Granby Halls was usually an ice-skating - roller skating arena but occasionally hosted concerts with standing only, no seats and about a 2,000 capacity.

Around the perimeter of the hall itself was a barrier and being so small and young my mate David and me, under the eye of his brother, hitched ourselves up on top of the barrier so we could see over the heads of the crowd. We were on the side of Bruce Foxton and had an amazing view as long as we could keep our balance stood on top of the steel barrier!

I remember before they had even come on stage there was 'smoke' rising from the crowd - of course it was the sweat and perspiration of an excited audience. During the wait, chants would suddenly ring out. The atmosphere was electric, really was brilliant.

The house lights dimmed and then went out. A spotlight hit the stage and the crowd roared. A grey haired fella - I had no idea at the time that it was John Weller - came on stage and stood under that spotlight and introduced The Jam on stage. The place just went absolutely ballistic.

I remember looking over that crowd and seeing it getting tighter and tighter down the front in anticipation and then they appeared.

This band I loved. A surreal moment - one I've never forgotten. I remember Paul Weller picking up his guitar and saying, 'This one's for you lot down the front - this is called 'Going Underground!' The place just erupted. From the opening clunking chords the crowd was just a writhing jumping mass of sweat.

I'd be lying if I said I remember everything they played - I simply don't. But I knew every word from every song they played even at that age. Me and David Bradley punched the air and sang our hearts out on top of that barrier that night. It was a truly life changing experience.

They finished with ''A' Bomb in Wardour Street'. I remember that and that then the house lights went back up. I saw an exhausted soaking wet crowd start to exit the Granby Halls.

I'd seen something so utterly brilliant - it is still to this day so hard to explain what that hour and a half meant and how it affected me.

I saw them twice more in 1982 in Leicester, at De Montfort Hall and Granby Halls once again, but there's nothing like your first time!

I would later see Oasis play at the Granby Halls in 1995 (they were just on the cusp of greatness), an older man obviously but another defining moment and as I watched Oasis I remembered fondly seeing The Jam as a kid and how the atmosphere was pretty much the same.

The Granby Halls sadly was demolished in 2001. It made way for a car park. The building may have been destroyed but memories last forever. Long live The Jam… and thank you. All three of you.

GUILDHALL

23 JUNE 1981, PORTSMOUTH, UK

I WAS THERE: RUSSELL HASTINGS

Although I saw the band many times from '77 to '82 and met them all at sound checks usually at Portsmouth Guildhall or the Brighton Centre, this recount is when me and two friends, James Perry and Mark Poffley, met Paul Weller back at the hotel.

It started with the usual hanging around backstage at the Guildhall Portsmouth for the coach to arrive. Sure enough Kenny Wheeler and Joe Awome jumped off the coach to clear the path of 20 to 30 fans and get the stage door open. Then all three – Paul, Bruce and Rick - came off followed by Steve and Keith, the brass section.

We all got into the sound check under the watchful eye of Kenny and Joe and were treated to my first live version of 'Carnation' which to this day remains stamped in my memory bank with colour and audio! I remember the fans (wind) blowing Paul's now French-cropped hair, much to the disappointment of the lookalikes!

A few more songs including 'Ghosts' and a great version of 'I Feel Good' and the band were off closely followed by us three teenagers in a Mark 1 Cortina all the way back to the Holiday Inn Hotel, Fratton (now the Marriott).

We waited outside in the car for ten minutes when I said I'd run the gauntlet through the lobby to see who I could spot. The game was on as that's what it was between us and Kenny and Joe the security. I walked straight in and walked to an open phone booth to make a call and give myself time to survey the joint!

All of a sudden Paul walked by and said, 'Alright?' Maybe my white Levi's and bowling shoes had given the game away? He sat in the corner on some sofas so I ended my call (to an old girlfriend) and took a deep breath and walked up to him and sat down opposite. I can't remember my opening line but it must have been OK as he asked if I wanted tea or coffee and ordered a tray and sandwiches.

After a good ten minutes, Mark and James came in to find out what the fuck I was doing and found me sitting with Paul. We chatted for a good couple of hours or so and witnessed Kenny playing pool with John and Steve and Keith coming down in their new suits, only to be taken the piss out of on exit from the lifts!

Time came to go to the gig and Paul asked if we were OK for a lift when Mark stupidly said, 'Yeah, we've got a car outside!' Mark, you wanker! You just blew my chance to arrive with the band to the venue!

As Paul walked out the door to the coach I noticed a check wool scarf on the floor so I picked it up, recognising it to be Paul's, when he came back and said, 'Nice one mate cheers', and took it back. It was later seen on the photo shoot for *Snap*, I think.

A great memory and one I've shared with Paul and Bruce of course over my other more relaxed encounters over the years.

I understood what the band meant to people. I saw and felt the energy, passion and excitement. I guess I was lucky to see them.

I saw the last show in Brighton too, but as they say, 'That's another story'.

BINGLEY HALL

27 JUNE 1981, STAFFORD, UK

I WAS THERE: STEVE SMITH

August 2019, and I am at a prog rock festival near Canterbury, organised by my brother. Curiosity has led me to watch Soft Machine, tuning their guitars, 25 minutes after taking to the stage. These boys are serious, I thought. My phone pings, and it's a text from my mate Andy. Apparently, a book is being mooted, with Rick Buckler's approval, about fan memories of seeing The Jam.

I am transported back in time, to a bizarre day in 1981. Myself, Andy, and my brother are driving up to Stafford from south London to see The Jam. This is the furthest I'd ever travel to see them. Andy's travelled abroad, and my brother was dragged kicking and screaming from his Jethro Tull albums in a vain attempt to get him into the best band to have emerged from the Seventies punk scene.

We arrived in Stafford early afternoon, gagging for a pint. The first couple of pubs we encountered were shut. Not closed down (doubtless that came later), just shut at that point in the day. Our third attempt brought moderate success. Another shut pub, but one with a burger van in the car park. Munching our prize-winning burgers, we enquired where we could get a drink. 'You'll get nowt in town today because of them concert people' we were told. We assured him we were part of 'them concert people', and any fears they had were unfounded. How wrong we were.

We tried one more pub (shut), whereupon I decided direct action was needed. It was now gone 5pm. I rang the doorbell. Eventually, an upstairs window was thrown open, and 'mine host' popped his head out. 'What?' he sneered at us, in that friendly northern manner. 'I just wondered what time you were opening?' I enquired, flashing him my winning smile, not to be outdone in the friendliness stakes. 'How would you like it if I came knocking on your door in't middle of night asking you what time you started work?' he responded. 'If you're them concert people, you'll not get served in Stafford today' he cheerily informed us. Deciding this relationship was going nowhere and puzzling over which time zone Stafford was in, I terminated the 'conversation' and we decided to leave town and try our luck in an outlying village.

At last, an open boozer! And welcoming, despite whatever plagues of locusts had been visited on the area by previous 'concert people'. Three pints of previously unknown ale to me (I was still in my teens), Ansells, were purchased and consumed with indecent haste. Happy with this new acquaintance, we speedily bought another three. Then another. What was in this splendid local brew I have no idea, but we quaffed like it was going out of fashion. Sadly, it was, as the local Aston brewery shut that year, merging and re-locating to Burton, where I believe they know a bit about that sort of thing. Anyway, I digress. After about five pints, we decided to head for the gig. This was 1981, remember, and whilst making no excuses, drink-driving didn't carry the stigma it does now. So, our (to remain anonymous) dedicated driver wended his merry way to Bingley Hall.

Steve Smith plays air guitar to The Jam

For those that have never been, it is a giant disused aircraft hanger (or if it wasn't, it should have been) seemingly plucked from civilization and dumped in the middle of a field - literally, nowhere. We picked a place about half way between the stage and bar at the back and waited for something to happen. It did. A swaying mass of people in front of us grew more and more lairy before splitting themselves into two groups - Wolves supporters and Birmingham City supporters. Punches were thrown and it got quite nasty. Suddenly there was a gap between the rival fans and a bloke stumbled out holding his side. He'd been stabbed. In a vain attempt to stop the trouble, the support band, Everest the Hard Way were brought on early. They were truly shocking, and this resulted in two eventual outcomes. 1) It stopped the trouble in as much as both sets of fans found a common bond and united to attempt to bottle them off. 2) As well as coming on early, they left early. As an aside, I went to see another band a week or so later in London (I can't remember who) and the announcer proudly introduced the 'special guests' - yep, them again.

Anyway, onto the main event, The Jam, who took to the stage accompanied by a frenzied chant of 'Jum, Jum, Jum' from the locals. I can't remember too much about the actual gig and have no idea of the set list. It had now become a gig to just get through - the setting, the crowd problems ('concert people') removing much chance of enjoyment - and just get out in one piece. We subsequently found out there had been trouble in town throughout the day, hence all the pubs had closed. We exited unmolested and even had time to stop off for a couple of quick pints on the way home.

Back to 2019, and I'm aware that Soft Machine have gone quiet. That's because they weren't tuning their guitars that was their set. For all the negatives of Bingley Hall, I still remember the day fondly, if not too clearly The Jam's part, and if we're going to live in the past, then I'd rather do it in Staffordshire than Kent. It makes sense anyway. They clearly live in a time warp. 'Middle of the night' indeed. Behave yourselves!

I WAS THERE: BRETT JANSEN, AGE 13

Paul Weller captured during their 1981 tour

An old mate sent me a late-Seventies, black and white (verging on sepia) photo of Bingley Hall recently which, apart from making Birmingham's long-since transformed Broad Street look genuinely Victorian, called to mind some of the best gigs I attended back in the day. This venue, eventually destroyed by fire in January 1984 and thankfully while no one was in it, was particularly notable for several performances by The Jam. I loved The Jam; still do, in fact. But in the interest of avoiding too much self-indulgence, I'll spare you a blow by blow account of their live musical sets on each occasion, and focus instead on the physical experience of attending a concert in the kind of place that would, I suspect, struggle to pass Health and Safety regulations in this day and age.

There's a two-abreast queue snaking around the building, the doors due to open at 7.30. Tim and I join it on a chilly Broad Street having timed our arrival pretty well. The line starts to shuffle forward, and we're soon around the corner into Oozells Street where the main entrance is, our random conversations betraying the fermenting excitement in our youthful souls. For a 13 year old (14 next week), this is going to be as good as a Tuesday night can get, let's face it. A couple of heavily accented touts try their luck, but we, and everyone in front and behind, are already sorted - £3 exceedingly well spent some weeks earlier, green no-frills tickets thrust deep in jeans pockets, ready to display.

We enter through a steel columned industrial lobby area and are issued forth into a presently well-lit space that seems quite large but is rapidly filling up, mostly with much bigger guys, the majority in Mod gear. *Quadrophenia* motif, red, white and blue target tops, Lonsdale sweat shirts, boating blazers, paisley or striped shirts, parkas, Sta-Prest trousers, Harrington and pilot jackets, bowling shoes, brogues and Docs abound. The front middle bulges with fans already, so we find a spot just to the right of that, about five short metres from the stage. Losing sight of the floor and quickly hemmed in from every angle, the hall looks much smaller now, and we're starting to feel it pack out.

presents
The Jam
+ SPECIAL GUESTS
Bingley Hall BIRMINGHAM
Tuesday November 11th 7.30pm
Tickets £3.75 Standing

Accustomed to standing on the terraces, being squashed and shoved around by hard-knocks doesn't faze me, but I'm keen to do a bit of wriggling so as to see past two six-footers in my way (in November 1980, I still have a lot of growing to do.) I've effected a sideways half-step when the lights go down, a loud cheer rises up and the support band are ushered on. A brief pause while amps are plugged in, then out screams the siren of sax that's been getting a lot of radio time of late, kicked along by a stomping drumbeat. It's The Piranhas, spotlights picking them out two bars in, and the whole place starts jumping to their one-hit wonder 'Tom Hark'. This is the musical equivalent of a goal going in at the Holte End, my feet lifted clean off the ground and carried diagonally forwards without coming down for five seconds, such is the kop-like surge from behind. I'm at the mercy of a collective human leviathan, the only control I can muster being to remain upright at all costs like a gymnast, tensing abdominal muscles and bracing myself against the jumble of rib cages and hampered elbows rolling me in this sea of 5,000 people, 99% male.

For the next two and a half hours it's like this. A throbbing, seething, pogo-dancing, gobbing, pulsating, singing, swaying, chanting, swearing, laughing, stumbling mass of abandon. Tim disappears into the throng, threaded to parts unknown by the physical phenomenon surrounding us. I'm dogged by a two-metre giant directly behind me for 20 minutes, whose 'Weller is God' mantra is delivered with an accompanying arm that continues to crash down on my bonce until I manage to extricate myself from that particular pocket of sardines.

I've watched footage on *YouTube* of a similar gig I attended two years later, recorded not long before the band split up, and the steam you can see rising off of the same squashed crowd reminds you this was a different age, when no one batted an eyelid at commonplace crushes, now consigned to the post-Hillsborough delete history bin. Nevertheless, The Jam are an exhilarating joy, their third encore bringing proceedings to a sweat soaked close a shade after ten o'clock. Heads buzzing, ears ringing and clothes hanging, we're tipped out of Bingley Hall like bedraggled trauma victims, suddenly frozen by sub-zero temperatures, but deliriously content on a drug-free high never bettered.

'Tour t-shirts, lads?' The predominantly Mancunian and Scouse hawkers flog their wares for a quid-fifty per item. I buy one and Tim two. We grab cans of Fanta and Vimto from the ice cream van parked across the main road, and discuss a truly memorable evening on the 126 bus home, hearing not fully restored till third period next day, bodies still aching in a nice way.

I saw them three times in 1982 as well, and at Stafford in 1981, 'Funeral Pyre' summer. I can't see past 80-81 being the best year of my life in terms of the experiences you know will never come round again, and I also count myself lucky to have been at those Jam gigs. Still the best live act I've seen.

I WAS THERE: SUZANNE KRENTZ

I've been a fan since the age of 15, most likely from having heard 'Down in the Tube Station' and loving the band's lyrics and energy. I've been lucky enough to see them live four times, including at the Civic Hall in Wolverhampton and three times at Bingley Hall, Stafford.

I worked at WHSmith in Dudley on a YTS (Youth Training Scheme). I earned £20 for a 39 hour week! The best part of my training was working on the record counter

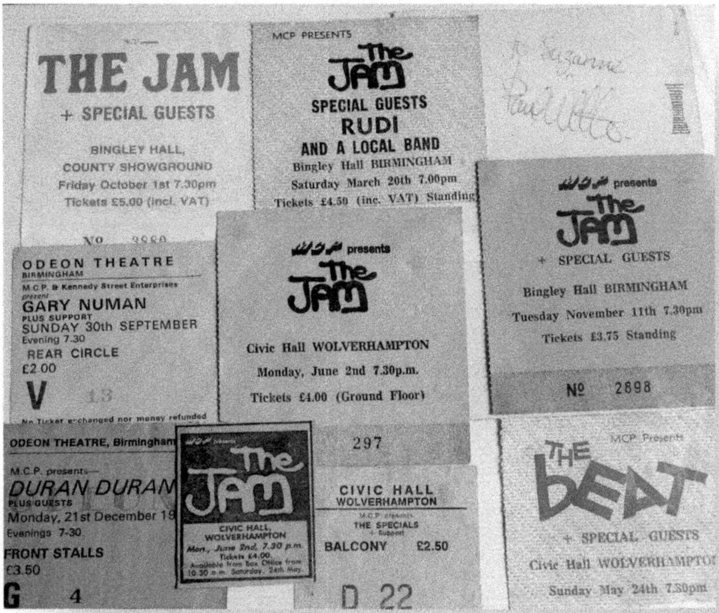

Suzanna Krentz saw the Jam four times

where I could choose what music was played. You've guessed it - The Jam were high on the list but I did have to vary the music to encourage customers to buy other music genres, plus the latest 45 singles or LPs. Whilst there, I managed to get hold of a load of empty *Setting Sons* LP covers which I arranged and stuck to the back of my bedroom door along with Jam posters and 45 single covers (as you do).

The highlight for me was meeting Paul Weller when I was 18. He was waiting for a bus at Victoria Station in London. I was visiting London with my mum when I spotted him. Even my mum knew of Paul Weller and asked why he'd be waiting for a bus - I could only imagine it was an easy way to get round London and as no one (apart from me) was taking any notice of him and he could obviously get round quite easily. I asked him for his autograph (he kindly obliged) - my mum happened to have a pen and Paul signed the back of a postcard for me. I was so star struck I could hardly speak and had to spell my name out when he asked me what it was. I told him I'd got tickets for Bingley Hall but sadly he didn't do a shout out (as if he would!).

I also met the band when they visited the HMV store at the Wolverhampton Mander Centre. I was attending Crestwood School's sixth form (in Kingswinford) at the time, so went to school to get my attendance mark and promptly caught the next bus straight to Wolverhampton where Paul, Bruce and Rick signed my picture cover copy of 'When You're Young'. Exciting days to meet your heroes, especially when it was before everyone had a camera to hand and obviously there were no mobile phones. I still have the signed cover hiding somewhere in a very packed spare room.

So many great memories with a few photos (taken on a 35mm camera, keeping your fingers crossed they came out ok after either posting the film off to be processed or taking them to your local Super Snaps shop), plus autographs and concert tickets as proof. I always stuck concert tickets in the back of my photograph albums.

To say I was gutted when The Jam split was an understatement. My other half has never understood why I didn't then follow The Style Council or Paul Weller as a solo artist. I think it's more to do with being a Jam fan as a whole and me feeling they could have carried on as a trio. We did see Paul at the Civic in Wolverhampton in 2009 and, although very good, I was extremely disappointed that he didn't play any Jam songs apart from 'The Eton Rifles'. Time flies but the music never dies - not many people will understand the thrill of purchasing *The Gift* when it came wrapped in a pink striped paper bag.

I WASN'T THERE: MALCOLM WYATT

I'm not fully sure when The Jam first popped up on my radar, but it was most likely late '78 via Capital Radio airplay for double-A side single 'David Watts'/"A'Bomb in Wardour Street' and epic follow-up 'Down in the Tube Station at Midnight'.

My brother - seven years older – soon snapped up *All Mod Cons*, and I was hooked from the moment this dynamic trio kicked into an adrenaline-driven 80-second title-track and 'To Be Someone (Didn't We Have a Nice Time)'.

By the time of 1979's non-LP 7"s I was smitten, a top-three chart position for next offering, 'The Eton Rifles' - out a day before my 12th birthday - suggesting similar reactions up, down and around the UK. And when *Setting Sons* followed, I was more than ready for that next amazing chapter.

Only later did I join the dots and see within the elements and influences that shaped this three-piece, not least the songwriting of Ray Davies and spirit of The Who. Early cynics suggested they were copyists, but I saw an inspirational outfit building on those influences, and they introduced me to so much more great music. As my Woking born and bred old man would say, this was all fresh ground to me.

There's a good reason I can't put a date on some evangelical awareness of The Jam. They were intrinsically part of everything I felt I was about from the start. Local lads made good, providing an inspirational soundtrack to my life.

Rick Buckler was a frequent visitor at the builders' merchants where my brother worked and my Nan lived in Woking - on a road our family moved to in the late 1890s, less than a mile from Paul Weller's Stanley Road roots and Maybury estate base - and later I became a Woking FC regular, so many home and away trips over the years involving in-car, pub jukebox or club tannoy plays of 'A Town Called Malice' and other masterpieces.

From *All Mod Cons* and *Setting Sons*, it was something of a revelation to go back and hear frenetic 1977 debut LP *In The City*, retrospectively making me aware of those old punk and new wave, R&B and '60s soul leanings and interpretations, its opening side's six-song salvo a sonic manifesto of intent.

I also found plenty to savour on that rushed second LP, its last four songs taking me back to the cassette player in my Ford Escort Mk I, leaving work on Friday afternoons, the promise of a punishing couple of days and nights ahead. *'Long live the weekend, the weekend is here!'*

With so many bands, mainstream success puts me off, seeing me quietly retreat - not bitter, just happy to let them go. But that was never the case with The Jam. Irrespective of sales figures, the songs still talked to me and they never stood still long enough to outstay their welcome and for me to lose interest. After the conceptual storytelling of *Setting Sons*, next long player *Sound Affects* took us on again, while threading me back to belatedly discover The Beatles' *Revolver* and much more.

I wasn't about tribalism, keeping a distance from the plastic Mod following in the same way I did from the postcard punks I saw around my hometown, Guildford, seven miles from The Jam's roots. Don't get me wrong, the true Mods were a class act. It was mob mentality that warded me off, the antithesis of what Weller and co. were about.

But I listened carefully when Paul talked clothes, dance culture, records and books, and his world view touched a nerve. By the time of *The Gift* he expressed himself all the better too, 'The Planner's Dream Goes Wrong' taking on the personal-political sentiments of the similarly-evocative 'Man in the Corner Shop' on the previous LP. This was no Paul Weller trio either. The Jam were a proper band, all three members integral to the sound, overall aesthetic and vibe.

I was upset when the split came, but accepted it. I was only pissed off that I hadn't got to see them live, having turned down a chance to get along to Guildford Civic Hall in early July 1981. It was barely a fortnight after my first visit for The Undertones, and I didn't feel I had the cash to snap up the opportunity on the spur of the moment. Complacency, I guess. I find that hard to accept now. I loved *Sound Affects*, out seven months earlier, and everything else – few bands come anywhere near when it comes to singles - and took it for granted that I'd catch them next time. Big mistake.

In early August '82, I was on the Isle of Wight with my folks – there's a dodgy shot of a long streak of piss in specs on a beach wearing an *In The City* era t-shirt (no doubt unofficial) that I won't be sharing – on our last holiday together, when I read in the *NME* about December's return to my hometown amid break-up speculation. I was gutted, knowing instinctively there would be no tickets left on my return.

Official confirmation followed three days after my 15th birthday, that Civic Hall show (admission £5) set to be the finale until feverish interest ensured an extra date at Brighton Centre. Proper fans and the band themselves saw it as the big one though. It was all too emotional from there.

I learned to love The Style Council and caught Bruce's solo album tour in May '84, aged 16, a first interview following for my *Captains Log* fanzine, via a postal Q&A. I finally caught Weller live for the first time in March '94, that Guildford Civic performance (I was in Lancashire by then, but regularly returned) one of my top-five gigs ever, Paul between the creative highs of *Wild Wood* and *Stanley Road*.

In late 2007 I had my first proper chats with Bruce and Rick backstage at Preston's

53 Degrees after a From The Jam show, each everything I'd hoped - easy company and great to be around.

I've been lucky enough to interview Bruce, bandmate Russell Hastings and Rick a few times since, still see From the Jam at least once a year, and met the lovely Nicky Weller when the *About The New Idea* exhibition visited Liverpool. I'm hoping one-to-ones with her brother and early bandmate Steve Brookes will follow.

I don't expect there'll ever be an on-stage reunion, and I'm alright with that. I get that they've all moved on. The peacemaker within me would like to see the band relationship reconciled though, the sooner the better. However, what really matters is their legacy. They were a force to be reckoned with for an all-too-quick five-year spell as a recording unit. Those records remain as fresh as ever, and will always be a creative inspiration to me.

Malcolm Wyatt, music writer, author of *This Day in Music's Guide to The Clash*

MAGNUM LEISURE CENTRE

30 JUNE 1981, IRVINE, UK

I WAS THERE: ROBERT STEVENSON

I saw The Jam 17 times. When they played The Magnum my friends supported them. They stayed in my hometown and Paul Weller went for a ride on my scooter. I had the side panel signed by the full band. They put us on the guest list for the next gig in Carlisle.

MARKET HALL

4 JULY 1981, CARLISE, UK

I WAS THERE: KEN SCOFIELD

I saw them at Carlisle Market hall in July 1981. It was my 23rd birthday. I slept in a van afterwards. Cracking night.

CIVIC HALL

7 & 8 JULY 1981, GUILDFORD, UK

I WAS THERE: MICHAEL FARRAGHER

This was part of the *Bucket and Spade* tour, although Guildford was nowhere near the sea. It was the closest I got to see The Jam do a hometown gig. It was a brilliant venue, sadly now demolished. Me and my sister had met The Jam during the day and we had got in to see the soundcheck.

The gigs were brilliant, fantastic atmosphere and boiling hot. Paul and Bruce were in shorts. I remember Paul running on stage and falling flat on his back even before he had struck the first chord. They were welcomed as homecoming heroes and the second night was one of the best ever. At the end Paul took his shirt off and had black tape over his nipples. We met them again after the gig, which was always the icing on the cake. Having nowhere to stay after the away gigs was hard going but nights like this meant it was worth it.

Paul Weller taken by Michael Farragher

CHISWICK HOUSE

31 AUGUST 1981

I WAS THERE: DEREK D'SOUZA, AGE 22

I heard 'In The City' on the radio - that opening bass line and then the drums, the energy. That was it - I was hooked! I first went to see them at The Music Machine in London on 2nd March 1978; I was 18 and had only recently started attending gigs on a regular basis. I had been to a few gigs, but nothing like this. The set was a mixture of songs from the first two albums and the soon to be released *All Mods Cons*. Stand out songs were 'A' Bomb in Wardour Street', 'Down in the Tube Station at Midnight', 'In The City' and 'The Modern World', but it was all great. The gig was a mixture of the threat of violence (it felt like it could kick off at any moment), being very loud, and the feeling of this was what I had been waiting for!

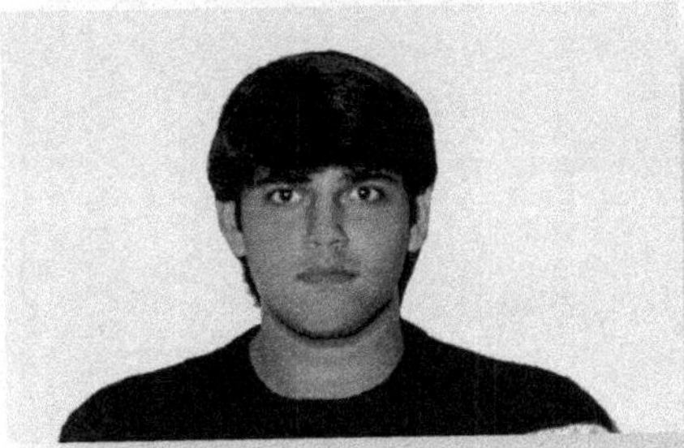

Jam fan Derek D'Souzas' first photo shoot was for The Jam at Chiswick House

I used to sneak my camera into gigs, which was a challenge in itself. The gigs were frenzied affairs and sometimes violent! People would knock into you all the time, making taking pictures very difficult. I would generally only take four rolls of films (max 190 frames) because of the cost of developing and printing. I wasn't a professional photographer. I just went along because of my love of the band and the music and I wanted to try and capture something of the atmosphere of the gigs.

I think The Jam was among the first gigs I photographed. Other bands I had photographed earlier were Dr. Feelgood, 9 Below Zero and The Inmates. The gigs were smaller and I only had the single camera, with one or two lenses and a flash. The first Jam gig I took photos was at the Rainbow Theatre in December '79. I only got a few half decent shots. I really didn't know what I was doing. There was no Google to look up for advice. The only other place I asked was the local camera shop and they didn't have any experience of that genre of photography, so it was really a matter of trial and error.

After a couple of years of taking pictures at gigs and sound checks (always unofficially), I decided to send a few of my photos to The Jam fan club and Paul Weller himself wrote to me saying he liked the photographs, especially some that I had taken off the TV.

After the gigs of summer 1981, I sent some more pictures and the next day I had a call from Paul's mum Ann (who ran the fan club along with Paul's sister Nicky) informing me that the band liked my pictures and were interested in commissioning me to do a formal photo session with the band.

This was huge! They were my favourite band and had a massive following, and

One of the 190 shots Derek D'Souza took of The Jam at Chiswick House © Derek D'Souza

here I was a fan with a camera that had never undertaken a photo shoot for anyone! I don't think something like this would happen now, a band would normally choose a big-name photographer.

After meeting the band at George Martin's Air Studios in Oxford Street, London, the brief was to take pictures of the band wearing dark suits (in contrast with the stone statues and greenery) in Chiswick House grounds. The shoot was for the cover sleeve and promotional material for the single release of 'Absolute Beginners'. I had limited amateur equipment but was very familiar with my gear. As with shoots of this kind we were looking to have a handful of possible images to choose from.

The band were great, very accommodating and helpful. Rick later said they knew I was nervous, understandable really, my first ever photo shoot, but it was enjoyable. I think being a fan of the band helped both ways. I certainly wasn't a professional photographer out on assignment. This was The Jam, my favourite band, top of the charts, and I was their photographer for this shoot!

We spent just over two hours, which really flew by. I had four rolls of Kodak Ektachrome slide film and a roll of negative film just in case.... 190 photos, not much really, and one of the restrictions of film. I'm sure if I did it today I would take a lot more photos, not to mention all the other advantages of modern cameras.

It really was a 'somebody pinch me' moment.... all things considered, the fact I was a complete novice at any kind of formal photo shoot. I had taken a few photos for fun and of course I was learning all the time from shooting gigs (I still am). I think in truth it said more about the band that they would give an unknown a shot (in true *Rocky* fashion), and hopefully I didn't disappoint. I have had a number of people say that my photos of the band, particularly from this shoot, were their favourites, a mixture of what I was able to capture and the fact they were experienced in front of the camera and looked very sharp!

Thankfully the shoot was a success and the band liked the photos I had taken and chose one for the reverse of the record sleeve and insert lyric sheet. And the rest as they say is history!

Many years later Stuart Deabill and Ian Snowball's *Thick As Thieves - Personal Situations with The Jam* really paved the way for my first book *In The Crowd - Images of The Jam*, with both published by Marshall Cavendish and we were introduced by designer Jon Abnett. As I had a reasonable sized collection of mostly unseen images, and with the interest in the band having something of resurgence, it seemed the right time to put together a book of my photographs. These were taken mostly from a fan's perspective, with me sneaking my camera in to many gigs over a period of four years.

The book was a largely personal account of how I saw the band and became involved, the highlight being the photo shoot in Chiswick House for the 'Absolute Beginners' sleeve.

The book sold out a couple of years ago, which still shocks me as we sold over 2,000 copies. Not a big number compared to record sales in the past, but a big number for a first book.

My second *book In Echoed Steps, The Jam and a Vision Of Albion* was published in August 2017, a collaboration with artist and designer Paul Skellett and writer Simon Wells. The book sees new life breathed into some old images and features a mixture of colour and B&W and both seen and unseen images. The book was a limited edition release of 1,000 books and has been very well received by fans of the band and the band themselves.

I have continued to take photographs and am still heavily involved with gig and band photography.

Among my personal highlights was when one of my photographs of The Jam was chosen for display in The National Portrait Gallery. I have also contributed to the two Jam exhibitions. *About The Young Idea*, firstly at Somerset House, and then a larger version at the Cunard building in Liverpool.

I would say the main thing that drives me on is the belief that the best photo I am ever going to take is one I haven't taken yet.

'Absolute Beginners' was released on 18 October 1981 peaking at number four on the UK chart and named after the Colin MacInnes novel of the same name. The book was one of songwriter Paul Weller's favourites, being chosen by him when he appeared on BBC's *Desert Island Discs.*

FINSBURY PARK

24 OCTOBER 1981, LONDON, UK

I WAS THERE: DAVID WILSON

The most memorable gig for me was their set on the back of a lorry in London during the huge CND march against cruise missiles in the early Eighties.

THE YOUNG VIC

30 NOVEMBER 1981, LONDON, UK

I WAS THERE: MICHAEL HOROVITZ

Paul and I met first in 1980 or '81, when I was revving up on the Poetry Olympics festivals. The early Jam recordings, as well as Paul's *December Child* and *Riot Stories* fanzines, had turned me on to the sensitive, poetic ends of the punk revolution, with both his song lyrics and his pure poems delighting my friends and me with their innovatory edge and personal soulfulness, plus the rebellious directness of 'The Eton Rifles', 'Little Boy Soldiers' et al felt like a direct pop/rock counterpart to the Beat Generation/protest/Jazz Poetry movement of the writers I related to most strongly and was publishing in *New Departures* and presenting in Poetry Olympics.

He gave a brilliant performance of his poems at the Young Vic to a full house largely populated by literary rather than pop fans, many of whom were instantly converted to his originality and intimate communication of his wordsounds. Paul's sound, style, ideology and voice are - like those of most authentic superstars - intensely unique to him.

MICHAEL SOBELL SPORTS CENTRE

12 AND 13 DECEMBER 1981, LONDON, UK

I WAS THERE: CHRIS JONES

Saw them as my first gig and loved it. Memory not great but I think Paul Weller ran on at the beginning and slipped on his backside and continued to play. Not a bad first gig!

I WAS THERE: MAXINE BUTLER, AGE 14

I was lucky enough to see them twice. I'm sure it had been snowing both times. Mum and dad sat outside the venue with soup and said they could hear it all.

I cried my eyes out thinking I would not see Paul anymore after the Brighton gig. My love for Paul still continues and after all this time I have been lucky enough to meet him and last year got a signed photo and plectrum from him.

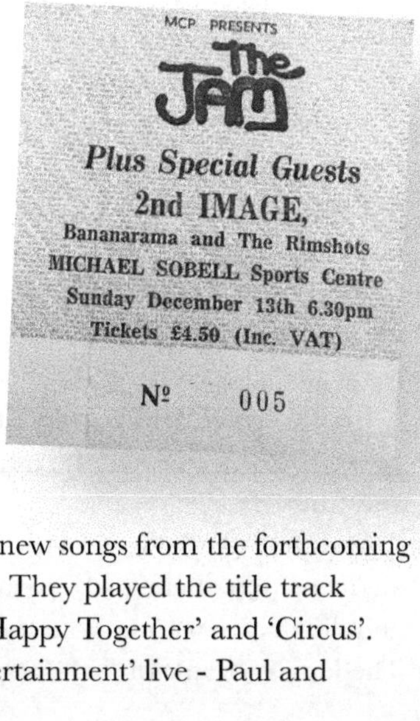

I WAS THERE: MICHAEL FARRAGHER

Michael Sobell Sports Centre was not a great venue and not built for concerts, unlike Hammersmith Palais which had a terrific atmosphere. The Jam previewed six new songs from the forthcoming album *The Gift* which would be released in three months. They played the title track 'The Gift', 'Ghosts', 'Town Called Malice', 'Precious', 'Happy Together' and 'Circus'. It was also the first time I saw the band play 'That's Entertainment' live - Paul and

Bruce both playing acoustic guitar. They did a cover of 'Big Bird' which would appear on the live album *Dig the New Breed* next year and a brilliant version of Chairmen of the Board's 'Give Me Just a Little More Time'. Little did we know then that in less than a year Paul Weller would call time on The Jam.

Michael Farragher snaps Rick Buckler outside the tour bus

BBC TV THEATRE

19 DECEMBER 1981, LONDON, UK

I WAS THERE: RAY BUTLER, AGE 17

When my friend at work said he could get free tickets to see The Jam, I didn't really think he could and I didn't think much more about his claim; after all he was a fan of The Stranglers and although we shared the same job title of 'messenger' in an art studio, we had little in common, except we were both 17 and had the same first name.

This was 1981 and a great time for diverse sub cultures to thrive – Mods, punks, skinheads, rude boys. In 1979 it wasn't unusual to be at a house party where all the different styles of clothing and music came together in a respectful and mutual acknowledgement that although we different fundamentally we all wanted the same thing, to be free of our parents and on a journey of discovery within our different groups. By 1981 this harmony had well and truly broken down and after many altercations down Carnaby Street, at Brighton, along Oxford Street and even at the same parties of the year before, the difference was that now we were sworn enemies. Ray had left school at 16 as I had and so when this new wave punk said he could get me a free ticket to see The Jam it was greeted with an 'Ok. Thanks'... but true to his word he arrived one day with the tickets and not only that he had a Jaguar car mascot that I could buy off him for a few pounds. This was the crowning glory for my heavily decorated Vespa150 Super scooter. I thought it was Christmas. Well it nearly was. This was mid December 1981.

It turned out that Ray's sister had contacts within the BBC who could get these 'gold dust' tickets and the irony is that Ray the Strangler fan was going because he liked the support band, Department S, who sang 'Is Vic There?' and Vic was Ray's girlfriend's name, whereas I was there for the greatest band I had ever hear. Their energy, their lyrics and, above all else, their sound.

Here you had the ferocious drumming of Rick Buckler, the wild, gunning sound of Bruce Foxton's bass and the soul cutting provocative lyrics sung with stabbing, realism and truth.

The atmosphere was electric and the anticipation was palpable, although some of the audience were there for Department S and some because they had nabbed a free ticket and didn't care who was on. It didn't matter a jot, I was there to see my band, the band, The Jam. A couple of 'casual' girls looked in our direction as the sound of 'It Must Be

Love' played as background. They swayed, sang and looked but I was here for The Jam and I didn't want any distractions, not tonight anyway.

Department S did their thing and then Gary Crowley burst on the stage with genuine excitement for one of his favourite bands. What made the night so memorable was not just hearing them for the first time, although their sound reached every nerve. Nor was it seeing them close up. This concert was not the usual crammed in, sweating, ducking and diving, to see the band. This was an intimate, exclusive seated event for the chosen few.

Not only was I already in heaven but Paul Weller announces that they will be playing their, as yet, unfinished and untitled album. Imagine - listening to a track so new that we become apart of the process. Your mind runs riot, as you are absorbed by the sound in every fibre, you try to imagine what you would call it... what did this pounding, pulsating instrumental track that ambushes you with a brass section. This was not just The Jam but a Jam evolution I was experiencing. It was a full on, wild sound cacophony of sound just like a circus and that is wh at it ended up being called.

'How could this gig at the Hippodrome, Golders Green, 19 December 1981 ever be topped?' I thought and 40 years on it never has been.

The Jam tracks have lived with me and through me. They have been 'my constant', they have been my voice and they have been my comfort. If I have something to express, something to shout about or something to remember, there's a Jam track. It can infuse energy, it can release frustration and it can take me back to a better time.

1982

The double 'A' sided single 'Town Called Malice'/'Precious' was released on 29 January 1982. The single debuted at number one on the UK singles chart preventing 'Golden Brown' by the Stranglers from reaching the top. EMI, The Stranglers' record company, objected to the sales of both versions of 'Town Called Malice' being aggregated, arguing that Jam fans were buying both and thus preventing their band from reaching the top of the chart.

I WAS THERE: PETE TOWNSHEND

The March issue of London's Time Out magazine published an interview with The Who's Pete Townshend where the guitarist had met Paul Weller.

When Weller and I met for the first time there was guarded mutual respect, not much else. We differed greatly on the importance of American music audiences. I have never seen The Jam live and don't listen to their records all the time. Weller only likes early

Who stuff. From my point of view it's peculiar because I still feel as angry as I ever did, as unhappy about the exploitation of the individual by the difficult-to-pin-down `system'. People like me don't give up being angry, but they start to channel their aggressive frustrations into hard, defined arenas.

Weller is so full of pent-up energy that when he writes he sometimes streams ideas on to a record. He rarely uses controlled metre and never bothers to rhyme a line. The words of his songs laid out in naked print appear art school self conscious but are actually far from it. Weller is a slasher. He cuts and mauls. He drags you from complacency. He buttonholes you so you feel an urge to defend yourself, then you are opened up and weakened. The attack touches your heart and you realise that the purpose of The Jam is Revolution. Both Weller and Buckler sing with the vengeance of men cornered. Their threat is that if you approach you will feel the full force of their anger: stay at a distance and you will hear their venomous condemnation of your cowardice. There is a fully fledged taunt in `The Eton Rifles'. A totally sweeping derision in `In The Street Today'. In both cases there is also the thread of merciless self-analysis; so typically British. I keep coming back to this, The Jam are so fucking British.

There is another inconsistent facet to The Jam, however. They are soulful individuals, concerned with a passionate but innocent resignation to a concrete world that reminds me of John Lee Hooker's blues. From London to the cotton fields. Their stance is not a show of `stiff-upper-lip', its an almost spiritual surrender to the inevitable. On their first album they ask: `Where is the Great Empire?' No one I know seems to give a shit. The question is asked with cynicism but it's asked nonetheless. Its almost as though they are saying: `Your badly run society fucks us up but it hasn't made the leader's lives any better either.' The Jam are a new kind of blues band.

I'm putting words into their mouth. But there's a lot of powder flowing in high places, a lot of intelligent people who should know better swaying in futility and unable to think clearly. Strangely, many of Weller's songs include lines that are addressed to the wealthy aristocratic families, to Lords and Ladies, to officers in the Guards, to peers of the realm and to all their spoon-fed offspring. Heroes and Junkies.

Weller takes on the whole of British society without a blink. The Jam are a small army dedicated to the awakening of a sleeping nation. It sounds a bit pretentious to say this, but I think it's true, The Jam actually do give a shit about the downtrodden soul bereft of spirit and direction, whether they are on the dole or living on handouts from decaying country estates.

The Jam are ostensibly Britain's top band. They figure prominently in all our polls and their shows sell out rapidly. Alongside UB40 they might not appear too successful as an alternative co-operative kick back at commercial record companies; alongside The Associates they might appear a little reactionary, but alongside The Who, a band I can just about speak for today, they represent everything that is vitally important in rock. No one likes musical categories, but The Jam are a great rock band in the old tradition. They have listened to the music that created the roots of the great bands of the Sixties and kept clear of the evolutionary demise of those groups. Weller's love of early Who stuff has never, for example, been affected by my own disenchantment with the Sixties.

He has his own gripes. But he has listened to The Who and to all the music we used to love: blues, Motown, reggae (blue-beat as it was called then). I am probably the most musically open minded person I know: if it has a few notes in it I like it. Yet despite their well-watered roots The Jam distress me musically. Weller strives hard as a composer; his yearning to be a great musician cuts through even his most scathing material. It's this that niggles at me. I feel a terrifying frustration there. It's a frustration I used to feel at his age (I had to start getting condescending and patronising somewhere!). Anyway, it is all part of The Jam's power.

Paul Weller: I'd never read the Nevil Shute novel, *A Town Like Alice*, but I must have seen the title. The music came from us jamming, which we were always doing. I remember us first hitting that groove and being fired up by it. Then I added the middle eight and sorted the song out, adding the organ. It was all done pretty quickly. I remember feeling good about it, and when we played it to friends in the studio, everyone went 'wow'.

The Jam clean up in the NME Poll Winners awards published on 28 February 1982 including Paul Weller winning 'Best Haircut'.

The Gift the sixth and final studio album by The Jam, was released on 12 March 1982. Also on the same day The Jam played the first date on their 25-date *Trans Global Unity Express* UK tour at The Guildhall, Portsmouth.

1982 NME POLL WINNERS

BEST GROUP: The Jam
BEST MALE SINGER: Paul Weller
MOST WONDERFUL HUMAN BEING: Paul Weller
BEST SONGWRITER: Paul Weller
BEST SINGLE: The Jam - "Town Called Malice"
BEST LONG PLAYER: The Jam - *The Gift*
BEST LIVE ACT: The Jam
EVENT OF THE YEAR: The Jam Split
BEST DRESSED MALE: Paul Weller
BEST HAIRCUT: Paul Weller
BEST GUITARIST: Paul Weller
BEST BASSIST: Bruce Foxton
BEST DRUMMER: Rick Buckler

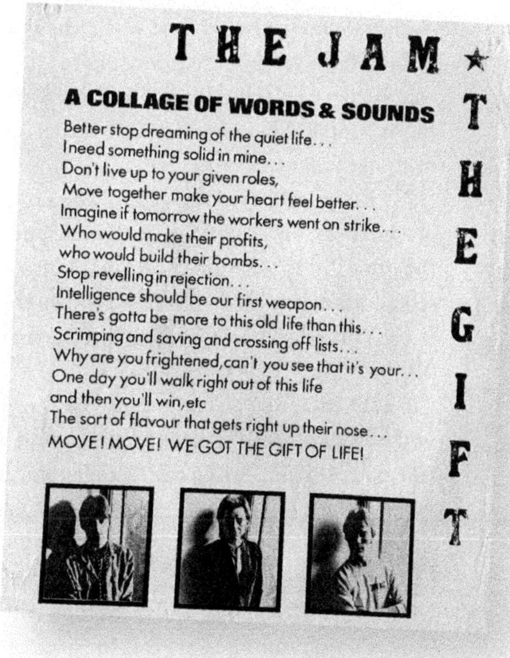

ROYAL BATH AND WEST SHOWGROUND

17 MARCH 1982, SHEPTON MALLET, UK

I WAS THERE: MARK STAGG

They were touring songs from *The Gift* album. I now live in Australia and am going to see Bruce Foxton in From The Jam at Hillarys in Perth next weekend.

I WAS THERE: STEVE JONES

The Gift Tour and my first live gig – I was 17 at the time and bought the t-shirt and the album (and since on CD).

AFAN LIDO

18 MARCH 1982, PORT TALBOT, UK

I WAS THERE: CLAIRE MAHONEY, AGE 14

It was their final tour and I was only 14 at the time. This was the first gig I'd ever been to and will always be the best. I have never experienced anything like the atmosphere or energy of that crowd. It made everything since then feel as if it lacked something.

BINGLEY HALL

20 MARCH 1982, BIRMINGHAM, UK

MCP PRESENTS
The JAM
SPECIAL GUESTS
RUDI
AND A LOCAL BAND
Bingley Hall BIRMINGHAM
Saturday March 20th 7.00pm
Tickets £4.50 (inc. VAT) Standing
№ 850

I WAS THERE: GAVIN JONES

I went with my friend Marc from Reaction to this one, and we went to the sound check hoping to get Marc on the guest list as I had a ticket. They played 'Carnation' and 'Precious', but we were kicked out straight after so couldn't chat to the guys. It wasn't how it used to be. I didn't recognise many people at the sound check. It felt different as there were more people there - you could tell this was a group getting very big.

We decided to find the group's hotel, which we did across town, and saw Paul in the bar and he was really good with us, and put Marc on the guest list written on his fag packet! We then got chatting to Gary Numan's manager, who bought us a drink. We had to run to the gig as we nearly missed the start. Paul true to his word had put Marc on the list. When we got in they were playing 'Happy Together'.

It turned out to be a great gig, Paul was really aggressive, kicking amps over and windmilling, Bruce jumping loads, great atmosphere. They did all the songs from *The Gift* except 'Planners Dream', and some *Sound Affects*. All in all a great gig, with The Jam coming back on for three encores.

I WAS THERE: RITCHIE WESTON

I went to the *Trans Global Express* tour with a few friends and myself and my mate Tich were filmed saluting as we left the arena.

We then went to the Holiday Inn for a beer and in the bar was John Weller, what a nice guy - he bought us a beer straight away. So then down came the band and Paul sat with us for over an hour just talking about music then up popped Dave Wakeling from the Beat with a tape he had of a friends band. Bruce And Rick were really friendly too such nice guys.

After an hour of chatting with Paul he asked if he could go and play cards with the roadies. I mean for fuck sake! - my hero asking me if it was OK? I have to say what a great guy, never meet your heroes - nah Weller is a legend.

BINGLEY HALL

21 MARCH 1982, BIRMINGHAM, UK

I WAS THERE: LAWRENCE BRACKSTONE, AGE 13

The year was 1979 and I was 13 years old. I was living near Solihull, on the edge of Birmingham. The mood of the city and the wider country was angry with factory strikes, apathy and violence aplenty. Punk rock was now moving on after giving the fashion and music scene a massive kick up the arse. I had always enjoyed music, but it was up until then it was without an identity.

'Eton Rifles' changed all that. I first heard its bass-driven, Rickenbacker feedback, drum-crashing sounds through the radio. I loved its differences to anything else musically at the time and its catchy chorus and choice of words in the vocals – I had to research what a 'catalyst' was.

With that full sound I was surprised to see on *Top of the Pops* that there were just three of them. At the time Bruce stood out more on stage to me than Paul, as I thought he stood back from the limelight looking cool in his wrap-around black sunglasses.

This in turn ultimately lead to me hearing the *Setting Sons* album. It was the first time I had listened to back-to-back tracks on any LP. It was on an illegally recorded cassette passed around my friendship group, which tended to happen a lot where I lived. Significant steps followed as I started to wear Mod clothing and was open to listening to the other revival Mod bands of the time. It has to be said that as far as I'm concerned The Jam had their own sound and, although Weller was clearly a Mod, The Jam as a band weren't in that camp and stood head and shoulders above the other bands of their time.

In 1980, another cassette recorded from Radio 1 was passed to me by a friend. This was to seriously adjust what I had experienced musically to that point in time. It was a live take of The Jam performing at the Rainbow in London in 1979. I actually listened to it first under my pillow when I should have been long asleep. The kick drum and Weller's broken up intro to 'Its Too Bad' will stay with me forever as capturing the atmosphere of the band. I knew then that I had to see them live at some point in my life as this was more than just music.

My parents, with some justification, had discouraged me from going to gigs. There was much negative press coverage of violence and drugs, so it meant that at the age of

16 I actually hadn't ever been to a music concert. In early 1982 the band had just released what was to be their final studio album – *The Gift* - and had announced a number of live dates for a UK tour to promote the album. Could this be my time?

Through The Jam's influence, two of my friends and I had started a band with me on bass guitar. It was the guitarist, Andy, who actually managed to get me a ticket for my first ever gig, the second night at Birmingham's Bingley Hall on 21st March.

The build up to this epic occasion had been frenetic, with each passing day excited teenage discussion as to what songs would be played, what would they open with, what would they wear?

Bingley Hall was an aging, huge open space building in Birmingham's city centre, built originally for exhibitions and now, owing to the Jam's growing popularity, was one of the few places in town big enough to cope with 5,000 plus fans.

It was pretty busy when we pulled up outside, with Mods sporting all sorts of Weller haircuts, Jam shoes, boating blazers and many fishtail parkas, which I did question may be a little over dressed for a gig.

We made our way as close to the front as was possible. The building had a number of pillars that obstructed the view if you were unlucky to be badly positioned. It was at that point we realised that the gig was to be filmed, a real rarity in those days.

The stage had a huge black banner strewn across it with the words 'Trans Global Unity Express' written on it. It was dark and had two huge stacks of Marshall amps positioned for Paul and Bruce, while Rick's massive ivory drum kit sat up on the riser awaiting his presence. The DJ and huge Jam fan Gary Crowley was playing a warm up act to the gig by spinning Northern Soul and Motown Classics, a nice touch. But the crowd were there for one thing, and one thing only – the trio from Woking.

The impatience in the crowd was noticeable as the clock ticked by. There was an almost football crowd feeling in the audience as people pushed to get forwards.

Soon the lights went down and John Weller appeared on stage to announce the now famous line of, 'Put your hands together for the best band in the fucking world - the Jam'. The band walked on stage and I thought, 'Oh my god, what's Weller done with his Marriot haircut?'

He had trimmed the 'curtains' for a short French crew cut and was wearing a black mohair suit, bowling shoes and a white Lonsdale t-shirt. After a courtesy greeting - 'Fank you' - to the crowd, they tore into my then most favourite track 'Strange Town' – I couldn't actually believe I was there.

The pushing was violent and constant while the power of the sound was completely amazing and very, very loud. I could actually feel the bass pulse beating in my chest. I had positioned myself in line with Bruce on the right hand side, about ten people deep from the front. As a bass player myself, I watched his fingers moving up and down his Fender Precision bass with fascination.

The roar of the crowd was huge after the first song and the band moved straight into 'Carnation', a real contrast without stopping for air. Song after song was reeled off in high tempo bursts of energy. Weller had brought in a two piece brass section to give a more soul approach to the sound and this was used to best effect when Weller announced, 'This is one of Rick's songs' with a real sense of irony and they played the Curtis Mayfield classic 'Move On Up', a new song for the band to play live and the first time I had heard that amazing tune.

The set was a mix of popular live tracks, eight from *The Gift* and songs that have since turned out to be Jam classics – 'The Butterfly Collector', 'When You're Young', 'Private Hell' and 'Tales From The Riverbank'.

Fans' favourites that were missing I suppose were 'Going Underground' and 'Tube Station', but you can't have it all!

Two things really stood out to me at the gig. Firstly, everyone was dancing, more of a 'pogo' actually, but I mean every one front to back, side to side - all 5,000 of them. I've been to hundreds of excitable gigs since and there's always a graduated divide between the mosh pit and the curious standers by at the back. This was none of that, and despite the aggression in the pushing there was a unity amongst the fans who were there. I have often since quoted that the place wouldn't get a safety licence these days and that it was a wonder no one got seriously hurt.

The other thing that stood out was the haze of sweat rising from the crowd, which was visible in the strobe lighting. It was seriously cold outside; indeed there was snow. It was seriously hot inside Bingley Hall. I had a blazer and Hush Puppies on at the time and both were literally wringing wet at the end.

Two days after, I caught a monumental cold from the extreme drop in temperature outside the gig.

I saw the Jam again at the same place on 8th December of the same year. Sadly it was their farewell and although another top night it left the word 'Why?' on most peoples' lips.

Looking back at my tickets from those two nights brings back amazing memories of the band. It's also interesting that they cost the princely sum of £4.50 and £5 respectively - what great value.

I did follow Weller with the Style Council afterwards and his pretty amazing (until *22 Dreams*, that is) solo career. The lasting part for me was that the band, primarily Weller, shaped my fashion and social outlook for many years. I even used his lyrics in my English exams and fared pretty well out of them. Nearly 40 years on, I feel lucky and proud to have been a part of it, lucky also that my first ever gig was captured on film. But overall, to really know The Jam was to see them live and I did – twice.

DEESIDE LEISURE CENTRE

27 MARCH 1982, DEESIDE, UK

I WAS THERE: BRIAN SOUTHERN

In 1980, in my final few months before leaving school, my record collection probably consisted of half a dozen singles and one LP, *Parallel Lines* by Blondie. I don't think I had heard of The Jam at this time although I had heard of the song 'Eton Rifles' – I just wasn't aware of who sang it. My mate Ian had an older brother, Dave, who was three years older than me, and an apprentice engineer at ICI. Dave was into his music and groups like the Stranglers, The Clash and the Skids. One day when I was round at Ian's he took me up to show me his brother's brand new Akai stack system and played me this record called 'Going Underground'. He told me, 'This record is number one in the charts.' I remember thinking how great the brand new picture sleeve looked - all my records were just in plain sleeves. I thought, 'I must get this record.'

The following Saturday I was out on my Saturday job as a van lad on a bread round and as soon as I was finished I was off to the local hardware shop where they sold the chart singles. The shop was known locally as 'Johnny One Eye's' as the guy who owned it had a glass eye.

'Have you got the new single by The Jam?' I asked. He had one left but it was only in a plain sleeve. He said he only got a few in picture sleeves, which were limited editions in those days. I had to have it.

Later that year I got my first job on a YTS scheme at ICI at £23.50 a week. Luckily for me, after a couple of weeks cycling to work, Dave said I could travel to work with him. Dave had a MK1 purple Ford Escort Mexico which had recently had fitted a sharp stereo cassette player.

This is when I really got into The Jam as Dave used to play the *Sound Affects* album every day on the way to and from work. I used to love the way the sound of the fly buzzing around on 'Music for the Last Couple' used to move from speaker to speaker.

Sound Affects was the first Jam album I bought and can remember playing it continually on my record player while playing darts in my bedroom with the arm off so it would keep playing over and over. I then spent the few months or so trying to get The Jam's back catalogue, not an easy job back then.

I got to see them live for the first time at Deeside Leisure Centre on the *Gift* tour in 1982 and then saw them twice more in the autumn at Liverpool where we got in to see the sound check and at Bingley Hall.

I would to have loved to have said I was into The Jam from 1977 but those two years from 1980 to 1982 seemed like a lifetime at the time and the music has been a soundtrack to my life. Even today not many days pass without hearing The Jam.

OPERA HOUSE

28 MARCH 1982, BLACKPOOL, UK

I WASN'T THERE: STEPHANIE HAUBER, AGE 13

The Jam were playing at the Opera House. They only played Blackpool once. I was 13 years old. My best friend talked me into camping outside the Winter Gardens over night to queue for tickets for The Jam as she fancied an older boy who was definitely going to be there to get tickets.

I did love the music, as everyone did, and just being part of the crowd was enough at that age. After lying to our parents about what we were going to be doing, we spent nearly all night freezing with all the cool older kids but had to give in and go home as we were just freezing children with no money.

The next day there was a story in the *Evening Gazette* about the fans queuing all night with a picture of the queue and I remember thinking thank god we had left. I'd love to see that picture in the *Gazette* archive if they still had it. There were lots of kids I would recognise and some of the names too. I did go on to see Paul Weller three times in my mature years but I will never forget that night.

I WAS THERE: STEVE JONES

I saw them many times but the two concerts that stick out and remember well are Blackpool and Paris.

What I remember about the Blackpool concert is that we were in the seating location balcony and when Paul, Bruce and Rick came on stage the whole place went crazy - everybody dancing jumping up and down and you could feel the balcony moving. It was that bad the security were asking us all to sit down, which never happened.

TOP RANK

29 MARCH 1982, SHEFFIELD, UK

I WAS THERE: DAVID WILSON

It was 1982. I had just left school, with no job or money. I had just started on a YOP scheme. The Jam were coming to the Top Rank in Sheffield. Having no ticket I thought I would go down in the afternoon and see the sound check. Getting there early, myself and many other fans hung around waiting for the band to arrive. While waiting I got talking to another guy that said he was from Manchester and couldn't make the concert and was trying to sell his ticket. 'Hold on to that ticket,' I told him and dashed home. Mum gave me the £16. Going back into Sheffield sat on the bus, I had the dreadful thought he may have been a tout and already sold the ticket and I might have missed the sound check as well. But he was still there with the ticket and we both got to see the band set up. It was a great night at a packed venue.

Sadly that was the one and only time I got to see The Jam together. Since then I have seen The Style Council at Sheffield City Hall and Bruce Foxton a few times at the Octagon, Sheffield University. More recently I have seen From The Jam a couple of times at the O2 in Sheffield, which is the old Top Rank building. It brought a lot of memories from that Jam concert back with Russell Hastings filling some very large shoes and giving an excellent performance - but not the same.

Jam fans are very diehard and after the band split in 1982 there was a pub in the centre of Sheffield called the Dove and Rainbow. This was the only boozer in Sheffield that had a full page of all the Jam songs and LPs as well on their jukebox. In the evenings, especially Sunday night, the pub was full of Mods in their gear with Weller and Foxton lookalikes and with Jam songs playing all night.

QUEENS EXHIBITION HALL

1 APRIL 1982, LEEDS, UK

I WAS THERE: STUART FREEMAN

The original 'spit and sawdust' music venue in Leeds, the Queens was the fourth biggest venue in the UK at the time, but my god it was a shambolic place. I remember looking up at the stars through the holes in the roof. It was anything but fit for royalty, showing the signs of its former life as a derelict tram shed right up until it stopped hosting gigs in the early Eighties. It was demolished in 1989 and used for a number of ventures since. It played host to a number of music's top acts including Kiss, Pink Floyd, The Clash, The Who and The Rolling Stones. Sure the acoustics were crap but nobody cared.

What I remember is it was so crammed full my feet were off the ground the whole gig and you just moved with the sway of the crowd. The floor melted so your shoes were covered in blue paint. I remember my mate lost his slip-on Hush Puppies in the crush and was reunited with them at the end of the night. The band were playing songs from the new album, *The Gift*, and everyone wanted to hear the well known songs. I remember Wellers response to the umpteenth shouted request for 'Down at the Tube Station at Midnight': 'It's nineteen eighty fucking two not 1978, grow up!' The support band The Questions were booed and bottled off.

I WAS THERE: GRAHAM CLARK

I saw The Jam only once – at the Queens Hall in Leeds. It was around the time of *The Gift* in 1982, shortly before the band broke up. The Queens Hall was the only big venue left in Leeds. During the day it was still an undercover car park and the place used to be a tram shed! The gig was hot and sweaty and the energy from the stage crossed over to the audience.

By this time the group were coming to an end and Paul Weller was rediscovering his Motown influences, which were to be fully discovered with The Style Council. I recall the band had a brass section on stage with them too. It was the first and last time I ever saw The Jam but I remember it well – they were very tight. It was a big celebration to go out on.

I WAS THERE: PETER FLETCHER

For some reason it was always just the two of us, my friend Mark and myself. We had lots of mates but it was like The Jam were ours.

It was like a repeat of the last queue experience - we weren't quite the first this time but we decided to wait by the right hand door because that one opened first last time. There were more fans early this time and we chatted to a lot of them, playing I Spy and all sorts of other tedious games to pass the day by. We warned the other fans about time slowing down nearer the opening time and it wasn't long before they were agreeing with us. Eventually the right hand door opened and we were in before the left door opened. We headed straight for the souvenir stall, bought a t-shirt and programme each, and we bought a plastic bag each to put the souvenirs in which we put under our shirts which we then tucked into our trousers.

This time we didn't go right to the front, aiming for the middle of the crowd. Red Lorry Yellow Lorry, a local band were on first. I had heard of them but none of their songs. There was another band on called The Questions - I think they didn't interest me whoever they were and were forgettable in my opinion. I just wanted my Jam fix.

The Jam came on stage but there was a difference this time - a horn section. I remember Mike Reid on the radio playing 'The Circus' on the radio - it was instrumental and had horns in it. He told the listeners that they would not believe who it was. I guessed correctly. I knew he was a Jam fan and their new album *The Gift* was released that day. But he was right - it was a different sound. The concert was brilliant even with the extra guys on stage. It was still The Jam. They did some old songs and of course the new album. Mark and I managed to get to the second row. We were up close again. Paul was dressed slightly differently with his scarf, while Bruce in his suit and Rick was wearing his polo shirt. It was a great concert but I felt the other two with their raw rough around the edges sound were better. Looking back I think that was the sign they were going to move in different directions.

When I heard 'Beat Surrender' was going to be the final single I was gutted - devastated was the word, and it was exactly how we felt. I hated the song. It signified the end of a way of life. We would have nothing to look forward to now.

Later the final tour was announced with two dates at Wembley. The Queens Hall was closed or demolished so by now we had no venue big enough in Leeds.

We decided not to go to Wembley - the band would be too far away and there would be too many people. I went to Cavendish Travel in Leeds. They specialised in concert tickets with travel to and from the venue. They had a trip to Bridlington, which was immediately after the Wembley concerts so I bought those. Meanwhile Wembley had three more dates added due to the demand for tickets.

I WAS THERE: CHRIS DUNN

I was 12 years old when I first heard 'Going Underground' on the radio one Wednesday morning while getting ready for school. It had gone straight to number one in the charts, which was a big deal back then. I had been listening to punk for a while with some older lads on the street I lived on. I liked the Sex Pistols, The Damned, The Clash, etc. but 'Going Underground' seemed a more polished sound and I was impressed when I saw they were a three piece producing that wall of sound.

Chris Dunn saw The Jam at the Queen's Exhibition Hall, Leeds

I bought the *Setting Sons* album and played it to death. I followed up buying 'Strange Town' and 'When You're Young' singles and loved the guitar sound. By this time I loved the Jam and Weller in particular. Whatever Weller said I went along with. I bought *Sound Affects* when it was released and quickly realised this was a different musical direction from the earlier stuff. I found it a little harder to get into, although 'Man in the Corner Shop' remains one of my favourite Jam songs.

I did my high school English language talk on The Jam and at the end played 'Funeral Pyre' to a mainly nonplussed English class.

Then came along *The Gift* and the news they would be splitting up came shortly after. I liked *The Gift* but *Dig The New Breed* was the album I had been waiting for. For me it captured the essence of The Jam, raw but polished at the same time.

The Gift tour was the farewell tour and I bought tickets along with two excited 14 year old friends, one of whom didn't end up going after contracting shingles and being too ill to go. I was blown away by them actually playing the songs I loved so much right in front of me. Not only was it my first ever concert but it was The Jam! I recall the crowd chanting, 'Tube Station, Tube Station' and Weller stating, 'Its my concert - I'll sing what

I fucking like' and not playing it. I was gutted because it was the song I most wanted to hear.

It remains one of the best gigs I have ever been to. My daughter recently bought me a vinyl LP of that tour which brings back some wonderful memories.

All too quickly The Jam were no more and I eagerly anticipated Weller's new project and The Style Council's first single, 'Speak Like A Child'. I remember seeing it performed on *Top of the Pops* and instantly hating, maybe unfairly, Mick Talbot for (in my mind) being the reason The Jam split up.

I still have a Jam playlist on my Spotify and it still seems fresh and real. The Jam set me up for the music I now listen to - Stone Roses, Ride, Pigeon Detectives, The Rifles, etc. A lot of my favourite bands – Stone Roses, Ride - have reformed and done tours around the world, including New Zealand where I now live, and I have been lucky enough to see them. I would love The Jam to reform one day but I know deep down it will never happen. Maybe it's a good thing. I would hate the memories I have to be tarnished by some half-hearted 'Top Up The Pensions' tour.

CITY HALL

3 APRIL 1982, NEWCASTLE UPON TYNE, UK

I WAS THERE: PETER SMITH

The Jam were back at the City Hall, this time supported by The Questions, who were signed to Paul Weller's record label. They also wrote some songs for Weller protégé Tracie Young (aka Tracie).

The ticket also mentions a local support act, but I'm afraid I can't remember who that was.

By 1982 The Jam had released six albums, and had hit the charts many times, including three number ones. 'Town Called Malice' was number one in 1982, and the band were riding the crest of a wave. However Paul Weller was beginning to feel that this was the end of The Jam and the band was soon to disband. I would see The Jam, once more. Looking back this band left a legacy of great singles, and some great live performances.

APOLLO

7 APRIL 1982, GLASGOW, UK

I WAS THERE: STUART MCDONALD

What a gig this was. I went with two mates and it was the first time any of us had been to the Apollo. The atmosphere was electric. Three and half thousand fans going nuts, I'd never experienced anything like it before - or since. Walking home we were soaking wet but it didn't matter. We knew we'd witnessed something very special.

It was from this night that the live recordings of 'Going Underground', 'Dreams of

Children', 'That's Entertainment' and 'Private Hell' were made and used on the live album *Dig The New Breed*.

I WAS THERE: MANDY SCOTT

I live in Glasgow and saw them at the Apollo twice and then Ingleston in Edinburgh that same year 1982. I had to bunk off school to get the tickets and although the Glasgow gigs were local getting to Edinburgh was on an organised bus, unbeknown to my parents. Boating blazer and Fred Perry as an outfit my friend and I thought we were the coolest girls ever.

My brother in law is my biggest musical influence and he bought me *All Mod Cons* which was the start of me going every week into town to buy a single in order to have the full collection. Including trying to get as many picture covers as I could. I still have them!

I love 'The Butterfly Collector', 'That's Entertainment', 'Strange Town' and 'Down in the Tube Station', which are all personal favourites. I've told my husband my funeral song needs to be 'Going Underground'.

JOHANESHOVS ISSTADION

16 APRIL 1982, STOCKHOLM, SWEDEN

I WAS THERE: SANDRA MEDIN, AGE 13

I discovered The Jam in 1980, at a Girl Scout camp in the archipelago in Stockholm, Sweden. We were camping on the lawn by our leader's summerhouse and were supposed to go hiking and do what Scouts usually do, but it rained most of the time. So we ended up in the summerhouse, bored, with nothing to do. A disaster for 13 year olds. There was a record player in the sitting room, and a pile of records. We listened to Peter Gabriel, David Bowie and The Jam for the first time. And I liked it, all of it. I still listen to these artists today. But The Jam is my number one band – and always will be.

Sound Affects is my favourite album, and the first album by The Jam that I bought. When I lived in a flat and my neighbours would play loud music, I would play 'Set the House Ablaze' on full blast to shut them up. It worked every time. And I got to listen to one of my favourite songs. I like all their albums, but *Setting Sons* is probably my number two. So many great songs.

I saw The Jam live in Stockholm on 16 April 1982 at Johanneshovs Isstadion. The ticket cost 85 Swedish kronor. I went to the concert with my classmate Karin Johansson, who had also been at the Scout camp. It was the *Trans Global Unity Express* tour. I don't recall exactly which songs they played, but I remember that I felt a bit disappointed that they mostly played songs from their brand new album *The Gift*. But I fell instantly in love with 'A Town Called Malice', and 'Precious' and 'Carnation' are now some of my favourite songs. And when they played 'That's Entertainment' I was as happy as can be. When the concert was over, we had to take the underground home, and the walkway was full of large groups of skinheads looking for some Mods to bash. We just slipped past them without any trouble.

I probably have The Jam, and especially Paul Weller, to thank for my career. We learn English from third grade in Sweden, and when I started listening to The Jam, I wanted to speak like Paul Weller. The lyrics taught me lots of words and expressions that we didn't learn in school. I developed an interest in languages and studied at universities in Sweden and Spain. I now work as a freelance translator, translating non-fiction and fiction from English and Spanish into Swedish. My interest in languages is most likely due to the great music and lyrics of The Jam.

'It's nice to be your own boss, really.'

PARADISO

24 APRIL 1982, AMSTERDAM, NETHERLANDS

I WAS THERE: CAROL LINTOTT, AGE 18

I was 18 and The Jam featured greatly in my life. My older sister was a fan and my two younger step brothers were Mods so it goes without saying they were fans too. Music from The Jam was played non-stop in our house. As the band were from Woking, which is relatively local to us, we felt an greater affiliation with them than other artists around at that time.

Having been to many gigs to see them, myself, my sister and two friends saved up to go to one of the two gigs in Amsterdam in April 1982. We arrived in London at Victoria Station in what we thought was good time to join our coach trip which had been specially commissioned to take budding fans to Amsterdam for the gig with a hotel stay. Turns out we were 12 hours late, the 24 hour clock was not widely used in those days and I got my AM and PM mixed up. Needless to say I was not popular! Never defeated I found that the next magic bus out of Victoria was headed for Amsterdam, so we forked out a further £15 each for our tickets and travelled overnight, missing out on the hotel stay.

We arrived early at the Paradiso to try to find our original coach group and to our amazement we were allowed in for the sound check - what a treat! That and the gig itself was absolutely fantastic, we had the best time.

At the venue in Amsterdam. Left to right, Carol Lintott, Phillip Cleeve and Carol's sister, Sue Rutter (nee Lintott)

The stand out song for me on the night would be 'Pretty Green'. It was and is my sister's favourite and so we went a bit mad for that.

We met up with our coach group just before the gig and made sure we were on the coach for the journey home, which was much less stressful!

We saw the band a couple more times in Guildford and Portsmouth, then later came the devastating news that Paul was breaking up the band. In December 1982 we attended the very last gig at the Brighton Centre. It was very, very emotional. Such a sad day but again, a fantastic gig never, ever to be rivalled.

The Jam on stage at The Paradiso

I still listen to all the albums, remember all the words and sing along. The music has surely stood the test of time and I love it!

I WAS THERE: EDWARD BIJL VAN DUIJVENBODE, AGE 17

As a 12 year neat Dutch boy I went in August 1977 from a middle class area elementary school in Amsterdam to a high school in a rather posh area of the city. The future seemed pretty bright and uncluttered. Although an average, neat and rather shy boy, musically I really hated most of the hit parade stuff - Smokie, Guys and Dolls, ABBA, Boney M, George Baker Selection, Father Abraham, Showaddywaddy, Bay City Rollers. I couldn't associate myself with these broadly smiling idiots.

The first record of The Jam I bought was *This Is The Modern World.* I think it must have been somewhere in 1978. It was a rush-recorded album as a follow up of their debut album *In The City*. So at first it didn't convince me, but the good thing about it was that it sounded different from the rest of the punk bands. I heard some strong Beatles/Who influences, which I knew, because my two sisters had those Sixties records. I can remember being four and five years old when I listened to those records when my sisters played them on their small turntable.

I also can remember listening to a Jam single 'All Around The World' and two lines I can remember very well:

'What's the point in saying destroy? I want a new life for everywhere'.

I give Paul Weller credit for writing this and so many other great lyrics about the situation in England. I think he had started already then to refrain from nihilism and too simple 'solutions'. He was damn serious, he meant what he said and wrote. That's a thing I will always remember about The Jam.

Musically they went from punk pop to power pop with some punk influences. Leaving the key principles of what punk should be. No more three chords on steroids, but great Sixties influenced turbo power pop music. Going their own way, going their way to success. They were often accused of being too British. But that's just the reason why I loved them so much.

In April 1982 I turned 17. Just a week after my birthday the best present would come to Amsterdam as part of their *Trans-Global Express Tour*. The Jam really became popular in the Netherlands after playing the 1980 Pinkpop festival and their single 'Going Underground'. So it was no surprise that the three gigs (two in Amsterdam, one in Nijmegen, near the German border) were sold out in no time. 'A Town Called Malice' was also a smash hit over here. Luckily I got my ticket on time.

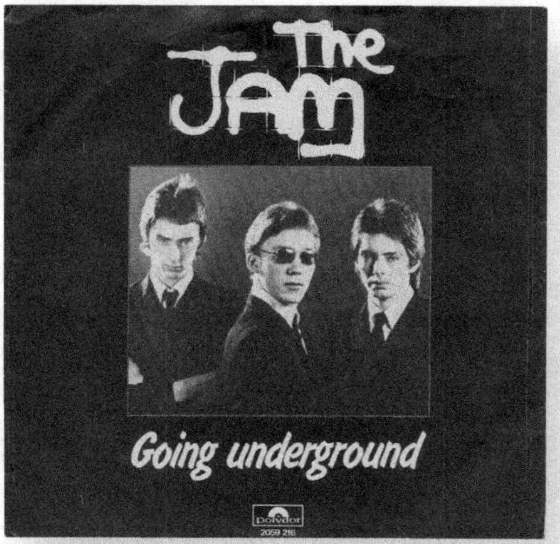

Saturday's kids went on the 24th of April 1982 to the former church named Paradiso. I can remember that myself and a school mate went quite early to the venue, hoping to see Paul, Bruce and Rick, maybe smoking a cigarette outside? I didn't see them, but I recognised some wild bearded guys between the huge trucks. I think it must have been Kenny Wheeler and Dave Liddle. But it seemed impossible to reach the band so we decided to go to the entrance. When we were inside the venue we immediately went to the front row, but there were already five or six rows of impatiently waiting fans right in front of us. When we had accepted this fact I looked at both sides of the relatively small stage. It wasn't really smaller than other occasions, but The Jam took a monstrous PA system with them so it thought we would be blown away. In a split second I thought we were attending a Motörhead gig. No sleep till Paradiso!

The support act was a Dutch band called Dance In Armour. All I can remember was that they were very nervous. Maybe because there were a lot of English fans among the audience and they were great, but also very noisy!

After the stage change-over Paul's dad ran onto the stage and did his famous yell: 'Put your hands togetheeeeer, for the best fucking band in the wooooooorld: The Jaaaaaaaammmmmmmm!!!' Paul wore a black Fred Perry suit, Bruce wore a grey suit and a red shirt and Rick wore an odd looking blue/white striped shirt. Starting the set list's first song, 'The Eton Rifles', it felt like all hell broke loose. The audience went nuts and as far as you could talk about moshpits or slam-dancing in 1982, it was sure that this is what happened. Paul's 'Jimi Hendrix act' (sawing or scraping with the guitar at the side of the guitar amp) during that song felt like it would last forever. It was very clear from the first second that this band had come to Amsterdam to tear off the roof of the former church. And that's exactly what happened.

'Running On The Spot', 'Trans-Global Unity Express', 'Pretty Green', 'Malice', 'Move On Up', 'Precious', 'Alfie' - each song was sung intensely. The English fans were fantastic, singing 'We are the Mods!' and waving their Union Jack. It felt sometimes a bit strange. Loving your country and hating it at the same time. But that's what I liked about them. And of course they didn't hate their country. They hated the predicament where they have got into the depressing situation through no fault of their own.

Talking about highlights is quite difficult, but if I had to call one the highlight I think it was 'That's Entertainment'. That song proved that this band didn't need a loud amplifier or loud drums to impress. Just two acoustic guitars (Bruce played also a six string) and some modest drumming. No fifty chord changes and modulations. And it was even written in 15 minutes as far as the story goes. 'The tranquillity of solitude', simple, but brilliant lyrics, a powerful and timeless song. If a song works on just an acoustic guitar you know it's good.

Was it all rosy and fun that night? No, to be honest it wasn't. Maybe it's a question of taste, but in my opinion the horn parts didn't match with the rest of the band and sounded very thin, far too thin. In the studio it worked well, but live there were maybe three or four wind instruments needed. There were no samplers in these days. That's a thing I kept always wondering about Weller, in particular after his Jam days. Please, do it right or don't do it at all. But of course, that's just my point of view.

I'm not sure, but I think they finished the set with 'The Gift'. I vaguely remember that the last sung words were the same words where Paul started the gig: One, Two, Three, Fourrrrrrr!!!

After the gig we were dazed. Really drugged without taking any drugs. I can't remember whether I bought something at the merchandise stand. But there's one thing I can remember very well: I desperately wanted the advert, the poster made by the (in Amsterdam world famous) Englishman Martin Kaye (London 1932-Amsterdam 1989), known as 'Martin the Mobile Maker'. I asked the Paradiso staff if I could get that poster, but they couldn't get one or they were too busy to pick it up for me. I was very disappointed, because the night felt historic and I wanted something as a trophy to remember. But a few days after the gig I went to a record shop called Boudisque, near Central Station. I remember staring or pointing at exactly the same poster at the front door. A lovely shop girl asked if I had attended the gig. 'Yes, of course it was great, wasn't it?', assuming she was there too. The girl said 'If you like the poster you may have it!' In my fantasy I kissed her a thousand times, but of course that wasn't part of the deal (unfortunately), but I could grab the poster from the front door window and take it with me. I did that very carefully. Maybe this was an even better present for my birthday than the gig itself!

Of course the shop girl couldn't know then that these so called Paradiso posters, made by Martin Kaye, are sold nowadays for hundreds of pounds at auction sites.

But that story left in later years a slightly bitter taste in my mouth. Martin Kaye was murdered in Amsterdam in 1989. The killer was caught in 2004 by chance in Austria while robbing a church.

Even so, the framed poster remains such a nice memento of that wonderful gig in Amsterdam played by the fantastic three men of Woking, Surrey and supported by their fantastic English fans. We are the Mods!

CIRCUS ROYAL

27 APRIL 1982, BRUSSELS, BELGIUM

I WAS THERE: GAVIN JONES

This trip started with a late train (on my own again!) to London Euston, then Victoria where I arrived about 3am for a 7am departure I met four other Jam fans from Worcester on the train so had company, along with about 20 others at Victoria, all from the north of England. We all had a good laugh trying to get some sleep, but not succeeding! As time went by others turned up to fill the five coaches, and off we went at seven in the morning. Our coach broke down so we were 20 minutes behind the rest, not a good start! The trip to Dover had The Jam playing on the sound system non-stop and we were all really getting in the mood.

On the ferry we changed some cash then went to the bar. A group of about 20 of us sat round singing Jam songs and drinking. Some holiday makers couldn't understand why we were going abroad to see a group. I guess you just can't explain The Jam feeling under your skin that draws you like moths to a flame! On the coach again at Calais where two lads got left behind and then spent loads getting to Brussels on a train, and then on the two and a half hour trip to a service station outside Brussels. A few toilet stops along the way, where we had some food, then into the gig.

The whole place looked a bit rough and run down, with a lot of road works, but we got our tickets on the coach then had an hour to kill before going into the rough looking concert hall. There was a big local police presence as Aston Villa had been there two weeks before and smashed the place up, so they weren't looking forward to another load of English fans. They had big riot sticks, adding to the imposing atmosphere.

When we got inside, it reminded me of a smaller, scruffier De Montford Hall, with a stage at one end and balcony all round with no seats. I decided to go upstairs for this one, right next to the stage, to get a different view to usual. There were a lot of Belgium Mods, skins and punks, which gave a good charged atmosphere like some of the punk gigs from a few years before. There were Union Jacks dotted around the crowd and stage, giving a patriotic feel, made more so when the Belgium crowd started singing 'Argentina' to taunt the Brits as the Falklands War was on at the time.

Eventually The Jam came on and delivered a fantastic gig. The set was similar to the *Gift* tour in the UK, with a few more older songs thrown in but all delivered with extra aggression and Weller was supreme! I was glad I picked the balcony, as all the way through the skins were fighting downstairs, and chants of England kept the atmosphere charged. At one point Paul said over the chants, 'Here's a song about fucking England', and did brand new song 'The Great Depression'. Once the main gig finished they came on for five encores, including 'Butterfly Collector' and 'David Watts'.

It was a really fantastic gig and great atmosphere. Then we had to go outside and wait for the coaches, which meant the skins started kicking off and the police came in with the batons hitting a few Brits. I just ducked out of the way of one. It was all over the top. I managed to grab a poster off the wall outside and stuff it under my coat. After a long trip back I got home in the Midlands around 4pm the next day, totally knackered, but elated at a great gig and great experience.

PANTIN HIPPODROME

29 APRIL 1982, PARIS, FRANCE

Steve Jones with the Modfather

I WAS THERE: STEVE JONES

(AKA The Modfather of Liverpool Lost Boys Scooter Club).

For Paris in 1982 I travelled by coach from my hometown Liverpool – the first time I ever went abroad. I was nervous but looking forward to the concert. Meeting the three band members outside the venue was great and having a cheap camera to catch the memories. Inside the venue you could feel the tension between the Brits and the French. The song I will always remember is the 'Strange Town', which I had found myself in. Again the whole place went crazy.

THE COLISEUM

24 MAY 1982, TORONTO, CANADA

I WAS THERE: TIM NICHOLLS

All I remember was total energy and sweat and then it was over and I was thinking it was the greatest show I'd ever attended! Still in my top five all timers. I still spin the records regular!

MICHIGAN THEATRE

25 MAY 1982, MICHIGAN

I WAS THERE: DAVID SKIDMORE

I loved The Jam, particularly when I was young. I grew up in Michigan, and I think I was the only person in my school who knew they existed. I bought *Setting Sons* in a bargain bin because I read about them in *Creem* magazine. At first it was weird, it was so English, but I grew to love it. 'Strange Town', and 'Thick as Thieves' are universal, once you get used to the presentation.

After *Sound Affects*, I was obsessed. I loved that album and still do. *Snap* was a particular pleasure, great music and they were so smartly dressed!

I saw them live at the Michigan theatre three weeks after I graduated from high school. So amazing, there was an incredible power, which I think was my youth in the end. I was very upset when I learned they had split, but in the end it was probably the right decision. We all have to grow up - Weller and me both.

ARAGON BALLROOM

26 MAY 1982, CHICAGO, ILLINOIS

I WAS THERE: ERIC BEAUMONT

Weller bashed his teeth on the microphone, slammed down his Rickenbacker to the ground (it landed flat with no apparent damage), and then stormed offstage. He reappeared within a minute, just blazing with intensity.

PERKINS PALACE

29 MAY 1982, PASADENA, CALIFORNIA

I WAS THERE: SANDY WACHS

Music has always been an important part of my life. In the Seventies I was listening to the basic rock that my skateboarder friends all listened to. Basic rock 'n' roll but I tended to be drawn to music that wasn't really being played on the radio. Around that time of my senior year in high school everything changed. First Quiet Riot with Randy Rhoads played in the auditorium for a Friday night concert (and I was blown away). And then it happened. I discovered punk rock. The energy was explosive. Me and a few of my close skate friends dropped anything that had to do with the old rock we used to listen to and dove head first into the growing punk rock scene. I had discovered an energy and a mindset that shaped me into the person I am today.

We also discovered local Los Angeles DJ Rodney Bigenheimer and his local radio show *Rodney on the Roq*. It was here we discovered all kinds of new music. Myself, and my friends would travel to Hollywood which was about 30 minutes away to see bands every weekend and sometimes during the week.

I first heard The Jam on Rodney's show - it was either 'In The City' or 'Going Underground'. I'm not sure which but I loved them instantly.

Though not a punk band they had this raw energy that I loved. Loud and raw with lyrics to match. I bought every album they put out.

I was finally able to see them in May of 1982 which was *The Gift* tour at Perkins Palace in Pasadena California, a suburb of Los Angeles. Me, my girlfriend at the time and a few friends piled into my friend's car and drove the 45 minutes to the show.

The Jam hit the stage full of energy, blasting into 'Running on the Spot'. Of course they had everyone on their feet for the whole show even during the slower numbers.

The songs that stood out to me were 'Running on the Spot', 'Start!', 'Town Called

Malice', and one of course one of my all time favourite songs, 'That's Entertainment'.

Though I wished I could have seen them earlier on, this was still a great show that I will never forget and The Jam are still on my music playlists today.

The Dutch import of 'Just Who Is the 5 O'Clock Hero?' peaked at number eight in the UK singles charts in July 1982. 'The Bitterest Pill (I Ever Had to Swallow)' was released on 6 September 1982, peaking at number two, for two weeks unable to dislodge 'Eye of the Tiger' by Survivor and 'Pass the Dutchie' by Musical Youth from the top spot.

KERRISDALE ARENA

5 JUNE 1982, VANCOUVER, CANADA

I WAS THERE: VIC GAILIUNAS

It's 1982 and my high school graduation weekend in Edmonton, Alberta, but The Jam are performing in Vancouver, British Columbia (the next province over in Canada). So I leave shortly after the Grad dinner and my Mod band - who worship Weller & co. covering tons of their tunes - and our roadie (which was exactly 80% of all Mods in Edmonton at the time – turns out we bumped into the other guy/20% at the show!) fly off to Vancouver and cram into a hotel room, which none of us are legally allowed to book at our tender ages.

We head to The Jam's soundcheck and the band lets the 30 of us hardcore fans in! We're literally right up against the stage front. After the check, we get autographs on the English pound notes we have brought and head for a bite before the show, ecstatic at our industriousness and good fortune.

Half an hour later while queued up at the front of the Kerrisdale Arena, I realise I've lost my autographed pound note! We rush back to the fast food place but no luck. I'm absolutely beside myself but what could I do?

We head into the gig and it's absolutely brilliant. It turns out, unbeknownst to us and likely even Foxton and Buckler, that this is their last North American show before they split up. They play a great selection of tunes, which, since we all knew literally every one of them by heart, was a given.

After the show, we're hanging out behind the arena waiting for them to run out to their tour bus. A Jam roadie comes out about 20 minutes later and says if you want to meet The Jam, come around to this door on the side of the building. A bunch of

Vic Gailiunas (center) in his group The Mods

fans make their way, but us, being suspicious this is a ruse so they can get into their bus unscathed, stay put. About five minutes later, the ones who went to the side door still haven't come back so we figure it just might be real. We head over and sure enough, we're let in for a five minute walk through the dressing room to sit with each of them for a minute or two, ask questions and get stuff signed! Out come our programmes, my *The Gift* t-shirt and more pound notes. Twice lucky I guess - or just the rock n' roll gods wishing me a happy Grad.

To this day, I have my t-shirt with all their autographs and the fab memory of that trip, although my Grad date was not quite as thrilled. I share a birthday with Weller, still play Mod-influenced power pop with my band and wore a *Start!* t-shirt at our last gig so, yeah, guess you could say I'm a fan.

I WAS THERE: DAN BARACH

Going to the show I noticed a lot of Vespa's and Lamberts parked outside. The Jam played a blinder that night. There were a couple of black gents in the coolest suits doused in purple light on trumpet and sax off to the side. One of the best shows I ever saw.

After the show I went to a Mod party in some mansion with lots of mods and cool chicks dressed in Mod gear. Partied till the early hours. Probably one of the best parties I ever went to. Tremendous R&B Sixties music blasting and the cutest, hip, knowledgeable girls in mini skirts, striped tops and officer hats! I felt like it was 1963 all over again. What a memorable night!

SHOWERING PAVILION

21 SEPT 1982, SHEPTON MALLET, UK

Guy Helliker age 15 who went on to work with Bruce Foxton

I WAS THERE: GUY HELLIKER, AGE 15

I was lucky enough to see The Jam twice. I was 15 at the time and I can say it certainly say it changed my life! My very first gig. I was on holiday in Somerset and sat in Taunton bus station going through the *NME* I saw an ad showing tickets were on sale from a record shop just around the corner. I ran there and handed over my last tenner of holiday money and patiently waited five weeks for the gig.

I recall it was an exciting atmosphere with parkas everywhere. I had sweat soaking through my Lonsdale sweatshirt. My main memory was someone throwing a glass cider bottle at the stage a shattering when it hit Rick's drum riser. Paul pointed, shouting 'You cunt', and then a mini riot broke out at the front.

My brother who drove me there wanted to go early to see his girlfriend at home so he had to drag me away half way through 'Trans-global Express' so I missed the encores including 'Funeral Pyre' and 'Eton Rifles'!

Guy Helliker with Russell Hastings and Bruce Foxton at The Jam Exhibition

The next day at school everyone wanted to know every detail - the set list, what everyone was wearing and what merch I bought. An amazing experience!

Almost 40 years later I now run Bruce's From The Jam websites and social media and see From The Jam whenever I can. I've gone from a fan to part of the team and I'm often seen at gigs running the merchandise. I even filled in briefly as Bruce's guitar tech which was an amazing experience, scary but amazing. I will never forget the two of us sat on a flight case at the side of a stage when he showed me how he likes his Fender bass re-strung!

The 15 year old me would never have dared to dream I actually know Bruce and have done for almost 10 years. They say never meet your heroes but I'm lucky enough to call him a friend.

I WAS THERE: DAVID OWENS, AGE 13

It was 1979 when my world changed forever. I was 10 and my older sister had a boyfriend who allowed me to borrow his copy of The Jam's *All Mods Cons* album. It was transparent, even to my pre-pubescent eyes, that he was trying to butter up his girlfriend by cosying up to her little brother, but still, I wasn't complaining (he made a pretty good job of it. He's now my brother-in-law and has been since 1986).

When the needle hit the record it was as if a bomb exploded in my mind. The intoxicating, adrenaline rush of furious guitars, sneering vocals and visceral thrills were like nothing I'd heard before.

Prior to this epochal introduction to new wave, punk and rhythm 'n' blues, I had experienced a series of half-baked liaisons with every child's favourite furry environmentalists The Wombles and teen pop teddy boys Showaddywaddy.

The Jam, however, were the real deal – a dazzling collision of serrated chords, sharp-suited chic, razor-sharp lyricism and an unstoppable self-belief that inspired rabid fanaticism amongst their adoring following.

For a time in the early Eighties, they were the biggest band in Britain and far beyond. I'd been set onto the path to musical fulfillment, and my guiding light was Paul Weller.

Picking up the album, with the ultra-cool trio of Paul Weller, Bruce Foxton and Rick Buckler staring back at me from the cover, I slid the black vinyl from the pristine white inner sleeve with a sense of excitement.

The Jam were my first love and my very first gig.

It was September 21, 1982. I was 13 years old, fast approaching my 14th birthday, and was being taken to the concert as an early present courtesy of my aforementioned sister – Nicky and her boyfriend, Stuart. I had unsuccessfully attempted to see The Jam two years earlier when they played Sophia Gardens in Cardiff.

As a fresh-faced 11-year-old I was laughed out of Virgin Records, then on Duke Street in the city centre, when I tried to purchase a ticket. Save for a stick-on beard and impromptu voice breakage, who was I kidding.

To cut a long story and long journey through the winding back roads of Somerset short, my very first time was at the decidedly insalubrious surrounds of the Shepton Mallet Show Pavilion. Astonishingly, thanks to the quick thinking of its owner, it was a venue that by day doubled up as a cattle market and by night staged live music. It was very much a case of the shit hitting the fan but luckily, the aromatic pungency of the building didn't last long in the memory – but one of the greatest nights of my life did.

Bedecked in purple two-tone Sta-Prest trousers and a black and white Prince of Wales check button-down Ben Sherman shirt topped off with obligatory parka – purchased from Gwyns in Cardiff Central Market - I believed I was the epitome of cool rather than what I actually was, an eye-boggling car crash of badly co-ordinated colour choices.

I've still got the Solid Bond In Your Heart tour t-shirt that I bought that night and if I eat just lettuce for the rest of my life, I might yet fit into it again.

My youthful mind's eye is littered with these sorts of epochal landmarks that have Paul Weller's footprint stamped all over them.

I also vividly remember the day The Jam announced they were to split and I fought back tears as I trudged my way to high school after reading those earth-shattering headlines in my copy of *Record Mirror*.

In the pre-internet age, there was no mass message board rumour-mongering, so no inkling of the devastating news that tumbled forth from the music mag's pages that fateful morning of 28 October 1982.

It was ironic that a music paper had dealt me such a hammer blow, as it was after all The Jam's music that would propel me to write my own Mod fanzines, firing my imagination and setting me on the road to journalistic enlightenment.

These most do-it-yourself of DIY publications hit a high in the late Seventies and early Eighties as did music with its all pervading do-it-yourself aesthetic.

And I was no different, having my own stab via the medium of Pritt Stick and a mate's mum's office photocopier.

My laughably stitched together *One Way World* fanzine (named after a song by Mod outfit Secret Affair) was strictly League Two compared to some of the glossily professional Premier League ventures that served as the pinnacle of amateur publishing.

Now, more than three decades after first discovering The Jam, I was set to be granted an audience with my idol. To not put too fine a point on it and deviate from grammatical elegance, I was shitting myself. I'd not been this tense and sweating so profusely since my daughter was born and my wife and I were locked into a hair-raising three-day labour.

Of course, as a journalist you're often afforded the luxury of meeting musicians, celebrities and all manner of people in the public eye. While I've been wielding my keyboard in anger as a professional hack since 1989, I like to think I've got this interview lark down to a fine art. However, no conversation has left me suspended in such a dizzying stupor as my meeting with the Modfather.

So what was the root cause of this anxiety? Why has this musician with the impeccable threads and improbable barnet to match had such a profound effect on my life?

Nevertheless, little did I realise that these formative foundations would decades later lead me to stand outside the stage door of the Cardiff Motorpoint Arena on an impressively arctic, sub-zero Saturday evening in November 2010, waiting for this long sought after rendezvous.

The air was sharp and icy, Wales had surprised no one by losing to the All Blacks at the Millennium Stadium that afternoon and Cardiff was awash with hordes of rugby fans, attempting to numb the cold by drinking to excess. It was a surreal evening in every sense of the word and it was about to get even weirder.

Accompanied by Weller's affable tour manager Bill Wheeler, I was ushered into the inner sanctum of the Motorpoint's backstage area past two burly security guards and into one of the arena's many dressing rooms. Despite spending that afternoon rewriting the questions I would put to the modernist icon and whiling away the rest in nervous anticipation, something surprising happened.

At that precise moment I felt totally relaxed; trapped in the eye of the storm there's no turning back, so it was as if I accepted my fate and the professional adrenaline kicked in.

My colleague Andy was busily setting up the camera to film the interview and I started checking my hair, adjusting my John Smedley top (hand-picked for the occasion) to accommodate a mic and polishing my shoes on my trouser legs. Well, one doesn't want to look unkempt in the presence of a fashion figurehead.

Then he appeared before us and sat down. 'All right mate, how you doing?' he inquired in a chirpy London accent. It's often said that Weller can be difficult in interviews, but thankfully and reassuringly, he was in an ebullient and playful mood.

My line of enquiry centred around just what it's like to be Paul Weller – as he occupies a unique place in British rock 'n' roll history. He's a musician who has reinvented himself through The Jam, his fan base polarising Eighties outfit The Style Council and latterly for 25 years as a hugely successful solo artist.

As the former voice of a generation and now as the music press's anointed Modfather, he perhaps means more in seismic shift terms to music fans than any other British artiste since The Beatles first bestrode the rock 'n' roll landscape. I put it to him that he means an awful lot to an awful lot of people – citing the effect he has had on my life as an ample example.

He, of course, had no idea of what this moment meant to me, but then he's had a lifetime of similar encounters with fans who have waxed lyrical with Weller eulogies, citing him as a mod god and a musical icon.

As Bill Wheeler signalled the allotted 15 minutes was up, our chat ended on this humorous high and frankly, I was buzzing like a bee with tinnitus.

We had just enough time to grab a picture. Stood there with Weller's arm round me I felt elated. It was as much out of an enormous sense of relief that I didn't embarrass myself as it was that I had finally met the great man himself.

Impromptu photo session over, Weller turned on his desert boots, shook our hands once more and with a cheery 'nice one lads' headed off for a pre-show pow wow with his band.

Don't ever meet your heroes they tell you. How wrong could they be.

I WAS THERE: DARREN HANNAFORD

I was fortunate to see The Jam twice in 1982 at Shepton Mallet where I had to bunk off school to see them and at the Cornwall Coliseum which fortunately for me was on a Sunday night. Not too many memories but I do recall a Mod from Exeter was beaten up by some guys from Plymouth (inter city rivalry).

GRANBY HALLS

23 SEPTEMBER 1982, LEICESTER, UK

I WAS THERE: MICHAEL BEASLEY, AGE 15

Back in 1980 I was 15 and at school and somebody gave me a copy of *Setting Sons*. I took it home and that was it, hooked. I was in Ireland a month later and picked up a copy of 'When you're Young' in the 10p bucket in Woolworths. After that everything was bought on the day of release as well as going back and buying everything I hadn't got.

My best memory was going to see them at Granby Hall Leicester in September 1982

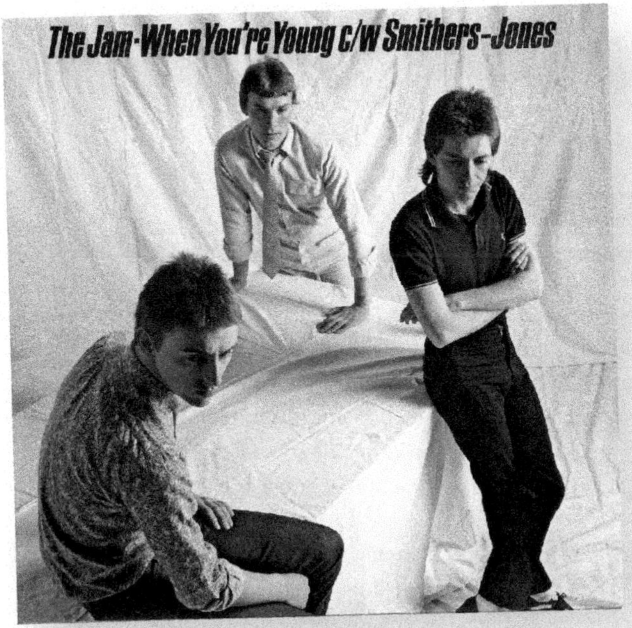

on the *Solid Bond* tour. My best mate was Leigh Foster and his mum knew someone on reception at the Holiday Inn in Leicester who had said the boys were stopping there after the gig. So when the gig finished, which was brill, we made our way down to the Holiday Inn reception and were given two passes to make it look like we were stopping the night. We went into the bar in our Jam t-shirts and cardies and got two pints and sat down and waited nervously to see if they would arrive. The bar was empty except for us. After about 15 minutes Paul walked in with Gill and I think Kenny Wheeler. We stood up to try and shake Paul's hand and say hello, when Kenny moved in front of Paul and told us to sit down or he would break our arms. We said we were sleeping there and showed him and Paul our room passes. Paul apologised and asked if they could sit with us and buy us a pint. We of course said yes! Then Bruce and Rick and their girls came in, Bruce sat with us but Rick sat at another table. We also had Jim Telford (keyboards) and the two guys who played sax sat with us. They all signed my programme, which I still have, and sat with us until we had to leave at 1am. Paul even asked us if we wanted to go on the tour bus the next day to Liverpool but we had both not long started work and didn't dare take a day off. In hindsight how we wish we had.

Going up! Stuart Iron captured Rick and Paul in a lift at the Holiday Inn Leicester

I WAS THERE: STUART IRONS, AGE 16

I met The Jam with my mates at the Holiday Inn in Leicester when they were getting on the coach to go to the sound check. My mate Dave tried to get us a ride on the coach, Weller was fine but Kenny said no chance. Great and great days for a 16 year old.

ROYAL COURT THEATRE

24 SEPTEMBER 1982, LIVERPOOL, UK

I WASN'T THERE: MICK HANRATTY

I grew up during late Seventies and early Eighties in Liverpool, a city ravaged by pain inflicted on it from others; mainly Government and a world changing with lightning speed. I, too, was changing as I entered my teens in 1980 and discovered the joy of music almost immediately at that point, despite a grandmother having a back catalogue to die for - including early and original Beatles, Stones, and...erm...Ken Dodd.

1980 still remains for me a crowning year on the pop charts culminating in the brilliant Jam and their two sparkling number ones. I mean how many records and bands get a mention on *News at Ten* for entering the singles charts at number one; except perhaps the aforementioned Beatles.

While for record buying Jam fans, 1981 was a barren year - two singles, months apart, and no LPs - it was a good year for me and my cousin to start going back in the record catalogue and buying up every piece of black vinyl with the words 'The Jam' written on them.

So when 1982 dawned and an advert for their new single was announced (with the words, 'Thanks to all our fans - *The Gift* is coming...') things started to liven up again.

The *NME* and *Record Mirror* were religiously scanned for news and when a tour was finally announced to promote their new album *The Gift* (it took a while for the penny to drop what that advert meant!) and with Liverpool Royal Court Theatre on the rota, we waited for a date which became the most important event of the year; O levels and other things be damned!

My cousin and I, while not being overly rich, begged and borrowed enough money to buy a ticket to see our heroes and some three weeks before the gig we made our way to Empire Theatre with the fee (a whole £5, I think) burning in our pockets.

Expecting a large crowd, we went early. Excited, the bus ride to the theatre seemed to take three days rather than the usual 30 minutes. Arriving at the theatre we were surprised to find no queues, no crowds, nobody other than an older woman behind a counter ready to sell tickets.

Now it's important to remember that this gig had been the most important thing on our mind for months; well maybe with the exception of finding a way of meeting the 19 year old girl who'd just moved in opposite my cousin, and who we both fancied. So I think we were a little stunned by the fact we were the only ones there... and that made us hesitate at the door. We literally stopped in our tracks and looked at each other... and never took another step forward.

Once more we looked at each other and almost in unison said to each other, 'Let's wait until next year...' little knowing what was to come. For some five months later, in December 1982, The Jam were no more.

All change for Foxton, Weller and Buckler. Pic Anton Corbijn.

JAM SPLIT

THE JAM are to break up right after their pre-Christmas concerts — and that is now official.

Paul Weller announced the impending disbandment this week, so ending speculation which has been simmering for three months, and which was first revealed by *NME* in the summer.

Rumours gained momentum last week following a report that their Christmas gigs may be their last. Despite inconsistencies in the report — which claimed that the band had cancelled their European tour because of internal disharmony and the split decision, whereas Weller's illness was the real reason for its curtailment — its credibility was heightened by the fact that all official sources remained tight-lipped and refused to comment.

But now Weller, in a statement addressed to The Jam's fans *(see below)*, has finally laid to rest the band which has won more *NME* Poll awards than any other act since The Beatles.

It's been common knowledge for some time that the three Jam members, as often happens with long-established groups, have become increasingly anxious to expand their activities outside the limitation of the band format — particularly Weller, with his songwriting and production interests. He said as long ago as July that, after a hectic year on the road, the bulk of 1983 would be devoted to individual projects.

Weller is also known to be keen on fronting a larger outfit, possibly including strings and girl back-up singers, which would give him wider scope than the present three-man line-up. But at this stage, he is still not saying exactly what the future holds in store for him — and neither are the other two Jam members, Bruce Foxton and Rick Buckler, though it's possible that they haven't yet formulated any definite plans. All three had this week retreated "out of town".

The Jam are to give their fans one last opportunity of seeing them in live action. Their two Christmas shows at London Wembley Arena (December 1 and 2) were announced last week, and they have now sandwiched these between half-a-dozen provincial concerts — which now become their official farewell tour.

Newly confirmed dates are at Poole Arts Centre (November 27), St Austell Cornwall Coliseum (28), Port Talbot Afan Lido (29), Bridlington Spa Hall (December 6), Manchester Apollo (7) and Birmingham Bingley Hall (8).

Guest acts at Wembley will be Stuart Adamson's band Big Country and the group in whom Weller has been taking a special interest, The Questions. As already reported, The Jam have a new two-pack single issued by Polydor on November 19, followed by a live album on December 10.

Tickets for the band's regional dates are all at the one price of £5, and they are available from box-offices and usual agencies. Additional outlets for Port Talbot are at Spillers Records (Cardiff), Roxcene (Newport) and Derricks Records (Swansea and Cardiff); and for Birmingham, there are extra outlets at Goulds TV (Wolverhampton), R. E. Cords (Derby), Selectadisc (Nottingham) and Cyclops and Virgin (Birmingham). Wembley booking arrangements (£6 and £5) were reported last week.

PAUL WELLER'S PERSONAL GOODBYE TO HIS FANS

THE JAM: A STATEMENT

At the end of this year The Jam will be officially splitting up, as I feel we have achieved all we can together as a group. I mean this both musically and commercially.

I want all we have achieved to count for something and most of all I'd hate us to end up old and embarrassing like so many other groups do. The longer a group continues the more frightening the thought of ever ending it becomes — that is why so many of them carry on until they become meaningless. I've never wanted The Jam to get to this stage.

What we (and you) have built up has meant something, for me it stands for honesty, passion and energy and youth. I want it to stay that way and maybe exist as a guideline for new young groups coming up to improve and expand on. This would make it even more worthwhile.

I have written this as a direct contact with you and so you hear it from us first. But also to say thank you for all the faith you have shown in us and the building of such a strong force and feeling that all three of us have felt and been touched by.

Here's to the future,
In love and friendship,
Paul Weller (Oct. 1982)

I haven't seen my cousin in a few years and yet the last time we spoke to each other we talked of little else other than that fateful day. I've been lucky enough to have had a little success in my business life. I've climbed to management / director positions and had to make decisions that had long term, often key effects on lives.

And yet I know that, through it all, the decision I made that day did have long term, lasting effects and was - by a very long chalk - the worst I've ever made.

Oh how I regret it still - 37 years later...

I WAS THERE: PHIL HUGHES

I was 11 or 12 years old when I went to see The Jam at The Royal Court in Liverpool. When I bought my ticket at the box office weeks before, with older friends who were taking me, the guy looked down at me and said 'you'd best take seats upstairs as you won't see a fuckin' thing otherwise!'

On the night of the gig my brother and I were in the upper circle whilst my mates were downstairs jumping around to the sounds. Next thing I knew all hell broke loose as men armed with bats and iron bars came running through the aisles. I didn't know what to make of it at the time but soon after rumours spread that fire escape doors upstairs had been broken and people had bunked in behind us. It was a bit like a scene from the movie *The Warriors* and just added more excitement to the night for a young kid wanting to see his favourite group live.

It was real eye opening stuff and catapulted me into the gig scene and from there I went on to see many bands live. It was a totally amazing first gig experience.

WHITLEY BAY ICE RINK

26 SEPTEMBER 1982, WHITLEY BAY, UK

I WAS THERE: ALAN LITTLE, AGE 16

I saw The Jam on the second night at Whitley Bay Ice Rink on September 26th 1982 on their *Solid Bond in Your Heart* tour. It was my first ever gig and what a way to begin my life journey of seeing great bands. I was 16 and had just started a YTS scheme (remember those?) working in the Investment Department at Northern Rock Building Society (remember them?).

Alan Little wearing his grey Lonsdale t-shirt a la Weller

Me and my best mate Gary had been into The Jam since 1978 and we were so excited at seeing our favourite band. We boarded the brand new(ish) Tyne and Wear Metro at Four Lane Ends to Whitley Bay where we joined the throngs of youths - mainly Mods - walking up to the Ice Rink. The atmosphere inside was electric. There was no support act but various Mod tracks were played. I particularly remember The Kinks 'Waterloo Sunset' getting a big cheer.

Then the lights went down and The Jam took to the stage to a rapturous welcome. Paul Weller was dressed in his customary (then) grey Lonsdale t-shirt. The first song they played was 'Ghosts' off their new *The Gift* album. They played for around 90 minutes. They played all the hit singles and various album track classics. Little did I know when they departed the stage after a second encore that it would be the last time I'd see The Jam as they would announce they were splitting up only weeks later. I can only say now that I am so proud that I saw my favourite band of all time

ROYAL HIGHLAND EXHIBITION HALL

27 SEPTEMBER 1982, INGLISTON, EDINBURGH, UK

I WAS THERE: PADDY DONAGHY, AGE 16

I was 11 when I first heard The Jam in 1977. My older cousin Tony got me into them. I remember him playing their music to me and when the stylus hit that vinyl and the sound exploded through his speakers I was hooked then as I still am now. Later on he somehow managed to get hold of two large advertising posters for the *In The City* album and gave me one of them for my bedroom wall. Any of my mates who were also into The Jam were well jealous.

I was lucky enough to see them several times in Glasgow but my best memory is of the gig in Ingliston just outside Edinburgh on 27th September 1982, supported by The Vapors.

Now I was 16 nearly 17 back then and my girlfriend at the time (now my wife) wasn't into The Jam. She preferred Adam and the Ants - Prince Charming version. The Glasgow Apollo had put on buses to shuttle us through from Glasgow and off I went. I had the usual Fred Perry, white jeans and parka on and I had also just purchased from Dunn & Co one of those tan cord John Lennon hats and thought I was the bee's knees.

Now for some reason I didn't have enough money for a tour t-shirt and a programme so settled on a programme but luckily enough there was a young lady standing near me wearing a tour t-shirt who took a particular shine to either me or my hat (for the purpose of the story we'll say my hat). Just after The Vapors finished their set she came up to me and asked me for my hat so I took a chance and said that I would give her my hat if she gave me her tour t-shirt. She thought about it then quick as a flash she whipped the t shirt off over her head. Now as a 16 year old I hadn't seen many females in a state of undress like this but believe me I was in my element! Not long after this moment The Jam took to the stage and were the cherry on the icing on top of the cake.

Paul Weller at the Royal highland exhibition Hall 27th September 1982

I returned to Glasgow with my head replaying what had happened that night over and over. Anyway a few weeks passed and I'm not sure how it came up but during an argument with my girlfriend I happened to mention that I had swapped my hat for the t-shirt including all the details of how I got it. Incensed, she took my tour programme and then proceeded to rip it to shreds. I must have forgiven her eventually as we are still together now and have been married 26 years.

So the moral of the story is...whatever happens on tour stays on tour.

I WAS THERE: HILARY FALL, AGE 22

I was 22 when I first saw The Jam, but bought my first Jam album at 21 (a late starter). I was going through a life change at that time… *Setting Sons* was the start of my being an ardent Jam fan. My two mates heard the album and were hooked. I think at that time girls in my area were not really into Mod, new wave, etc.

Paul Weller became my hero, his song writing and his take on life at that time was so true. I was very inspired by his lyrics. I still have fanzines which have poetry written by Paul. Their songs changed my life.

My gig memories were seeing The Jam play Edinburgh Playhouse, on the *Global Unity Express* tour. Also one at Carlisle and on the last tour at Edinburgh Exhibition Centre. Sadly it was a flat venue and me not being the tallest I couldn't see them. I remember being gutted as it was their last gig.

I WAS THERE: IAN BERESFORD, AGE 15

Ian Beresford stood inside Wembley Stadium

My first time seeing The Jam was on September 27th, 1982 at Edinburgh Ingliston Exhibition Centre on *The Bitterest Pill* tour. I was 15 years old. The gig was extra special as I only found out I had the chance of a ticket a couple of days before as an older friend had bought four and someone had to drop out. We travelled with a work colleague of my friend and for some strange reason I can remember he played the cassette of a live album by Bob Seger, which was pretty far removed from The Jam.

At the venue we had to go through metal detectors which was a bit of a surprise for a country boy from Berwick Upon Tweed. I remember all the people with parkas on who must have been melting in the heat! Support band was The Questions who got a reasonable response from the crowd with their recent single 'Price You Pay' and the fact they were on Weller's label.

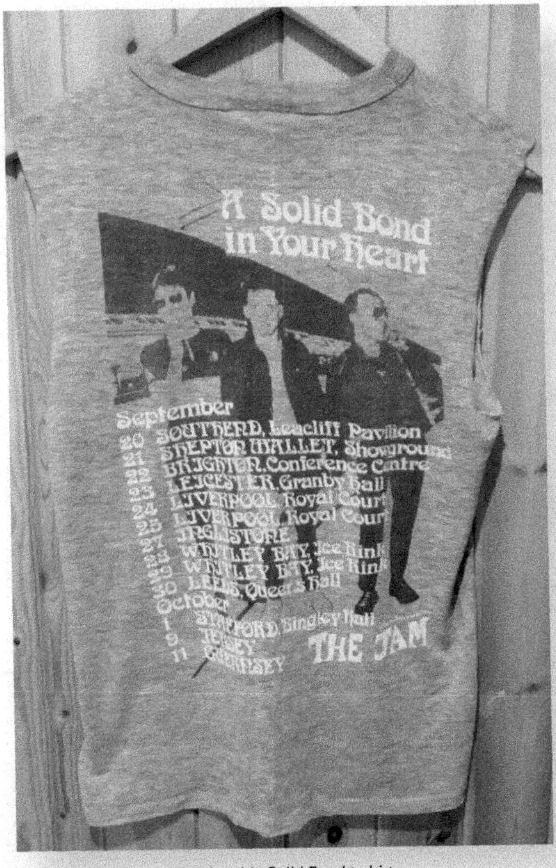

Ian Beresford can still fit into his Solid Bond t-shirt

When The Jam came on it was a different matter as the crowd swayed and pushed and I remember thinking that I had gone from one side of the stage to the other in the melee.

The set list was obviously amazing with everyone singing along and jumping about although unsurprisingly 'Bitterest Pill' didn't get an outing. Paul was his usual reticent self on stage in terms of taking to the crowd but I remember someone had thrown a toilet roll on the stage and he said 'Cheers, I'll use it on my arse later'. There were the regular chants of 'We are the Mods' through the gig. In all to short a time it was over and we exited sweaty, bruised and ecstatic. I purchased a t-shirt and programme on the way and we headed off back to Berwick. Next day was a day off school on account of the late night and the fact that there would be no way of concentrating whilst reliving the night before.

I had first got into The Jam proper in early 79 with the 'When You're Young' single although I had been aware of earlier ones and especially 'The Modern World' which was regularly used as an ident on Radio Luxembourg. My friend was an even bigger Jam fan than me with a bedroom plastered with posters of the band and was always the first to buy the albums. I made a mixtape of their songs, which I played so much that whenever I heard a tune on the radio or wherever I could remember what came next on the tape.

The Jam breaking up was monumental to everyone our age given how much they meant to us and probably like a lot of people I drifted away from them as I got older to the point where I sold all my records to the second hand shops as CD's came to prominence and it was only in the mid Ninties I ended up with a full collection of their albums again.

I did follow The Style Council and 27 years after my first solo Weller gig and I still catch him each tour and even made a trip to the USA in 2014 to watch shows in Cleveland, Detroit and Minneapolis. Have also been to see From The Jam five or six times. Only this week I was giving *The Gift* full blast on the car cd.

WHITLEY BAY ICE RINK

28 SEPTEMBER 1982, WHITLEY BAY, UK

I WAS THERE: PETER SMITH

The last time I saw them play was at the cavernous (and cold) Ice Rink in Whitley Bay. This was the first gig to be held at the Ice Rink, which was used as a venue for large gigs before Newcastle Arena was built. The Jam played two nights in the massive venue and once again showed what a great band they were. I saw the Style Council a few times, and couldn't really get away with them, and saw Paul Weller in concert a few years ago, and he was just great. But nothing compares to The Jam in the late Seventies and early Eighties.

NEW BINGLEY HALL

1 OCTOBER 1982, STAFFORD, UK

I WAS THERE: TOM LANGLEY

It's fair to say that since I got into The Jam in early 1978 till the split I was a massive fan. I saw about 30 times live during their short lived career and as someone said in the music press in the Eighties on their day The Jam live (and the Undertones) could raise the dead.

The last concert was always the best... ears buzzing the next day and feet and legs aching from standing for hours. The last Wembley shows were standouts but as a Brummie lad my favourite show was always Birmingham Bingley Hall.

The Birmingham gig that sticks in my memory was the last one. Me and my friends always managed to get into the sound check via Kenny Wheeler and found ourselves chatting to Jill, Paul's then girlfriend. Only about 100 to 150 fans managed to get into the afternoon sound check. We saw Weller on stage with this white Lonsdale top and guess what? Me standing there with my grey one on.

The sound check ended and we thanked everyone and went for a walk around Birmingham for a few hours. I was the only one of our group to drive and our usual trip was to find out which hotel The Jam were staying at and get in the bar after the concert. The usual venue was the Holiday Inn but at the sound check and because of the announcement of the split everyone was keeping tight lipped.

We went back to Bingley Hall early doors and managed to get right at the front. After a couple hours, the Questions came on to loads of booing. Then a load of fighting broke out in the crowd. This soon subsided when John Weller came on stage and announced 'Put your hands together for the best fucking band in the world - THE JAMMMMMMM.' All of sudden we were whipped into an absolutely frenzy - burning hell. They set the house a blaze. 'Thick as Thieves', 'Going Underground', 'Tube Station', 'Malice' - it was like being thrown into a washing machine and someone had shut the door. You could lift your feet off the ground and move around the hall, the sway of the crowd. All too soon it was over - the last ever show in Brum.

Tom Langley's collection of Jam souvenirs

Fortunately, we had a whisper that The Jam were staying at the Albany Hotel instead of the usual Holiday Inn. I managed to get to the back of the hall and get out pretty sharpish and get the car started. I think it may have had ice on the windscreen. Joined by my mates, me and my Triumph Dolomite raced around to the Albany Hotel and parked outside and waited. About 30 minutes later a coach pulled up behind me and proceeded to blast his horn. Eventually someone got out the coach and asked us to move. I reversed behind the coach and my mates and me left the car and raced into the foyer of the hotel. Within three or four minutes, Paul walked in followed by Bruce with Kenny Wheeler. Kenny wanted to know who owned the Triumph Dolomite, I reluctantly owned up and he said I was a barmy fucker and I had left my lights on!

We had our photos taken with Paul and I got him to autograph various pieces of paper and records, which I had in the car. Bruce was very chatty but I guess with what had gone on in the previous month this was understandable. Before we got thrown out I got Bruce to sign a £5 note.

Paul Weller looking a bit surprised when he entered Albany Hotel

I WAS THERE: MICK HOOLE

I saw a great band in a terrible venue.

The City Centre Exhibition Hall burned down two years later and the International Convention Centre is now on the site. During the Seventies and Eighties it was a popular venue. Bob Marley & The Wailers, Status Quo, The Stones, Pink Floyd, The Who, Sabbath, David Bowie, Queen and Bruce Springsteen all played there.

THE TUBE

5 NOVEMBER 1982, NEWCASTLE UPON TYNE, UK

I WAS THERE: PAUL BROMLEY, AGE 18

I was lucky enough to see The Jam 57 times from 1978 to the last gig in Brighton and to think when they split up I was only just 18, but the gig that stands out for me was the first ever *Tube* appearance.

I was lucky enough to get guest passes and spent the day with the band. When you see most programmes on The Jam the footage from *The Tube* is nearly always shown and I am fortunate enough to be there in the audience and always visible on the big screen. Memories that were made and will never go away.

I am about the sixth person to your left (just out of screen), however, very visible when they did 'Ghosts', not that I've watched it and freeze framed it and shown it to any unlucky person who will watch, honest! Personally, although I think the performance is outstanding, I think they could've done a better set, it being the last ever live TV performance.

Paul Bromley in the audience at The Tube

I WAS THERE: IAN TURPIN

I was born in 1964. I grew up in Northern England, so I was in my early teens when the punk explosion found its way to my home town. I liked the energy and rebellion, but not the ripped clothes and spitting. I heard about a band called The Jam who had played a gig at Seaburn Hall, which some older lads had seen and kept talking about, and after some quick research I thought they were about right for me. Cool, spiky haircuts, black suits, skinny ties, power-pop, high-energy music … what's not to like?

I started to emulate their style, which gave me a starting point in the search for that identity which so many young teens are seeking – a way to belong but at the same time be individual. I didn't even realize at the time that in doing so I was entering not the world of punk, which was already giving way to the more palatable 'new wave', but on my way to becoming the first Mod in my school.

In the autumn of 1982 my band had been together for around 18 months and had achieved some success locally but were looking for some way to step up to the next level. We had made a demo tape and schlepped it around various radio stations and record labels without much response. In the late summer of 1982 we had heard about a new TV show that was going to be broadcast from the Tyne Tees studio in Newcastle. I was friends with Maxine Deas at school, and her dad, Max Deas, was a big cheese at Tyne Tees Television, so we asked her if she would pass our tape on to her dad, with the naive aspiration that we might get on the telly!

We did get a response from Tyne Tees along with a handful of passes to the inaugural episode of the show, which we found out was going to be called *The Tube*. You can imagine how chuffed I was to find out that The Jam were going to be playing live in the studio.

So me and the other lads from my band made it through to Newcastle. The entrance to the studios resembles the eponymous Tube and whilst we were waiting in there Jools Holland – who had probably been chosen as presenter following a documentary he had done following The Police around the Caribbean – walked down the queue cracking jokes with those of us in line. Who knew he would go on to have such a successful career as a TV host?

The Toy Dolls were playing some cacophonous power pop in the lobby. I nodded at Olga as we walked past, as I used to often see him down at Pete Dodds' rehearsal rooms where both of our bands practiced and stashed our gear. Then we were ushered into the main studio for a lot of standing around while various interviews were going on around us. Sting was on camera and Pete Townshend too but I don't really recall if they had anything earth-shattering to say.

I was right up front to see Heaven 17 perform a few songs. I used to frequent an 'alternative music' nightclub with my band mates around this time where along with the likes of Kraftwerk, early Human League, Bauhaus, Killing Joke and Japan, and 'We Don't Need This Fascist Groove Thang' was regularly played. I was surprised Heaven 17 were on the bill as they had no new stuff coming out and they often stated that they had no interest in touring or playing live. True to form, their keyboards weren't even plugged in but they had a horn section who were playing live over their pre-recorded backing tapes. Keyboardist Martyn Ware would soon go on to produce Tina Turner's comeback single, a copy of Al Green's 'Let's Stay Together', and a few years later he was at the controls for the recording of *Introducing The Hardline According To Terence Trent D'Arby* – one of the best debut albums ever in my opinion. Too bad Terence swiftly faded away, but I digress …

During the next interval (commercial break – this was live TV!) I bumped into a lad in the crowd I knew who told me he'd heard a rumour that The Jam were packing it all in, but I didn't want to believe it. Due to being in a non-Mod band I had naturally started to expand my music tastes way beyond what would normally be expected from a revivalist Mod in 1982, but I was still fully dedicated to The Jam and couldn't believe they would throw in the towel when they seemed to be at the height of their success and setting up for world domination. To this day I don't remember when I finally heard the news. On reviewing the video of the whole performance, prior to The Jam going onstage Tube presenter Muriel Gray announced, 'As most people already know The Jam are splitting up…' I certainly didn't know, and that bit wasn't shown to us in the studio so I lived on in blissful ignorance for a little while longer. When The Jam finally took the stage Weller made no mention of it, either to the live audience in the studio off-camera, or to those watching on TV.

By now I would guess that most people reading this who were interested in The Jam will have seen this show, either on TV or on the *Complete Jam* DVD. I got near the front and was surprised to see Bruce's bass. He had previously exclusively used a series of Rickenbacker 4001s in the early years and more recently a black Fender Precision, but he came out sporting a beautiful gold-coloured neck-through Aria SBR. I had just happened to get the exact same bass in padauk red a few weeks previously and still own it now!

The band blasted through a short set of nine or ten songs, which was a pretty good cross-section of their career to date. There was a huge trolley camera right behind me, so if you're really sad you can take a look at the DVD and see the back of my spiky head bobbing up and down in the foreground in many of the shots. Towards the end of the show, as 'Move On Up' is playing out, the camera angle reverses and there's a clear close shot of me clapping.

The show ended, the crowd were ushered out and that was that! I was on the train home in a bit of a dazed state not quite believing my luck that I'd just seen my heroes in such an intimate setting. Of course, not long after this show the news filtered through that the rumours were true and The Jam really were breaking up. Because it was obvious to so many people that I was a big fan (even if they didn't know me, they could tell I had that look!) I was asked over and over what I thought about it. I was friendly with an older Mod named Rob Baker and ran into his brother – who I barely knew – in Annabel's nightclub. He came rushing over to commiserate with me and told me he had been growing his hair out like Jim Morrison's as he'd become a huge fan of The Doors but when he heard the news about The Jam he'd cut it all off in mourning!

The Jam released their final single 'Beat Surrender' on 22 November 1982, their fourth and final UK number one. Paul Weller wrote the song as a valediction for the end of the band's career, which he broke up by walking away from shortly after its release. 'I wanted it to be a statement, a final clarion call saying, 'Right, we're stopping, you take it on from here." The sleeve for the single, including the 12' and the double single pack, featured Gill Price, Weller's girlfriend at the time.

APOLLO

25 NOVEMBER 1982, GLASGOW, UK

I WAS THERE: COLIN PORTER, AGE 18

It was like the end of our Mod days when we heard The Jam were splitting up. It was 1982 and the last concert at the Glasgow Apollo. What a concert and a way to end my Jam days - well that's what I thought. On the way home my mate who was a massive Weller fan said his mum worked in the Excelsior Hotel at Glasgow airport and The Jam were staying there. Well I had just picked up my 'Beat Surrender' EP that day and a Manish Boys single I had left at the pub I worked at. I picked them up after the concert and we headed down to the hotel and once in we got a pint and just waited.

Colin Porter in front of his Jam collection

Well our faces must have been a picture when Paul, Bruce and Rick walked into the lounge. We didn't know what to do! I was the first to go over and I asked Bruce if he wanted a drink. He said, 'No thanks lads I'm with company', but he signed my EP and my concert programme. Paul was a little quieter and he also signed my EP and programme. Rick was amazing. He signed both and then asked what else I had in the bag. I showed him the Manish Boys single and he asked if he could buy it from me – I agreed and he gave me a signed fiver for it.

What a night and what an end to my Jam career. The fiver ended up being spent the next week on a carry out. Well I was only 18!

POOLE ARTS CENTRE

27 NOVEMBER 1982, POOLE, UK

I WAS THERE: STEVE PARK

On the *Beat Surrender* tour, I was all suited and booted by midday as I had a first date with a girl who I was meeting for lunch. Well I met her for lunch and all these years on, Lisa and I are still together. She still doesn't like The Jam but I get brownie points for remembering our first date every November!

I WAS THERE: DAVID SHEPPARD

Saw them three times, all in Poole. I just remember all the Parka coats and chants of 'we are the Mods'. I remember the Vapors as one of the supports. Don't seem to have any of the tickets but I still have t-shirt and a small advertising leaflet from the time.

Dave Sheppard still has his Jam t-shirt from the Poole gig

WEMBLEY ARENA

2, 3 ,4 & 5 DEÇEMBER 1982,
LONDON, UK

I WAS THERE: MARTIN ROSE

Martin Rose (middle) on his way to Wembley

I was young, very young when I first got into The Jam. I knew I'd never get to see them being as young as I was but their music, lyrics and image hit home straight away. I knew they meant something to me and would be with me to this day; I'm now 52 and still wear the clothes, listen to the music and still ride a scooter.

The Jam came to Bracknell Sports Centre on (I think) the *Sound Affects* tour. I begged and begged for my mum to let me go but it was pointless, I was absolutely gutted especially as I had to hear from mates at school who's parents let them go how good the gig was.

It would be another few years until I managed to skip school on 2nd December 1982 and get on a bus and get to Wembley to see the heart breaking farewell tour. Nothing was going to stop me this time. I remember getting to the venue and feeling so excited that I was actually in the same room as the three members of The Jam! Me, and 10,000 others, but to me this was in my eyes a private gig, I was in the same fucking room as Paul, Bruce and Rick! The concert was everything I'd imagined it to be - exciting, fast, and passionate and moving, yet also upsetting, as I knew it was over! I now had to get back to Bracknell and sneak into my house without my mum asking where the hell I'd been. And I managed to get away with it.

So from that day on I was obsessed with The Jam even though they had split prematurely. Myself and two friends found out where Rick lived in Lightwater. As a young kid that seemed miles away – so far away that I couldn't get there, although it was only about 10 miles from Bracknell where we lived - but we went to Lightwater to find him! We had no idea the town was so big. We went from house to house asking residents if they knew who Rick Buckler was. It was madness but we didn't care. Eventually I had a brain wave and went to the local paper shop and asked if he had papers delivered. The woman in the shop didn't let on but a young kid in the shop told me where Rick lived, so that was it. Bold as brass I marched up to his house and knocked on the front door, and to my amazement Rick answered it!

I didn't feel flustered or scared. I just asked him question after question after question and he gladly answered all of them. He must have thought, 'What the fuck?'

As we were about to leave I told him I was learning drums and it was all down to him. He then said, 'Wait here,' and he went off and came back two minutes later with a set of Premier drum sticks! Can you image how that felt?

October 1982.

Dear All,

Hope you all managed to see the Jam on tour.

We went to Brighton Conference Centre, and thought it was great. It was good to hear all the old songs again.

Gig list for November/December.

28th November - St.Austell Lido.
29th November - Poole Arts Centre.
30th November - Day off.
1st December - Wembley.
2nd December - Wembley.
3rd December - Wembley.
4th December - Day off.
5th December - Manchester Apollo or Mansfield Leisure Centre.
6th December - Bridlington Spa.
7th December - Birmingham, Bingley Hall.
9-8th December - Guildford Civic Centre.

All these dates are subject to confirmation.

Tickets £5.00 from;

M.C.P.,
P.O. Box 124,
Walsall,
West Midlands.

Please do not write to the fan club for tickets.

Wembley tickets will be £5.00 and £6.00. The Jam will have a live album out in the last week in November or first week in December. The single will be an E.P. out the second week in December. Sorry we can't tell you the title yet but, Paul keeps changing his mind. (Beat surrender)

The Jam will be on the new Channel 4 on November 5th on a half hour live show.

There will be a new book out in December called 'All our Yesterdays' about the Small Faces written by Paul and Paulo Hewitt. The book will be mail order, any enquiries on the book send a s.a.e. to Riot Stories, c/o Nomis Studios, 43/53 Sinclair Road, London, S14.

Competition Time. - Prizes will be signed live Jam albums. It's a crossword sent in to us by Emma Reid, London, club number 4055. Please make sure you mark COMPETITION on your envelope and do not enclose anything else in the envelope otherwise it could be destroyed.

The Questions, Paul's group on Respond Records, have re-recorded their single called 'Work and Play' available on 7" and 12". If you have any difficulties in obtaining this single then you should be able to get it from one of these shops;-

Virgin Records, Oxford Street.
Boots, Union Street, Glasgow.
H.M.V., Churchill Square, Brighton.
W.H.Smith, Church Street, Liverpool.
W.H.Smith, Eldon Square, Newcastle.
W.H.Smith, Queen Street, Cardiff.

Hope this helps.

Last correspondence from The Jam fan club in January 19

The Jam always had time for their fans, and that day stays with me to this day. I went on to play drums for some cool indie bands in the late Nineties as well as doing a bit of session work and a Radio 1 John Peel session - all this is down to The Jam and Rick. Without being obsessed with all of them I wouldn't have felt the need to play music. I mean, I doubt many kids that listened to Duran Duran felt the same!

A couple of years later I got to go to see the Style Council and met Paul Weller and his dad. His dad was so cool with me and got me in the changing room and gave me an access all areas pass for the next night.

I don't have the drumsticks any more. Lord only knows where they went – gutted to this day! I met Rick again at his book launch in London a few years ago and recited my story to his wife, who laughed out loud at the ballsy teenager knocking on their door.

I WAS THERE: CHRIS WILLIS, AGE 14

My first ever gig was The Jam in their last tour - I was just 14. Inside the cavernous Wembley Arena or at least it was to me then, I watched Big Country, the then little known support act but don't remember them at all due to the excitement of seeing my heroes.

The Jam were unbelievable and were no longer the three piece I knew as they were joined by a horn section, Merton Mick on keyboards - a Style Council precursor - and the three girl backing singers. Stand out songs I remember were 'Beat Surrender', 'Absolute Beginners' and a cover of Curtis Mayfield's 'Move on Up'. Hot, sweaty, deafening magic!

Chris Willis found The Jam to be a deafening magic

I WAS THERE: GAVIN JONES

Well here it was, the final tour, and once the disappointment of the split announcement had worn off, we were going to another Jam gig!

Off in the Beetle again down to Wembley with my friends Marc and Steve. We actually all had tickets and got there about 1.30. There was no one there at that time, just touts, so we went to a pub and then back about three to see if we could get in for the sound check. Stuart Adamson of Big Country came over for a chat and then the band arrived in separate cars. By this time there was quite a crowd trying to get in. Then we heard the sound check start and realised no one was getting in this time.

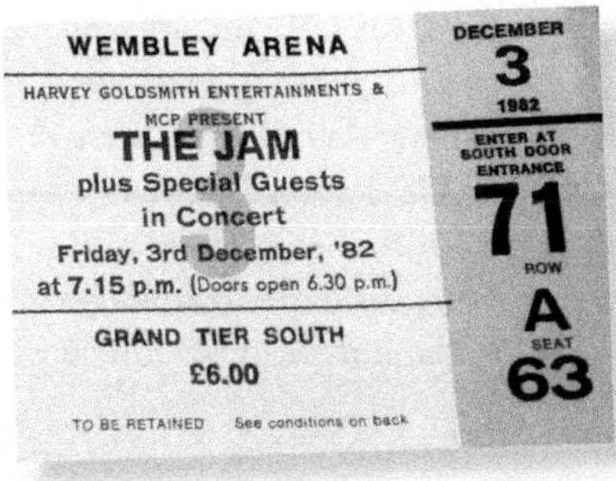

WEMBLEY ARENA
HARVEY GOLDSMITH ENTERTAINMENTS & MCP PRESENT
THE JAM
plus Special Guests
in Concert
Friday, 3rd December, '82
at 7.15 p.m. (Doors open 6.30 p.m.)
GRAND TIER SOUTH
£6.00
TO BE RETAINED See conditions on back
DECEMBER 3 1982
ENTER AT SOUTH DOOR ENTRANCE 71
ROW A
SEAT 63

We went with a crowd of about ten London lads down the side of the arena and found a fire door slightly open, which got more open as we pulled it, and we all squeezed through to sneak into the sound check on the balcony - a massive place with just us in there! The Jam did a couple of songs and then were just mucking about with soul covers, etc. possibly a preview to Paul's new direction. We were kicked out by a security guard and went and sat in the car till the doors opened.

When we went in and found our seats were right at the back on the balcony, it was like watching the television when Big Country came on! They did a good set, with a great guitar sound from Adamson, then after about an hour on came The Jam.

It was a good set, starting with 'Start!', followed by 'In The Crowd', 'Away From The Numbers', 'It's Too Bad' ,'To Be Someone', 'Ghosts', 'Smithers Jones', 'David Watts' and 'In The City'. They only did one encore, 'But I'm Different Now' and 'The Gift', then said, 'Thanks for the last five years.' The set was good, but only lasted about one hour and fifteen minutes which was a bit short for a farewell gig. Still we went home happy, looking forward to the next show in Birmingham a few days later.

I WAS THERE: STEVE JOEL-DICKS

I was at their supposed last gig ever at Wembley, but I think they did a local gig in Woking just after. The highlight for me was hearing them perform 'Butterfly Collector' live.

I WAS THERE: MARK EATON

Me and my mate got our photo in *Smash Hits*. Remember it like yesterday. Beer cans everywhere, brilliant gig.

ROYAL SPA HALL

6 DECEMBER 1982, BRIDLINGTON, UK

I WAS THERE: PETER FLETCHER

We caught the bus at the train station. We were early so we could secure the best seats on the bus. This was going to be different - we were travelling to the concert and we would not be early so we decided early on that we would go for a pint on arrival rather than queue. The coach filled up and pretty soon we were on our way. As we were on a coach we started a sing song - only Jam songs allowed – and opened up with 'Strange Town' which we managed to sing the whole way through. 'Tube Station' and 'Butterfly' followed we even sang 'Ghost'. There was only me and my friend Mark that knew most of the lyrics. We weren't great singers but at least we knew the words which is more than could be said for the others. As far as we were concerned we were the veterans and they were all newbies. We deserved better.

Arriving at Bridlington we charged to the Harbour Lights for a beer or two and then wandered into the venue last, which was a first. We bought the programme, what the hell? It was the last time we would be able to do so and it was with a heavy heart that we did.

I don't remember seeing the support - we might even have missed it. We went for a pee and didn't rush ourselves into the hall. When we did it was quite small inside and the atmosphere was subdued - more like just before an eclipse. The Jam walked on stage and it felt like there was an elephant in the room. But it was soon forgotten as they banged out our favourite songs. Somehow me and Mark got to the front, shouting out all the lyrics. We were both a little tipsy and the atmosphere became electric again. We were back at the Queens Hall, Leeds in the early days and the guys were on fire. Eventually 'Beat Surrender' was played - I still hate that song. Encore done and Bruce thanked us all and was very emotional about it. Paul said thanks and they all took a bow. Bruce had tears in his eyes and so did we.

On the trip home we were very quiet. The newbies tried to sing songs they thought they knew.

I WAS THERE: GRAHAM HEALD

I first heard The Jam in 1977. My mate bought *In The City* - I was about 14 and loved the punk scene but The Jam stood out for me.

I would have been about 17 or 18 at the time of the gig - I lived in Leeds and our mate had just passed his driving test and bought an old Escort van. About five of us travelled to Bridlington. We had a few pints round the town then went to the gig.

They played all the classics. We hung about in The Spa afterwards and were being chased all over by the bouncers. Then Paul, Bruce and Rick appeared from backstage and Paul shouted to leave us be - there were about 30 or 40 fans gathered round the band asking questions. The band signed tickets and t-shirts and other bits of paper!

I WAS THERE: DAVID BRADSHAW, AGE 15

My sister and all her friends were Mods/scooterists and avid Jam fans. The tickets had sold out but she contacted Hamilton's in Middlesbrough and luckily someone had cancelled last minute and the rest is history. I had a can of Yorkshire bitter on the bus and into the gig! I can't believe how scary it was. Like being in a pressure cooker, the atmosphere was something I've never witnessed since and I've been to quite a few gigs over the years. It changed my life forever and it's just a shame it was the final tour and this chance would never come round again. I'm glad in a way that they never reformed as you cannot recapture an era and atmosphere generated by a youth movement that lived and breathed The Jam.

I WAS THERE: DAVE MOLLISON MOLLA

I went to 1979 79 Newcastle City Hall and 1982 farewell tour at Bridlington Spa. Both occasions were just electric. At the City Hall gig I always remember Bruce looking up at the balcony and I'm sure to this day he was staring at me thinking to himself, 'Look at that young kid giving it all to 'Strange Town'.'

I WAS THERE: TRICIA ROBINSON

I drove all the way to Bridlington from Scunthorpe with the exhaust tied up on my mum and dad's Hillman Avenger car, just so I didn't miss them. I still have my programme and still own every single, twice. One lot played and the others still in mint condition. I also have the single that has 'YMCA' by Village People on it, but the Start label on the record. Best band ever.

APOLLO

7 DECEMBER 1982,
MANCHESTER, UK

I WAS THERE: MIKE LEE

No sooner had my older brother walked in the house with a copy of the album *In The City* than I just knew I had to have it. I was 13 at the time and after some persuasion my mum and dad eventually let me go to a gig. I then saw The Jam both nights of every tour they played when they appeared at the Manchester Apollo.

My fondest memory is the last tour in December 1982. I missed out in the queue for tickets as they sold out - I was gutted! On the night of the gig I went to the Apollo and managed to get let into the building for the sound check (which I'd done many times before). I then just hung around town all day. As gig time grew nearer I tried getting a ticket but the touts outside the venue were asking way more than I could afford.

I moved round the back of the Apollo waiting for show time. Eventually I heard the familiar bass line for 'Start!' We're off!

After a couple of songs I found it too upsetting only being able to listen through the back stage door and decided during 'Away From The Numbers' I should go home. Then suddenly the door flew open and big Kenny Wheeler stood there and said, 'Right, no fucking pushing and you can come in.' There were around 15 of us – we all froze, looking at each other in disbelief. We marched in like little boy soldiers behind big Kenny and made our way around the back of the stage and came out in the Apollo stalls, opposite Paul. To top it all they were playing my favourite song - 'Ghosts'. Best night ever!

I WAS THERE: MICHAEL HARRISON

I saw them at the Apollo in Manchester in the Eighties, I was only young, and it was all a blur even then, but I'll never forget the excitement and the energy they brought. The place went crazy when the lads came on stage. Great show - one of the best.

I WAS THERE: PAUL TANSEY, AGE 17

I was 17 years old and had been a Jam fan from the very beginning but due to my age I had never been allowed to attend a gig up to that point. Once the announcement to split up had been made that summer it almost became a pilgrimage to get to the Manchester Apollo gig before it all ended.

My first driving test was on the morning of the gig itself, December 7th 1982, three days after my 17th birthday and realistically it was my only possible way of making the journey.

Paul Tansey took his driving test on the morning of a Jam gig

Fortunately I passed first time, and without asking my mother (whose Mini Clubman Estate I had used to learn and take the test), I drove straight to Manchester after the test and joined the queue for the gig.

Not the coolest mode of transport by some margin and still not sure how I made it there, or back home, but my one and only Jam gig was worth the adventure and the severe bollocking I got when I arrived home in the early hours of the following day.

I WAS THERE: ANDY COCKAYNE, AGE 15

I was 15 and went on the coach from Sheffield with my mate Steve - we had matching red cardigans with blue pinstripes! We were stood queuing outside when the bands coach arrived.

I remember at the end of the gig, grown men were crying, all these years later I now know why. Fantastic memories – I've seen Weller loads of times since and also From The Jam on a number of occasions.

I WAS THERE: DAMIEN MORRIS

I watched the Jam on many occasions (I think it was 12 in total) mainly Manchester but also Leeds, Bingley Hall and Saddleworth Arts Festival. I can still remember the day they split and being absolutely gutted about it. This was made worse by missing out on tickets for the farewell tour at Manchester Apollo.

The night of the gig me and a mate decided to try and get a ticket outside but they were pretty scarce - the touts were asking £20 which was more than we could afford in those days. After a time we went in the Apsley Cottage (the pub at the back of the Apollo), had a pint and agreed to have one last walk around the venue to try to find a ticket.

We walked past the stage door where there was a group of about 20 people so we went over to find out if anything was going on. After a couple of minutes John Weller opened the door and said 'give me five minutes and you'll all get in'. We pushed a little further into the crowd and right enough a few minutes later the door reopened and John let us all in. He lead us under the stage (by this time The Jam were on stage) to a door and at this point he said once he opened the door (which led into the downstairs seating) it was 'everyman for himself'. The door opened and there was about three bouncers with their backs to us, completely unaware we were about to charge in and with the element of surprise we manage to avoid them and run into the crowd. A great night - I only missed about two or three songs and earned great bragging rights over my mates who never went.

BINGLEY HALL

8 DECEMBER 1982, BIRMINGHAM, UK

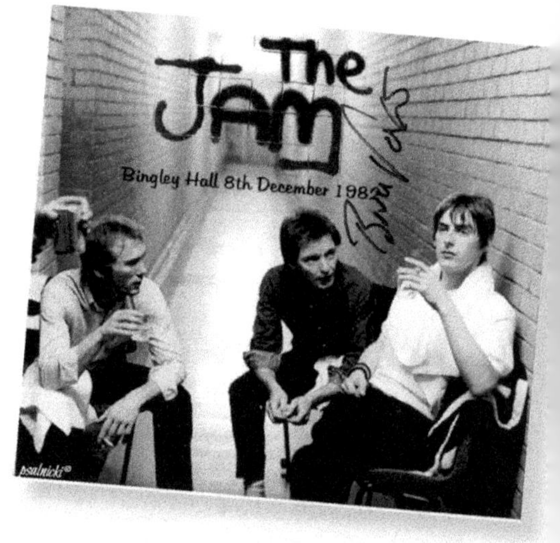

I WAS THERE: PETER SALNICKI, AGE 21

In the late Seventies, I was more into new wave bands like The Police and Blondie. I had heard some of the early Jam singles like 'The Eton Rifles', but really got into them when, in a pub, a couple of my mates, Mark and Anthony, started singing the lyrics to 'Saturday's Kids'. The next day I bought the *Setting Sons* album on vinyl and from then on I was hooked. I still have that album and some of the singles I bought.

By winter 1982 I had already been to see The Jam live three times, at Stafford and Birmingham. However, this concert at Birmingham was going to be very different. The band had just announced that this was going to be their last ever tour before splitting up. There were only two more Jam concert dates in England after this one (Guildford and Brighton). So it was up to Birmingham early one very rainy morning to join an already large queue for tickets as, remember, there was no internet back in those days to book tickets on!

THE JAM
+ SPECIAL GUESTS
BINGLEY HALL, BIRMINGHAM
Wednesday December 8th 7.30pm
Tickets £5.00 (incl. VAT)
Nº 0803

The real bonus was the concert was just three days after my 21st birthday. Birmingham Bingley Hall was a very large indoor venue, which was used mainly for exhibitions. For concerts it was virtually all standing for the crowd, which suited the type of crowd that followed The Jam, rather than the Birmingham Odeon which had just seats for about 3,000 people.

Outside the venue on the night it was chaotic. There were loads of fans outside without tickets, either trying to buy spares or attempting to rush the entrance to just get inside. I was glad to just get in OK, but was gutted I didn't get chance to get a t-shirt, but did buy what I thought was the programme – which turned out to be just some magazine on the group, but it was a souvenir anyway.

I was never into being crushed at the front of crowds, and preferred to stand a bit further back, but that night the whole hall was packed and very hot! Even before the band came on, the crowd were singing various Jam and football songs. The atmosphere was electric, but at Jam concerts you always felt they were also on the edge of violence.

Peter Salnicki (second from left) in the pub with friends

Eventually Paul Weller's dad came on stage, and announced, 'This is The Jam - the best band in the fucking world' and the place erupted, as the guitar chords of 'Start!' sounded. They went through all the different albums that night, loads of songs from *All Mods Cons* and *Setting Sons* as well as the more up to date songs. It was so hot in there you could see the steam rising off the crowd. I'm sure I remember being disappointed though that the last song they played was 'The Gift', as it didn't seem very poignant.

After the concert ended, there was quite a large gang of skinheads hanging around outside the venue, obviously looking for trouble. I don't think they anticipated though how many Mods were going to come streaming out and chase them all the way down Broad Street, chanting 'We are the mods, We are the mods', just like in the film *Quadrophenia*.

It was sad to think that even though they were brilliant that night, it would be the last time I would see them live. But maybe it was better that they went out at the top.

Fast forward to 2017, and I was lucky enough to be invited to a sound check of From The Jam with Bruce Foxton. It was fantastic hearing them play some of The Jam songs, like 'Ghost'. I actually got to meet them afterwards as well, and had my photo taken with Bruce. He also very kindly signed a photo I had of The Jam from that actual concert I went to in Birmingham in 1982. It's now stored away safely with my tickets that I kept from the concerts I went to.

I WAS THERE: GAVIN JONES

So the final day had come. My last ever Jam gig. I picked up my friends Trev and Tracy and then went on to pick up my other mate Marc. We got there about two in the afternoon and went for a drink, and then to the hall when the pub closed. The sound check wasn't until five, so we went to their hotel and saw Bruce who had a chat then got on the coach. Then Rick came down and stood talking for a bit. Marc asked him what he was going to do now and he said he had no plans yet, but he'd been back to ask for his old job back and they turned him down!

Then Paul came out, signed some autographs and got on the coach. We went to the hall and got let in the sound check by a very cheerful Kenny. I smuggled a tape recorder in and got a muffled recording of the sound check, where they did 'Beat Surrender', 'Precious', 'Planner's Dream' (rare to see live) and 'Reach Out'.

Once we had been kicked out we went to a cafe past the band's hotel, and saw comedian Jim Davidson there. We went to a pub and met mates Hoppy, Lisa and Penny, then to the gig and caught the last half of support act Apocalypse, not bad. We went right down to the front, and after half an hour The Jam came on. The set was similar to Wembley, but delivered with a lot more venom, leading to a great atmosphere, hot and sweaty. They finished with 'In The City'.

After about 10 minutes they came on for an encore, doing 'A Town Called Malice', 'Butterfly Collector', 'But I'm Different Now', and last song I ever saw them do live, 'The Gift'. Then Bruce knocked his mic stand over and Paul threw his guitar on the floor and walked off.

I grabbed a *Final Tour* poster, then went back to their hotel, freezing as the cold air froze our sweaty bodies! Bruce was there signing autographs, then went to bed. Then Paul and Rick came down after about half an hour. We chatted with them and thanked them for the last few years, almost shaping our lives with powerful music and inventive, insightful lyrics, as well as never forgetting the fans. I shook Paul by the hand and that was it - the end.

John said he could get us in to the Brighton gig if we turned up at the sound check, but I couldn't afford to get there. I was skint!

I WAS THERE: JUDITH SCULLY

I saw the Jam several times but on their farewell tour we couldn't get tickets for our hometown gig in Birmingham. There were four of us and we decided to go anyway to see if there were any touts. We had no luck so decided to head home. Walking up past the end of Bingley Hall a coach comes past with the boys on it. We started waving manically and Bruce started pointing ahead. We walked round the corner and there was the stage door. We hung around for probably 30 minuets when suddenly John Weller comes and lets us in. The best bit was we had to run across the stage in front of the huge crowd. Pure magic for us.

CIVIC HALL

9 DECEMBER 1982, GUILDFORD, UK

I WAS THERE: DEL BOXALL

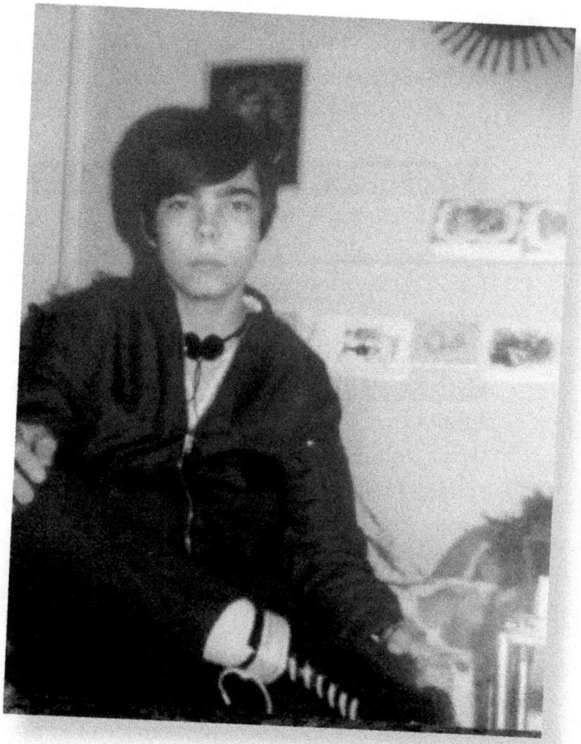

Del Boxall wearing his Sony Walkman headphones

I first heard The Jam on the radio and had always liked them but it wasn't until 1982 when 'The Bitterest Pill' came out that I thought, 'This is the best track I've ever heard and this band are now my favourite.' I straightaway started buying the old records but sadly they announced they were splitting within a couple of weeks.

This was their penultimate gig. I'm from Guildford and I lived about two minutes walk from the Civic Hall. I didn't have a ticket but was trying to watch through the doors from outside but got really lucky when a bloke turned up and wanted help taking some boxes in. Me and another guy helped him carry them in and got to stay. 'Down in the Tube Station at Midnight' was brilliant. It was December 1982 and the next night was the final gig in Brighton.

Fast forward about five or six years and I used to drink in the Plough in Guildford and Bruce Foxton also used to drink there. He would sometimes watch us play darts on Monday nights.

About eight years ago, Rick Buckler's mum had a flat in the same block as my mum and I used to clean her carpets (I'm a carpet cleaner) and I remember her showing me a photo book of The Jam. She also told me her son isn't really called Rick - his name is Paul - but I don't think Weller wanted two Pauls in the band. I often see Paul Weller in Ripley where he has a recording studio. He was in the baker's last week when I was in there. Small world.

The two tracks I have played the most in my life are 'The Bitterest Pill (I Ever Had to Swallow)' and 'The Boy with the Thorn in his Side' by The Smiths.

I WAS THERE: WOODY JONES

I went to the Guildford show and had my cassette machine confiscated on the door. What a bummer. In those days it was normally easy to get your cassette recorder in. I was just unlucky!

I first heard the band in 1976, and had always loved their sound. I loved the energy and fast pace of the early days, and then later the softer sound of *The Gift*. I will also argue that The Jam were the greatest band ever. Oh, and it was a belter of a show.

I WAS THERE: ALISON WHIBLEY, AGE 15

I saw them at the final gig at the Guildford Civic Hall - then they added Brighton! I was 15 and got right to the front by the stage and was warned to get back by some concerned fans. I didn't move and awoke to a black eye the next day! It was fantastic and I'll always be grateful to my big brother for buying me two tickets as a loan so I could go with a mate!

I WAS THERE: MARTIN WILLIS

I first heard The Jam at a friend's house on April 29th. He'd bought a copy of the first single, 'In The City', on the day of release. I was blown away by the sound and instantly hooked on the raw, aggressive melody - it was a light bulb moment in my life and I knew things would never be the same.

Martin Willis drank, smoked and chatted backstage with The Jam

My first gig was at the Reading Top Rank in 1977 and I subsequently travelled far and wide all over the country and once to Reims in France (in 1979) to see them. I was lucky enough to get back stage and meet the lads at Reading University in February 1979 - we drank and smoked and chatted.

On the 9th December 1982 The Jam's final tour before splitting up was drawing to a close with the penultimate gig at Guildford Civic Hall for their farewell to their Surrey fans.

Having seen them 26 times since 1977, I was determined to go although I didn't have a ticket, hoping for the off chance of getting in on the door. We left Reading in two cars and travelled to Guildford. When we arrived there was a massive crowd buzzing around outside and we found out that most of these people didn't have tickets and that the venue was sold out and practically full to the rafters so my friends tried to push to the front to get to the main doors.

Thinking it highly unlikely that anyone was going to gain entry at the front, I slipped around to the rear of the building and made my way to some double glass doors where I saw a large doorman standing. I gestured to him, 'Could I come in?' and he slowly shook his head. I even waved some money at him but to no avail.

I stood there for about 15 minutes and by this time The Jam were playing and the crowd was cheering. It was a cold winter's night and I was wearing my blue mohair suit (it was freezing) and I was about to give up and walk back to my mate's at the front of the venue when a stocky silver haired middle aged guy walked up to the doorman - I knew straight away it was Paul's dad, John Weller. As he chatted to the doorman he glanced at me through the glass doors, seeing me stood there suited up and looking cold. He told the doorman to open the door and let me in, which the doorman did, telling me it was my lucky night.

Once I was inside John Weller said, 'Come with me'. So I followed him as he guided me up onto the balcony, directly off the side of the stage where family and friends of the band were sitting. He told me I'd be OK there and went on his way.

I had a great seat only a few feet from the band and had the most memorable Jam gig of them all. Paul's dad was such a lovely guy for giving me a night I will never forget!

Sadly my mates weren't so lucky and spent the night outside the venue on that cold December night.

I WAS THERE: PAUL RUSSELL, AGE 13

I've been a massive Jam fan since I was 10 and still am. I was lucky enough to go to their penultimate gig at Guildford Civic Hall (now G Live) on 9 December 1982.

My mum bought five tickets for me from the *Surrey Advertiser* classifieds as a birthday present as my 13th birthday was on the day of the gig. As I was too young to go on my own so I went with a cousin of a school friend. It was a cold December night and it was packed outside the Civic Hall. My friend's cousin had three remaining tickets to sell and I remember there being heated discussions outside between prospective buyers and my friend's cousin.

Inside the Civic we were right at the top, in the area they now call the circle, as I was too young to go down the front. It was my first gig. Once The Jam came on stage the atmosphere was electric. I remember the steam coming off the wave of kids at the front and Bruce saying, 'It's all right for you lot – it's fucking hot down here'.

Paul Russell takes his latest look into the garden

It seems a long time ago now and I will be 50 this December but I do have a bootleg CD copy of the gig and photographs to remind me. My memories are now not that clear - I was nervous, excited and in awe the whole night.

Paul Russell's shoes

I WAS THERE: DAVE BAILEY

It was a cold December night in 1982 and I was off to see the Jam for the very last time at the Guildford Civic Hall, the closest venue to my hometown of Woking. My feelings were mixed - this was the end, after all - but the excitement of a Jam gig was something special, indescribable to those who never got to see them in the flesh. On a more practical level, I was wearing my uniform Lonsdale short sleeved sweat-shirt and green bomber jacket (the look adopted by the band, especially Rick, in that year). I'd also worn this combination at the previous gig I'd attended - in Brixton that March to promote the *Gift* LP, but I'd made one terrible mistake: I didn't take off the bomber jacket and ended up in what I can only describe as a full on sauna situation. By the end of the gig I was soaked in my own sweat, having spent the previous hour being swept up and down in a continuous mass pogo. The venue was jam-packed (pun inevitable) and we moved as one the whole night. So this time I thought I'd be smart and take the jacket off before the start.

We got there early and managed to get to the front, where I stood clutching the jacket until one of the road crew asked me if I wanted to leave it on top of the flight cases for the PA system. Great, I thought - leaves me free to pogo the night away. And it was a strange night - first up the 'Eton Rifles Dance Troupe' improvising to the strains of 'Aquarius' from the show *Hair* (memorable for one of the girls' boobs falling out the side of her dungarees!), then the crowd verbally abusing compere Mike Read, and finally the very last time I would see the only band I ever loved.

Dave Baily and his mum after a Carnaby birthday shopping spree - the boating blazer and a pair of Jam shoes in the bag from Melandis!

It was a strange gig, mixed emotions, a set of amazing memories in song and then the end. We walked out into the cold night along the street to our waiting lift - probably one of our dads (we were 15 years old and had school the next day!) and I think it had begun to snow and that's when I realised I'd left the jacket on the flight case. I rushed back to the hall and much to my surprise, the doorman let me back in to the auditorium. An almost empty space, except for the road crew breaking down the gear. I stood there watching the drum kit being taken apart and the amps being wheeled off stage, wondering if, and hoping that the magical night would end with a glimpse of the band, when one of the crew said to me 'this your jacket mate?' and tossed me the green bomber from the stage. And that was it - Paul, Bruce and Rick didn't appear, but I felt their presence. I mean it would be difficult not to with those tunes still ringing in my ears. The tunes that for five years had been an ever present source of inspiration.

I WAS THERE: ANDY WELLBELOVE

I saw them around 20 times, from The Rainbow in London in 1979 to Guildford in 1982. Being from my home town of Woking they were 'our' band. I saw them many times in Guildford Civic and even at Sheerwater Youth Club in 80/81.

I've got to know Paul Weller since then and have renovated two of his houses and his recording studio just outside Woking. Top man.

I WAS THERE: RICHARD WALTER

I saved up all my paper round money, bought a ticket from Bonaparte's record shop and saw The Jam for the first and last time at Guildford Civic Hall. I believe that was their second to last gig ever. They played Brighton the next night - I'm honoured to have been there.

CONFERENCE CENTRE

11 DECEMBER 1982, BRIGHTON, UK

I WAS THERE: ANDY ROSEN

Paul Weller rang me up and asked me if wanted to photograph the last gig since I had covered so many of their concerts. The band gave me an all-access pass. I got good stuff before and after the gig. I even got a classic shot of John Weller walking across an empty arena after the gig. Everybody has gone and he looks pensive as he contemplates the end of The Jam.

The only shot I had never taken of the band was from behind the stage. I had many from the side. I wanted to capture the last moment looking through the band and to the audience. All the others I took could have been taken on any night, but the band 'saying goodbye' to their fans was the shot I had to get. On the last song, I dived back behind Rick's drums and got my chance. After that shot, I rushed back to the dressing room before they arrived and got the last shots of them coming backstage as The Jam.

I WAS THERE: JOHN GRAY

I saw them 10 times from 1979 until that last night at Brighton Conference Centre. The atmosphere at the front of the crowd was unbelievable, it's hard to explain the buzz you got. Great memories.

I WAS THERE: NICKY WELLER

I was one of the dance troupe. We came on stage before The Jam. Paul decided that it would be good to have this hippy dippy dance troupe on the last show and we all dressed like something out of San Francisco, with flowers in our hair - it was awful. There was me, Gary Crowley, Pete Barrett, Louise Court - there was about eight of us. We got booed off stage and stuff thrown at us but Paul thought it was hilarious. We first did it at Guildford, then down to Brighton. It was a bit mad but it was a laugh. We weren't on stage for very long because we had everything chucked at us.

But the night was very sad. I remember my dad being really sad. There's a picture of my dad that I used at The Jam exhibition walking across the floor with it all empty, he had his head bowed, it was just sad. It was an end of an era really. But Paul never really sat around, he was always wanting to go on and do something else. He keeps reinventing himself. He'd always be doing something, books, poetry. He's all about making the next best record or making something completely different.

We'd made an official announcement breaking the news about the end of The Jam in a newsletter to fan club members. During this time we had so many people hanging around outside our house. Some came with tents. We had a big green outside our place in Bramwell Drive - The Boundary - and they were pitching up their tents. There were people arriving on scooters and just hanging around all day, they were so upset. It really hit a lot of people.

Nicky Weller dressed as part of the dance troupe Eton Rifles with her brother Paul

I WAS THERE: MICHAEL FARRAGHER

A fellow Jam fan was supposed to get us tickets for the final gig at Brighton Centre which had been added late on after Guildford but he had let us down, so we had no tickets. We decided to go anyway and keep our fingers crossed we would get in by hook or by crook. Luckily we got let into the soundcheck. We hung around outside the stage door, desperately hoping by some miracle we would get in. Thankfully John Weller and Kenny Wheeler came out with a handful of complimentary tickets and we were let in. It was a strange and strained atmosphere onstage and in the crowd. Someone threw a bottle of beer on stage which just missed Bruce and the band walked off stage but they came back. The last song they played was '*The Gift*', a few farewell words were said and that was the end.

Michael Farragher's collection of signed Jam goodies

A fan said after the gig that it was the end of our youth and in a way it was. I was 18. I felt a huge sense of loss. I went to The Jam exhibition at

Somerset House in London and the Cunard Building in Liverpool which brought back so many memories for me. The Jam will always hold a very special - and a solid bond - in my heart.

I WAS THERE: ANDY ROSCOE

Whilst driving to work in Croydon, Mike Read made an announcement on Radio 1 that The Jam were going to play at Guildford Civic Centre as the last gig and tickets would go on sale that morning. So I drove straight to Guildford and got tickets. The very next day, again driving to Croydon, Mike Read announces they have added Brighton Centre to be the very last gig with tickets on sale that morning. Guess what? I turned around and drove to Brighton and got tickets. I'm very fortunate to have been at their last two ever gigs. A great band the likes of which we haven't seen since.

I WAS THERE: STEVE KEEN

I saw them at Guildford Civic Hall in December 1982 and then at Brighton Centre - their last gig. Fabulous days for a star struck 15 year old and Bruce became responsible for my lifetime of playing bass.

I WAS THERE: STEVE HUMBERSTONE

I saw them many times but the one time that sticks in my mind is the gig in Brighton. Living in London, I borrowed a Ford Escort estate and took myself and six passengers to the gig and straight back afterwards! The clutch had to be replaced on our return - but it was worth it!

I WAS THERE: CAROL LINTOTT, AGE 18

I guess I probably first heard of the band from the radio and then our friends playing their tracks. We soon bought our own vinyl copies and between myself, my sister and our step brothers we probably had all the albums. Then we started going to see them live.

I love pretty much all The Jam songs. A special favourite of mine is 'English Rose' from *All Mods Cons* followed by 'Precious' from *The Gift*.

I don't think any of us really believed that it would be 'the end'. A group of us went from Midhurst and my sister and her now husband stayed over in Brighton. I just remember us all being really sad. The place was packed. The last number, 'The Gift', went on for ages and ages, I guess

Carol Linott at Somerset House exhibition wearing the T-shirt bought in Amsterdam in 1982

that really was their parting gift, then I recall the band coming out on stage and waving and that was that! We didn't even save our ticket stubs; we have plenty of those but not from the last gig, which is a shame.

Set List:
Start!
It's Too Bad
Beat Surrender
Away From the Numbers
Ghosts
In the Crowd
Boy About Town
Get Yourself Together
All Mods Cons
To Be Someone
Smithers-Jones
Tales From the Riverbank
Precious
Move On Up
Circus
Down in the Tube Station at Midnight

Encore:
David Watts
Mr Clean
Going Underground
In The City
Town Called Malice

Encore 2:
The Butterfly Collector
Pretty Green
The Gift

I WAS THERE: BARRY CAIN

'Time is short and life is cruel…'

Sad, bleak words from the pen of the ever-acerbic Paul Weller, written when he was young and uncertain but also capable of dressing up those feelings in melodic finery that The Supremes would've died for. That's genius. That's understanding teenage souls implicitly. That's communicating. That's saying I know what you feel because I feel it too – the uncertainty and the despair, the passion and the love. Let's face the music and fucking dance…

That's Paul Weller and that was The Jam, a rock 'n' roll band that dished out the passion and love to those uncertain and despairing wasteland teenagers more than any other band I've ever known. After a shaky start, they cornered the market in credibility and cool and no doubt would've carried on cornering for many years if Uri Weller hadn't broken the silver spoon and adopted a Style Council estate of mind.

Was he right? I used to think not. I used to think he was insane. I used to think The Jam would've gone on to achieve greatness but they managed to throw it all away.

Now? Now I think in the 35 years that have passed since the split, they've gone on to achieve greatness anyway. And Paul Weller has gone on to achieve greatness in his own right, in his own way, on his own terms. The Jam were, in effect, his teenage years, y'know, hanging out with your mates and railing against the world and constantly thinking of girls and booze and football. Bruce and Rick were in his gang, watching his back, making him, them, tick, creating a unit of imperious measurement that delighted and provoked, the very essence of rock 'n' roll.

Jam scooter belonging to Steve Jones from Liverpool which was part of the About The Young Idea exhibition

From 1977 to 1982, I followed them every step of the way. The Hope & Anchor, spring '77, was the first time I saw them live. The Royal College of Art, the Rainbow, the opening show of their debut UK headlining tour at Barbarella's in Birmingham on the same night as the Pistols silver jubilee boat trip, Newcastle, Battersea, Stuttgart, Munich, and more, many more. First interview, a boutique in Carnaby Street, May '77, when they were swathed in Union Jack jackets and rancour – 'I can't imagine how anyone can go on stage at the age of 32 and sing 'My Generation' and still be a force.' Last interview, Paul and Rick in a West London pub autumn '82, days after after the end was announced. Bruce was a no show. He wasn't ready to talk about the break up.

I lived the dream with The Jam and when I saw them in Brighton for that last show I shed a tear. Our paths crossed rarely after that. Marriage, kids, lives in overdrive heading in different directions. From around 1984, I never saw any of them again for 25 years until I hugged Bruce and Rick at the funeral of Bruce's first wife, Pat.

Another five years went by before I bumped into Rick at a pub in the West End where a band he managed was performing. I asked him if he wanted to do a photo session and interview for a revamped online version of *Flexipop!*, a magazine I co-created in 1980 in which The Jam often appeared – even providing the exclusive flexi disc for issue two, 'Pop Art Poem' and a 'Boy About Town' remix. He agreed and a few weeks later, Rick asked me to read his book, *That's Entertainment*, before it came out and he kindly mentions me in the 'Thanks' section. Reminded me of 'Special Thanks To Mr. B. Cain' on the back of *This Is The Modern World*. Teenage blue anyone…?

A year later, the *About The Young Idea* documentary, coupled with The Jam exhibitions at Somerset House and the Cunard in Liverpool, threw me into their paths again. I ended up having a coffee and a fag with Paul at the café in Somerset House, our first meeting in over 30 years. A few months later, he agreed to appear in the republished version of my book *'77 Sulphate Strip* as the final interview.

In common with many supremely successful bands, there seems to be none of the one for all, all for one attitude between these three musketeers. The last time Rick saw Paul, Mr. Weller was fatherless. now he's the proud dad of eight kids. Time flies when you're having fun. It's always sad when friends fall out, it borders on the tragic when those friends were once members of the biggest band in the land. Shit happens, especially in your own backyard.

But let's not dwell on the shit. We should be concentrating on the legacy – the six glorious studio 33s, the stream of classic 45s, the hundreds of spectacular gigs, the style, the Mod osmosis or mosmosis as it never came to be called, the indefatigability, the joy. Above all, the joy.

As the musician said to his colleagues in the Titanic movie – and let's face it, we're all sinking ships – 'Gentlemen, it's been a privilege.'

THE JAM, JOYBRINGERS

Sometimes, just sometimes, I don't envy my kids their ages…

Here is that last interview I did with Paul and Rick after they announced the band were going to split.

OK, so how do you feel about it, Rick?

Rick: I personally think we could have had more to contribute but at the back of my mind I knew we shouldn't go on forever. We all knew it would happen eventually.

But you would rather it happened later rather than sooner?

Rick: Depends how you think.

But if Paul hadn't decided to end it, The Jam would've continued?

Rick: Yeah.

Paul: I told Rick and Bruce in the middle of August. In my own mind I've been thinking about it for some time. There are a lot of contributory factors as to why, but it's mainly on a personal level, the way I feel as a person. That's what really made my mind up. One day I just woke up and thought about the whole secure situation The Jam was in and it terrified me. The fact that we could go on for another ten years and have hits and be successful, which we know we could do, really frightened the life out of me. I'm 24 and here I am SECURE. That's when I decided I wanted it to end.

What do you mean, 'secure'?

Rick: To know what's going to happen to you in the future.

And you don't like the idea of that?

Rick: No. It's similar to the feeling people get when they suddenly realise they've done everything that's required of them in normal circumstances – marriage, house, children, job. And then you get to thinking it's gonna be that way for the rest of your life. That's all there is left.

But The Jam has given you both security which in turn has enabled you to do what you're doing now.

Paul: Right and I'm not knocking any of it. I can understand if Rick and Bruce are pissed off about the split. That's fair enough. But at the same time, I don't want to get too sad about it. We've really achieved a lot in six years. We've done everything a group could do.

Rick: I haven't got anything to be sad about at all.

Paul: It's best to quit while you're on top. You can't go much further than The Jam. Splitting now means you can hold your head up high. I hear the Who are going to split up soon but who really cares? I'd hate us to go on like that because people don't look at all the good things you've done. They just focus on the crap. All the good you've done gets cancelled out. To me, The Jam will always mean something and it will never lose that meaning.

How did you break the news to Bruce and Rick?

Paul: I just told them.

What was their reaction?

Paul: Hard to say. You'll have to ask them. I think they took it pretty well.

Were you worried about telling them?

Paul: Yeah. It's a difficult thing to do.

What did you say? Was it something like, 'Look, I think we come to the end and it's time we did something different'?

Paul: Something like that

Were they surprised or were they expecting it?

Paul: They were surprised.

I heard they were expecting it.

Paul: That's crap. All these papers talk crap. It's like all these 'close friends' we've suddenly acquired. Y'know – 'A close friend of the group tells me.' Utter crap.

But you're upsetting a hell of a lot of people. Doesn't that concern you?

Paul: Sure – but you've got to put yourself first. Look, if I carried on doing what I've been doing over the last few years – touring, releasing albums, choosing the singles – I'd go mad. I need time to get out of this whole insular set up. We're not public property. Never have been and never will be.

But isn't that a selfish attitude?

Paul: Yeah, maybe it is. But at the same time they are important reasons to help me keep sane. Oh sure, aside from that I still firmly believe that we've achieved everything. Sure, if we didn't give a fuck about it and decided we were only in it for the money we could plough on forever. But The Jam has always been much more than that. Right from the start it has always transcended just being a group and just being music. It's much, much stronger.

In what way?

Paul: The whole feel about it. The contact with our fans or always trying to stand by what we've said or always remaining the same people. I'm proud of what we've done.

But hasn't the fact that you haven't sold records outside of the UK in any significant amounts played a part in the decision to split up?

Paul: No! I read something in *The Sun* that said I want to expand and have a brass section and girl singers and that Rick and Bruce want more success in America. That's bullshit. Never believe the rumours. The fact that we haven't been successful elsewhere is just hard luck on those people. We've always played whatever we wanted and if people pick up on that, great. We've never tried to change to capture another market.

Have the personal relationships between the three of you – which have remained something of a mystery – had any effect on your decision? Have your attitudes towards each other changed much?

Rick: Obviously they do. At the start you're mates and then as it grows you become business colleagues. You're there for a different reason then when you started the band.

Can you honestly describe yourself as friends?

Rick: I think we could. OK, so we don't socialise. But we're still friends.

Paul: If anything, our relationship has gone onto a more polite level, which in a way is a bad thing. When we first started out we used to hang out with each other all the time and get on each other's tits and argue and say exactly what we felt. A lot of it was to do with our age. We were so young. But now our relationship has mellowed and as a result, maybe it's lost some of its edge.

Can you talk to each other or are there embarrassing silences?

Paul: Don't you think that happens with everybody? We all live in different areas, we've all got girlfriends, we've all got our own circle of friends. You haven't got so much to talk about. It's not that the band falls apart, it's little things like when one of you meets a girl so you wanna be with that girl as much as possible. In fact. I'm the worst offender for that. When I first met Jill I totally cut myself off from Rick and Bruce, which I now kinda regret.

Why?

Paul: Because I think we could have been, well...we are still mates, still close, ain't we?

Rick: Yeah and we always will be.

Paul: When it boils down to it, I guess you're talking about going out and getting drunk together, which ain't so very important.

But can you honestly say now you've split up you'll remain friends?

Paul: When you've worked with people for ten years you're bound to.

But people work in jobs for that length of time, build up close relationships with their workmates yet when they leave they never set eyes on them again. Doesn't it worry you that that might happen?

Paul: I haven't thought about it.

What are your plans?

Paul: No concrete ones. The last thing I want to do is go out and get a really tight, insular thing again. I certainly don't want to recreate what we three have done.

Will you ever work together again?

Rick: It's possible but I can't see it happening, to be honest. The break will give us breathing space. I suppose we can do anything we like. But most problems you don't see until they happen.

Won't you be lost without Paul? After all, you're used to being part of a band where one member is so obviously the front man.

Rick: Well, if I just sit back and wait for something to happen it's going to be a lot worse. There are lots of things I want to do.

Like what?

Rick: Photography for one thing. And seeing friends. I guess they'll be the first things I'll take off the shelf.

Paul: Music will be first with all three of us because it's in our blood. The big mistake people make is adopting the 'I'll be all right' attitude. The Jam was a group. OK, I was projected as the front man but it was still a close knit group. The letters from the fans reflect that.

But you alone have been promoted as The Jam.

Paul: The fans don't see it that way. A lot of people, record company included, think I'm gonna blast in where The Jam left off and go straight to number one. That's bullshit. It just won't happen that easily and why should it?

But you do get pissed off when a Jam record doesn't get to number one.

Paul: You've got the wrong man.

But I know you think it deserves to be there.

Paul: Oh, I think all our records deserve to get to number one and I always have done since 'In The City'. But it doesn't choke me if they don't.

But how are you going to feel if you don't achieve the success in the future you achieved with The Jam?

Paul: But that's just what I've been talking about. That'll do me good and that's not because I'm arrogant. I'm less arrogant than all the other pop stars around. I simply need the challenge as an individual. It's not the success; perhaps I can't articulate it properly. Let me give you an example – when a Jam record gets to number one I can't find it in myself to be as elated and I should be.

Highs and lows of the last six years. What was the best time?

Rick: When we started off doing places like the 100 Club. When it was so fast it was unbelievable.

Paul: That era was the best. All the club dates. Everything was really moving. Not just us, everything. 1976 was so exciting.

Favourite Jam records?

Paul: The first two singles. *All Mods Cons* which was a whole new step. *Sound Affects*, the chain of singles from 'Tube Station' to 'Going Underground' which all had a similar sound.

So, you think Jam music was becoming a bit samey, a mite predictable and that might be another reason to quit? A lack of ideas?

Paul: I'm not sure about the lack of ideas. As a group we could go no further. But as individuals...

Rick: Though I do think about all the things we could have done, in the future. Maybe a change of direction.

Paul: Yeah, but then we could have ended up our own arses doing that. You said earlier you hadn't changed over the last six years. Is that really true? In some ways, maybe it isn't, but there's been no major change. I've always tried to stick to my word.

I don't think there's another band that would split up at this point in their career.

Paul: Right! No-one. You'll see The Clash celebrating their twentieth anniversary like The Stones are now. To me, that's disgusting.

So, what now? A low profile? It's been impossible to pick up a paper in the last two years without something about The Jam inside. I thought you decided a while ago to stop doing interviews.

Paul: I only ever do the ones I feel like doing. I haven't done *NME* or *Sounds* for a very long time.

Why?

Paul: Because I don't agree with their policies. Most of them stink. It's the same with the national press. I'll do *Flexipop!* and *Smash Hits* because I like them.

Will your dad, John, still manage you?

Paul: He understood the reasons behind the break-up. Him and me will always carry on – it's a partnership. We'll never split up.

Do you think the band will ever get back together again?

Rick: That would be a mistake. The only reasons would be either trying to recapture a memory which is impossible or for the money. Both would be wrong.

Paul: I know people will say it's easy to talk like that now and that we will get back together in the future. But those same people were saying I'd gone back on my word and that The Jam will never end. Well, they can now eat their fucking words.

OTHER ENCOUNTERS

I WAS THERE: STEVE SMITH

Around 2015 when I was driving a taxi, I had a traditional 2.4 family in the car. As we passed Bromley College of Technology, the mum said, 'And that, kids, is where your mum saw The Jam in 1979.' So I said, 'And that kids, is where your cab driver saw The Jam in 1979.' A top journey ensued, dad and kids feeling well left out. She was flabbergasted as to how we got tickets and I asked her how she got hers. Turns out she was events organiser at the college, and also a friend of Nicky Weller. Only 200 capacity that night. I remember it being small, but not that restricted.

I WAS THERE: LYNDA GATT

In the Seventies I went to a pub in Westfield, Woking Surrey - I didn't know it was Paul Weller's local. The rest of the band were there so they did a few numbers for us but asked us to contribute 50p for charity. My mum also worked as a clerk at the school Paul Weller attended.

I WAS THERE: PAULA MCLLROY

I never saw The Jam but I met Paul Weller in Milan Airport. He was very engaging and didn't mind that I approached him and said how much I enjoyed the music.

I WAS THERE: GAVIN UNDERHILL

About 10 to 15 years ago I was in London and walking along a main road in the Notting Hill area when I noticed a vintage Mini. I always like to take a closer look at such vehicles as, unlike today where they all look the same, cars from the Sixties, Seventies and Eighties which I remember fondly from my youth all had distinctive and easily recognisable designs. So as a result of doing that, I recognised the driver as none other than the Modfather – Paul Weller! But what was more strange was that he was looking at me just as curiously as I was looking at him, if not more so. This was probably because like many others at that time he thought I was Ricky Gervais, as I supposedly bore a strong resemblance to him.

People were even telling me I should become some kind of Gervais - David Brent tribute act, although I could never really see the similarity myself. Anyway, just to be on the safe side I've worn my hair pretty long since then in order to head people off at the pass!

Steve Park with Paul Weller at Heathrow Airport, December 2018

I WAS THERE: STEVE PARK

I met Paul Weller at Heathrow last December. We'd just dropped my boy off at the departure lounge and we were waiting while he went through Customs. I said to my wife, 'God, there's Paul Weller!' I called out and he came over and shook hands. We had a brief chat and, bearing in mind it was 7am, he looked bloody sharp!

I WAS THERE: RAY DAVIES – THE KINKS

The first time I saw Paul Weller on Marylebone High Street, he was wearing the same scarf as I was, and we were both wearing crombies. So he always had style.

NICKY SAUNTER

A few years ago we went to a Band of Skulls acoustic gig at Madam Jojo's and after we had a wander up Wardour Street. Paul Weller was doing a photo shoot. I lost the power of speech, like a complete tit... all I could think of was how many years I'd loved his music. How can that possibly be 40 years ago? *All Mod Cons* has to be one of the best albums ever!

JAM EXTRAS

After this book had gone into production we continued to receive more stories from fans – here is a selection of those memories:

CIVIC HALL

12 MARCH 1977, WOLVERHAMPTON, UK

I WAS THERE: PETER WRIGHT

I saw The Jam at Wolverhampton Civic very early in their career - I might still have the ticket stub somewhere. I remember a hail of spittle directed at the band (this was the tail end of punk) and Paul Weller threatened to wrap his guitar around someone as a result.

They were electric as were many of the other bands I saw at The Civic through the mid-Seventies and Eighties. I always thought the Civic was an ideal venue, unlike the aircraft hangars often used these days.

Punk rockers in tour row

A RIFT between two of Britain's biggest new wave bands has forced the Jam to quit the Clash tour. But the Jam, who embark on their own British tour next month, have added three London shows to their schedule — and all three concerts will be part of the Silver Jubilee celebrations,

The Jam, whose "In The City" album is number 30 in this week's MM chart, were originally due to play 10 concerts with the Clash. But, after playing at London's Rainbow theatre last week, the Jam left the tour.

WINTER GARDENS

9 JUNE 1977, EASTBOURNE, UK

I WAS THERE: ADRIAN FITZGERALD, AGE 17

I remember the gig well and still have the poster and ticket in safe keeping (alas not getting it signed by Paul Weller when he was in the pub after the concert). I was 17 at the time and working as an apprentice compositor at the *Eastbourne Herald*. I believe the support band was Wire. Rumour has it that The Jam were booked by mistake as folk act Wilbury Jam was the intention. It's hard to believe Paul Weller was only 18 at the time and writing such classic songs.

I WAS THERE: ELAINE HUGGETT

I was lucky enough to see them in Eastbourne at their gig at the Winter Gardens. It's hard to believe that was 42 years ago now! The Jam (along with a few other bands from that time) were new, young and exciting and a real breath of fresh air on the music scene, which had become a bit staid and boring. I could not believe they were coming to Eastbourne and rushed out to get tickets the day they became available. (There was no booking on line in those days!) The Winter Gardens was not even the biggest venue in Eastbourne, so I was very fortunate to get those tickets.

They looked sharp, sounded great and powered through the set list at a rapid pace. The audience were jumping up and down and cheering them on, as they treated us to songs such as 'All Around the World', 'So Sad About Us' and, of course, the mighty 'In the City', which stills sounds fresh and relevant today.

I cannot recall all the songs now, but I do remember them playing the 'Batman' theme!

The Jam went on to produce many other great songs before Paul Weller called it a day, and I am grateful I got to see them in those early days. I'm pleased to say I still have my treasured ticket too!

I WAS THERE: MARIO RIDDFORD, AGE 19

I was at one of their first gigs, which was held at the Winter Garden in Eastbourne, a very popular and a typical, rather conservative seaside town down on the south coast and a place where many people would come to retire. There were the usual pubs and nightclubs in town but the jewel in the crown for big names in entertainment was the Congress Theatre. This was built in the early Sixties and hosted touring West End musicals and plays, ballet, opera, comedy, TV celebs and live music. Unfortunately for me, my genre of music did not often come to Eastbourne which meant a trek over to Brighton's Top Rank or The Dome amongst other venues. However times were changing, and from middle of the road safe entertainment being booked at the Congress and in order to be keeping up with the latest trends, bands were now being booked next door at the Winter Garden, a Victorian exhibition centre where you could stand and jump around!

Enter The Jam. I was 19 years old. I couldn't believe it. After hearing them on the radio and seeing them on the television I was now going to see the real deal. The time had come. I was standing at the front when they came out on stage, sharply dressed in black suits, white shirts (top button undone) and loose black ties, plugging in their Rickenbacker guitars and with Rick fired up and ready to go on the drums. Bang! We're off.

From the opening chords Paul and Bruce were leaping around toing and froing to the mics with us jumping around at the front. It was not packed out and there were still a few people standing around at the sides and at the back of the venue. But with so much energy coming from the stage we were all bouncing around by the end of the gig, which seemed to be over in a flash. I wish you could have seen the smile on my face. So, what do we do now? Go for a drink in the pub next door - The Buccaneer - and, after a few pints to wind down, who should walk in? Yeah, only the band themselves plus, I believe, Paul's dad who I'm sure at the time was their roadie/manager driving a Ford Granada Estate car as the bands transport. Anyway, there they were having a pint, not being hassled too much and I'm thinking, 'Do I go over or do I leave them be?' By the time I decided what to do, a couple of girls (who my mate had recognised from school days) were chatting to them, so I figured they would rather chat to them than have me pestering. I'm guessing they had one or two things in common because soon after them meeting they all left the pub together.

Fast forward to 1982 and Saturday 11th December. A couple of mates and I got tickets for the extra date added to complete the final tour. Yep, the very last day of the final tour at the Brighton Centre. So here we are, sold out, packed out, sweat dripping and waiting for Paul, Bruce and Rick to take to the stage for the very last time as The Jam with everybody shouting and cheering. Then, the moment comes. The announcement, the spotlights, the cheering. There they are. Paul comes to the mic and says something. I can't hear a thing.

Then it's - bang! Here we go! Looking up at the balconies I can see that every single person is standing. Scarves and banners were being waved. It was more like a football cup final. Back down on the floor and it's just utter mayhem with no let up for the whole gig. I think the band asked a couple of times for people to chill a bit. Obviously that was never going to happen. Halfway through the gig I thought I'd hit the bar for a quick breather. I eventually managed to scramble my way out only to see my mate was already sitting there with a small gash on his head. Unlucky for him, he was in the line of fire from one of the missiles that were being thrown around. It was like a battlefield in there. Anyway after a quick refresher it was heads down and back in we go to see The Jam's final gig. Not a bad Saturday night out!

Since the breakup of The Jam I've seen Paul Weller a few times but have probably seen Bruce Foxton's From The Jam far more. Obviously it will never be the original Jam but I have to say that, with eyes closed, it's a close call. They usually play at the Concorde 2 down on Brighton seafront, a classic Victorian venue. Even now I still enjoy going to their gigs which tend to be every December and quite often on a Friday and Saturday night, with both nights being sold out, and playing a different Jam album each night, usually an album anniversary or a particular topic, ie. A-sides and B-sides of singles, etc. Bruce is still looking great, still managing the leaps, sounding as good as ever and playing to sold out venues. Thank goodness!

VILLAGE BOWL CONCERT THEATRE

15 JUNE 1977, BOURNEMOUTH, UK

I WAS THERE: PAUL LEACH

We started off in the Badger bar as we always did. From there it was only a stone's throw to the Chelsea Village situated in a block in Glen Fern Road.

We walked to the Village, showed our tickets and made our way down the stairs. On the right was the club. I think they still had super heroes painted on the walls. We had a look round for anyone we knew, got a beer and went into the Village Bowl next door. It was a small venue and your view was restricted by what I imagine were building support pillars.

As we made our way back to the disco before the bands played, the support band The Boys came down the stairs and we had a brief chat with them. We had previously seen them support John Cale.

The three members of The Jam were chatting to people in the club. We saw Gene October and several other members of the group Chelsea plus a group of punks from London showing off the latest ideas of fashion – zips everywhere and earrings a-plenty.

We made our way back to the Village Bowl and headed towards the stage. It was small and there was not a lot of room for the bands to perform.

The Boys came on first and I remembered some of their set from the John Cale gig – 'I Don't Care', 'Soda Dressing' (I bought the single) and 'Sick On You' from their 1977 debut album. They were better than the first time I'd seen them.

Then the much-awaited Jam came on, all suited and booted like they had just stepped out of Carnaby Street in the Sixties. The first thing that struck me was how graciously Paul Weller accepted the spitting. He ended up looking like a dressed Christmas tree, although why spitting was popular with the punks is beyond me. The set was really the single 'In The City' and the first album. They were slick and together with a good live sound. The crowd pogoed all the way through the set and there was just music with very little talking.

Three tracks that stick out for me were 'In The City', 'London Girls' and 'Theme From Batman'. After the gig everyone went straight into the club where both bands stood having a drink and chatting with the punters.

THE CAT'S WHISKERS

29 JUNE 1977, YORK, UK

I WAS THERE: GRAHAM MOISLEY

I was not only at The Jam gig at the Cat's Whiskers in 1977, but I was actually working there. The promoter, called something like Grobs, were evaluating a new PA system and mixing desk. I think the supplier was a company called Malcolm Hill, based in Maidstone, Kent, and they sent a 'professional' sound engineer who was showing us 'amateurs' how to operate a 16 into 4 into 2 desk.

We were still clueless at the end of the night, but I remember the guy was not into 'punk' and instead of headphones to monitor the sound, he had on a pair of ear defenders. The long hair and Afghan coat kind of gave it away as to where his musical interests lay. I can't remember if the PA system was bought or not.

The next gig was in Middlesbrough. I was a mere roadie carrying kit in and out. What made it memorable was that it coincided with my 20th birthday, and I am told I was very drunk in the Dragonara hotel afterwards, and that at least one round had been bought by John Weller, Paul's dad, who was their initial manager. I spent a year chasing the dream, then got a 'proper' job in IT!

MANIQUI HALL

14 JULY 1977, FALKIRK, UK

I WAS THERE: JOHN THOMSON

I was at the Maniqui in Falkirk when The Jam played there in July 1977.

I had seen them appear on *Top of the Pops* a few weeks earlier performing their new single, 'In the City' and thought they were fantastic on that. When I learned they were to appear at the Maniqui I quickly bought a ticket and couldn't wait to see them live.

The Maniqui is not a huge venue but big enough to attract a decent sized crowd and the place was fairly bouncing that evening. The Jam were something else and seeing a new wave band live for the first time on stage was an exciting and memorable occasion.

John Thomson saw The Jam at the Maniqui

The sound they made was very loud and aggressive but even at that early stage in their career you could recognise that they were very special and going places. I was there with some of my mates and we all had a great time and finished off the night with a few beers in the bar.

I kept my ticket from that gig.

TOP RANK

7 DECEMBER 1977, BRIGHTON, UK

I WAS THERE: DAVID WALLACE, AGE 16

I was a bored 16 year old in the summer of 1977 who'd led a fairly sheltered life. We'd grown up in rural Sussex listening to Led Zep/Pink Floyd/Genesis, etc. after the glam rock thing as young kids and life seemed very dull. Rumours were filtering through about this new phenomenon called punk rock.

My mate Jerry had heard The Jam were promoting their debut album on tour and off we went to the gig at Brighton Top Rank. We didn't really know what to wear as all we had were flared trousers and big collared patterned shirts, etc. so we adapted our school uniforms which included the only straight-legged trousers we owned. We just about got away with it, although there were a lot of older urban punk types in the long queue outside.

It was pay on the door - no problem! Admission was £1.10 - advance would have been £1.

Inside the atmosphere was quite scary and violent. People were pogoing and spitting at the support band, Essex's New Hearts, who later became Secret Affair. Their front man

Ian Page was very streetwise and cocky and a few glass pint pots came flying through the air in his direction. In the circumstances they played a blistering set (promoting their debut single 'Just Another Teenage Anthem') and I was surprised later that their recorded output was more power-pop than punk. They were therefore the first new wave band I ever saw and as such will always have a place in my heart.

When The Jam came on I was absolutely astonished by their energy and attitude. I was amazed at how loud it was. I was surprised that Paul Weller was swearing at the audience (with good reason as the pint pots and the airborne phlegm hadn't stopped). They were basically playing the first album and maybe some of the second. It was my first exposure to such high energy up-tempo tunes and life was never really the same again.

By 1980 I would have seen hundreds of new wave bands but that night in July 1977 was where it all started.

KING GEORGE'S HALL

12 JUNE 1978, BLACKBURN, UK

I WAS THERE: JOHN HALTON, AGE 16

I was gutted to miss The Jam on the *Setting Sons* tour just before Christmas, but three UK gigs, sandwiched between appearances at the Pink Pop and Loch Lomond festivals, gave us a second chance. When Paul, Bruce and Rick returned to the King George's Hall less than six months later had to be there.

'Going Underground' had entered the charts at number one. Polydor had reissued the group's older singles. The charts had never looked better and The Jam's profile had never been higher.

There was no alternative but to plead with our parents to queue for tickets outside Ames Records in the Market Square first thing on Monday morning for us, whilst we went to school.

Then on a cold wet June evening in 1980 - typical East Lancashire weather - we boarded the train at Burnley Central for the short journey to Blackburn - a risky place for two young Clarets to visit!

Safe inside the King George's Hall, our early arrival meant that the queue for the bar wasn't too long. Luckily being just 16 didn't stop us both getting served with pints of Thwaites.

We entered the auditorium and took up position in front of the huge Marshall speaker stack to the right of the stage. This was my first gig so a visit to the mosh pit was still a few gigs away.

We wondered who the support act would be. Our mates had been impressed by The Vapors who had that distinction in December. This time it was the turn of The Expressos. The highlight of their set was the excellent single 'Tango in Mono', but the large crowd gave them a lukewarm reception, at best.

Incessant chants of 'We want The Jam' were finally silenced when John Weller boldly strode on stage to introduce 'the best fucking band in the world'.

The power of guitar and drum filled the room with energy - The Jam were a powerhouse live. The set list was largely made up of favourites from *Setting Sons* and *All Mod Cons*. 'Going Underground' featured early on, whilst 'But I'm Different Now' gave fans a glimpse of what was to come on *Sound Affects*.

All too soon it was over. The force and directness of their lyrics spoke volumes to me and Andy - a couple of teenagers whose eyes were opened wide by a band whose songs had far more style and substance than their punk and new wave contemporaries. On a high from our experience, the journey back to Burnley was simply a blur.

VICTORIA HALL,

13 JUNE 1978, KEIGHLEY, UK

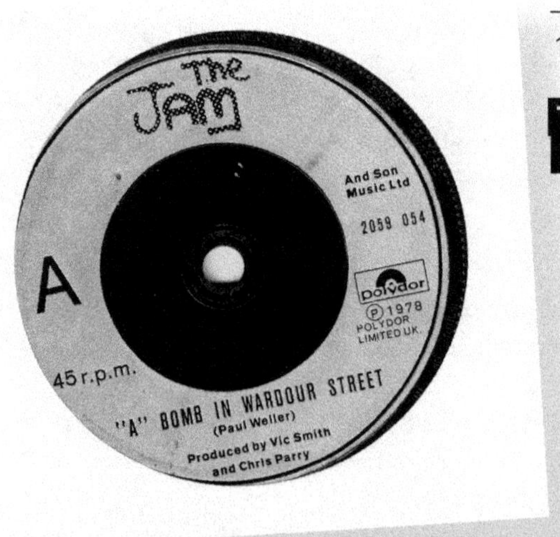

THEY WEREN'T THERE: GRAHAM SMITH

The Jam gig in Keighley in 1978 never went ahead. It was cancelled by the local council due to the noise limits being exceeded a few weeks previously by AC/DC. Years later Paul Weller played a solo gig at the same venue and anyone who had a ticket for the original gig in '78 could get in for free, which several of my mates took advantage of.

BARBARELLA'S

15 & 16 JUNE 1978, BIRMINGHAM, UK

I WAS THERE: DAVID JONES

I was a big Jam fan back in the days of punk and was at Victoria Hall, Trentham Gardens and Bingley Hall. I also saw them at Barbarella's night club in Birmingham and if I was to pick the best gig I would pick this one as it was when they were touring after *Modern World* (which had been panned by the critics) and just before *All Mod Cons.* I think ''A' Bomb In Wardour Street' had just been released as a single. I can honestly say it`s the only gig I`ve been to where I wanted the group to play new songs. 'Tube Station', 'Mr Clean' and 'To Be Someone' sounded so good, even though I`d never heard them before!

As for the Stoke gigs I remember being so excited before the first at the Vic Hall in December 1977 and although they were tremendously energetic and sounded great, my abiding memory is being disappointed it didn`t last very long, perhaps 40 or 45minutes.

DE MONTFORT HALL

2 NOVEMBER 1978, LEICESTER, UK

I WAS THERE: KEVIN GREENHILL

I went to see The Jam at De Montfort Hall in Leicester and I remember the concert very well. It was the time when punk rock started and was in its infancy. The concert itself was brilliant but sadly the crowd were not. This was the time when punk rockers started spitting throughout the concert, so I stayed to one side of the auditorium. However that aside, the thing I found bad and a little unnerving was after the concert had finished, a number of drunk concert goers started to smash the internal windows in the wall of the hall which was just crazy. It was such a shame as I have attended dozens of concerts and I had never come across this before. It certainly made me angry, as this was my favourite venue being a local to Leicester. Sadly not many big bands come to the venue any more unless they are at the start or end of their careers in the industry. It made me smile digging out my concert tickets again and just seeing how many concerts I used to go to. I just wish the prices were like they were back then - £2!

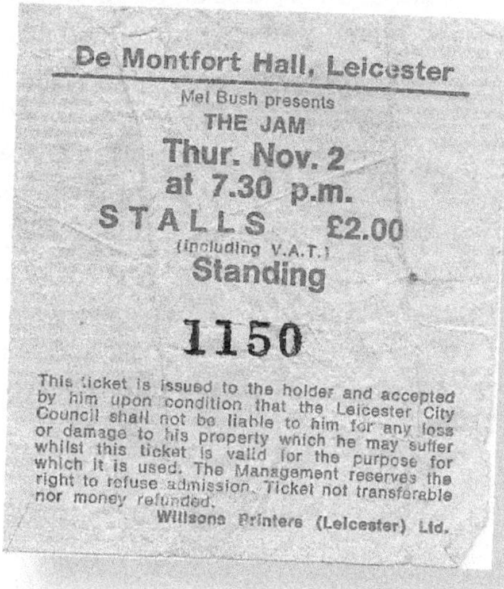

Kevin Greenhill's ticket to see The Jam at Leicester's De Montfort Hall

CIVIC CENTRE

22 NOVEMBER, 1979, WOLVERHAMPTON, UK

I WAS THERE: STEWART JEENS, AGE 17

I saw The Jam at Wolverhampton Civic in 1979. It was my first live gig. The Vapors supported them. I was 17. I still love the band with a passion. I queued up in Dudley for the release of 'Going Underground' in 1980. I was the first to buy it in the picture cover. It's still my favourite Jam single. I joined the Army soon after. The band are one of the seminal English groups, up there with The Beatles, Who, Kinks and Slade.

I WAS THERE: ANDY HIPGRAVE, AGE 16

I first saw them at the Laf (the Lafayette) in Wolverhampton in 1977. I was 13. I couldn't actually get in but fortunately the brother of one of the girls at school was a doorman and so I got in that way. I couldn't see because I was short – I still am – but he managed to sit me on the end of the bar. So that's how I got to watch 'em first off.

I was into the punk thing in. I'd read about the Pistols, etc. at the time and I went along just because they'd got a cool name. I'd not heard any of their music before.

It was just the energy of it that got me. I just got hooked – it was love at first sight. Or love at first chord! I was one of the lucky ones – I saw them 26 or 27 times. It was the brashness of it, because they were doing *In The City* at the time. As a three piece they sounded so good, particularly in a small environment like that.

They used to play Wolverhampton on a regular basis. Even if it wasn't on a tour they'd do a pre-tour gig. But I saw them in loads of places. I was the first one at my school to really be into them. There was a punk at my school that I looked up to who was about three or four years older than me. I just liked the fact that he wore a donkey jacket, really! But then I started going to gigs and you get to know local people who would go as well so we would go together. Bingley Hall, Stafford was quite a good one. We'd go there on a regular basis. Bingley Hall in Birmingham - which is no longer there – was good too.

And then we'd go further afield. If you could get tickets on a tour it was dead easy to get to London and back. So we could go to Hammersmith, for example. We'd just go wherever we could get tickets. We went to Newcastle a couple of times. It was a bit like being away fans for a football team. If we could all go, we would. There was never animosity in it.

I started reading poetry and George Orwell. Weller made me aware of things like Tamla Motown and Stax, because they had some of that on the inner sleeve of *All Mod Cons*. It was an education. I know he doesn't like being called a spokesman but he was like a big brother, going, 'I think this is cool.' It was an influence rather than a dictatorship.

Tour dates would normally be in the *NME*. Sometimes you'd send off postal orders.

Sometimes, because a few of the guys had scooters, we would go on the day that tickets were released, bunk off school and go down to wherever it was and queue up outside the box office. As they became ultra popular it became harder to get tickets but we'd be there from early doors to make sure we did. At the time they'd normally allow you to buy four.

When they played Wolverhampton, just before the *Setting Sons* tour, I'd hurt my ankle playing football. It wasn't in plaster but I could hardly move my leg so I couldn't be downstairs as I normally would be, in the crush, and I remember sitting on the balcony and I was quite close to the stage, maybe 20 feet from Paul. He came out and he had a grey suit on, like Sting wore in *Quadrophenia*, and grey patent shoes on that matched the suit. I remember looking at him and thinking, 'Wow, this is ultra cool.'

They started playing and I don't know whether we caught them on a bad night but he was so angry he was just spitting out the lyrics. And he looked so cool in that suit and those shoes. I was thinking, 'I would never get away with wearing that stuff', but after I thought, 'You can wear what you like. If you're a Mod and you think you're cool, you do look cool.'

People were angry at their situation. Youths all seem to go through that rebellious phase. It was the Thatcherite era, so people were pretty angry and lots of people were unemployed. Nobody knew *Setting Sons* was coming out and we didn't expect them to tour then. We'd already seen them a month, maybe six weeks, before and then they did the *Setting Sons* thing. That was a really, really good concert.

'79, '80 were great because Paul was at his angriest and the music was superb. It was before they were mainstream. They were still our band then.

It was that anger and energy which made you read those lyrics and think, 'What's he saying here?' In 1980, I was doing my 'O' levels. It helped me because it helped me read. It helped me want to read poetry. It made me look at words more. I perceived all of the songs to be a poem and I would read them like that. You would read every word off the vinyl sleeves and you would learn every word off by heart. It was a coming of age.

I was with a friend when I heard about the split. He was in a band at the time. When *The Gift* came out, he said, 'This'll be the final album' and I laughed in his face. 'No way.' And so when we heard the news he just said, 'Told ya.' I couldn't believe it. In retrospect I think they did the right thing.

I was obviously very sad because I had such good times with them and it would be the end of an era for me as a social life. We all knew that it was a kind of disbanding for the fans too. You'd see a lot of the same people at the gigs, particularly in the Midlands area. You'd go to Leicester De Montfort and you'd see the same girl as you saw at Bingley Hall and the Civic. There was one girl who stood out who used to wear green suede pixie boots. I was absolutely infatuated with her. I never spoke to her! I used to think, 'If only I could get the guts to talk to you.'

I thought it would be a break and that they'd get back together. I didn't understand his motivation for it. And all these people now who say they want The Jam to get back together? Well I've seen From The Jam and Paul on his own but I actually wouldn't like them to get back together. Because it was so special then. Paul has mellowed now. He can't sing the words the same way that he did before. It's not the same energy.

At a From The Jam concert, all the fans are singing along almost like karaoke but to me that's almost the football fan. To me, it's not what The Jam were about originally. To me, The Jam was about social documentation. I was in love with the lyrics and they mirrored what I thought and what my feelings were. So for people to be singing along to 'Town Called Malice' or 'Going Underground' now hasn't got the same bite as it had then. It hasn't got the same meaning.

My favourite track is 'When You're Young'. Weller said people have described it as the epitome of pessimistic. And he said, ' I don't think so at all.' And neither did I. That was a mirror of what like was like then, with the careers officer coming in and asking you what you wanted to do. People didn't get a job. They ended up on schemes.

I see guys jumping up and down at From The Jam concerts now and I think, 'You weren't there. You're drunk. You don't know what it means.' Maybe they were there and maybe now they're just drunken old men. For me, that's why I wouldn't want to see them get back together. Because you couldn't recreate it.

I've brought my son up on it and told him how great it was and if I took him to a Jam concert now it would be an anti-climax. You can't tell me that Paul's going to be spitting the lyrics out, angry, jumping up and down on stage, and stamping his feet. Because he's not that person any more. And it was the angry young man that influenced me enough to follow and to read everything he wrote about and to listen to everything he wrote about.

I'm grateful to him that he opened my eyes and made me know that it's okay to read poetry and think it's cool, and be open minded about music and listen to The Kinks and Stax and Tamla and Blues. Because back in the day you were either a Mod or a New Romantic or you had to fit in one of the other boxes, and I didn't feel like that. The message was, It's okay to be like that. I'm very lucky to have grown up when I did.

Didn't we have a nice time? I had a great time.

TRENTHAM GARDENS

26 NOVEMBER 1979, STOKE-ON-TRENT, UK

I WAS THERE: BILLY TIDESWELL, AGE 20

I saw them on the *Setting Sons* tour. I still have the ticket somewhere at home. I also saw them twice at Victoria Hall, sweet and good memories of a band that spoke where others couldn't be heard and only a fiver too. I went to see Weller at Sherwood Pines in 2019 too. It was an awesome gig with a great back catalogue of the things you wanna hear.

DEESIDE LEISURE CENTRE

29 NOVEMBER 1979, DEESIDE, UK

I WAS THERE: LESLEY CROFT

I first saw The Jam play on our local news channel, *Granada Reports*, back in 1976. I was barely 11 years old and I think it was Tony Wilson (before I knew what an influence he was on new bands) who introduced them at the end of the show. The segment was barely two minutes long. I remember the bass of 'In the City' just hit me, and me and my sister were hooked.

We made our brother drive on his moped to Deeside in North Wales to get us tickets for the up coming show. It was at Deeside Ice Rink. We travelled up on the bus and had to queue outside to go in. It was full of punks and skins and I was a little girl of barely 11. I didn't care, or worry about the crowds getting gobby, but Weller was having none of the spitting or beer throwing. He told them straight. I think Weller may have offered to meet a few outside after the gig!

The security sectioned us all off and me and my sister were in the middle crowd section. The band looked like they do on the cover of the *In The City* album, with black skinny suits and Foxton's spiky hair. It was the first gig I had ever been to and is still one of the best, with raw guitars and biting lyrics. To this day I still think *In The City* is The Jam's best album.

We couldn't get home that night. Bus services in Wales were crap even before Thatcher had got hold of them. We hitched home... all the things you shouldn't do but my god it was worth the risk. I went to see them again at the ice rink in Deeside but it's the first one that has stayed with me.

RAINBOW THEATRE

4 DECEMBER 1979, LONDON, UK

I WAS THERE: ANDY PHILLIPS

My first memory of The Jam was hearing 'Strange Town' on the radio and immediately after that I bought *All Mod Cons*. I loved it. That album also got me into The Kinks via 'David Watts'. I was 14 at the time and I think that might have been the crest of the Mod revival. I just loved The Jam and didn't really like the Mod-associated acts like Secret Affair and Squire, etc.

I saw The Jam at the Rainbow in December 1979 with two mates. You had to send a cheque to the box office and my mum did it for me. I remember we were in the stalls, half way back on the left facing forwards. The support act was The Vapors who were actually great. I do remember that it was really hot. I also remember feeling very young compared to everyone else there! The energy was incredible. I have seen hundreds and hundreds of gigs (I was a musician in my twenties so I have seen a lot of bands!) and I will always remember the intensity of that gig. Paul Weller seemed very angry to a 14 year old. I saw them a few times after that – Wembley Arena with Big Country supporting springs to mind – but it wasn't the same. I'm not sure a venue that size suited The Jam.

I haven't followed Rick or Bruce if I'm honest. I quite liked the Style Council but haven't followed Paul's work particularly. I still listen to The Jam. *Setting Sons* is probably my favourite album, which is the album they were touring at The Rainbow. I doubt they would reform and if they did I wouldn't go and see them. I'd like to remember them as they were.

KING GEORGE'S HALL

12 DECEMBER 1979, BLACKBURN, UK

I WAS THERE: JACKIE LEIGH

I have a signed *Setting Sons* album cover from the gig. My friend and I went and she also had a ticket stub signed. I have a plectrum off Bruce somewhere too.

THE CIVIC HALL

2 JUNE 1980, WOLVERHAMPTON, UK

I WAS THERE: DAVID POTTS

Having played *Setting Sons* to death, I couldn't believe my luck when I read that The Jam were coming to play live at my local venue -

David Potts saw The Jam six times

Wolverhampton Civic Hall. It was to be only the second concert I had ever attended.

The Jam had recently gone straight into the UK charts at number one with 'Going Underground', ensuring the tickets had sold out fast.

The first thing I remember about the gig were the cheap t-shirts. They were selling for £1 each - cheap even then!

The magic moment took an age to arrive but finally the support band disappeared, the lights went down and the three heroes ran on stage to a deafening welcome. Up came the lights and The Jam thrashed into their opening number, 'Thick as Thieves'.

The concert was a highly charged affair with Weller and Foxton leaping around the stage in front of the steady and powerful Rick Buckler.

Around halfway through, Weller and Foxton picked up acoustic guitars and Weller introduced a new song by saying that he thought it would provoke a Jam backlash. He said it was the first time the song had been performed live. It was called 'That's Entertainment' and it brought the house down.

Other highlights included a fast and furious 'Going Underground', 'Dreams of Children' and a sublime 'Little Boy Soldiers'.

Of course the gig lasted too short a time - about an hour and a half - but I always preferred quality to quantity and everyone came away wanting more.

During the next two and a half years I was to see The Jam another five times. They were superb at each gig, but none was so special as that first one at Wolverhampton.

VICTORIA HALL

4 JUNE 1980, STOKE-ON-TRENT, UK

I WAS THERE: MICHAEL CONLON, AGE 12

I was 12 at the time. My only memory of the Victoria Hall concert was meeting the band on the car park before the event - we must have gone early. Bruce, I think, saw me and my equally 12-year-old friend and said, 'They're getting fucking younger every day.'

I have clearer memories of the Clash and Police concerts at the Victoria Hall. It got a bit rough down in front of the stage, so we used to sit on the balcony on the right of the stage, where you could see the band running onto and off the stage. We usually managed to grab a drum stick from the drummer (one from Stewart Copeland, I remember) when he left the stage. The Clash concert was particularly good because it had been cancelled a couple of times, so they made up for it with two or three encores. I remember the crowd shouting for 'White Riot', which they then played in the encore.

I went to one of The Jam's Bingley Hall concerts and remember the crowd being a bit rowdy. Paul Weller's dad came onto the stage at one point and asked the crowd to calm down. I also remember Paul Weller's microphone not working during 'Mr Clean'.

I WAS THERE: ROGER MALKIN

When The Jam arrived it was absolutely fantastic for a late teenager as they were a brilliant band. Paul was a genius. I was at the Victoria Hall and Trentham Gardens concerts and these were absolutely brilliant nights, especially Victoria Hall. It was a small venue and I was near the front.

ROYAL COURT THEATRE

27 APRIL 1981, LIVERPOOL, UK

I WAS THERE: MARK SMITH, AGE 15

I went with six of my close friends – Billy Gibson, Trevor and Bill Davies, Harry Hazlehurst, Steve Stone and Simon Deer. We were all around the same age and from West Kirby and Greasby on The Wirral. It was about my third ever gig and I still regard it as my best ever gig, even though I have been to hundreds since and seen so many great bands including The Who and The Wedding Present on many occasions. I feel fortunate to have seen The Jam live and still hold their songs close to my heart, which helped me during hard but great times while I was growing up. I remember feeling absolutely gutted a couple of weeks later when they announced on *The Tube* that they were splitting up, but in a way I'm glad they did so those memories didn't fade.

OTTAWA TECHNICAL HIGH SCHOOL

24 MAY 1981, OTTAWA, CANADA

I WAS THERE: MICK KERN

I saw them in Ottawa, Canada during the 1981 tour at Ottawa Technical High School. It was bloody hot in the school auditorium, and packed. It was a fantastic, intense show. I wanted to stay afterwards to meet them but chickened out. I then saw them in Montreal at the Verdun Arena in the spring of 1982. The 'new' sound. The Jam and the Clash were my bands in high school. They translated well to a frustrated, suburban Canadian student.

To me, The Jam spoke of a universal frustration that transcended English politics/class system struggles. Many of the same themes are woven through our life over here in the colonies. Which is why I was somewhat surprised the band never broke here in North America...until 'A Town Called Malice'. 'When You're Young' - that was my life!

THE RITZ

26 MAY 1981, NEW YORK, NEW YORK

I WAS THERE: KEITH AULD

The first time I heard of The Jam was in the late Seventies on a New York AM radio station. They played 'Modern World' and I was hooked. But it wasn't until the *Sound Affects* album that I actually got to see The Jam live. It was at the Ritz in the Village. I remember standing about five people back from where Paul Weller would appear. As they came out the crowd surged toward the stage. The air was full of energy and excitement. I don't remember what order the songs were in, but I remember watching Paul thrash his guitar against the mic stand, Bruce dancing across and then jumping off the drum stage, and Rick keeping up a furious pace on the drums.

The second time I saw them was at a larger venue in Midtown New York called The Palladium. It was during their *Trans Global Unity Express Tour*. I remember Paul being angry or upset during the set. At one point he quipped about his guitar saying, 'Bloody American guitars' which drew some boos from the crowd. The show wasn't like the first time. It felt more polished with the horn section. And Paul seemed a little distant from the audience. 'That's Entertainment', 'A Town Called Malice' and 'Precious' were a few highlights.

MICHAEL SOBELL SPORTS CENTRE

12 DECEMBER 1981, LONDON, UK

I WAS THERE: DAVID O'DOWD

Living in a small town in the south of Ireland in the late Seventies, I always felt that punk and new wave was kind of passing me by. We ordered LPs from COB Records in the UK but not many bands came to Limerick to play.

In December 1981, I was working in a local travel agent. My brother Tom was living in Dublin. Browsing the *NME* listings I noticed that The Jam were touring and playing a couple of gigs in Finsbury Park. On an impulse, I called the brother and said, 'Let's go'! We were both massive fans. He said yes of course so I 'wrote' us a couple of train and boat tickets to London. Off we went. Hardly any cash, no tickets, one bag of weed!

Arriving in London, it was freezing cold, snow and ice everywhere. I had booked us a room in the Atlantic Hotel in Paddington so we stopped off there, had a few pints and then headed on the tube to Finsbury Park Station. The gig was at the Michael Sobell Sports Centre. We arrived at the station and as soon as we got off the train, there was a guy selling two tickets which we bought immediately. We heading for the gig and got there just as they came on stage. The place erupted and I didn't see Tom for the whole gig it was that crazy. It was, in a word, the best gig I've ever been to.

I met Tom outside after the gig - we were both soaked in sweat and completely knackered. The afterglow was incredible! I have read since that the gigs at the Michael Sobell are legendary and I managed recently to download an audio of the whole gig. I write this with some sense of poignancy as my dear brother and best mate Tom passed away last year at the tender age of 52. The memory of the trip and the gig itself live with me every day.

It was definitely our 'down in a tube station at midnight' moment.

R.I.P. Tom and long live Paul Weller!

BINGLEY HALL

21 MARCH 1982, BIRMINGHAM, UK

I WAS THERE: CRAIG PULLEN, AGE 16

I'd heard friends at school talking about The Jam but never really paid any attention. That Thursday night in 1978 when I saw them perform 'David Watts' on *Top of the Pops*, changed everything. From that day on I joined the rush at lunchtime to race into town to be the first to buy the new record by The Jam, back in the day when singles were singles, B-sides were classics and nobody went straight in at number one.

Fast-forward four years. I was 16 and finally got to see The Jam live. John Weller, 'the best band in the whole fucking world', and on they came. My first thought was where was Weller? The Steve Marriott hairstyle had gone for a crew cut (so a trip to the barbers in the morning for me) but then they played 'Strange Town' and the whole place erupted. Whilst a tour to promote *The Gift*, the set list covered the whole catalogue and I was mesmerised - Weller so cool, Foxton (my favourite) dressed so sharp and Buckler was the steady presence. The whole night would be a blur but luckily it was recorded and released as a video which I still have to remember a fantastic night.

The next tour didn't go anywhere I could get to by train from home and then came the split. One final tour and, when it was announced, the final date was to be Birmingham Bingley Hall and a ticket was secured. Eventually two dates were added, in Guildford and Brighton, I wouldn't see their final concert but at least I'd see them one final time. From 'In The City' to 'Beat Surrender', the set list was a greatest hits. No 'Bitterest Pill' but as the beat surrendered one last time we were left with 'The Gift', a song of hope and promise for the future.

As one fan wrote at the time, The Jam were our Elvis, our Beatles and won't become our Who or Rolling Stones (and add U2 to that list now). Remember them as they were and don't call for them to reform as it could never be the same again. They were our band of that time - I've never seen their like since. Move, move, I've got the gift of life.

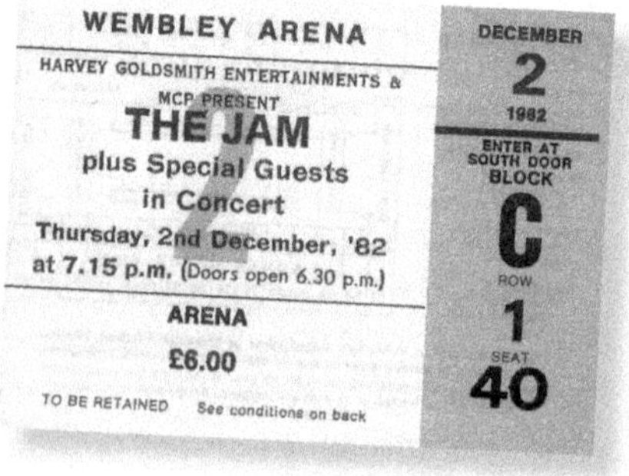

WEMBLEY ARENA

DECEMBER 1982, LONDON, UK

I WAS THERE: SAM WESTHEAD

Being born in '63, I was a bit of a late developer re music. I was never into Bowie or

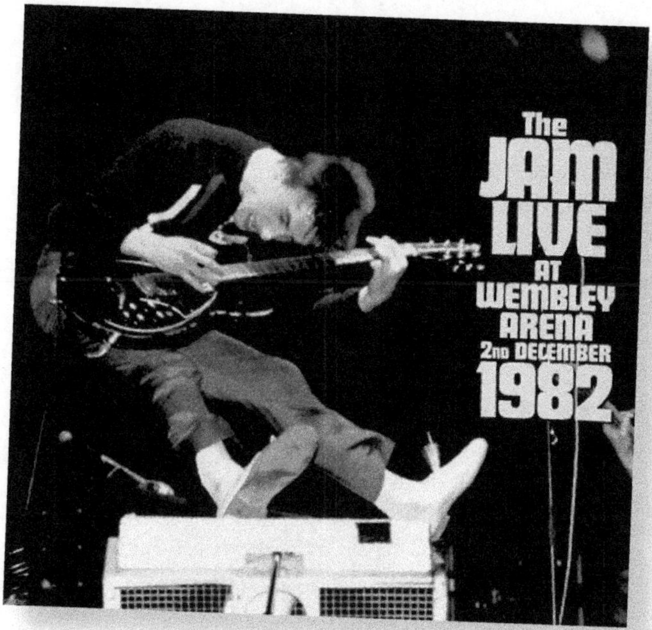

Queen, I was more into pop or - slightly later – Jean-Michel Jarre, which would have been around 1977. But my first concert was the Jam *Beat Surrender* concert in late '82. My friend and his pal had a spare ticket for Wembley Arena. I'd been to London before, watching my beloved Man City. What set this apart was the fact I wasn't that bothered - that was, until when we went in and our seat tickets were in fact about eight rows from the front. The supporting group were Big Country and I absolutely loved them. They were brilliant. The atmosphere was electric. The speakers seemed about the size of a double decker stood on end. There I was in amongst my friends who were dressed as Mods as, it seemed, was everyone else, and there was me - just a normal kid in

t-shirt, jeans and trainers. On came The Jam and blew me away. I wish I had a digital camera! The crowd surged forward so any semblance of seating was gone but it was all good-natured pushing and dancing. Now in all honesty I can't remember the set list apart from a couple of songs, 'Beat Surrender' being one of them. But I suppose my experience is how I felt after I left the concert. I was absolutely on cloud nine. But more than that it gave me a taste for live concerts like Bowie at Maine Road, Queen, Fleetwood Mac, Pet Shop Boys, Ultravox and James (a firm favourite of mine) plus lots more. But for the pure magic and debut The Jam have always held a special place in my heart, and always will.

THEY WERE ALSO THERE

I WAS THERE: PRAFUL SOLANKI

Saw them at Granby Halls and was chased by skinheads. On stage they were loud. Awesome gig.

I WAS THERE: PAUL STACEY

Newcastle City Hall supported by the Piranhas.

I WAS THERE: DONNA GOODWIN

Top Rank Sheffield in 82. I was 17 and hero-worshiped Paul Weller. They were amazing!

I WAS THERE: NEIL AARON

Saw The Jam more times than I can remember. The best band in the fucking world.

I WAS THERE: GARY SMITH

Saw them three times at Glasgow Apollo just before they split. Best days of my young life.

I WAS THERE: ANNE-MARIE RIDGEON

I've told the tale many times! Meeting Bruce Foxton in town and getting his autograph up my arm then it was all rubbed off when I got home. I lost one shoe too that night but thankfully found it when everyone had left! Great memories!

I WAS THERE: JANET DEAN

We went round for the sound check in Leeds. I was squashed against the garage doors. They rolled up and I fell on the floor and the tour bus rolled over the top of me. I was escorted to hospital but I wouldn't tell them who I was or where I lived because we'd legged afternoon off school to get the best spot. Got a signed t-shirt, scarf, back stage pass but didn't get to meet any of them. Best day of my life.

I WAS THERE: PAULA FOTHERBY

I remember thinking for fucks sake its Janet - we're gonna get caught now'! Not - I hope our buddy is OK. She got whisked off to the hospital and as much as I love her I was more concerned with not losing my place in the queue. Fast forward a few hours and who should we see lording it up back stage? Only our bloody squashed mate! The Jam were amazing but we'll never forget the day our mate got run over by the tour bus!

I got crushed at the front and dragged to the back so all that queuing was for nothing in the end! I remember being stood on my own at the back and listening to Weller thinking 'this is it. This explains everything'. It was a euphoric moment.

All the trouble we'd be in if the school and our parents found out went out of the window! I think the attendance at school for that afternoon must have been down by 50%. We were all in the queue outside the Queens Hall.

I WAS THERE: PAUL BRENNAN

Loch Lomond music festival 1979. Chords, Bad Manners, The Cuban Heals, The Only Ones, Ra Bears, The Regents, Punishment of Luxury, Stiff Little Fingers, The Tourists, The Jam.

I WAS THERE: LARAINE MANLEY

Saw The Jam at the Marquee, London. Amazing, those where the days!

I WAS THERE: DAVE ROSE

Still have my ticket stub from Whitley Bay Ice Rink Gig 1982. Great Gig.

I WAS THERE: STUART DAWSON

Preston Guild Hall July 5 1981. Bruce played almost the entire gig facing Rick!

I WAS THERE: GERRY CLARKE

Rainbow Finsbury Park, London, 1979.

I WAS THERE: TIM BRAUND

My friend Bill Walker and me got a 52 seater coach up to see them at Bath Pavilion.

I WAS THERE: KEVIN BONNOT

Last ever at Brighton, also Wembley and Bingley Hall.

I WAS THERE: STEPHEN KING

I took their equipment to *Top of the Pops* when they did 'Going Underground'.

I WAS THERE: GARY SMALE

First concert I saw was The Jam at Manchester Apollo 1979.

I WAS THERE: MARK STEPHENSON

Newcastle City Hall 1979 as a 13 year old was the first time. Last time Bridlington Spa Dec 82 farewell tour. In between a few more City Hall and Whitley Bay Ice Rink.

I WAS THERE: JOHN DRISCOLL

I saw The Jam twice at Leeds Queens Hall around 1980. Not sure if second time counts though. Couldn't afford ticket so stood on bike looking through a broken window at the back.

I WAS THERE: CHARLIE GRAYLING

Deeside. I was there. Great gig but loads of trouble. I think The Piranhas were support.

I WAS THERE: DAVE J JOHNSON

Deeside leisure centre, Queensferry N. Wales, *Sound Affects* tour. Remember there was blue effin murder going on inside and outside the venue, happy days!

I WAS THERE: JAMES SCOTT

Saw them at Loch Lomond Rock Festival think it was 1979. They played after Stiff Little Fingers. There was cans getting thrown everywhere. The Jam stopped playing two or three times but in the end all the punks and all the Mods surrender to the brilliant music of The Jam.

I WAS THERE: SI ALLEN

Yeah Granby Halls Leicester, 1981 £5 a ticket.

I WAS THERE: JENNIE ANN PAYNE

The last gig they did at the Brighton Centre before splitting up.

I WAS THERE: PHIL SPALL

December 4th 1982 Wembley age 14. Blown away.

I WAS THERE: ROBERT PAUL GLENDINNING

1980 Hammersmith Palace then 1981 Brixton Academy.

I WAS THERE: ANDREW SHUTE

Saw one of their last concerts in Whitley Bay. Remember it well as Weller managed to mess one of the songs up, 'Thick as Thieves' I think.

I WAS THERE: LOUIE BOTHA

Saw them (front row too) at the Winning Post pub in 1977 in Twickenham. They played the whole of the *In the City* album. They were sweating even before going on stage. Mr Weller armed with his Rickenbacker slid past me before getting on. The week before the gig they were on *Top of the Pops* doing 'In the City'. From that moment seeing them, I was hooked. Best ever gig I ever went to. Exciting and £1.50 entry fee.

I WAS THERE: JACKIE ORCHARD

At Wembley on their farewell tour. Paul Weller slipped over and left the stage in a strop but did eventually come back.

I WAS THERE: MARK PROUSE

Beat Surrender tour at St Austell in Cornwall.

I WAS THERE: WILLIAM DORNING

The Palladium in New York City, 1982.

I WAS THERE: JOHN NEWLANDS

Bucket and Spade tour 1981, Irvine Magnum. There was a cine 8 camera filming it on a balcony. I'd pay to see that.

I WAS THERE: TIM RYLAH

Saw them at the Rainbow and Hammersmith Odeon.

I WAS THERE: TIM HARRIS

Saw them for the last gig of five at Wembley; don't remember much except the guy I was queuing with was in the seat next to me!

I WAS THERE: PAUL JARDINE

1982 Wembley Arena December 4th *Farewell Tour*. I was 13 years old and right at the front on my older mate's shoulders. True story. It was ace.

I WAS THERE: PAUL LEWIS

Saw the band 12 times and loved every gig. First one in 79, but one of the most memorable was the Sobell gigs in Dec 81. The band were on fire and got stuck in the snow on the way home from the Sunday gig.

I WAS THERE: TAMMY STRINGER

1979 at The Rainbow - that was my first Jam gig, I was blown away. We waited outside after and got their autographs.

I WAS THERE: GINA GUARNIERI

Last gig was a bloody disaster. Weller moody, crowd upset and arsey – got covered in beer from fighting.

I WAS THERE: KRAM GREIG

St Austell Coliseum, Nov 82.15 years old, my first ever gig, lived with me forever since, pure raw sound, lyrics of a genius.

I WAS THERE: CHARLIE MONEY

St Austell Coliseum, Nov 82 aged 13, also my first ever gig. Big Country supported, and announced that The Jam had cancelled so they'd be doing the gig instead. Being young and gullible I believed them at first.

I WAS THERE: IAN PICKARD

Three times in Poole. The feeling was like nothing else ever again. The rawness, the attitude, the tunes. They were our band and always will be. It never goes away.

I WAS THERE: JOHAN GODDIJN

I saw them in Sweden, in a town call Lund. Both their next last tour probably 1980 or 1981 and the *Gift* Tour. The other tour must have been the *Sound Affects* tour. Anyway they were brilliant. I was not glad when they quit as a band.

I WAS THERE: RUSSELL SMITH

West Runton Pavilion '77 around the time of their second single. I think they were support to a band called Tonight?

I WAS THERE: DAVE JONES

Had at chat with the band after their Sheffield Top Rank gig in '82. Rick Buckler gave me some of his chips! Top blokes.

I WAS THERE: KAREN SMITH

Saw them a couple of times at Whitley Bay Ice Rink, once at City Hall Newcastle and then at the *Beat Surrender* tour in Bridlington. Also have a set of tickets that we never got to use for Whitley Bay Ice Rink when the car broke down getting us there. I've seen From The Jam a few times and still go every year to see Paul Weller, was at Dalby Forest this year and he was amazing.

I WAS THERE: SARAH ALLEN

Poole lighthouse theatre about 1979. Got knocked by a punk pogoing and nearly ripped the long t-shirt off my mate Deb L Marsh as I fell. The floor was literally bouncing. Happy days.

I WAS THERE: ANDY NEAVE

I saw them at the old ABC in Great Yarmouth on the 17th November 1978, great night.

I WAS THERE: JANICE DOCHERTY

Met Paul and Bruce twice in Glasgow, once at the Apollo after the sound check and at the Excelsior Hotel at the Airport. I saw The Jam umpteen times. I'd sell my soul for one last Jam gig.

I WAS THERE: ALAN S. TILLER

I saw them on Long Island. I can't remember the name of the venue. One of my all time favourites.

I WAS THERE: STEVE JONES

Saw The Jam March 1982 at Shepton Mallet. *The Gift* tour and my first live gig 17. At the time I bought the T-shirt and the album now a CD.

I WAS THERE: CHARLIE PROUD

Saw them in Portsmouth... before they were famous.

I WAS THERE: PAUL GUILFORD

Shepton Mallet showground 1982, on my 14th birthday, got in with my older sister.

I WAS THERE: CHRIS WAKEFIELD

I was 15, saw them in Brighton, sang along to every song.

I WAS THERE: JACKIE TAYLOR

I saw them twice at Bingley Hall Stafford and they were awesome and then again at Bingley Hall Birmingham when I got turned away from a pub for being too casually dressed.

I WAS THERE: LORRAINE MANN

Farewell Tour 1982 Wembley. Cried our eyes out. Fantastic but also a very sad night.

I WAS THERE: PAUL FITZGERALD

Bromley Tech pre tour warm up. Only 100 or so people in a school gym. They came out and chatted to the fans afterwards. They were all really friendly. Still the best live band I've seen.

I WAS THERE: MICHAEL MILTON

April 1st 1982. Leeds Queens Hall. Bunked off school for the only time in my life to queue all day to make sure we got to the front.

I WAS THERE: JAVKIE MCGEOUGH LEES

Odeon New Street Birmingham November 1978. Bingley Hall Birmingham twice plus sound checks. *Setting Sons* album promo at HMV New Street signing. Brilliant.

I WAS THERE: MARK SALMON

Preston Guild Hall, the first gig for my sister and me. I just remember the stage presence of Paul and the energy from the band. First album was *Sound Effects*. I'm lucky to have seen Paul Weller a number of times and he never disappoints.

I WAS THERE: BARRY JOHNSON

1979, Rainbow, London. I found a wallet - it paid for my ticket.

I WAS THERE: DAVID LINGE

I did twice, once at the Rainbow in 79, can't remember a thing then on the farewell gigs at Wembley Arena also a long time ago.

I WAS THERE: CHRIS THOMPSON

Birmingham Odeon Nov 1978, one of my first ever concerts. Fantastic energy. 'Down in the Tube Station' is still one of my all time favourite tracks.

I WAS THERE: STEVE BARK

First ever concert. Amazing! Queens Hall Leeds. Bruce wrapped his guitar round one of the pillars on stage because he broke a string.

I WAS THERE: MICHAEL THWAITES

Saw them at Whitley Bay Ice Rink. My brother won a competition in *The Sunderland Echo*. I was only 12 at the time and managed to sneak in but hey what a night - loved it.

I WAS THERE: DARREN WITTS

First time was Bracknell Sports Center 79. I think and the last time was Brighton Center, last ever Jam gig and about 15 times in-between.

I WAS THERE: DICKIE MCSPANGLE

I queued for hours outside the venue to buy tickets for The Jam. I was first in the queue, rode there on my motorcycle. Funnily enough I met a couple of blokes from Overton, also queuing. I think the tickets were delayed in transit. I can't remember if we got the tickets that day or not.

I WAS THERE: KEN SCHOFIELD

Saw them at Carlisle Market Hall. July 4th 1981, my 23rd birthday. Slept in a van afterwards. Cracking night.

I WAS THERE: DAVE WASHER

Saw them at Queens Hall Leeds in 1977. Vapors were support act. Absolutely brilliant.

I WAS THERE: DOUG GRAY

First saw The Jam in Bracknell 1981. My big mate from Newcastle who had moved south at the time had already seen them up North.

I WAS THERE: DOUGIE TODD

Saw them twice, at Loch Lomond Festival and the last tour at the Edinburgh Playhouse.

I WAS THERE: KONRAD WILKINSON

Travelled from Belfast with a friend to see them four times. We met Bruce Foxton walking down Princess Street in Glasgow and he told us what hotel they where staying at for the Birmingham gig. He put us on the guest list. I have tickets from gigs and pics with the band too. Best band ever!

I WAS THERE: HERBIW ELIAS

Seen them loads of times in the UK plus once in Paris! Great memories.

I WAS THERE: GEOFF MARSHALL

Only once - Reading Festival in 1978. Hope to see From The Jam one day.

I WAS THERE: KRISTOFER MAGNUSSON

I was at the Grand Hotel Royal Ballroom for the televised show Måndagsbörsen on October 5 1981- the interview with Paul was an embarrassment for Swedish television. The interviewer focused on the fact that Jam in Swedish meant the stuff you put on toast - never giving a thought to the fact that it does mean the same thing in English. I bet Paul considered her an idiot.

On the show The Jam played 'Absolute Beginners', 'Tales From The Riverbank' and 'Funeral Pyre' - introduced by Paul as 'Chicken in a Basket'.

I WAS THERE: DENISE HILL

Saw them seven times. My favourite band ever. First time at Loughborough University when I was 15. Then every time they came to Leicester. Still watch Bruce and From the Jam whenever they are in Leicestershire. No band has ever come close.

I WAS THERE: GARY PESCOD

Went to *The Tube* in Newcastle. Me and my mates all got drumsticks after the TV program finished.

I WAS THERE: DAVID SHEPHERD

Saw them three times, all in Poole. I just remember all the Parka coats and chants of 'we are the Mods'. Remember the Vapors as one of the supports. Don't seem to have any of the tickets but I still have a t-shirt and a small advertising leaflet from the time.

I WAS THERE: GARY MASON

At Stafford Bingley Hall 1981 *Bucket and Spade* tour in the middle of Staffordshire.

I WAS THERE: GERARD TOOHEY

78 in the De Montfort Hall. I was 14 and my mum let me go to my first concert. Changed everything there and then.

I WAS THERE: BRIAN JAMES O DRISCOLL

Saw them loads of times. Weller, Foxton and Rick were unreal.

I WAS THERE: IAN CLARKE

Upstairs at Ronnie's (Scott's). About 1976. Paul Weller smashed up a stingless guitar a la Pete Townshend. Then saw them a few says later supporting Little Bob Story at The Marquee.

I WAS THERE: MARK MCGINNESS

Saw them loads of times. Might write a book!

AND FINALLY

EMPIRE THEATRE

1 NOVEMBER 1978,
LIVERPOOL, UK

I WAS THERE: GLYN MCGAULEY, AGE 18

Looks like someone is giving Glyn the bird

I started following The Jam in 1978. My first concert was at the Empire, Liverpool and from there I followed them right to the end. I think I went to see them about eight times in total in various locations around the North West. I was 18 when I first saw them and after that I saw them at Manchester University and then Liverpool University the following year and then I saw them at Deeside Leisure Centre. The last time I saw them was in Blackpool just before they split up in 1982.

They were being supported that night by The Vapors because Bruce Foxton managed them with John Weller at the time. The Empire is similar to the Apollo in Manchester. We were upstairs on the balcony. They had just released 'Going Underground' but the album didn't come out until a week later. There was a poet on at the beginning and then there was a group called The Dickies, who did 'Banana Splits'. The crowd started bottling them from the balcony so they had to go off. They did their one hit and they had to go off. They didn't last five minutes. Everybody just wanted The Jam to come on. There was nobody there over 20 or 22. The age range was 14 to 21.

It's the most memorable concert I've ever been to because it was the first time I'd seen The Jam and they went through the whole catalogue. It was strange because the new album hadn't come out and they normally toured with the album - when the album came out I bought it the following week.

As a Jam fan you felt that they belonged to you. They hadn't become commercialised but in the autumn of 1979, when *Setting Sons* came out, when the Deeside Leisure Centre gig took place, it felt like they didn't belong to you anymore.

They called the Deeside Leisure Centre gig the 'bloodbath one'. It was just when they were getting popular, when The Specials and Madness came to the fore. It tied in with the Mod thing so all the ones from Liverpool who went watching them and the North Wales lot. There was a fight halfway through the concert and the concert got stopped. Paul Weller's dad and Bruce Foxton basically said, 'If you don't stop we're going to pack it in and we are walking off.' There were sporadic fights during the night. They weren't proper Jam fans. They were just into whatever was flavour of the month at the time.

The last time I saw them, in Blackpool, in March 1982 they had a brass section. That was a cracking concert as well. The Opera House was a similar theatre to the Empire, Liverpool. Everybody was bouncing around.

I was obviously devastated when I heard they were splitting up. We just didn't expect it - you thought they would go on for ever. I saw the Style Council three times and I must've seen Paul Weller over the last 20 years at least 20 times.

WEMBLEY

5 DECEMBER 1982, LONDON, UK

I WAS THERE: ANDY SUMMERLY, AGE 14

I saw The Jam live at Wembley in 1982. If was one of the last shows of their farewell *Beat Surrender* tour. My dad took me as I was only 14 at the time, and although he loved music he was a little less enthused than I was. The Jam were my favourite band, I owned every single and album that they had released and listened to them all religiously. I remember the show from the support band Big Country getting booed by a bunch of Mods that only wanted to listen to The Jam. Then the excitement of them coming on stage - I stood up and sang along with every song. I remember a tear coming to my eye when Rick Buckler threw his drum sticks into the crowd at the end of the show, knowing it was literally all over.

'I'm still adamant that The Jam will never reform; that's a god-given even though I've been asked about it every day for the last 30 odd years'

PAUL WELLER

'After the last show we went our separate ways, as happened often at gigs that our friends and families attended – but this time we stayed apart. It didn't really hit me until the next morning. I woke up in the Grand Hotel on the seafront with a very thick head, thinking, 'Well, that's that then. What do we do now?'

BRUCE FOXTON

'You talk to any Jam fans and they really felt we belonged to them as much as they belonged to us and calling it a day didn't seem to make any sense to anybody. I think Paul came up with all sorts of funny ideas about how it would make the band mean something if we split it up. But I think the band already did mean something to anybody who was a fan anyway'

RICK BUCKLER

The authors would like to thank Rick Buckler for all his help in making this book possible and Nicky Weller for contacts, stories and photos. And of course all the Jam fans who are featured within these pages. Without you there would be no book!

For news on Rick Buckler visit:

https://www.facebook.com/ RickBucklerThatsEntertainment/

And Rick's site http://www.thejamfan.net/

We would like to say a big thanks to all the fans that sent in photos. John, Ed and John Silvester, Michael Farragher, John Campbell, Anne O'Rourke, Neil Crud and Derek D'Souzas. And special thanks to Catherine Corrighan and Olly Walsh at UMG for their support.

We reached out to the following publications and on-line resources for help and research.

NME, Sounds, Melody Maker, Record Mirror, Smash Hits, Time Out, Uncut, Muzins, Stroud News, Link2Wales, Richard Buskin from Sound on Sound, Birmingham Music Archive, Vintage Rock, Steve Hoffman Forums.

https://writewyattuk.com/2016/09/15/waiting-for-the-vapors-return-the-dave- fenton-interview/https://whycontrol1977.blogspot.com/2008/06/bombsite-fanzine-1977. https://111- max.co.uk/streetsounds/vapors.htm, https://nonstopdancin.wordpress.com/category/ the-jam/ https://mylifeinconcert.wordpress.com/2011/05/13/004-this-is-the-modern- world-the-jam-with-the-mods-april-10-1979/#more-143

https://www.thejamarchive.co.uk/

https://thejam.org.uk

Thanks to Omnibus Press for kind permission to use an excerpt from *Shout To The Top - The Jam* by Dennis Monday

Richard Houghton would also like to thank: Neil Cossar, Liz Sanchez and Emily Powter-Robinson at This Day In Music Books; Malcolm Wyatt; Chris Green and Kate Sullivan.

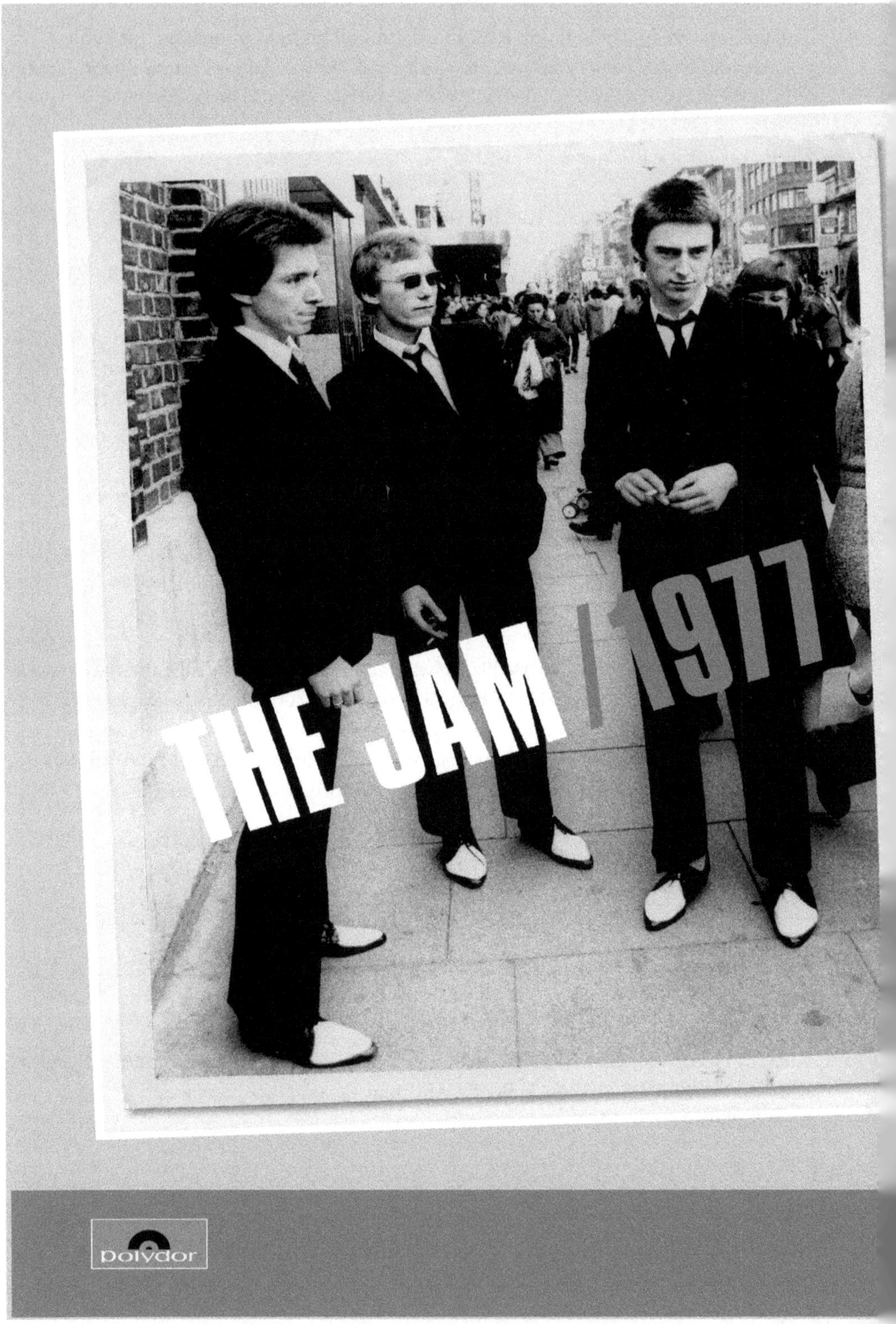
THE JAM / 1977
polydor

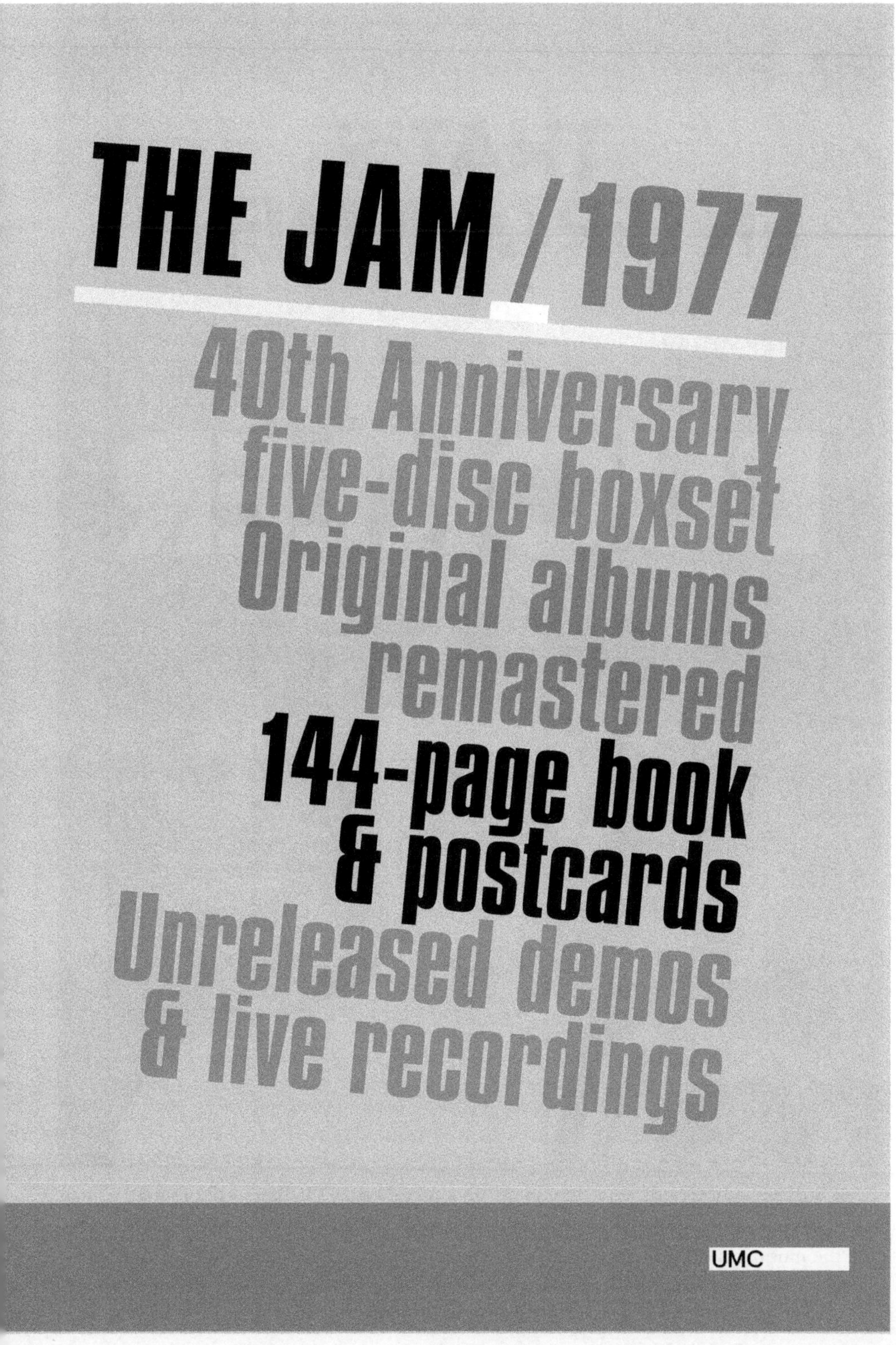
THE JAM / 1977
40th Anniversary
five-disc boxset
Original albums
remastered
144-page book
& postcards
Unreleased demos
& live recordings
UMC

Also by Sandra Turner...

Tales of unrequited love; a haunted house; a defiant old man; temptation; an unwelcome return; mistaken identity; a love triangle; forgiveness; poetic justice; a stolen talisman; a glimpse of sepia.

A GRAVE MISTAKE

EVERY ACTION HAS ITS OWN CONSEQUENCES

by Sandra Turner

Michael Terence
Publishing

First published in paperback by
Michael Terence Publishing in 2022
www.mtp.agency

ISBN 9781800943285

With thanks to my partner, Peter Sartori, for his essential support and my publishers, Michael Terence Publishing, for making this possible.

To Helen
Best Wishes
Sandra Turner
18/6/22

A Grave Mistake

The landlord of the Fiddler's Cat was growing tired of the group sitting at a table near the window. One man in particular, Derek Gardener, who was in the pub most nights had become unpleasantly loud and was now singing "Molly Malone" at the top of his voice.

'OK lads. Can you keep the noise down to a decent level please!' the landlord said, raising his voice to be heard above the melee.

'Sorry George. I guess it's about time we all headed for home anyway,' one of the men called back.

All of the men stood up and put their coats on and left. All of them except Derek Gardener who walked up to the bar with a swagger, pint glass in hand and asked, 'How about one more for the road George? And I'll have a whiskey chaser.'

The landlord looked at Derek, who stood at about five feet six inches tall with thick black, greasy hair. He wore a dirty, hard-to-tell-what-colour anorak and grey wellington boots. There was something about this man that the landlord didn't like. It was rumoured that Derek Gardener was a bully, mostly

to his wife. Having lost his own wife to a long battle with cancer two years previously, he found Derek objectionable.

'I think you've had enough to drink for one evening Derek. Didn't you mention earlier that today is your anniversary? You should be getting off home to your wife!'

'Do ya mean Molly? She won't be expecting me home before midnight anyway!'

'Well, if you leave now, you should just about make it home by then.'

'I need another drink to keep the chill out!' Derek said, slapping his hand on the bar.

'Well, you won't get it here Derek. Neither will you get any more credit from the off-licence till you've paid the money you owe them!'

'I've a good mind not to drink in this pub any more. It's a shit-hole anyway!' Derek screamed.

'That's right. You won't, because I've just barred you. Now get out of here before I throw you out!'

Derek looked at the landlord who towered above him, then decided not to say any more. He'd come back another time with his pal Joey and trash the

bloody place!

***

Derek stormed out of the pub, letting the door slam behind him. His mood was fuelled even further as a light drizzle began to fall and the last bus was just leaving the bus stop. He grabbed a handful of mud and threw it at the pub window. 'Bastard. It's all your fault!' he screamed. The pub landlord let his dog out, a black and beige German Shepherd, which chased Derek along the road until the landlord whistled for it to come back.

Derek lost his footing trying to run away from the dog and tumbled down a hill, landing in a puddle at the bottom. He tried to scramble up the hill again, but now the rain was falling at a steady pace so he kept sliding down again into the puddle. 'I'll kill that fucking dog! I'll slit its throat and watch it bleed to death!' Derek screamed. Derek searched the pocket of his anorak, for a handkerchief or tissue to wipe his hands and face. He came across something folded, took it out and his mood instantly changed. He laughed as he unfolded the ten-pound note which he had pocketed from the whip round on the table, the other men had contributed to. He kissed it and said, 'I'll get a bus into town tomorrow to buy half a bottle

of whiskey and some cans in the supermarket.' He was able to see now as his eyes became accustomed to the dark. 'Shit. I meant to buy a bunch of flowers from the garage for Molly. Not that she deserves them.' He remembered that when they were first married, a cooked meal would be waiting for him every evening when he came home. Now he was eternally having to live off sandwiches as Molly was too busy with her voluntary work. 'Well, she'll have to wait until tomorrow. I'll buy her a bunch of flowers from the supermarket, if I have any money left after my purchases.'

Derek decided to take a short cut through the cemetery which would cut his journey by fifteen minutes. Having made this decision, he walked off in the direction of the church, the bell tower was just visible in the distance.

***

The single storey grey-stone church stood tall on the hill.

It had a huge arc-shaped stained-glass window to the right of the entrance door. Built onto the back of the church and looking like the turrets of a medieval fortress, stood the bell tower. This was open to the

general public from May to September on Sundays, after morning service, for a small donation into the box on the wall next to the spiral staircase on the ground floor. A recent addition to the churchyard, were railings with a lockable gate. This wasn't much of a deterrent as a fit youth could scramble over the dip between the gates when they were closed, but it was better than the wooden fence and gate which had stood there, before a vehicle had backed into it, knocking it to the ground. It was never found out if the driver had done this intentionally or not – he, or she, was never identified.

***

Derek was not fit, and at fifty-three, was not a youth either, but he had managed to climb over the gates before and did not consider it would be a problem tonight. What Derek didn't know was that the previous week, the vicar had, with the help of donations from the people of the parish, had a security light installed, so as Derek managed to find his footing and pull himself up the railings, the security light came on. 'Oh, Christ!' he cried out, but there was nothing he could do so he hauled himself to the top of the gate and in his rush to remain undetected, fell onto the Viburnum bush below. He

received scratches to his face and hands. A piece of the broken bush had torn through his trouser leg; piercing his knee. The wound, although not deep, trickled blood into his sock. 'Aargh!' he yelled out, in shock and pain. His heart pounded as he expected the noise he made to bring the vicar running after summoning the police. All was silent. Then Derek remembered that the vicar had been called away to Nottingham where his sister and her husband lived, Molly had informed him. She also mentioned that the vicar's brother-in--law had had a heart attack, a mild one, as far as heart attacks go, but enough for the vicar to take the first available train from London St Pancras.

Derek began laughing. The gods were smiling on him for sure, but he realised he must get out of here as soon as possible. Cautiously, he scrambled out of the bush and sat on his bottom on the ground, trying to gather his thoughts. He wondered if his injured knee would support any weight? The pain was more like a dull ache. He flexed his ankle, up and down, then a small circle. Although this movement was painful, his ankle did not appear to be injured It suddenly occurred to Derek that if he'd gone the long way round, he would almost be home by now. He needed someone to blame for the situation he found himself in. If he'd been at the bus-stop five minutes earlier,

he would have caught the bus and the reason for him missing the bus was his argument with the Landlord at the Fiddler's Cat. 'Bastard!' he said. More pressing now though was for Derek to get out of the churchyard. 'Some nosey bastard might come to see why the security light keeps turning off and on,' Derek grumbled. He would deal with the landlord in his own time, in his own way. Derek turned onto all fours, he straightened his legs and pushed himself up into a standing position, then hobbled away to the back of the church.

***

As Derek walked along the path, past the gravestones, something caught his attention. It wasn't the recent addition of this particular grave, but the fresh deep pink roses placed in the appropriate container which interested him. 'What a bloody stroke of luck,' he thought. 'I'll take them home to Molly.' This meant that he could spend the ten pounds on himself tomorrow and there was still fifteen minutes to midnight, the right side of his anniversary. As he snatched up the flowers, he didn't see the card which fluttered to the ground, nor the words written on it. "To mummy. I miss you all the time. Love Sarah". Derek would not have concerned

himself, even if he had seen the card. He now thought how providential it had been for him to choose this way to come home. Molly would surely agree to have sex with him tonight. She had slept in the spare room for the past week. He wasn't to blame for her split lip, he had been trying to put his side across during an argument they'd had about him spending all their money on drink. He'd thought that she was going to attack him with the wooden spatula she had been waving around. He was only trying to defend himself after all.

***

'Molly I'm home,' Derek said as he stepped through the front door of their tiny, one bedroom, one box room, terraced house, which Molly had suggested they sell as they couldn't afford the many repairs that needed to be carried out. Derek had fiercely been against this idea at first, but had reluctantly thought that, for once, Molly might just be right.

***

'Molly. Are you awake? I've got something for you.'

'What is it?' Molly called out.

'Come downstairs and see!'

‘Can’t it wait until morning?’

‘No it fucking can’t! You’re the one who complains that I never remember our anniversary!’

Molly came slowly down the stairs wearing a blue, fleece dressing gown over blue, striped pyjamas. On her feet were brown check, bootee-type slippers. Derek thought how she’d let herself go. She wasn’t the attractive, smart young woman he’d married. She didn’t even wear skirts any more. Always dressed in jeans and brushed-cotton shirts. Her once chestnut, now grey hair, had no style. She always had it pushed behind her ears. Derek wondered why he still stayed with her. Well, he had made a vow to stay together through thick and thin, but she did try his patience most times.

‘You’ve trailed mud into the kitchen again. You should have taken your boots off in the porch before you came inside!’ Molly scolded.

‘Sorry, I forgot. I just wanted to give you these flowers,’ Derek replied, smiling, hoping that his annoyance towards her didn’t show.

‘Where did you get these?’ Molly asked.

‘From the garage near the pub,’ Derek replied.

‘But there’s no cellophane around them.’

‘That’s why they were cheap. They were the last bunch and the owner was going to chuck them out, but I persuaded him otherwise.’

‘Thanks. I’ll just put them in a vase,’ Molly replied, still suspicious.

‘Can you cook me something please? I’m starving,’ Derek asked.

‘Ok. I’ll do you some beans on toast, then melt some cheese on top under the grill. Will that do you?’

‘Great!’ Derek agreed. realising he was too hungry to wait whilst bacon and fried bread cooked.

‘What have you done to your leg? There’s blood on your trousers,’ Molly asked.

‘The landlord at the Fiddler’s Cat was out walking his dog when it slipped its lead and chased me. I fell over trying to get away. Thankfully he caught the bloody thing before it jumped on me. That dog is dangerous.’

‘I suppose he had to get a dog after those two break-ins last year,’ Molly offered.

‘Yeah, but it could have been a kid the dog was chasing. The outcome could have been a lot more serious.’

‘Do you want me to clean and dress the wound first?’

Molly asked.

'No, don't worry love. I'll clean up in the bathroom and get changed. Can you make a pot of tea to go with the food? None of that Earl Grey stuff you like. Just regular red label tea please,' Derek replied pleasantly.

***

In the bathroom, Derek had intended just to clean his wound and apply some antiseptic cream but suddenly he felt very cold and began to shiver. 'It must be the after-effects of tonight's events,' he thought. He decided there was only one way to warm up – in a hot shower! He stripped off, leaving his clothes in a pile on the floor and stood beneath the flowing hot water. He reached for the shower gel and soon worked up a nice lather on the sponge. He washed his neck, shoulders and stomach. As he reached the wound in his knee, it began to bleed again, just a few spots at first, then it began to trickle. Derek washed it gently, but this seemed to make it worse, the blood flowed from the wound, down his leg and into the drain. He grabbed a flannel and held it against the wound, applying pressure, trying to stop the flow of blood. He'd read somewhere this is what you should do, but the blood soaked through the

flannel, and spurted out like a hosepipe. Derek began to panic, what was happening? 'Molly, Molly… come quickly… please help me,' he wailed. In his panic, Derek lost his balance, fell and hit his head on the protruding soap dish. He landed heavily and lost consciousness.

***

Derek woke to see Molly kneeling next to him, wiping his forehead and face with the cold water-soaked sponge.

'Thank God you're OK. What happened?' Molly asked.

'The blood… I couldn't stop it! I tried putting pressure on the wound but that seemed to make it worse!' Derek sobbed.

'Which wound Derek? You are not making much sense.'

'The bloody wound in my knee you stupid bitch! Call for an ambulance!'

'Don't use that type of language, Derek. I am not stupid. The small wound in your knee is not even bleeding.'

Derek looked down at his knee. It was not bleeding.

There was no blood on the flannel. No blood anywhere in the shower.

'I don't understand,' he said. 'The blood was pouring out of that wound. I couldn't stop it.'

'I think you had too much to drink, fell asleep in the shower, hit your head and then you had a bad dream whilst you were unconscious!' Molly replied. 'Put some clothes on and come downstairs. Your food is getting cold.'

***

Derek slept badly that night. Every time he closed his eyes, he relived the experience in the shower. Was it, as Molly had suggested, because he had hit his head on the soap dish and what he believed to be real was part of his concussion? When he finally drifted off to sleep, just as dawn was breaking, he had a nightmare.

***

He was back in the church graveyard and had just removed the roses from their container when he heard someone sobbing.

'Who's there?' Derek called out into the dark.

No reply, but the sobbing continued.

'Who's there?' Derek asked again.

This time the sobbing stopped. A white orb appeared, similar in size to a tennis ball. It hovered above Derek's head for about thirty seconds, then floated, silently, towards the grave, pausing behind the headstone. The orb started to grow in size. A grapefruit soon became the size of a melon, a pumpkin, a salver and finally it looked as though the moon had fallen from the sky. Then the orb changed shape, it was more like a huge rugby ball. Derek stood transfixed, frozen to the ground, mouth wide open staring straight ahead, unable to even blink. The orb changed colour from white to orange, then began pulsating like a heartbeat. Boom-boom. Boom-boom. The heartbeat grew louder and louder, so loud that Derek had to cover his ears with his hands. The heartbeat seemed to throb through his entire body, enveloping him, causing shortness of breath. Derek felt as though he were being suffocated. His own heart was constricted, as though it was being held in a vice. Then he felt the pain, so sharp, like a knife through his heart. He heard his own muffled sobs. He took a large inhalation of breath and with every ounce of his strength, managed to scream out, 'Help me!' He awoke, drenched in perspiration, shivering and crying on the floor of his bedroom like a baby.

Molly rushed in shouting, 'What on earth is going on!'

'Molly, Molly. I thought I was dying. I couldn't breathe. I've never been so scared!'

'You must have hit your head harder than I thought. I should call for an ambulance.'

'No. No ambulance. I might never come home again! But I don't want to sleep in this bed. In fact, I don't want to sleep ever again!' Derek wailed.

'It was just a nightmare,' Molly said soothingly, 'I'll get you a clean pair of pyjamas. You can sleep in my bed. These sheets are damp from your perspiration. Shall I make you some hot chocolate whilst you change?'

'Can you put a drop of whiskey in it, just to warm me up?' Derek asked.

'No alcohol. Besides you drank the last of the whiskey before you went out last night. I'll get you a hot water bottle,' Molly replied walking out of the bedroom, down the short, narrow staircase and into the kitchen.

As Molly took the milk out of the fridge to make two cups of chocolate, the roses caught her eye. They were dead. 'No wonder they were cheap.' Molly thought, then wondered if the garage owner had

thrown them out with the rubbish and Derek had just happened along at the right time to retrieve them. 'Sounds about right,' Molly said with a deep sigh.

***

Derek waited until he heard the click of the front door as Molly left. He put on a navy fleece dressing gown, thick socks and slippers he normally only wore in the winter. He felt cold even though the sun was peeping out from behind some clouds. The weather forecast had promised a fine afternoon. Still feeling fragile, he slowly descended the narrow staircase, went into the kitchen, put the kettle on to boil, then sat at the kitchen table. He went over the events of the previous night in his head. Had he really hit his head and passed out in the shower? What other explanation could there be? The terrible dream came back to him seconds later. He recalled the feeling of being unable to breathe, how his heart felt, as though it was bursting. Maybe the dream was his subconscious sending him a message, a warning. Maybe his blood pressure and cholesterol were too high. Maybe he should make an appointment with his GP for a complete health check. He decided that was just what he should do. In fact, he would call the surgery to make an appointment as soon as he had

made coffee and toast for his breakfast.

The kettle had just boiled and turned itself off. Derek took the jar of instant coffee from the cupboard, put a heaped teaspoon into a mug, adding two spoonfuls of sugar, milk and finally the hot water. He sipped the liquid at the same time as looking for the bread in the fridge. There wasn't any there. Not to worry, there would be some in the freezer, Molly had just forgotten to take it out.' The good thing about bread is that you can toast it straight from the freezer,' Derek thought. There wasn't any bread there either. Then he saw Molly's note, on the door of the freezer, held there by a fridge magnet, it read: "Derek, forgot to get bread yesterday at the supermarket. There's Cornflakes or sugar-free malted wheats in the cupboard, or a box of eggs in the fridge. It's my day to help out in church. Will get some bread on way home. Back about three. Molly". 'Oh, well. I'll fry myself two eggs, although it won't be the same without toast,' Derek said to himself. He took out the frying pan from the cupboard beneath the sink and suddenly an ice-cold shiver ran up his spine. He had an overwhelming feeling of dread. He clutched at the edge of the sink so tightly, his knuckles turned white. Slowly he turned around and what he saw made him grab a chair for fear of falling over. A woman stood in the space between the kitchen and the hall. At

least, it looked like a woman. Derek wasn't sure as blood was flowing from a gaping wound in her head, down her neck and onto a pale blue blouse, which was already soaked in blood. Then as swiftly as she had appeared, she disappeared, leaving a bewildered and horrified Derek wondering who or what he had just seen. His head felt light and dizzy, he heard a buzzing noise in his ears, he thought he was about to faint. Hadn't he read somewhere that high blood pressure could cause hallucinations? He wasn't sure, but he decided to believe this as the alternative was something far worse and unimaginable.

***

When Molly arrived at the church, she was surprised to see Reverend Halliday standing outside the church talking to a policeman. She hesitated, but Reverend Halliday motioned for her to approach. The policeman got into a car and drove away.

'Anything wrong Reverend Halliday?' Molly asked.

'Molly. I've asked you to use my Christian name.'

'But it doesn't seem right to call you John.'

'As you wish Molly. All the other volunteers call me John.'

‘Have you been burgled?’

‘Nothing quite as dramatic as that. When I arrived back this morning, I noticed the viburnum bush was broken, its white flowers scattered everywhere. It was obvious to me that someone had managed to scramble over the gates and the bush must have broken the fall. I rang the police immediately. Half an hour later, a constable came.’

‘Oh, no. How dreadful!’ Molly exclaimed.

‘The policeman said it was probably some drunken youths messing about after a visit to the pub. Without CCTV it was virtually impossible to find out who the culprit was. The thing that upset me is that flowers were taken from one of the graves and the empty container thrown on the ground.’

‘Some people have no respect,’ Molly said distastefully.

‘Yes, I agree with you. The security light would have come on. Maybe that was enough to scare them off. It would be possible to see an intruder if someone were passing by.’

‘I am so sorry,’ Molly said.

‘The constable was right about CCTV. But where am I going to find the money?’

'Don't worry. the other volunteers and I will think of something. We'll have a raffle. Ask some of the local shops to donate whatever they can as prizes.'

'I think it's a splendid idea!'

'Then that's settled,' Molly said smiling.

***

Derek had to get out of the house.

He rushed back upstairs, threw on a pair of jeans, long sleeved sports shirt and some trainers. He suddenly remembered the £10 in his pocket from the night before and immediately felt better. He went back down to the kitchen and took a jam jar out of the cupboard half full of loose change. He counted out one-pound sixty. That should be enough for a couple of loaves from the supermarket and Molly wouldn't notice this small amount missing.

Derek went to fetch the ten-pound note and his mobile phone from the pocket of his coat he had been wearing the night before which was hanging on a peg beside the front door. His mobile phone was missing! 'Oh, shit!' he yelled. He got down on his hands and knees and searched every inch of the hall carpet to see if it had dropped there. No sign of it. He wondered if Molly had found it and put it on the

kitchen worktop or in a drawer, but it was nowhere to be found. Derek re-read the note Molly had left for him. It didn't mention his mobile phone. Where could it be? Maybe he'd left it at the pub? That would mean him facing the landlord of The Fiddler's Cat. He didn't like that thought. Maybe the bastard would set that ugly, ferocious dog on him again. Then Derek remembered the fall into the ditch. Perhaps it fell out of his pocket as he slid into it, or worse still, he may have lost it when he climbed over the gate at the church. If Halliday found it that was evidence he had been there and he would surely report it to the police. All thoughts of going to the supermarket left Derek's head. There was only one avenue left for him to follow. He had to retrace his steps.

***

Molly enjoyed helping out at the church. She felt useful. Her efforts were appreciated by Reverend Halliday and she got on well with the other volunteers, she had found her niche. Molly had connected with another lady, Barbara Woods. They had similar interests, watched the same dramas and soaps on TV. Barbara's talents were in her sketching and drawing, whilst Molly's flower arrangements were admired by all who visited the church. The

difference between the two women was the relationships with their husbands. Barbara's husband was the manager of the local building society, he enjoyed photography in his spare time. Barbara spoke about their holidays in Cornwall where the light was perfect for sketching and photography. Barbara's husband supported her in everything she did. Molly had Derek. She sighed when she thought about him. Molly had attended Flower arranging classes for a term a couple of years ago until Derek complained that it was a waste of their money. It was a pity he never had the same views about spending their money on alcohol, her father's money to be more precise. Molly's father had never liked Derek, even though Derek had been respectful to him. Molly's father had worked hard at his job as a BT engineer. He had been both father and mother to Molly after her mother died when she was thirteen. 'Look after your money. It will ensure you are not dependant upon Derek,' he had said to her. That's why she had her own secret account at the building society, separate from their joint bank account.

Derek's attitude towards Molly had changed dramatically when her father died and Derek was made redundant from his job at the electrical retail store, which closed completely eight months later. He was verbally abusive when she complained about his

drinking habits. Then one day, less than a year ago he had slapped her so hard her lip had split. It had been a shock and she'd lied to Barbara about drinking from a chipped mug. She realised Barbara had not believed her, but neither Barbara, nor Reverend Halliday had challenged her version of events. Molly had been wary of Derek ever since, always leaving the room if she thought Derek was reaching boiling point. Barbara had taken her aside one day, tactfully saying to her, 'If you ever fancy a change, or feel in need of a break, you can always come and stay with us.' So far Molly had not taken her up on her offer, even though Molly had come close several times.

***

Derek stood opposite The Fiddler's Cat. He wasn't looking forward to facing the landlord. Derek saw the windows being opened and heard the door being unlocked. One door was pushed open. A Lorry pulled up outside the pub, the driver jumped down and Derek, although he couldn't hear the conversation, knew it was friendly, the Landlord and the driver were laughing. The Landlord opened the delivery hatch and walked back inside the pub. This was Derek's chance, he crossed the road and walked through the open door.

'Derek Gardener, don't come any further. You've been banned from entering these premises.'

Derek put his hands up, palms facing forward. 'I've not come to make trouble George. I just want to ask you a question.'

'OK. What is it!'

'Did you find a mobile phone last night or this morning when you were clearing up?'

'No, I didn't. The cleaner would have told me if she'd found one this morning, but she didn't.'

'Is it possible she put it in her pocket and forgot to mention it to you?'

'I don't like what you are insinuating, Derek. The cleaning lady has been coming here for seven years. You wouldn't believe some of the stuff she's found fallen down the back of the chairs. Besides, I've seen your phone, it ain't very smart, so I doubt she'd get anything for it on the internet or amongst her acquaintances. Now if your question has been answered, leave my pub and don't come back. I have a delivery to check.'

Deflated, Derek turned around and left the pub.

***

Molly and Derek were not blessed with children. They were not certain why.

Molly had asked Derek if he would come to speak to their GP about it. Derek had refused to go, so Molly went alone to see her GP, who in turn referred her to hospital for tests. When the results came back, it was concluded that there was no reason why Molly could not conceive. When she told Derek about the results, he changed the subject and they never spoke about it again.

***

Molly's younger brother had two children a girl and a boy, whom she doted on. She liked her sister-in-law and the feeling was mutual. Only problem was that they had moved to Leeds, where her brother ran a Wholesale Stationery business.

Molly would go to visit them as often as she could. Derek went a couple of times, then lost his job. Molly went a few more times on her own, then it became difficult to afford the train fare. She travelled up once by coach, but the round trip in a single day was so long and exhausting she had to stay overnight. Derek complained about this so Molly stopped going on a regular basis. She sent presents on the kids' birthdays,

Easter and at Christmas to make up for this. One time, Molly's brother and his family drove down from Leeds to visit Molly. Derek's welcome had been less than luke-warm, coupled with the fact that Molly and Derek's house was not big enough for them all to stay in, they had to book into a bed and breakfast before travelling home the next day. Molly's brother had said to her before leaving, 'Molly, you are welcome to come and stay with us any time, for as long as you wish. I'll send you the train fare. We all love you.' There had been no mention of Derek. 'That's the trouble,' Molly thought. 'Derek doesn't make it easy for people to like him.'

***

Derek stood on the grassy verge looking down, trying to identify the place where he slid down the bank the previous night. He thought he had landed in a ditch, instead, there was a long trench the persistent rain for five days had caused. As if to mock him, the sun came out from behind a cloud, he could feel the heat on his face and he unzipped the top of his jacket. Even if the weather stayed like this for a week, it wouldn't be long enough for this area to completely dry out. Derek realised what a huge task it would be to find his phone. He wasn't even sure he had dropped it

here. For a moment it seemed hopeless, but he knew what was at stake. He let out a long sigh. At least he'd had the sense to wear his wellingtons. Shoes would be ruined in mud. He carefully made his way down the bank to begin his search.

The bell tower from the church was further to his right than it had appeared last night. He deduced that he was not too far from the original fall. As Derek walked slowly along the rut, his eyes scoured the muddy track. The first thing he found was a half-empty carton of cigarettes, squashed and flattened. Derek had never smoked. He'd tried it a couple of times with the other boys at school. All cigarettes had done for him was make him cough and feel sick. Alcohol on the other hand, has a completely different effect, he'd found. He liked the feeling. It gave him a high when he felt low. Blotted out his feelings when Molly nagged him. Gave him courage which he otherwise lacked. Helped him to sleep. Who needed pills when there was alcohol? The one and only thing, which Derek hardly admitted to, even to himself, was the problem caused by Whiskey. The first shot would make him feel relaxed and sociable The second, very talkative and jovial, (loud, most people would say). With the third shot, Derek was able to put his view across very clearly. Molly had said it made him argumentative. Derek remembered one night after

four shots, he had stepped up onto the stage in a pub and sang Karaoke. He'd enjoyed himself so much he'd kept on singing until a couple of guys stood up from their chairs and shouted, 'Get off the fucking stage and give everybody else a chance!'

Derek could rarely afford more than four whiskies, but on his last birthday someone had bought him a double at the Fiddler's Cat, rather he thought someone had, the next thing, he was being accused of drinking somebody else's Whiskey and the landlord had asked him to leave. Derek remembered leaving the pub, then crossing the road to the bus-stop, a car narrowly missed him, the driver stuck his head out the window and swore at him, 'Stupid bastard!' The next thing Derek remembered was waking up the following morning. Still fully clothed, on the sofa with a splitting headache.

***

Derek continued his search. He found a woman's ring. At first he thought it might be a significant find. Maybe the diamond was real! As he turned it over between his fingers, he discovered it wasn't even gold. The colour was coming off in places, revealing a rusty, silver-coloured metal underneath. 'Bloody bloke who gave it to her was probably a cheapskate.

No wonder she threw it away!' Derek said. A short way on, he found a few empty cans of beer and an empty bottle of Vodka. 'No bloody good to me empty!' Derek muttered. Except for a few broken branches and twigs the rest of the trench was clear. He stopped and looked up. He was in line with the church, there was no sign of his mobile. 'I'll walk on a little further, just in case,' Derek declared, knowing this was futile.

***

As far back as he could remember, John Halliday wanted to be a teacher.

He studied hard at university. Always had his head in a book, much to the annoyance of his friends, who preferred to be out clubbing, whenever possible, chatting up girls.

John sailed through his exams, obtaining the necessary qualifications in English, Maths and Science to gain him entry into Teacher Training at Nottingham University, a short commute from where he shared a house with his sister and cousin. He was awarded a BA Hons degree in English. He decided that he wanted to teach in or around London. Five months later, he was offered a position

to teach a class of eleven-year-olds in a school on the North London/Hertfordshire border.

Everything in those first two years made John extremely happy. He found a small, one-bedroom flat to rent, not far from the school. He passed his driving test first time and was able to buy a second-hand car. He drove up to Nottingham for his sister's wedding. He had a very healthy social life and although never in a serious relationship, he was popular with females, enjoying their company and their natural ease and camaraderie with other females. He found them fascinating. Then in 2008 everything changed.

He was in the playground talking to another teacher when a fight broke out between two pupils. His instinct was to intervene, try to diffuse the situation. One of the boys he recognised from his English class, the other boy was unknown to him. As he approached, he could hear their raised conversation. The unknown boy said, accusingly,

'You treated my sister like shit. She told me.'

'I have no idea who your sister is!' the other boy proclaimed.

'Helen Armstrong. You kissed her and then when you stuck your hand inside her blouse and she resisted you, you spread the word amongst your

mates that she was a slag. Remember now?'

'What's all the fuss about? It was only meant as a joke!'

'She didn't find it funny and neither do I!'

As John stepped between them, he saw a flash of metal out of the corner of his eye. The unknown boy had a knife, it was meant for the other boy, but it was plunged into the right arm of John Halliday. The two boys fled in opposite directions when their victim cried out in shock and pain.

The sight of his own blood gushing out of the wound down his arm, was enough to make John faint. He regained consciousness several hours later in hospital.

***

John went through a range of emotions and questions. 'Why did this happen to me?' … 'If I hadn't intervened, this would not have happened to me!' … 'Why did I survive?' After his discharge, he was still so traumatised that he couldn't leave his flat. His friends stopped inviting him out after he refused, several times to join them. He stayed in bed, refusing to eat, take a shower or get dressed. He was finally persuaded, by his worried sister, to go to see his GP,

who prescribed anti-depressants. He further chose to attend counselling at his GP practice.

***

John read in the newspaper that the two boys involved in the incident had appeared in court. The boy with the knife, because of his age, received a supervision order. The judge decided that, 'because of the seriousness of this offence, you must reside with your parents and be placed under house arrest from 6pm every evening until 8am the following morning, for the next six months, thereafter this decision will be reviewed.'

***

Things slowly started to improve for John, for a while anyway. He took up a leisure centre membership, swam three times a week, occasionally working out at the gym also. He was in touch with his friends again. If they went to the cinema or a music gig, he would go along. He even went to Nottingham to visit his sister, who was happy to see signs of the old John returning, she told him.

***

The day that John read in the local newspaper that the boy with the knife would not receive an extension to the judge's first ruling, was the day that he began his downward spiral again. The descent was so drastic and so fast that one of his friends, after several attempts to contact John had failed, let himself into the flat with the spare key he had insisted John give him. 'John are you there?' he called loudly, noticing as he entered, the empty bottle of Vodka and John sprawled on the sofa. He immediately dialled the emergency services. Twenty minutes late, with blue lights flashing and sirens wailing, John was taken away.

John was in hospital for a week, during which time he spoke to a psychiatrist. The decision was made to increase the dose of John's medication. Twenty-four hours later he was discharged from hospital. Nobody came to meet him. Probably because he didn't inform anyone.

***

John wandered the streets alone. All thoughts of his return to work had dissipated. He didn't know how long he wandered the streets. Time meant nothing to him. At one point, he stood outside a pub, wrestling with the idea of going in and drinking himself into

oblivion. He decided against it and carried on walking.

The light had just begun to fade when his wanderings brought him to a little church. He could see a light on inside. Exhausted and hungry, he tried the door. To rest, even for a short while, he decided, might revive him. To his surprise, the door was open. He crept in, hardly making a sound, chose a pew to his far right to sit on. Within minutes, he had fallen asleep.

He dreamt that he was a child again, on holiday at the seaside with his sister, under the protective eyes of his mother and father. He didn't know why, it felt like someone was gently shaking his shoulder. It lasted for a few moments longer until he realised that somebody was, in fact, shaking his shoulder. He opened his eyes to see the dog-collar of a priest.

'Hi son, would you like a cup of tea and a sandwich?' the priest asked. John found this kindness so overwhelming, his eyes filled with tears.

'Yes please,' he replied meekly.

Half an hour later, John tucked into two cheese and tomato sandwiches, washed down by tea.

'Now, do you want to tell me your name and why a young man like you has ended up in my church at this

hour of the night?' the priest asked. 'Father, I am not of your faith.'

'That's OK. God forgives you for the error of your ways,' the priest joked. John found himself pouring out the whole story. The priest never interrupted until the end when he said:

'It seems to me you have lost your faith in everything you have believed in. Why not put your faith in God?'

***

Molly took the bus to the local supermarket after leaving the church. She told Reverend Halliday she would return at 7.30 that evening. Reverend Halliday was facilitating an eight-week Alpha Course. He explained that "it aims to bring Christians and the wider community together to consider the meaning of life, through discussions and texts from the bible. Participants are encouraged to ask questions and share their experiences".

Molly liked this idea. She enjoyed a good debate and the opportunity to meet like-minded people, even if she didn't always agree with their views, but wasn't that the point? John was always trying to find ways to encourage younger people into the church. This might be a great way.

One of the parishioners, Mrs Harper, eighty-nine, had recently acquired a mobility scooter, because Reverend Halliday, as well as other members of the church, had petitioned their local council. Now she was able to attend coffee mornings, book clubs, knit and natter and any other groups which took her fancy. Molly thought, the Reverend was a real "people person". Possibly because he had been a teacher, with a lot of life experiences before coming to the church.

Molly had noticed how Sandra Burrows, a recent addition to their community, looked at him. Sandra had been carer for her mother in her mother's latter years. She'd had a career as a proofreader, but had to give it up when her mother's health deteriorated. Molly wasn't sure if Reverend Halliday had noticed how Sandra's face blushed a little every time she spoke to him. If he had, he'd made a good job of hiding it! Molly hoped Sandra would be at the meeting tonight. In her mind, Sandra and the Reverend made a perfect couple.

Molly treated herself to a cab. She had bought more from the supermarket than she intended. It was too heavy for her to struggle with on the bus. The cab driver was very helpful, carrying her shopping as far as the front gate. Molly gave him an extra three

pounds for his trouble.

She opened the front door, carried the shopping bags, one at a time into the kitchen, putting things away before bringing in the next one. She was just about to close the front door, when she saw something to her left, in the small flower bed. Upon closer inspection, she discovered it was Derek's mobile phone. 'He must have dropped it last night,' she said to herself, picking it up, putting it in her pocket. She hung up her jacket on the peg behind the kitchen door, washed her hands, put the kettle on and mad herself a cheese and cucumber sandwich. Just as she sat at the table, she heard Derek come through the front door.

'In here,' she shouted, 'Would you like a sandwich?'

Derek walked into the kitchen looking dejected and dishevelled.

'What sort of sandwich?' he asked.

'I've been to the supermarket. There's ham or cheese. Tomato and cucumber. Sliced bread or half a French Stick.'

'Cheese and ham on sliced bread would be nice with a mug of tea. I'll just go to the bathroom first.'

Molly put her unfinished sandwich onto the plate,

stood to put the kettle on again and make Derek's sandwich.

Derek re-entered the kitchen, he meekly took the plate Molly offered him with his sandwich on it and sat at the table.

'Are you OK Derek?' Molly asked. 'You seem preoccupied.'

'Lost my mobile. Tried retracing my steps. No joy.'

'Then you'll be pleased to know I've found it.'

'What? Where?'

'In the flowerbed,' Molly replied, putting a mug of tea down on the table for him.

'I don't know what I'd do without you Molly!' Derek said, surprising Molly by taking her hand and kissing it.

'I'll get it for you. It's in the pocket of my jacket.'

'Wonderful. Did you buy any pickle?' Derek asked, a broad smile spreading across his face.

***

The relief Derek felt was exhilarating, invigorating. He danced around the table, laughing wildly. He had,

up until the time Molly told him she had found his phone, believed it to be somewhere in the grounds of the church. He reflected upon the last forty-eight hours. Everything had turned out in his favour. All the worry of the whereabouts of his mobile had manifested in a series of bad dreams, nightmares, he rationalized. All he needed now was a drink. He'd meant to go to the supermarket to spend the ten pounds on alcohol, circumstance had dictated differently. Surely there had to be some alcohol somewhere in the house? Determined to find it, Derek retrieved the step stool from beneath the sink, and unfolded it. Standing on it he was able to look above the fitted cupboards. There were disposable cups still in their original packaging, kitchen towels, twin box of tissues and two packets of cereal, but no alcohol. Derek opened the cupboard doors, one by one, moving jars of marmalade and tins of beans, reaching to the back, no alcohol. Where was it? Suddenly, Derek remembered the cooking sherry, where did Molly keep it? Of course, in the cupboard beneath the sink! Derek got down onto his hands and knees, took out the washing powder, fabric conditioner, spray starch, cream cleaner, finally finding his prize, albeit just a quarter full bottle. 'Better than nothing,' he said. Laughing, he stood up and cracked his head on the cupboard door he had

forgotten to close. Unconscious, he fell to the floor.

***

Derek awoke and found himself curled up on the bench beneath the Magnolia tree at the church. It was in full bloom. 'What am I doing here?' he asked aloud. Then he remembered he had been looking for his mobile phone. He sat up, searched in his pockets, the mobile phone wasn't there, then he remembered Molly had found it somewhere. Where did she say?

'In the flowerbed,' he heard Molly's voice say.

'Which flowerbed?' he asked.

'The one outside our house, silly!' Molly replied.

'What am I doing here then?' Derek asked.

'It must be for some other reason. I have to go now, I should be at home. Derek needs me.'

'I am Derek!' he replied, vexed, but Molly had gone.

***

It was dusk. There was a golden glow behind the church where the sun was setting Derek realised it was not the glow from the sun, it was a fire burning. He needed to raise the alarm. He reached into his

pockets again, he needed to call the emergency services. He didn't have his phone! He ran to the church and pounded on the door.

'Reverend Halliday. Reverend Halliday. There is a fire!' Derek shouted. 'You need to call the emergency services before the fire reaches the church!'

There was no reply. Derek ran around to the back of the church, hoping to find a hose fitted to an outside tap. There was no hosepipe. He found an empty bucket, filled it with water, ran towards the fire, then stopped in his tracks. The fire was still burning but the earth beneath it was unscorched. The bush behind the fire and branches above remained untouched by the flames. It looked like a scene from the bible, but there was no man in long, flowing, white robes, with a grey beard. What emerged from the flames was not what Moses had seen.

***

It was human, in that it had two arms, two legs, and a head. The face was white and skull-like, with two sunken black holes where the eye sockets should have been. Its hands covered its ears and the mouth hung open in a silent scream. Something on its head writhed and squirmed. It reminded Derek of a story

he'd read at school. A creature from Greek Mythology who turned her victims into stone, just for daring to look at her face.

Although not engulfed by the flames, the clothes were smouldering and smoke rose from them. Everything was black and charred. The smell of burning flesh was sickening.

The creature emerged from the fire, slowly making its way towards Derek on stump-like legs, leaving a trail of ash and smut behind it. It laboured when it moved, groaning with the effort of each step, determinedly pushing ever closer to Derek.

Derek felt a hot flush rising from his feet, up his shins, into his knees, his thighs, his groin, up into his stomach, rising into his chest, where he felt crushing, searing pain, like a fire in his chest. Still the creature moved ever closer. It stopped close enough to Derek that he could inhale the putrid smell of flesh and death. The creature raised its right arm and pointed at Derek, uttering one word, over and over again, 'Thief!'

The pain in Derek's chest rose up into his throat. He heard a loud, piercing, primeval scream, so loud it almost deafened him. So loud and resounding he fell to his knees, realising it was his own scream. He

bucked and twitched with the effort but he was unable to stop screaming. There was terrific pain in his chest and head. He was sobbing and screaming at the same time, 'Sorry… sorry… sorry!'

He drifted into some kind of conscious awareness and heard Molly shouting, 'Derek… Derek what happened? You are covered in blood. I'm phoning for an ambulance!'

He suddenly felt warm and safe. His emotions were overwhelming, then everything went black.

***

'How's Derek?' John Halliday asked Molly.

'I'm not sure. I think he may be having a breakdown.'

'What makes you say that?'

'He's having hallucinations. They seem to be getting worse,' Molly replied.

'What type of hallucinations?'

'The latest one sounded like something out of a horror movie. It involved this black creature who wanted revenge.'

'For what.'

'Derek said it accused him of being a thief. He felt pain in his chest, thought he was having a heart attack.'

'Has he been drinking more than usual?' John asked.

'I don't know. I'm usually in bed before he gets home. Sometimes I hear him stumbling up the stairs. I have moved into the spare room.'

'Can you pinpoint when these hallucinations began?'

'Yes. It was the night of our anniversary. He came home a few minutes before midnight with a manky bunch of roses he claims to have bought at the garage. I asked him why there was no wrapping around them. He said it was because they were the last bunch. The owner had let him have them cheaply. I think they had been thrown away. Derek must have found them in the waste bin. They were dead the next morning.'

'Did you say roses? What colour?' John asked.

'Deep pink. Why?'

'That was the colour of the roses taken from the grave the same night.'

'No. Derek wouldn't do that!'

'Are you sure?'

Molly was silent for a few moments, reflecting on this question.

'The truth is, I'm not certain.' she replied.

***

Derek grew up in a village four miles from Bedford. It might as well have been four hundred miles for all the difference it made to him.

The village consisted of a school, a small supermarket with a flat above where the owner lived. A Corner shop which doubled as a post office selling stationery, stamps, pens & pencils, writing & drawing pads, staplers & staples, crayons & pastels, artists paintbrushes & paints. A bus ran from the village, twice an hour, to Bedford, except for Sundays when there was only one per hour.

Derek had a brother, Kevin, two years his senior. The two boys were completely different from one another. For a start, Kevin had fair hair like their mother. Derek's father had mid-brown hair, which left him wondering if he was adopted as his hair was so dark. 'You take after your grandfather,' Derek's mother had said one day when he'd asked her. He never found any photographs to prove or disprove this.

One Easter, Derek's parents had organised an Easter egg hunt, hiding them in various places not too difficult for the boys to find. Derek managed to find one, then gave up when he became bored. Kevin found three, but later gave one to Derek so they had two each.

Kevin tried to encourage Derek to take up some activities with him like canoeing on the local river. Kevin excelled. Derek just got wet.

Derek's parents bought the boys some roller skates, the type you could strap to your shoes, which is all that was available in the 1970s. Kevin managed to stay upright first time and was soon skating up and down the pavement outside the house. Derek could not maintain his balance. Several attempts and many falls later, Derek gave up.

'What a stupid idea. If humans were meant to have wheels on their feet, they'd be born with them,' Derek decided later.

The hub of the village was the Community Centre which had a youth club twice a week. Table tennis, billiards, table skittles, and board games, were available. At one end, a bar sold soft drinks. Once a month, there was a dance night with a band playing the latest hits. Derek had avoided attending the

centre as he preferred his own company, but on his fifteenth birthday, Kevin had persuaded Derek to attend the community centre.

'Derek, I'd like you to meet Rachel,' Kevin said.

Derek suddenly felt embarrassed as he looked into the face of a very pretty girl, with dark blonde hair cut into a long bob with a full fringe, slightly parting, naturally to one side. She wore a round necked, sleeveless, blue gingham dress, with white piping around the neck and armholes. The dress ended about three inches above her knees. She also wore long, white lace-up boots. She looked as though she had just stepped from the pages of a fashion magazine,

'Hi Derek. Nice to meet you. Kevin has told me a lot about you,' Rachel said.

'He hasn't told me anything about you,' Derek replied, blushing.

'Rachel is coming to tea on Sunday to meet mum and dad,' Kevin said, holding Rachel's hand. How much smaller and slimmer girls' hands are, Derek thought.

'Hi. As no-one has introduced me, I'll introduce myself. I'm Molly.' Derek looked into the face of a second girl, who wasn't as pretty as Rachel, but there

was something about her warmth and smile which immediately put Derek at ease. Her rich chestnut brown hair, was cut into layers, making her look a bit boyish. She wore blue denim dungarees which flared at the bottom, almost sweeping the floor, beige, slight platform shoes, and a white, long-sleeved, cheesecloth top. Her large hazel eyes were framed by dark lashes and her freckles danced when she wrinkled up her nose.

'Would you like a Coke? Kevin's buying,' Derek blurted out, suddenly deciding he wanted to know more about this girl. They all laughed and headed in the direction of the bar.

***

'How do you know Rachel?' Derek later asked Molly when Kevin was dancing with Rachel and they had stepped outside for some air.

'We met at a caravan park in Exmouth one summer, we were both six. I was bored and lonely. Most of my parents' time was taken up with my four-year-old brother who was always running off somewhere if he could escape! I was sitting on a bright orange and blue beach towel, building sandcastles. 'Hello,' a voice said. I looked up to see another girl standing

over me in a pink swimsuit with a frill at the bottom. 'Can I help you to build sandcastles?' We hit it off straight away and we've remained friends ever since. Tell me something about you now…'

'Not much to tell,' Derek replied.

'What do you want to do when you leave school?'

'To get out of this shit hole for a start. Go to London. See some real groups live at The Roundhouse. I just don't fit in here. I'm too tied down. I reckon if I can stick it out for another year, do odd jobs for people, make some money. I've already started to deliver the papers every morning, seven days a week and I get pocket money. I have my own building society account, enough to get me started.'

'Where will you live?'

'I'll worry about that nearer the time. Do you fancy coming back inside? I have just enough money for two cokes.'

'It's OK. Save your money. I'm paying. I have a Saturday job.'

***

A couple of months short of his sixteenth birthday Derek packed as much as he could into a battered

black suitcase. He crept down the stairs whilst it was still dark, pausing briefly outside his parents' bedroom door, listening to the rhythmic sound of his father's snoring.

Once in the kitchen, he opened the Oxo tin, which housed his building society savings book, and put it into the pocket of his denim jacket. He put the tin back into the drawer and saw his mother's purse on the shelf next to the mugs. Derek opened the purse, took out three five-pound notes, hoping this would be enough for the train fare to London. He put the purse back on the shelf, tore a sheet of paper from a notepad and wrote:

"Dear Mum, I'm off to London. Can't stand it here any longer. Sorry, I've taken fifteen pounds from your purse. I promise to pay it back as soon as I sort myself out. Derek".

He placed the note on the kitchen table, weighting it down with the egg cup, shaped like a chicken. He suddenly felt very sad. He was certain his parents had done the best they could for him, but he could never live up to their expectations of being as good as Kevin. Derek could achieve nothing whilst he remained here. He silently made a vow to make his parents proud of him one day, when he'd made something of himself. With a deep sigh, Derek picked

up the suitcase, telling himself he would return, but he never did.

***

Molly stood at Derek's bedside. He looked as though he were sleeping peacefully.

'Mrs Gardener?' A man wearing a white coat with a stethoscope around his neck asked as he approached her.

'Yes, I am.'

'Hi, I'm Mr Gardener's consultant. Mr Gardener was very agitated upon arrival, and talking incoherently. He has been heavily sedated to calm him down and to enable doctors to examine the wound thoroughly.'

'Oh, my goodness!' Molly replied.

'We have applied a pressure bandage. This is usual for a head injury. When Mr Gardener wakes up, we will run some tests to establish if there are any signs of neurological injury.'

'Is that likely?' Molly asked.

'Just routine. Try not to worry. We will keep Mr Gardener under sedation for twenty-four hours. Someone will let you know when he's awake.'

'Can I sit with him for a while?'

'Yes, of course. There's a coffee shop just down the end of the hall, if you need refreshment.'

'Thank you doctor,' Molly replied.

***

Molly took some hand cream out of her bag, squeezed a little into one of her hands, then started to massage Derek's right hand. First the back of it, then the palm, then each finger one by one, first in silence, then she asked, in a half-whisper, so that no-one else could hear:

'What have you been up to Derek? I've been talking to Reverend Halliday. He told me that someone took flowers from a new grave. The woman died in a car accident and the flowers were from her seven-year-old daughter.' Molly squeezed more hand cream from the tube and started to massage Derek's other hand. She continued speaking. 'The flowers were deep pink roses, rather like the ones you gave me for our anniversary.' Molly continued to massage Derek's other hand, the same way as the first, finishing the massage with Derek's little finger, then bent down and whispered in Derek's ear:

'It was you Derek wasn't it. You stole the flowers

from the grave of that poor woman. Her daughter was heartbroken. How could you do something like that? Then you brought them home and gave them to me. You have sunken to even lower depths than I could ever have imagined. No wonder you're having nightmares. It's your guilty conscience!'

At these words Derek's fingers on his left hand began to twitch, then his whole hand, arm and head. Molly pressed the alarm.

'Nurse, come quickly. I think my husband may be having a seizure,' she cried out.

***

Derek had not seen Molly looking so pretty for a long time. Not since that day she had come to meet him at Camden Town Station, a year after he'd moved to London. In fact, she was wearing the same clothes, a white puff-sleeved blouse under a pale pink denim pinafore dress.

Her legs were bare, with a slight tan, her strappy sandals had a slight wedge. He called to her:

'Hi, Molly. I'm over here!'

Molly's hair had grown a little longer into a page-boy style. She smiled and waved at him. Derek walked

towards her, carrying a bunch of deep pink roses, a gift for Molly.

In the distance, Derek could hear a rumble of thunder. The glorious sunny day began to change. The blue sky turned into a washed-out grey colour. As Derek walked towards Molly, he felt the first spot of rain. He looked up and saw dark clouds on the horizon, travelling at speed towards them. Lightning danced amongst the clouds, thunder rumbled overhead and the wind picked up speed. The branch from a nearby tree, snapped off, it flew through the air and smacked Molly on the head, she fell to the ground unconscious.

'Molly!... Molly!' Derek screamed running towards her.

The rain became heavier, turning to hailstones it stung Derek's face and eyes. He could see blood trickling from a wound in Molly's head. He battled against the storm-force wind, trying to get to her, save her.

Something was blocking Derek's way. He couldn't see it, but it was palpable. 'Get out of my way, damn you. Can't you see Molly is hurt?' he screamed.

'What is it like to feel helpless, unable to help someone you love?' a voice asked.

'I don't have the fucking time for stupid questions! Let me go. Molly needs my help!' Derek spat.

'There is no need for aggression, this helps nobody,' the voice continued, the presence still holding Derek steadfastly.

'Can't you see that Molly's in trouble? Her breathing seems laboured!

'I can't see, because I have no eyes. I can sense your urgency, feel your distress,' the voice replied.

'You are preventing me from helping her. The injury may be serious!' Derek wailed.

'You are not usually so concerned about Molly's wellbeing,' the voice said.

'You don't know me and you don't know Molly. You don't have any reason to say such a thing!'

'Oh, I know all about you Derek. All about your tiny, insignificant life. You think the world owes you a favour. You've been dealt all the wrong cards throughout your life. Why did your brother Kevin succeed whilst you failed? Your parents must have been to blame. They never gave you the same support they gave to Kevin.'

'It's true. My life could have been so different!'

'Poor Derek. You never went to your brother's wedding, even though you were sent an invitation. Neither did you attend your father's funeral.'

'They didn't really want me there,' Derek replied.

'No of course not. They were unreasonable people. What about Molly? Did you ever love her?'

'Of course, I did. I do!'

'You have a peculiar way of showing it. You have made her life pretty miserable in the last ten years.'

'It wasn't my fault. I lost my job at the electrical retailers. I became depressed.'

'It wasn't the fault of the store where you worked either. It was the recession.'

'It was the reason I started drinking. Nobody understands how useless I felt. Still do,' Derek declared.

'So Molly had to suffer the consequences.'

'I didn't treat her that badly!' Derek said in his defence.

'The slaps, the split lip, the berating was all for her own good, was it?'

'It wasn't me. It was the depression.'

Why did you not seek professional help?

'I don't like taking medication.'

'You couldn't even be bothered to buy Molly flowers on your anniversary. So you stole them from a graveside. They look rather like the roses you are carrying.'

'These are not the same flowers! How do you know so much about me anyway?' Derek asked.

'Like you, Derek, I had a life. I had a husband and a daughter, whom I love dearly. I was driving her to school one morning, as usual. She was in the back of the car, listening to music. My mobile phone on the seat next to me rang. My attention was momentarily distracted, but it was long enough. The handbrake was not properly secured. The car rolled forward slightly. I did not see the van which crashed into my door, until it was too late. I was killed instantly. Thankfully my daughter and the van driver were not seriously injured. Although both were deeply in shock.'

'Oh, my God. I've never heard of anything so horrific!' Derek said.

'The grave you stole flowers from was my grave, Derek. By doing so you made it even harder for a

husband and daughter to grieve.'

'I am sorry, so sorry for all the pain I've caused. Can I go to Molly now?'

'Molly is dying, Derek. That blow to her head was fatal.'

'No. It can't be so. Molly can't die. Can I go to her please?'

'There is a way you can save her, Derek,' the voice said.

'How? Tell me. I am willing to do anything.'

'Would you exchange your life for hers? Think carefully, Derek. What you decide now cannot be undone.'

'Will you let me say goodbye to her if I agree?' Derek asked.

'I would not deny you that, Derek. You may go to her.'

Derek felt the oppression lift. The wind stopped howling, the rain ceased its onslaught. Derek went to Molly.

'Molly. It's me. Derek,' he whispered, stroking her face gently, dabbing the blood from her wound with a tissue. He placed the roses next to her on the

ground.

Molly's eyes flickered. She opened them.

'Did you steal these flowers, Derek?' she asked.

'Not these ones Molly. I promise you.'

Back at the hospital, the doctors were frantically trying to save Derek's life. His consultant tore off Derek's pyjama top. The defibrillator was charged and applied to Derek's chest. Three times CPR was given without success. The monitor flatlined.

'I'm sorry, Mrs Gardener. Derek has gone.'

Sandra Turner

A Grave Mistake is the second book to be published by author, *Sandra Turner.*

Her first book, *11 Stories on the Go*, is a collection of short stories, designed to read, during a break with coffee; during the journey to work on the underground or bus; or as a companion to take on holiday, to pick up and put down at your leisure.

"I believe we are the key holders to our own destiny. Never give up on your dreams, no matter how rocky the road. Keep your destination in mind even though the journey may not be the one you had in mind."

Sandra Turner

www.writingcreatively.co.uk

Printed in Great Britain
by Amazon

81239537R00041

A WARTIME CHRISTMAS AT ROOKERY HOUSE

ROSIE HENDRY

A Wartime Christmas at Rookery House

ISBN: 978-1-914443-22-0

This is a work of fiction. All characters and events in this publication, other than those in the public domain, are fictitious and any resemblance to real persons, living or dead, is purely coincidental.

Published by Rookery House Press
Cover design by designforwriters.com

For Isobel,
with love.

CHAPTER 1

Monday 4th December 1939

Hettie Brown leaned her bicycle against the wall of Barker's grocery shop and went in, the brass bell above the door jangling to announce her arrival.

'Good morning!' Grace Barker greeted her cheerfully from behind the long, dark-wood counter where she was piling up packets and tins. 'Has it stopped raining yet?'

'Just about.' Hettie removed her round glasses, pulled a clean handkerchief out of her pocket and used it to dry the lenses. 'Can I leave our grocery order with you – I'll pick it up later after The Mother's Day Club?'

'Of course, but if you like, Alf can deliver it to Rookery House for you, as he'll be taking this lot up to the Hall. He can drop yours off on the way.'

'All right, thank you.' Hettie took the list out of her handbag and handed it to Grace, who scanned down it.

'Good job you don't want any dried fruit because this lot…'

She laid her hand on some packets on the counter, 'has cleared out the last of my stock until the delivery comes in tomorrow. Looks like Mrs Shepherd, the Hall's new Cook, is going to be making the Christmas cake and puddings.'

Hettie's stomach clenched. 'What? In that case she's *late*! They won't have as long to mature, or taste as they should. I always make them on Stir-up Sunday, as is traditional.'

'So do I,' Grace agreed. 'But every cook has her own ways of doing things.'

'I suppose so.' Hettie frowned as she plunged her hand into her coat pocket and ran her fingers over the soft wool of her glove. It wasn't any business of hers when the Hall's Christmas cakes and puddings were made, she chided herself. It *had* been her job though when *she'd* been Cook at Great Plumstead Hall. Now it belonged to someone else. Hearing this snippet about the new Cook had been strangely unsettling.

Hettie had started work in the kitchen as a fourteen-year-old scullery maid and had worked her way up until she became Cook – a post she'd held for twenty-one years. Deciding to retire had been bittersweet but, now she was sixty, Hettie was ready to take life at a slower pace. The long hours had become more tiring than they used to be. Being responsible for all the meals at the Hall, be it the everyday cooking for Lord and Lady Campbell-Gryce and their family, or for their extravagant dinner parties, had been a heavy burden. So earlier this year, when Thea Thornton, the daughter of Hettie's best friend, had asked Hettie if she'd like to come and live with her at Rookery House, she had snapped up the chance and given in her notice to retire in June. Thea's return to Norfolk after years of living in London had been fortuitous timing.

Now Hettie couldn't be happier living with Thea, and in September, Marianne, an evacuee expectant mother from

London, had joined them. Together they made a happy household, and that's what was important now, Hettie reminded herself, not when someone made their Christmas cake!

'This'll be the last year we'll be able to make proper cakes and puddings,' Grace said, a note of sorrow in her voice. 'Once rationing starts there'll be a shortage of dried fruit and an end to baking traditional fruit cakes.'

'Then we must enjoy this year's all the more.'

'I intend to!' Grace smiled, her eyes meeting Hettie's. 'I love a bit of Christmas cake with a glass of sherry.'

'So do I. This year's cake should be a good one; it was made on Stir-up Sunday with plenty of wishes stirred into the mixture.' Hettie's heart warmed as she recalled the afternoon at the end of November when she, Thea and Marianne had all made their wishes as they took a turn to stir the glorious, fruity cake mixture.

'At least you don't have to make so many cakes and puddings now. It must have been a burden all that cooking up at the Hall – so much work!' Grace said.

Hettie nodded. 'I had help to do it. Though I must admit it was a lot of work and responsibility. Now I'm retired I've got time to do other things that I never had the chance to before. Like helping at The Mother's Day Club.'

Doing different things was a joy. So why, Hettie wondered, had she felt that sudden wrench at the thought of another cook making the Christmas cakes and puddings up at the Hall, instead of her? She'd had many years there doing it and had willingly left to begin a new phase of her life. And she loved this new life of hers. Hettie hadn't had any regrets or unexpected jolts of envy over the new Cook's role before. Why had it tugged at her heart now? Whatever the reason she wouldn't dwell on it. She had other things to do. Her life had

moved on, although clearly part of her hadn't quite made the break and caught up with the rest.

'I'd better get going. I'm helping Prue set up before the mothers arrive. Thank Alf for delivering the shopping – Thea's there, so she can take it in.'

'Have a good time at The Mother's Day Club.' Grace took a packet of biscuits from the shelf behind the counter and held them out to Hettie. 'Here, take these for the tea break.'

'Thank you very much.' Hettie took the packet of Garibaldi biscuits with a grateful smile. 'These will be most welcome. I'll tell the mothers that they came from you.'

CHAPTER 2

Gloria Jessop was in the kitchen at Oak House, drying up the bowl she'd used for her breakfast when her billeting host, Mrs Sylvia Kirk, strode in.

'Are you finished in here?' Sylvia asked, her well-modulated vowels sounding like someone on the wireless.

Ignoring the first cheeky reply that popped into her head, Gloria took a deep breath before she turned to face the older woman, pasting a pleasant smile on her face. 'I'll just be two ticks. I'm almost done 'ere.'

'Good. Joyce will be here soon and it's best you don't get under her feet or distract her when she's got work to do,' Sylvia informed Gloria coldly, then, without waiting for a response, turned on her heels and left the kitchen, closing the door with a crisp snip of the latch behind her.

No doubt heading for her sitting room, where she seemed to spend most of her days unless she was out, Gloria thought. Her host didn't do any housework. That was all left to Joyce, who came in 'to do' for Sylvia every day except Sundays. Joyce

was the friendliest thing about being billeted here at Oak House.

Gloria put her clean bowl and spoon into the cupboard she'd been allocated to store her things. She cooked separately from Sylvia and was allotted certain times to use the kitchen to prepare and eat her meals. Sylvia stuck precisely to the requirements expected for billeting evacuee mothers, providing a place to sleep, use of bathing facilities and a kitchen, but *no more*. Gloria knew from other evacuees that not all hosts were like this. Marianne, who lived at Rookery House, was like part of the family there, eating with everyone else and not regarded as a barely tolerated lodger like Gloria.

If it weren't for the fact that this was a lovely house, much grander than her modest, terraced home back in the East End of London, then Gloria would have asked to be moved elsewhere. But she'd decided living at Oak House was worth biting her tongue for and not responding to Sylvia's remarks, because she could end up somewhere far worse. Thankfully, they didn't see a great deal of each other as Gloria suspected Sylvia avoided her as much as possible. Though how things would be once she'd had her baby, Gloria wasn't sure. Would Sylvia tolerate all the inconvenience of having a tiny baby in the house? Gloria sighed. She would not think about that now, as her baby wasn't due until March. She had other more pressing matters on her mind to deal with first.

The back door opened and Joyce came in with a gust of cold, damp air.

'Morning Gloria! How are you today?' Joyce asked, smiling cheerfully.

'I'm fine, thank you. Pleased to see a smilin' face.' Gloria beamed at the woman who had shown her nothing but kindness since she'd come to live here.

Joyce threw an exasperated glance at the closed kitchen door. 'Has she been hurrying you along again?'

Gloria gave a shrug. 'It's like water off a duck's back to me now!'

'Pity she hasn't got anything better to do.' Joyce took off her coat, which was speckled with dark spots of rain, and hung it on a hook by the outside door. 'She should be glad to have you here. You could be good company for her if she'd give you a chance and spend some time with you.'

Gloria wrinkled her nose. 'I ain't quite the sort of company she aspires to.'

She knew that Sylvia, who had been widowed the previous year, preferred her friends to be from a higher social sphere than the working class one Gloria came from. Her host spent a lot of time with Rosalind Platten from the Grange. The pair of them had looked down on the evacuee mothers from the moment they'd arrived in Great Plumstead, only providing billets because they were required to by law. Although Rosalind's evacuee hadn't stayed long, returning to London after little more than a week of living with her.

'Then she's missing out.' Joyce opened the cupboard where she kept her cleaning equipment and got out what she needed for her work. 'You never know, she might come to appreciate you one day.'

Gloria snorted. 'Not if she can 'elp it! Anyway, I 'ave plenty of others I like to spend time with at The Mother's Day Club. If Prue hadn't set it up, I'm not sure I would still be 'ere. I'd probably 'ave gone back to London by now.'

'I'm glad you haven't!' Joyce put a hand on her hip and gave Gloria a stern look. 'You're in the safest place here. You've got your baby to think of. There might not have been bombing in London yet, but it could happen any time.'

Gloria stroked her swollen belly underneath her emerald-

green dress. 'I know, it's why I came here – to protect this one. And why I sent my others to Devon…' Her voice wavered, tears flooding her eyes as the memory of when she'd last seen her five older children came back to her. It was the day they'd been evacuated, when she'd waved them off at the station, feeling like her heart was breaking into pieces. 'Gawd, I miss 'em, Joyce.'

The older woman nodded and placed a hand on Gloria's arm. 'Of course, you do. It's only natural, but remember, they're *safe* there. Take comfort in that. Don't go upsetting yourself – it isn't good for you or the baby.'

Gloria squared her shoulders and pulled herself up to her full height on her high heels. 'You're right, I must look on the bright side.'

'That's the way.' Joyce nodded. 'Are you going to The Mother's Day Club this morning?' she asked, wrapping her paisley-print apron around her small, wiry frame.

'Yes, but I've got shopping to do first at the grocers and butchers and then bring it back here before I go to the club, so I 'ad better get a move on. I mustn't be late.'

'And I must make a start, or she'll want to know why.' Joyce's eyes met Gloria's, a look of understanding passing between them. 'Have a lovely time at The Mother's Day Club.'

'Thanks, Joyce. I'm sure I will. It's *the* place to be in Great Plumstead!'

CHAPTER 3

'I remember your little lads playing with these.' Hettie smiled fondly as she took two wooden toy horses, on wheels, out of the box. She and Prue Wilson were setting up the play area in one corner of the village hall, ready for today's Mother's Day Club meeting.

'They loved these. It only feels like yesterday when they were pushing them around on the floor at home,' Prue said, a note of longing in her voice. 'Where did that time go? Jack's away in the army and since Edwin's tribunal last week he's now officially a conscientious objector. Who knows how long it will be before he'll leave as well to train with the Friends Ambulance Unit?'

Hettie put the toy horses down on the floor, then laid a hand on Prue's shoulder and squeezed it. 'Children grow up. I'm glad I had the pleasure of watching you and your sisters and brothers spread your wings. It's the way life goes.'

Prue smiled tremulously as she blinked back tears. 'I know you're right. I'm being silly.' She put a hand over her mouth.

'I'm not used to people coming and going so much. I had a letter from Sally yesterday. I do miss her.'

'How is she?' Hettie had liked Sally, Prue's evacuee mother, very much and had been devastated when the young woman had given birth to a stillborn baby. Understandably, after that, Sally had returned to her home in London.

'Fine, she's got a job in a garment factory making uniforms. It's the one where Marianne used to work. She sounds upbeat and says that keeping busy is helping her.' Prue removed the last of the toys from the box and arranged them in the play corner. 'I hope she'll come and visit us some time.' She glanced at the clock on the wall. 'It's a quarter to ten. We'd better get a move on, or the mothers will be here, and we won't be ready.'

When Hettie opened the village hall doors at ten o'clock, there was a group of mothers waiting outside despite the chilly, damp day.

'Good morning!' Hettie greeted them, stepping to the side and ushering them in with a welcoming smile and a wave of her hand.

She'd enjoyed getting to know these young women and their toddlers since The Mother's Day Club had been founded. Before her retirement, she'd never have had the chance to spend time with them, other than meeting them briefly at the monthly WI meeting. Hettie loved how helping here at the club had broadened her horizons, introducing her to women from the communities of London's East End, which were a sharp contrast to those of a rural Norfolk village. It had been an opportunity to learn from each other and that was part of the joy of being involved with The Mother's Day Club.

'Mornin', Hettie.' Gloria gave her a beaming smile, her lips painted in her usual pillar-box red lipstick. Hettie caught the scent of Gloria's light floral perfume as she took off her coat, revealing an emerald-green dress – one from her wardrobe full of colourful dresses which suited her personality, along with her bottle-blonde, pompadour hairstyle. Her distinctive, bright style was a contrast to what most of the local women wore. Amongst their plain or tweedy colours, Gloria stood out like a gloriously colourful peacock.

'How are you today, Gloria?' Hettie asked, returning the younger woman's smile.

'I'm fine, thank you Hettie! Though I need to get the last pullover finished this side of Christmas. It's for Ernie, my littlest one. I'll be knitting faster than I can talk this morning!' She gave a throaty laugh, headed over to one of the sets of chairs and tables that had been arranged, and unpacked the knitting from her basket.

'Hettie, will you teach me 'ow to turn the 'eel on my sock again?' Annie, another of the expectant mothers, asked. 'I tried to do it on my own after you showed me last time, but 'ave made a right mess of it.' Her brow creased in a frown. 'It looks simple enough when you do it, and I can manage when you're watching over me to 'elp, but when I try again on my own… well it ends up more 'ole than 'eel…' She threw up her hands in exasperation.

'Of course, I will. Don't worry, we'll sort it out. It took me plenty of goes to get the hang of it when I first learned. My mother despaired of me ever learning how to do it.' Hettie put her arm through Annie's. 'Let's get your knitting out and we'll make a start.'

Five minutes later, sitting beside Annie, Hettie watched as the young woman carefully picked up a stitch at the end of the row.

'That's it, you're doing it – I knew you could! Well done,' Hettie said, delighted to see the young woman was gradually mastering how to turn a heel. 'You *can* do it.'

'Not all the time, that's the problem. When I 'ave you 'ere beside me showing me what to do so I don't get in such a muddle, it's all right.' With that row finished, Annie turned her knitting around in her hands, ready to go back the other way. 'You always spot if I've done something wrong straight away before I make too much of a mess.'

'Keep practising and it will get easier each time. If you like, why not finish the heel you're working on, then pull it out and do it again while you're here and I'm around to ask if you are unsure of anything?'

'All right, I will,' agreed Annie, looking up and smiling at Hettie. 'Practice makes perfect, as they say!'

Hettie patted the young woman's arm and stood up. 'I'm going to get the hot water urns on so we can all have a cup of tea. If you need me, I won't be far away.'

Annie smiled gratefully. 'Thank you, Hettie, you're ever so patient with me – I appreciate it.'

'You're welcome,' Hettie returned the young woman's smile.

As Hettie walked across the village hall towards the kitchen, she looked around at what the other mothers were doing. Some were knitting like Annie, chatting and laughing together as they worked. Others were flicking through magazines at the table organised as a little library with donated books and magazines. Marianne, who'd arrived from Rookery House, was doing some sewing while she talked to Prue. In the toy corner, a group of mothers were deep in conversation while they watched over their children playing.

Starting The Mother's Day Club had provided these women with a place to come to, somewhere to meet others in

the same boat as them. It was building a sense of community once more for the women who had been ripped out of their homes and away from their families due to circumstances beyond their control. Hettie was happy to be involved because helping here made a real difference to these women's lives. Without The Mother's Day Club some of these young women would have returned home to London.

~

'Cup of tea and a biscuit, Gloria?' Hettie held out a tray with two cups of tea and a plate with the last two Garibaldi biscuits on it.

'Ta ducks.' Gloria took a cup and a biscuit. 'I'd lost track of time with focusing on this.' She touched the jumper she was knitting, which lay on her lap.

'Mind if I join you?' Hettie took the last cup of tea for herself and put the tray on the table.

'Course not, sit yourself down. I saw you 'elping Annie again with her socks. She's desperate to get them finished so she can send them to her 'usband, in the Air Force, in time for Christmas.' Gloria dipped her biscuit in her tea, then bit off the softened end.

'And she will – she's doing fine,' Hettie said. 'How are you getting on?' She reached over and stroked the soft, blue, cable-patterned pullover which Gloria was knitting. 'It's lovely. Your little one will look smashing in this.'

'I'm getting there, though it's taking longer to make than if I was just knitting it in plain stocking stitch. There's just the other sleeve to do, then sew it all together and knit the neckband,' Gloria said. 'I must get it done in time as I can't let my Ernie down. Don't want 'im to be the only one without a new pullover. It'll be 'ard enough being away from 'ome...'

Gloria's voice caught, her brown eyes filling with tears. She put her cup and half-eaten biscuit down on the table and rummaged in her handbag, fishing out a handkerchief and using it to dab her eyes. 'Take no notice of me. I don't know what's the matter with me today.'

Hettie's eyes met Gloria's. 'You miss your children. That's nothing to be ashamed of. It's hard for families to be split up.'

Gloria nodded, sniffing. 'I ought to be used to it now – it's been months since they were evacuated to Devon and then me 'ere, but sometimes it just gets to me…' Her voice wavered as emotions churned across her face. 'You know I sometimes wonder if I did the right thing 'aving them evacuated.'

'Couldn't you have gone with them to Devon?' Hettie took a bite of her biscuit, followed by a sip of milky tea.

'Perhaps, but when I agreed to them going, I thought I'd be living at 'ome in London and that wouldn't 'ave been so bad. I didn't expect I'd become an evacuee myself. I only came 'ere because my husband, Charlie, persuaded me. He found out about expectant mothers being evacuated after we'd already sent the children. Otherwise, I'd still be in London. Now I'm even further away from my children, and none of us at 'ome!'

'I'm glad he persuaded you,' Hettie said. 'He wanted you to be safe.'

Gloria nodded, dabbing at her eyes. 'I know, but I can't 'elp doubting whether I should be 'ere, and if my children would be better off back with me at 'ome in London. There ain't been any of the bombin', like they said there would be.'

'I understand, and it's harder still with Christmas coming up, but your children are *safe* in Devon. Just because there hasn't been any bombing yet, it doesn't mean there *won't* be. You wouldn't want them caught up in that, would you?'

Gloria shook her head. 'Course not! And that's what I keep tellin' myself. Being safe is more important than me missin'

them. But I still wonder if I should go 'ome and have them sent back to me…'

Hettie turned so that she was looking directly at Gloria. 'You're not *seriously* considering going back, are you?' she asked in a hushed voice. 'I know a few mothers went home in the early days before Prue started The Mother's Day Club, but I thought you were settled here.'

'I am, but…' Gloria sighed. 'It's just hit me 'ard lately how far I am from my children, and I have no idea when I'll see them again. It could be months… years even. All I can do for them now is write to them and knit things to send them.' She stroked the blue pullover lying on her lap. Gloria looked at Hettie, their eyes meeting. 'It ain't that I don't like it 'ere because I do. It's because part of me feels lost without my children and that I've let them down somehow, sendin' them off to be looked after by strangers.'

'You haven't let them down. In fact, I'd say you've made an enormous sacrifice to keep them safe.' Hettie put her hand on Gloria's arm. 'And you have your unborn child to think of.'

Gloria laid her hand on her swollen stomach. 'I'm looking forward to it being born and 'aving a child to cluck over again.'

'And the best place to do that is here, in Great Plumstead. Please don't go back to London, Gloria. And if you're feeling tempted, then come and talk to me first. You will, won't you?' Hettie said, her voice serious. 'Don't do anything rash.'

'All right, I promise I'll come and see you first.' Gloria glanced over to the other end of the hall where Prue was reading a book to a toddler sitting on her lap. 'Please don't tell Prue about my doubts, I know 'ow upset she was when the other mothers went back. She's been good to me. I don't want to cause her any trouble.'

'Don't worry, I won't say anything to Prue,' Hettie reassured her. 'Just take it one day at a time.'

'That's what my old Ma used to say. All you can deal with is today. The past is history. Tomorrow is yet to come, so concentrate on today.' Gloria looked around at the other mothers in the hall. 'Though it's a funny old time we're livin' in, ain't it? Everyone's affected by the war. We've all got to make sacrifices until we get through it.' She took a deep breath and lifted her chin. 'And sitting 'ere complaining about it ain't going to get this pullover finished, is it?' She picked up the remains of her biscuit, dipped it in her tea, ate it, then finished her drink before returning to her knitting and starting to work on it again.

'You're right, the war has affected every single one of us. Even in this village it's changed our lives.' Hettie paused for a moment considering how her own life had changed since war had been declared back in September, followed shortly by the arrival of the evacuee expectant mothers. 'But it's not all bad, Gloria. I'd never have met you for a start if it hadn't happened.'

Gloria gave Hettie a wry smile. 'I know I was a bit of a shock to some, with my bright clothes and fancy hair.' She chuckled. 'The looks I got from some people when they first saw me!'

Hettie laughed. 'You've brightened up the place no end. Seriously though, having you and the other evacuee mothers come here has been a boost to the village in my opinion – a real tonic. You've shaken things up a bit and, believe me, they needed some shaking up. New faces and ways of doing things are good otherwise our lives can become too staid and narrow-minded.'

Gloria raised her eyebrows. 'That's good to know, Hettie, thank you. And we've learned things from being 'ere too. I'd

never been blackberry picking till I came 'ere. I loved it! And can't wait to do it again. The jam we made was delicious.'

'Once rationing starts in the new year, there'll be even more need to pick blackberries next summer, so you'll get your wish.' Hettie drank the rest of her tea. 'Right, I'd better get the cups collected and washed.' She stood up. 'I meant what I said. I am glad you came here.'

Gloria beamed at her. 'Ta, ducks. I appreciate that. And I'm sorry for getting all maudlin…' Her brown eyes were earnest. 'It ain't like me, I think with Christmas on the horizon, well… it's stirred things up a bit, that's all.'

'I understand.' Hettie laid her hand on Gloria's shoulder for a moment. 'Everything will be all right, you'll see.'

CHAPTER 4

Gloria quietly closed the front door of Oak House behind her and slipped off her peep-toed, high-heeled shoes. Lovely as they were, the shoes made a loud clicking noise when she walked across the tiled hallway floor wearing them.

After her encounter with Sylvia that morning, Gloria would rather avoid drawing any more attention to herself. Her host might be out visiting her chum, Rosalind, but it was better to be safe than sorry, Gloria thought. She didn't want Sylvia popping out of her sitting room the way the troll did from under the bridge in one of the fairy tales her children had loved. The memory of how they used to snuggle on her lap as she read to them made her heart ache with missing them. A wave of longing to see them crashed over her. Not for the first time today, doubts about both her own *and* her children's evacuation to the countryside weighed heavily in her chest.

Confessing her feelings to Hettie during their chat at The Mother's Day Club had helped for a while. Gloria had felt better while she'd been there, but now the uncertainties were

creeping back, circling like dark crows, and plaguing her thoughts. What on earth was she doing here, hundreds of miles away from her children, making herself feel so miserable? Was it really for the best? she wondered. Gloria sighed. She needed a cup of tea and a sit down to mull things over.

As she plonked her basket on the kitchen table, she spotted an envelope propped up on the dresser, her heart leaping as she recognised her husband's handwriting. Abandoning her plan to make tea, she snatched up the envelope and eagerly tore it open. Contact with Charlie, however fleeting and even if only via words written on paper, was exactly what she needed right now. Oh, how she missed him. Although she should be used to him being away. His work in the Merchant Navy had meant that he spent more time absent from home than there even before the war. But when he was on leave and with her, what joyful times they had together. He was a great big bear of a man who always looked on the bright side of life, laughed and smiled a lot, making those around him feel good. Her luck was in the night she met him.

She unfolded the sheet of paper and began to read

New York, 23rd November 1939

My darling Glorious,

She smiled at Charlie's special name for her. He'd called her that ever since they'd first met and she'd introduced herself. His response had been to say she was Gloria by name and glorious by nature – and so his unique way of addressing her had been born. She read on,

We're loading up here in New York, ready for the next

convoy, so I've got time to write to you. How are you? You and our little ones are always in my thoughts, Glorious. We are thousands of miles apart, and with me doing this job, I know I should be used to it by now, but with the war on, it feels different. I'm grateful every day that you and our children moved out to the countryside. From what I've seen working on the convoys, the enemy is ruthless and when they attack, they mean business. I fear it's only a matter of time before it will be London's turn to face the enemy's wrath and if you were still there... But you're not! Thank you darling, Glorious, for putting all our children's safety first, the ones we have and the one yet to be born – even though it means you are all far apart. I know it can't have been easy for any of you to up sticks and move to live with strangers and somewhere so unlike what you're used to, but you did it and I'm for ever grateful. What you've done may well prove to have saved their lives before this war is done.

Memories of being evacuated from London came back to her. It had been on the third of September, the day war was declared and when Charlie had been home on leave. Two days earlier, they'd tearfully waved off their children who'd left with the rest of their school. Gloria had never planned on being evacuated, like she'd told Hettie. It was only after Charlie had spotted a poster encouraging expectant mothers to take up the chance to move to the countryside that he'd persuaded her to go. If he hadn't been back on shore then, Gloria would never have come here, and would still be living in London.

Gloria had dismissed the idea of being evacuated to begin with but had eventually given in after seeing how passionately Charlie felt about it. He wasn't the sort of man who always had to have his way in the home like some women's husbands

she knew. Charlie was easy-going, and it was Gloria who was in charge. But on this occasion her husband hadn't backed down. His strong conviction that evacuation was the safest and most sensible thing for Gloria and their unborn child had convinced her and she'd agreed to try it.

Charlie had accompanied her to Liverpool Street station and embraced her tightly when the time came to say goodbye. 'Thank you for doing this,' he'd told her, acknowledging how difficult it was for her to leave their home, friends, family and all that was familiar, for a life with strangers in the countryside. Gloria had been like a fish out of water here at first, but had gradually settled into Great Plumstead, made friends, and come to realise that Charlie had been right. It was only in the past few days that the niggling doubts about being here had crept in. Whether that was to do with Christmas being on the horizon or not, she wasn't sure.

She read more.

I just wish Ma and Father would move out of the East End, but I know I'd be waiting for ever for that to happen. There's no shifting them.

Gloria's parents-in-law, Ruby and Stan, still lived in the same street, just a few houses down from where she and Charlie had rented a house for their family. She knew they would never leave. If Gloria returned to London, she'd have to live with them as her and Charlie's home was leased out to his cousin now. The thought of living with her mother-in-law wasn't a pleasant one. Ruby had never approved of Charlie marrying Gloria, not liking the way she did her hair, dressed or did *anything* come to that. Although whoever Charlie had married would not have been good enough for Ruby. After several spats between Ruby and Gloria in the early days of the

marriage, the pair of them had settled into an uneasy truce, spending as little time in each other's company as possible. Regardless of how she felt about her mother-in-law, Gloria hoped no harm would come to Charlie's parents. Or to any of the people back home in the streets of the East End. But there were no guarantees in life, especially in wartime. That was what evacuating children and expectant mothers was all about, wasn't it? Protecting those who might be at risk – an insurance policy of sorts.

Returning her focus to the letter once more, Gloria read on.

We'll be leaving on the next tide. I hope this crossing is smoother than the one we had out here, but at this time of year it's more likely to be a bumpy ride! I'll sign off now so I can post this to you.

Look after yourself darling Glorious. I long for the day when I will see you again and hold you in my arms once more. In the meantime, I send you all my love,

your loving husband,

Charlie XXXXXXXXX

Gloria smiled as she traced her finger over where he had signed his name and the row of kisses. Charlie's letters were never long, but always filled with his love for her and today's had given her a welcome boost just when she needed it. She knew exactly what he'd say if she confessed her doubts to him. He hadn't changed his mind since he was last home on leave in September. His conviction was even greater now and knowing that his wife and children were safe was an enormous comfort to him as he worked on the convoys

ploughing across the rough seas of the North Atlantic. He had enough to worry about with enemy U-boats hunting them down, without adding more anxiety about the safety of his family. It made sense for Gloria to stay where she was, and the children too. Though it wasn't easy when her head told her one thing and her heart said another!

CHAPTER 5

Rookery House

'I've never seen Gloria upset like that before,' Hettie said, drying a clean plate with a tea towel. She'd confessed her worries about Gloria to Thea and Marianne while they ate their evening meal.

'She's usually one of the most cheerful and positive people at The Mother's Day Club.' Marianne rinsed the plate she'd washed and stacked it in the wooden rack on the sink draining board.

'Exactly!' Hettie agreed. 'And that's why it was a shock to see her so upset this morning.'

Thea carried the kettle over from the range, where it had just come to the boil, and poured hot water from it into the large brown teapot. 'Do you think she'll go back to London?' Thea asked, putting the knitted tea cosy over the teapot, its colours cheerful in the light from the lamp on the table. 'Prue would be worried to hear Gloria was even thinking about it.

Remember how upset Prue was when those other mothers went back? They'd only been here just over a week. She tried to persuade them to stay and give it another chance, but they wouldn't. It would be far worse if Gloria left as she's seemed so settled and has been a stalwart member of The Mother's Day Club since it started!'

'Gloria asked me not to tell Prue – and I promised I wouldn't.' Hettie looked from Marianne to Thea. 'So please don't say anything to Prue.'

Thea looked at Marianne who gave a nod of agreement. 'Don't worry, we won't,' Thea reassured Hettie.

'One reason those other women left was to look after their husbands,' Marianne said. 'Is that why Gloria wants to go back?'

Hettie shook her head. 'Not in Gloria's case – her husband's away at sea in the Merchant Navy.'

'So he's hardly at home to need looking after then,' Thea said.

'It's because of her children,' Hettie explained as she dried some knives and forks. 'She desperately misses them. They're evacuated down in Devon and she's here, hundreds of miles apart, and with Christmas coming up, it's hit her hard that she's so far from them.'

Thea collected some clean cups off the kitchen dresser for their tea. 'Why didn't she go to Devon with them? They could all have gone together.'

'Gloria never planned on being evacuated herself. She agreed to her children going, then after they'd left her husband spotted a poster encouraging expectant women to be evacuated too and persuaded her to go, only she ended up here…' Hettie waved her hand. 'In Great Plumstead and even further away from her children. It's being separated from them, and the fact that there's been none of the feared

bombing in London, that is making Gloria have doubts about staying here.' Hettie sighed. 'If she went back home, then she could send for her children, and they could all be together again.'

'But they'd be living in a potential target area,' Thea said solemnly. 'It's not *if* the bombers will attack London, but *when*. My friend Violet, who's the station officer at Ambulance Station 75, says it is only a matter of time – and they're prepared for it.'

'*You're* not planning on leaving, are you?' Hettie asked Marianne who'd just finished the washing up.

'Definitely not!' Marianne declared. 'I don't want my baby born in a place that could be attacked any day.' She placed her hand on her round belly. 'Remember though, a lot of the mothers found it difficult to settle here at first,' Marianne reminded them. 'They didn't have much to do before Prue set up The Mother's Day Club for them. Being busy always helps when someone's unsettled or having doubts.'

'Gloria goes to The Mother's Day Club every day it's on,' Hettie said, 'but there's a limit to the number of days the village hall is available. We're already running the club as often as we can.'

'Come and have some tea,' Thea said, pouring out three cups of hot, steaming tea from the teapot.

'I'll just put these away and then I'll sit down.' Hettie picked up the pile of clean, dried plates and bowls and took them over to the kitchen dresser.

'If you don't mind, I'm going to take mine upstairs. I'm tired out. This little one was doing somersaults last night, keeping me awake.' Marianne took one of the candle holders and lit the candle before picking up her cup of tea. 'Good night.'

'Good night!' Thea and Hettie chorused.

Left on their own, they settled down in chairs either side of the range. Thea rested after a busy day in the garden, her hands cradling her cup, while Hettie worked on the sock she was knitting, her fingers moving in a steady rhythm. They sat in companionable silence for a few minutes with the clicking of needles, the ticking of the clock on the dresser and the gentle hiss from the fire in the range providing a calming background sound.

'Are you going to tell me what else is upsetting you apart from Gloria?' Thea suddenly asked, startling Hettie.

She looked at her friend, her eyes meeting Thea's bright blue ones. 'Why do you think there is?'

'Because I know you.' Thea raised an eyebrow. 'You've got that look you get when you're upset but trying to hide it. Has something happened?'

Hettie gave a wry smile. 'Yes and no!' She knitted faster, not needing to watch what she was doing, as the strange, unsettling tug at her heart that she'd first experienced in the grocery shop that morning nudged her again. 'It's something and nothing. It shouldn't matter.'

'But it clearly *does* matter to you!' Thea said kindly. 'And enough to upset you.'

Hettie sighed and laid her knitting in her lap, her eyes fixed on it for a moment before she raised them to look at Thea. 'Grace was putting together an order for the Hall when I dropped our shopping list off at Barker's this morning. It was for the ingredients to make Christmas cakes and puddings, sent by Mrs Shepherd, the new Cook.'

'She's a bit late making them, isn't she?' Thea took a sip of her tea.

'Precisely!' Hettie leaned forward in her chair. 'But it's none of my business what she does, or when she makes them. She's the Cook there now – not me! I retired of my own free

will and I *love* my new life living here with you and Marianne. Now I have the chance to do things I've never had the time to before but…' she hesitated.

'But…?' Thea prompted her.

'Well, I minded for the first time since I retired, that it wasn't *me* working as Cook at the Hall. That it wasn't me making their Christmas cakes and puddings.' Hettie's breath caught in her throat. 'I don't know why because I've made enough of them over the years.' She rolled a knitting needle between her finger and thumb. 'But for some strange reason it niggled at me that I wasn't the Cook there anymore, though *why* I felt like that, I'm not sure. It's not because I'm not happy – because I am! The only thing I can think of is that it's because it's a Christmas tradition which I did there for so long, but now I'm not part of it any more.'

'You made our Christmas cake and puddings, the first ones here at Rookery House – you started our new tradition. That's good, isn't it?'

Hettie nodded. 'It is and they were the first of many, I hope.'

'Nothing in life lasts for ever, things change, new opportunities come along.' Thea paused, looking thoughtful. 'This time last year I'd never have guessed I would be living here with you and Marianne, and yet here we are. And it's wonderful!'

Hettie reached over and patted Thea's arm. 'You're right and I'm so glad you asked me to come and live here.'

Thea took hold of Hettie's hand. 'When our lives alter it's a chance to do something new or perhaps old things differently. This is going to be a new type of Christmas for you. For all of us. I know it's a big change after so many years at the Hall, but why not challenge yourself – embrace it?' Thea suggested.

'You could even involve Gloria somehow; it might help her get through a difficult time, too.'

Hettie considered what Thea had said for a few moments. 'What do you suggest I do?'

'That's up to you to decide.' Thea stood up, smiling. 'I'm sure you can think of something. Right, I'm off to bed. Good night.'

Sitting by herself next to the warm range, Hettie carried on knitting, bathed in the cosy yellow light from the lamp, her fingers weaving the wool in and out of the needles, working of their own accord while her mind mulled over what Thea had suggested. Was there a way to settle her disquiet about no longer being part of the tradition up at the Hall, *and* help Gloria at the same time? What, she thought, would make a first Christmas here at Rookery House special, and wholeheartedly embrace the festive season? This was a chance to do things differently, to embrace new opportunities. With Gloria's help, it could be something extraordinary. But would Gloria be interested? There was only one way to find out, she would have to ask her.

CHAPTER 6

Tuesday 5th December

Gloria knocked on the front door of Rookery House, then stuffed her gloved hand back in her coat pocket. It was a chilly day, with an icy wind needling its way through any gaps in her clothing. She'd covered her head with a rose-pink silk scarf that Charlie had brought her home from one of his voyages, tying it under her chin.

While she waited for the door to be answered, Gloria admired the colourful panels of stained glass in it. She hadn't been here before and so far she liked everything about Rookery House. It had a friendly-looking façade. There were bay windows on either side of the front door and three windows above on the second floor. It was smaller than Oak House, which was in the village centre, but had a lovely setting out in the countryside surrounded by fields and woods. She could see why Marianne loved it so much. It had been Marianne who'd passed on the invitation for Gloria to

come here this afternoon when they'd met at The Mother's Day Club that morning. Why Hettie wanted to see Gloria, she wasn't sure. Was it to check whether she was still here and hadn't sneaked off back to London despite her promise to talk to Hettie first? She was about to find out as the door opened.

'Hello Gloria,' Hettie greeted her with a welcoming smile. 'Come on in out of the cold.' She stepped to the side and ushered Gloria into the hallway. 'I'm glad you could come at such short notice.'

'I'm curious about why you've asked me 'ere,' Gloria admitted.

Hettie looked amused. 'I'm sure you are. The kitchen's this way; it's lovely and warm in there. We'll have some tea and cake and have a chat.'

Gloria followed Hettie along the length of the hall, her heels tapping on the black and white tiled floor. At the end, they went through a door into a large kitchen at the rear of the house where the smell of fresh baking made her mouth water.

'Something smells good!' Gloria sniffed appreciatively. 'Can I smell cinnamon and nutmeg?'

'You can indeed. I've made Welsh cakes,' Hettie said. 'I got the recipe from a Welsh housemaid who worked at the Hall while I was Cook there. She was homesick and longed for a taste of home – so she told me her ma's own special recipe and I made her some Welsh cakes. I've used that recipe ever since. I thought you might enjoy them. Let me take your coat.'

Gloria removed her scarf, folded it and tucked it in her coat pocket, then took off her red coat and handed it to Hettie. 'Thank you.'

'Sit yourself down at the table, I won't be a minute.' Hettie draped Gloria's coat over the back of a chair near the range.

'This will warm it ready for when you have to go out in that icy wind again.'

'That's kind of you, thank you. Can I 'elp you with anything?' Gloria asked.

'No, it's all in hand. I'll just get the tea brewing.'

While Hettie busied herself pouring boiling water into the brown teapot, Gloria took the opportunity to look around her. The first thing that struck her was how different it felt from the kitchen at Oak House. This room was cosy, warmed not only physically by the range tucked into the chimney breast at the far end, but by something more precious – the people who lived here. It was welcoming and clearly the heart of the home.

It reminded Gloria of her house back in London, where her kitchen had been the centre of their family home. Meals were eaten there, life lived there. The front parlour was kept for best – for high days and holidays. Gloria had loved her kitchen, it was where she could talk to her family while she worked, cooking or washing. Now Charlie's cousin and his family had her kitchen while Gloria's own family were scattered elsewhere. She hoped it wouldn't be too long before they could all go back, the war over and life returned to normal. But in the meantime, she was here and had to make the best of it.

'This is a lovely kitchen, Hettie,' Gloria said, noticing the two dressers lined up along one wall, the blue and white crockery stored on them looking fresh and crisp. The windows by the sink were framed with pretty yellow curtains with a pattern of blue flowers.

'Yes, it is. I like it because it feels homely. Though it seemed small to me when I first moved here. I'd been used to the huge kitchen up at the Hall.' Hettie put a plate of freshly baked Welsh cakes down on the table, then sat down opposite

Gloria. 'But this place is much easier to cook in as I have things closer to hand.'

'Do you miss being Cook at the 'all?' Gloria asked.

'If you'd asked me that last week, I'd have said *no*!' Hettie poured out two cups of tea and passed one across to Gloria. 'Help yourself to milk and sugar, and some Welsh cakes.' Hettie paused for a moment as she took two of the little cakes and put them on her plate. 'I'm happy being retired, but when I heard about the new Cook making the Christmas cake and puddings yesterday, I felt... a sudden wrench. It unsettled me. Upset me. I didn't expect that,' Hettie said in a heartfelt voice. 'It's not as if I haven't made enough of them for the Hall over the years. I've lost count of how many.'

'Why did it upset you?' Gloria asked, stirring milk into her tea.

'I've been mulling it over and I think it's because it was a constant tradition for me for so long. It was an important job for the Christmas celebrations, both for the family and the staff. They all loved a slice of Christmas cake or the pudding. Now it's gone and someone else is making them in my place.' Hettie waved her hands as if flicking away the idea. 'It sounds daft, I know.'

Gloria nodded sympathetically. 'It's sometimes 'ard to change things, ain't it? There's a lot this year that's different all round and Christmas especially!' Gloria ignored the sadness that threatened to well up inside her and helped herself to a Welsh cake. She took a bite, savouring the mouth-watering buttery, cinnamon and nutmeg taste, along with the fruity currants on her tongue. 'This is delicious, Hettie!'

'I think using a proper Welsh recipe makes all the difference.' Hettie took a sip of tea then asked, 'How are you feeling today? Are you still having doubts about staying in Great Plumstead?'

Gloria shook her head while she chewed her mouthful of Welsh cake. 'I've made up my mind to stay. Though I miss my children so much it feels like one of my arms 'as been cut off, but I ain't going back to London and the children will remain where they are in Devon – where they're safe.'

'What made you decide?' Hettie asked.

'My husband, Charlie!' A picture of his dear face filled Gloria's mind. 'There was a letter from him waitin' for me when I got 'ome from The Mother's Day Club yesterday. He said he was glad that me and the children are evacuated so he didn't 'ave to worry about us so much. If we were still in London, he'd be worrying 'imself sick about what would 'appen when the bombers come. He's got enough on his plate working on the Atlantic convoys with them being 'unted down by U-boats. He needs to focus on 'is job and not get distracted worrying about his wife and family being in danger. So I am staying put!'

'I'm glad to hear that. You're doing the right thing.' Hettie reached across the table and patted Gloria's hand. 'I know it's difficult, but it is the safest thing for you all, and for your husband, too. You and me are both facing a different sort of Christmas this year, and we aren't the only ones. All the other evacuee expectant mothers and anyone who's got family away serving in the forces is going to miss them. Prue's going to feel the absence of her son, Jack. This Christmas will be out of the ordinary for so many.' Hettie took a sip of her tea. 'I've had an idea that we should do something *extra*ordinary. Celebrate Christmas in a different way. Turn this odd time of so many changes and missing people into something fun and happy.'

'What were you thinking of?' Gloria took another Welsh cake.

'I'm not sure. That's what I need to discuss with you, and part of the reason for asking you here,' Hettie explained. 'I

wanted to see how you were and ask if you'd help me do something for our first Christmas here, and for everyone in the village who's affected by the war in one way or another.' Hettie's eyes were hopeful behind her round glasses. 'It would keep us busy, give us less time to dwell on things and what we're missing. What do you think? Are you interested?'

Gloria chewed on her mouthful of Welsh cake while she considered Hettie's proposal. Did she want to be involved with organising something for this strange first Christmas away from her home and family? she wondered. As Hettie said, it *would* keep her busy and it could be fun, too.

She nodded, smiling at Hettie. 'All right, if we can find a good idea, then I'm on board!'

'I'm so glad you said yes!' Hettie held up her teacup in salute. 'Here's to our first Christmas doing something different, and to making it a wonderful one.'

Gloria picked up her teacup and chinked it against Hettie's. 'To a marvellous first Christmas.'

~

Hettie scanned down the list of Christmas ideas she and Gloria had come up with over the past half an hour while they'd drunk the teapot dry and devoured the plate of Welsh cakes.

'This is enough to keep us going for several Christmases,' she said, tapping a finger on the piece of paper she'd listed them on. 'We can't do everything, so we need to work out what we can do in the short time we've got.'

'I agree, but at least we have a good starting point. How about if we organised a Christmas party and include different things? Instead of going carol singing around the village

separately, we could 'ave a sing song and include carols as part of it,' Gloria suggested.

'We could hold it at the village hall. I like the sound of a sing song,' Hettie said enthusiastically, putting a tick against carol singing on the list. 'We can have food at the party.'

'And dancing,' Gloria added, 'and some entertainments. We'd better hold some auditions to make sure they are suitable and good enough to perform. I'd be 'appy to organise auditions. Before I got married, I was a singer, so I know how these things work. That's 'ow I met my Charlie. I was singing with a band at a dance he came to and he approached in the intermission and swept me off my feet!' She threw her head back and let out a throaty laugh.

'Then we must use your experience – play to our individual strengths,' Hettie said. 'You can be in charge of the entertainments, and I'll look after the food side of things. How about if we ask for donations of prepared food on the day, or ingredients beforehand that I can use to bake things for the party?'

'Good idea,' Gloria agreed. 'When are we going to 'old it?'

'Not Christmas Eve because everyone's too busy getting themselves organised at home then. How about Saturday the twenty-third?' Hettie suggested.

'Sounds perfect. Shall I go and see Prue about booking the village 'all on my way 'ome? The sooner we get it sorted out the better,' Gloria said. 'Let's 'ope it's free that afternoon.'

'Good idea,' Hettie agreed. 'I hope Prue might want to help with the party too. She's so good at getting things done.'

By the time Thea and her nephew Edwin came into the kitchen for a tea break, after working in the garden, Hettie and Gloria had drawn up a list of what they needed to organise.

'You've been busy.' Thea glanced at the list as she made up

a fresh pot of tea and Hettie refilled the plate with Welsh cakes.

'We have a plan.' Hettie looked at Gloria who nodded her head encouragingly. 'We're going to hold a Christmas party for any evacuee expectant mothers and villagers who want to attend.'

'There will be food and entertainments,' Gloria added. 'I'm organising auditions for anyone who would like to perform.'

'You could audition to play the piano, Edwin,' Thea suggested as he sat down next to Hettie.

'You should, Edwin, you're a marvellous player,' Hettie encouraged him.

He nodded. 'All right, just tell me when they are.'

'I'm not sure yet as I'll 'ave to find out when the village 'all is available. Don't worry, *everyone* in Great Plumstead will soon know what's goin' on. I'll be putting posters up to advertise it. I'm calling in on Prue on the way 'ome to get it sorted out. The quicker we get started, the better.' Gloria smiled at Hettie. 'You and I are going to be busy getting this Christmas party organised. We won't 'ave time to be worried about other things!'

A lightness filled Hettie's chest as she smiled at the younger woman. 'That is *exactly* what we need!'

CHAPTER 7

'That sounds like a fantastic idea.' Prue leaned back in her armchair after listening attentively to the plan for the Christmas party.

'I'm glad you think so.' Gloria met the older woman's steady gaze. 'You've done a lot for us evacuee mothers – made such a difference to our lives 'ere. Hettie and I 'oped you'd approve of the plan.'

Prue smiled. 'I do. It's just what we need this year with everything that's going on. Do you have a date for it?'

'December twenty-third if possible. We'll have to 'old auditions before then as well. That's why I'm 'ere, to ask if we can book the village 'all, I 'ope it's available then.'

'We'll need to check the village hall diary. It's in Victor's study, as he's chair of the village hall committee, so let's have a look.' Prue stood up and led the way out of the sitting room.

'Ughh!' She grimaced as she pushed the study door open and the overpowering smell of tobacco hit them. 'He smokes too much in here.' Prue hurried over to the window and pulled up the sash, letting in a welcome blast of fresh air.

Gloria followed Prue in and looked around, noticing everything was as neat as a pin. A large, dark-wood desk, inlaid with a green leather top, was in the middle of the room. Papers and what looked like accounts books were on it, everything placed in precise neat piles. A pot containing sharpened pencils stood beside them.

'The diary should be in here.' Prue opened the drawer of a filing cabinet and took out a blue book. 'This is it. The twenty-third is what you wanted, isn't it?'

'Yes, it's the Saturday before Christmas.'

'It's free! Look...' Prue smiled at Gloria as she pointed to the blank space in the diary for that day. 'I'll schedule the Christmas party for then.' She grabbed a pencil from Victor's desk and wrote in the party, along with Gloria and Hettie's names as organisers. 'You also need a booking for the auditions...'

As Prue turned the diary pages, Gloria saw they'd been lucky to find the 23rd free judging by the many bookings for the hall already pencilled in the diary – many of them during the daytime for The Mother's Day Club. The village hall was well used in the evenings too, for things like committee meetings, Girl Guides or the Women's Institute.

'The only evening free for your auditions is Tuesday the twelfth. Will that do?' Prue asked.

'Yes, it's perfect. It will give people time to think about what they might like to perform, practise it, and if they're chosen, then prepare for the party.' Gloria gave an appreciative smile. 'Thanks, Prue.'

'You're welcome. I'll let Victor know about the bookings. Not that he'll be auditioning or will even go to the party – it's not his sort of thing.' Prue raised her eyebrows. 'But I will definitely be there.'

'Will you audition?' Gloria asked as Prue returned the diary to the filing cabinet.

Prue laughed. 'Oh no, not me! I'm no good at entertaining. I am better at organising and doing things, so if you need any help, I'll be glad to do whatever's necessary.'

'Thank you — Hettie and I 'oped you'd say that! We're going to be busy getting everything organised in time, so all offers of 'elp will be gratefully accepted!'

'Just let me know what you want me to do, as long as it's not providing entertainment.'

'Edwin's auditioning, playin' the piano,' Gloria said as Prue closed the window. 'I saw him at Rookery House earlier.'

'Is he? That's good.' Prue's voice was over bright, as she turned to face Gloria. 'Edwin's a talented player and has always loved music from when he was small. He inherited his musical ability from his late mother, so I've been told. She would have been very proud of him, as am I. It's a privilege to be his step-mother. I just wish he still lived here at home.' A look of sadness washed across her face.

Gloria had heard about Edwin being thrown out by his father after he'd registered as a conscientious objector which was why he now lived at Rookery House. She admired the young man for standing up for his beliefs. It took courage to do that. But clearly Edwin's father, Victor, didn't share her conviction. Gloria had only seen Prue's husband a few times since she'd arrived in Great Plumstead, but she hadn't liked the look of him. In fact, it had surprised her that Prue was married to him.

'We'll need a good pianist to accompany the sing song, so Edwin's talent will be very useful,' Gloria said.

'I think a party is an excellent idea. It will bring some joy to what's going to be a strange Christmas for us all,' Prue said as they left Victor's study.

'That's the plan. Now we've got the dates sorted I'll make some posters to put up around the village to spread the word.'

Prue nodded. 'Knowing Great Plumstead, news of the party will soon get around. The village hasn't had anything happen quite like this before. It will cause a stir!'

CHAPTER 8

Wednesday 6th December

Hettie stood at the front of the village hall facing her fellow members of Great Plumstead's Women's Institute. She was wearing the blue, flower-patterned cotton dress that Marianne had designed and made for her, and which fitted her perfectly. Hettie loved its style with three quarter length sleeves, a V-neck, a button opening down the front and a swishy skirt. She always felt good when she wore it and more confident as she knew she looked her best. Hettie needed that confidence boost right now. Being part of a WI meeting from this angle was a lot more daunting than her usual place in the audience with the rest of the members.

'Ladies, can I have your attention, please?' Prue's loud, crisp voice cut through the hubbub of chattering as the women returned to their seats after the tea break, where mince pies had replaced the usual biscuits in honour of this being the last meeting before Christmas.

The room fell silent, faces looking their way. Hettie felt members' eyes falling on her as the stragglers took their seats, no doubt wondering what she was doing here at the front.

'Thanks again to Mr Shaw for his interesting and most informative talk.' Prue gestured to their guest speaker who'd given a lecture in the first half of the meeting. 'What you've taught us tonight will help us all grow more and better vegetables next year.' Prue led the way in another round of applause.

When the hall was silent once more, Prue continued, 'Hettie would now like to tell us about the Christmas party she and Gloria are organising.' After introducing Hettie, Prue sat down in her seat beside the WI's president.

Hettie took a small step forward, her heart beating fast. She glanced briefly at Gloria, who sat nearby in the front row and gave her an encouraging smile. After taking a deep breath, Hettie began.

'I'm sure many of you will have seen the posters we've put up around the village, so already know that we're holding a Christmas party here in the village hall on Saturday the twenty-third of December at two o'clock. Everyone from the village is welcome.' Hettie's confidence, which had wavered along with her voice, grew as she got into her stride, talking about something she felt passionate about. 'There will be food and entertainments. We're holding auditions for anyone who'd like the chance to entertain the party goers. So if you're a singer, dancer, juggler, magician or can play an instrument, then we'd be delighted to see what you can offer.'

'When are the auditions?' a woman shouted from the back of the hall.

'Next Tuesday, on the twelfth of December, starting here at six o'clock. So that gives anyone interested a chance to practise beforehand.'

Hettie paused for a few moments while the noise level rose in the hall as the women made comments to each other.

'The other thing I wanted to talk to you about, and which I hope you can help with, is the food. We need food suitable for a party, things like sandwiches, cake, sausage rolls – things that you eat with fingers. If you could make or bake anything and deliver it to the hall on the day of the party, we'd be very grateful. Or if you'd prefer, you can donate some ingredients a few days before which I'll use to bake things for the party. Whatever help you could give would be most welcome.'

Prue stood up and waved a sheet of paper in the air. 'If you'd like to volunteer to help with the party food then please put your name down on here. Remember to say what you'll make or the ingredients you'll donate so we get a balance of different items. I'll send it round so you can add your names while we get on with WI business before our social games to end the meeting.'

Prue passed the paper and a pencil to a woman sitting at the front and sat down again.

'Are there any questions about the party?' Hettie asked, gazing round at the women.

'Can my children come along?' a woman asked.

'Yes, the party is for *anyone* who lives in Great Plumstead, whatever their age. It doesn't matter whether they've lived here all their lives or just arrived in September like our evacuee mothers.' Hettie's gaze settled on some of the evacuee mothers who now came along to the WI meetings like Gloria, and she smiled warmly at them. '*Everyone* is welcome!'

'We've never had a village Christmas party before!' Rosalind Platten declared. She was sitting next to Sylvia, who Gloria lived with. 'May I ask, *why* are you organising one? Surely now there's a war on we should focus on that, not

partying!' Her voice was loud and imperious, as she regarded Hettie through narrowed eyes.

Several women said things which Hettie couldn't hear clearly, but from their tone, they clearly didn't agree with Rosalind's sentiment.

'It's because of the war that we're having a party!' Hettie gave Rosalind a cool stare. Trust her to question their motives and try to pour cold water on the idea. Rosalind was known throughout the village for her stuck-up attitude. 'The war has affected us all in one way or another.' There were many nods and murmurs of agreement from women in the audience. 'The party is a way of bringing some fun and joy to a Christmas which will be a different one for many of us here tonight and for others in the village…'

Gloria sprang to her feet and turned to face Rosalind, hands on her hips. 'Last Christmas I was at 'ome in London with my children and 'usband. But this year, I'm 'ere with my children evacuated to Devon and my 'usband sailing in a convoy across the North Atlantic being hunted by U-boats!' Her sharp voice brooked no argument. 'This is going to be a Christmas turned on its 'ead! Having the party will 'elp keep me going. 'Elp to fill part of the massive 'ole left by not being with my family. And I ain't the only one in 'ere tonight who's facing a Christmas missing their family neither.'

'Well said, Gloria!' one of the evacuee mothers shouted.

Prue got to her feet. 'The Christmas party is an excellent idea and will be fun. Of course, it's completely voluntary to attend or contribute food. I for one will be baking some cakes to donate and going along to enjoy it!'

Cheers of agreement filled the hall. Hettie glanced at Rosalind who had a stony expression on her face, her arms folded across her chest, which was mirrored by her friend, Sylvia. Their attitude was a sharp contrast to the other

women, who looked excited by the idea of Great Plumstead's first village Christmas party.

Mrs Baden, the WI's president, stood up. 'If that's all then we shall push on with the business part of our meeting. Thank you, Hettie and Gloria. I've already added my contribution to the list and look forward to a most enjoyable party.'

Hettie rejoined Gloria in the front row and they sat down.

'You were brilliant!' Gloria whispered to her. 'Everyone is in favour of the party apart from those two sour pusses.' She nodded towards Rosalind and Sylvia. 'As the saying goes, you can't please everyone!'

'Do you think they'll come to the party?' Hettie asked.

Gloria raised her eyebrows, her eyes wide. 'Who knows, *everyone* is welcome – even them! They might even enjoy it!'

CHAPTER 9

Sunday 10th December

In the past, when Hettie had thought what her retirement might be like, she'd never imagined it would turn out like this. She'd pictured herself living alone in a cottage with just a dog or cat for company. Thea's invitation to come and live here at Rookery House had altered that likelihood. Hettie's retired life was full of people and everyone sitting around her in the kitchen had become her family. It filled her with joy.

'Tell me more about this Christmas party,' Lizzie, who was Thea, Prue and Reuben's youngest sister, said. Lizzie had come for a visit for the day from where she lived in Norwich and would be coming again to stay for a few days over Christmas.

'You know where it is, when and why we're holding it,' Hettie said, having already told Lizzie about it as they'd eaten their Sunday roast pork with all the trimmings. Now they had

moved on to the pudding of apple pie and custard. 'Are you thinking of auditioning for the entertainments?'

Lizzie's eyes widened as she shook her head. 'Not me! But I'll willingly help in other ways, with the cooking or decorating the hall. Although should I go if I don't live in the village now?'

'You grew up here and are willing to volunteer so you can come!' Hettie informed her. 'There'll be plenty to do to get everything ready, so we'll appreciate your help.' She scooped up a spoonful of apple pie from her bowl, glad that Lizzie could be a part of it.

'There'll be a Christmas tree,' Reuben said. 'Lord and Lady Campbell-Gryce are donating it from the estate.'

'That will give a festive touch and fresh pine smell. I love the scent of Christmas trees!' Prue said, reaching for the jug of warm custard and pouring some over her pie. She and her daughter Alice had joined them for the Sunday meal, her husband Victor having gone off to one of his regular Sunday meetings in Norwich.

'Will you deliver it to the village hall?' Hettie directed her question at Reuben, who worked on the Great Plumstead Hall estate.

He nodded. 'Yes, on the morning of the party. I'll cut it down just before I bring it, so the needles won't have dropped off.'

'Many of the WI members have agreed to provide food or donate ingredients,' Prue added. 'Hettie did an excellent job appealing for volunteers at the meeting on Wednesday.'

'Though not everyone was so keen on the party. Did Rosalind and Sylvia put their names down to help?' Marianne asked. Like many other evacuee expectant mothers, Marianne had joined the village WI and went along to their monthly meetings.

Prue shook her head. 'I'm afraid not, but that's their decision. They probably won't attend.'

'Best they don't come if they're only going to sit there looking disapproving.' Hettie declared, waving her spoon in the air. 'We want it to be a joyous occasion.'

'It might do them good if they went,' Thea said with a wry smile. 'Perhaps you could suggest Rosalind try it when you do her next dress fitting, Marianne.'

Marianne looked thoughtful. 'I could drop it in to the conversation that Lord and Lady Campbell-Gryce are giving a Christmas tree. It might tempt her. We know how Rosalind holds them in such high esteem.'

'Where they lead, she likes to follow,' Hettie said, with a slight edge to her voice.

'What about you, Edwin? Are you going?' Lizzie asked her nephew, who'd been sitting quietly tucking into his pudding.

Edwin finished his mouthful before answering. 'I'm going to audition to play the piano.'

'What pieces will you play?' Lizzie asked.

'I haven't decided yet.' Edwin replied. 'It will be something festive and another piece which is good to dance to.'

'I'm sure they'll snap you up with your talent, Edwin.' Lizzie turned to Hettie, sitting on her other side. 'Who's in charge of the auditions?'

'That's Gloria's job,' Hettie informed her. 'She knows what she's doing with entertainments as she used to sing professionally before she got married.'

'I bet Gloria looked good on stage with her bright style of dressing,' Thea said. 'Her colourful dresses were a shock to some of Great Plumstead's residents when she first arrived here. It was like a glorious peacock landing in a flock of grey pigeons.'

'She's brightened the place up,' Prue said. 'Our evacuee mothers have made such a difference to the village.'

'Even though you weren't expecting us! But I'm glad we came here. Our luck was in that day.' Marianne's tone was heartfelt.

Prue smiled across the table at her. 'As you know, we were expecting children, but I think it was a fortunate mistake that they were sent elsewhere. Lovely as they are, children wouldn't have brought so much change to Great Plumstead – like you with your design and dressmaking skills, Marianne, and us starting The Mother's Day Club.'

'Every cloud has a silver lining, as they say!' Hettie said in a bright voice. 'We've got to roll with the way life twists and turns, and you never know what opportunities and good things will come out of it.'

CHAPTER 10

Monday 11th December

With no Mother's Day Club on this morning, Gloria was busy doing her laundry in the wash house that joined on to the back of Oak House. She folded the dripping-wet sheet into four lengthways, then slotted it between the mangle's rollers and turned the handle. Keeping an eye on the sheet as it fed through, squeezing out water, she sang softly to herself for a few moments before stopping abruptly... She was singing! It was the first time Gloria had sung since arriving here. Stranger still was the realisation that she hadn't even noticed that she *had* stopped.

Gloria bit her bottom lip and let go of the mangle wheel. Back home in London, she was always singing: while she did the housework, cooking or while walking to the market. A song was never far from her lips or else playing in her mind. They were as much a part of her as breathing.

The wash house was quiet, except for the drip, drip of water plopping from the mangle into the tin bath standing underneath it.

What had happened to make her stop singing and *why* hadn't she noticed her songs had fallen silent until now? Why had they suddenly come back this morning? Being evacuated here and separated from her children and home had affected Gloria far more than she'd realised. The sense of loss had crept up on her over the past few weeks, growing the doubts that had made her seriously consider going back to London. Charlie's letter had put an end to that possibility. She had to stay here for everyone's sake: her children's, Charlie's and for this little one, Gloria thought, placing a hand on her swollen stomach, which was covered with a blue, flowery wrap-over apron.

Was it having the Christmas party on the horizon and being busy organising it that had unleashed her desire to sing again? she wondered. Whatever it was, singing once more had felt good. Like coming back to somewhere comforting and familiar. Gloria smiled to herself as she turned the mangle wheel again. This time, instead of singing softly to herself, she sang out loud and clear, filling the confined space of the steamy wash house with her favourite song. Her heart swelled with joy as the music swirled within and around her.

Gloria had almost finished working her way through the pile of wet laundry, ready to hang it out on the line to dry, when a figure appeared in the doorway.

'What on earth is all that caterwauling?' Sylvia shouted to make herself heard. 'I can hear it in my sitting room!'

Gloria fell silent and let go of the mangle handle. 'I was singing! Practising for the party. And…' She put her hands on her hips. 'It wasn't caterwauling because I'm a good singer. I

used to sing professionally so I know what's good singing and what ain't!'

'That's as may be.' Sylvia folded her arms across her twin set jumper and cardigan. 'But I don't want that noise in my house. This is a quiet, respectable home and if you are to remain living here, then I expect you to keep to my wishes. No more singing, Gloria. Am I understood?' Sylvia's voice was curt.

Gloria's immediate reaction was to let fly and tell Sylvia a few home truths. Say that this place and Sylvia herself could do with a bit more joy, fun and singing in them. But her host's words had been clear. If Gloria wanted to stay living at Oak House, then she couldn't sing as she'd just been doing while she was inside the house or even out here. This was too good a billet to give up for the sake of being allowed to sing, Gloria reasoned. She could practise her singing elsewhere. Somewhere like the church would be a perfect place with its good acoustics. She could have a word with the vicar. He was always in favour of doing things to help the community. He and his wife had been very welcoming to the evacuee mothers.

'Fair enough. I won't sing here,' Gloria agreed, sticking her chin out. 'I was only rehearsing for the party. It's been far too long since I last sang so my voice is out of practice.'

'I hope I have made myself clear. No singing here. I like peace and quiet.' Sylvia turned on her heels and left without waiting for further discussion.

Gloria sighed and turned the mangle wheel to finish the laundry. It was a fine winter's day with a steady breeze, so this lot should dry well. The song she'd been singing before Sylvia had interrupted her burst out of her again, only this time in a humming version. Gloria stopped and laughed. Sylvia hadn't said anything about *not* humming, had she? If Gloria kept it soft and well out of Sylvia's earshot, then Gloria could still

enjoy some music while she worked. Her billeting host might not appreciate the joy that songs could bring, but Gloria did. She might have forgotten it for a while, but now it was back, and she didn't want to lose it again. Music was part of her, like her family was. It made her happy and, right now, anything that brought happiness to her life was most welcome!

CHAPTER 11

Tuesday 12th December

'I posted the parcel off to Devon today with all the Christmas pullovers in it,' Gloria told Hettie as they worked together setting out chairs in the village hall ready for that night's auditions. 'I'm glad to get 'em all finished in time, especially now there's plenty to do organising the party.'

'I'm sure your children will love them. That blue, cable stitch one is especially lovely,' Hettie said. 'They'll have you with them every time they wear their pullovers.'

'They will, won't they? I like the idea of that.' Gloria beamed at her friend. 'Thank you, Hettie.'

'How many do you think will turn up tonight?' Hettie straightened the last chair she'd just put in place. 'I know Edwin and Thea are coming for sure.'

'That's two then.' Gloria tucked a loose blonde hair behind her ear. 'We'll soon find out.' She glanced at the clock on the wall. 'Five more minutes till it's time to open the doors and

begin.' She bit her bottom lip. 'I've got to admit I'm nervous, Hettie. I ain't ever done anything like this before on the judging side of things. It's always been me doing the auditioning for singing in a pub or dance 'all.'

'That's more experience than me! You'll be fine, Gloria,' Hettie reassured her. 'Remember, this is just for a bit of entertainment for a village Christmas party, not a show at a big London theatre!'

'Yes, I know, but I want it to go well and the party to be a success.'

Hettie put her arm around Gloria's shoulders. 'It will be all right.'

When Gloria opened the village hall doors a few minutes later, she was pleased to see that a queue had formed outside. As well as Edwin and Thea, a good number of villagers had turned up to show off their talents. Alf Barker, Grace's husband, had brought along his piano accordion to play.

'Good evening, everyone and welcome! Come on in and take a seat.' Gloria ushered them in with a wave of her hand.

After going around to each person taking their name, if Gloria didn't know it already, along with what entertainment they had to offer, she had a list of potential acts. Sitting at a table opposite the stage next to Hettie, Gloria ran her finger down the names.

'We've got a selection of different acts and I suggest we mix up the order we see them in, so not one similar act after another. It will give us a better idea of what works well, and that's how we should organise it at the party. Like they do in variety shows at the theatre. Variety's the spice of life, as they say.' Gloria raised her eyebrows. 'Are you ready for this?'

Hettie nodded. 'Yes, I'm looking forward to seeing the different acts.'

Gloria stood up and faced the villagers who were now

sitting in the chairs they'd set out. 'Thank you for coming along 'ere tonight. Each of you will audition your act and then we'll decide by the end of the evening who'll be asked to perform at the Christmas party on the twenty-third.' She gave them an encouraging smile. 'Without further ado, let's get started. The first to audition is... Edwin.'

Gloria returned to her seat as Edwin made his way over to the piano, sat down, and began to play. As the well-known notes of *Silent Night* filled the air, Gloria had to rein in the urge to burst into song and sing along with him. Instead, she sang in her mind. After the carol, Edwin played a contrasting, jaunty tune that had both Gloria and Hettie's toes tapping to the music. It would be perfect to dance to, Gloria thought. Each piece he'd played had been perfectly executed and with considerable flair. Hettie had been right when she'd said he was a talented musician.

As Edwin finished playing and stood up, the hall burst into loud applause. He gave a small bow, his cheeks flushing.

'Thank you very much,' Gloria shouted, clapping enthusiastically. Once the applause had faded away, Gloria called for the next act. 'Can we have Hilda, please?'

As Hilda, one of the expectant evacuee mothers, went to the front of the hall and climbed up on the small stage, Gloria put a tick beside Edwin's name and nudged Hettie, pointing to the list. Hettie nodded in agreement and then they both turned their attention to the next audition.

Hilda, who attended The Mother's Day Club, took five potatoes out of her cardigan pocket, and started to juggle them. Watching them fly through the air, up and down, round and round, was mesmerising. Then, without dropping a single potato, Hilda caught them all and gave a bow. Once more, the hall erupted with applause.

'How on earth do you do that?' Gloria asked.

'With practice. My Dad 'as a fruit and veg stall on the market back 'ome and he taught me. He juggles with some of the goods to show 'em off,' Hilda explained.

Gloria had seen market stallholders doing that, and it always made for entertaining shopping.

'Thank you, Hilda.' Gloria ticked the woman's name, thinking what a good turn it would make for the party and again, Hettie nodded her agreement.

'Next, we'd like Alf playing the piano accordion?' Gloria announced.

By the time they'd seen all the potential acts, Gloria was delighted with both the variety and the quality. No one who'd come here tonight had been terrible. Everybody had performed well, and the combination of acts would make an interesting mix of entertainments.

'Are you happy to include them all?' Gloria whispered to Hettie as the last act returned to their seat to more applause

'Absolutely! They're all good and entertaining,' Hettie agreed. 'And such a variety.'

'I agree. There'll be something to please all our party goers.' Gloria got to her feet and turned to face everyone.

'Thank you for auditionin' tonight. I'm delighted to tell you we'd like *all* of you to perform 'ere at the party if you're willing.' She paused as murmurs of delight filled the hall from those who'd auditioned, before continuing. 'You've shown us a thoroughly entertainin' mixture of acts from playin' instruments, singin', jugglin', poetry and dancin'. Together they will make a wonderful show for the party goers. So, keep on practising and we look forward to seeing you perform 'ere again on the twenty-third at Great Plumstead's first village Christmas party!'

CHAPTER 12

Wednesday 13th December

Hettie was bicycling back to Rookery House after a morning helping at The Mother's Day Club where last night's auditions had been the main topic of conversation. Two mothers, who'd been chosen to perform at the Christmas party, had been entertaining everyone while they practised their singing routine.

The party wasn't just about the actual event itself; it was growing into something much more, having an effect even before it happened on the 23rd, and perhaps it would continue to change things in small ways afterwards too, Hettie pondered, as she pedalled along. Rather like a stone dropped in a pond, ripples spread out in all directions.

She'd almost reached Rookery House when she heard a vehicle approaching just before it came around the bend from the opposite direction. Hettie recognised it at once since few people owned a car in the village and those who did didn't

have one as grand as this. The Rolls Royce belonged to Lord and Lady Campbell-Gryce from Great Plumstead Hall. Hettie braked, stopping at the side of the road for it to pass by and putting her hand up to the chauffeur whom she knew from when she'd worked at the Hall. But instead of driving past, the car slowed and came to a smooth stop beside Hettie, and a passenger window opened.

'Good morning, Hettie,' the plummy voice of Lady Campbell- Gryce called from her seat in the back.

Hettie bent down so she could see inside and smiled at her previous employer who was swathed in a warm fur coat.

'Good Morning, your Ladyship.' Hettie greeted her with a friendly smile. She liked the woman who'd always been kind to her and appreciative of her cooking skills.

'I'm glad to see you, Hettie. I heard about the Christmas party that you're putting on from Rosalind Platten when I saw her last week.'

'Rosalind was at the WI meeting where I asked for volunteers to help.' Hettie explained, thinking it was curious that Rosalind had been spreading the word about the party, perhaps thinking her high-class friends wouldn't approve of it.

'I think it sounds an excellent idea and just what's needed in the village right now.' Lady Campbell-Gryce smoothed down the tartan travel rug covering her legs. 'I'd like to offer some help. If it's acceptable to you, I will ask Mrs Shepherd to prepare some food for the party. Or I can have ingredients sent to you at Rookery House. I understand that's another option. Which would you prefer?'

Hettie considered for a moment, delighted that even Lady Campbell-Gryce wanted to contribute. Those ripples from Great Plumstead's first Christmas party were spreading out far and wide in the community.

'That's kind of you, thank you. I'm going to be busy, so if Mrs Shepherd could do some cooking for us, it would be a real help.'

'Excellent!' Her Ladyship gave Hettie a warm smile. 'I'll instruct Mrs Shepherd to make food suitable for a Christmas party and have it delivered to the village hall for you on the 23rd of December. I'll send a gramophone and some records too, if that would be useful.'

'A gramophone would be most welcome, thank you.'

'Jolly good. Goodbye then.' Lady Campbell-Gryce closed her window, and the chauffeur pulled smoothly away, heading towards the village.

Hettie watched them go with a wry smile on her face. It was hearing that Mrs Shepherd was about to make the Hall's Christmas cakes and puddings that had sown the seed for the party. Now the Cook would prepare food for it! Perhaps she might even like to come along on the day, Hettie wondered; it would be good to see her there. Although whether she'd have time was another matter as Hettie knew from experience how the run-up to Christmas at the Hall was always hectic in the kitchens. Not so for Hettie this year. Now she was retired she had time to get involved with organising a Christmas party for the entire village. It was something she could never have dreamed of doing before!

CHAPTER 13

Friday 15th December

Gloria was on her way back to her bedroom after paying a visit to the bathroom. The baby had woken her up a little after eleven o'clock, feeling like it was tap-dancing on her bladder. Not for the first time since she'd moved into Oak House, Gloria was thankful for the luxury of an indoor bathroom, and an upstairs one at that! At home in London, she'd have had to use the chamber pot or traipse outside to the lavvy in the back yard. A bathroom inside the house was a treat she wholeheartedly appreciated and was one of the things that made it worth putting up with Sylvia's exacting ways.

She'd almost reached her bedroom, treading softly along the carpet, when she heard groaning coming from Sylvia's bedroom at the far end of the landing. Was her hostess hurt? Gloria hurried over and stood outside Sylvia's door listening The groaning came again. Without hesitating, Gloria knocked on the door, calling out, 'Sylvia!'

There was no reply, just more groans.

Knowing under normal circumstances Sylvia would be horrified if Gloria entered her bedroom without her permission, Gloria pushed the door ajar and called in again.

'It's me, Gloria. Are you all right? Only I heard groaning sounds.'

'Help!' Sylvia's voice was weak.

Gloria pushed the door wide open and the smell of vomit hit her. Instinctively, she covered her nose as she reached for the light switch just inside the room. She gasped when the soft glow of the electric bulb showed a dishevelled Sylvia lying in bed wearing a voluminous white night gown, her arms clasped around her stomach, and evidence of her having been ill on the rug beside her bed.'

Sylvia squinted in the sudden light. 'I'm…'

Gloria hurried over to the bed and laid her hand on Sylvia's forehead. It was hot, and the woman's hair matted with sweat.

'You've got a fever, no doubt about that,' Gloria said sympathetically.

'Been sick,' Sylvia whispered in a hoarse voice.

'So I see. Don't worry about that, ducks, I've dealt with plenty of illnesses with my children. It ain't nothing that can't be cleared up.'

Sylvia nodded. 'Thank you.'

Gloria patted the woman's shoulder. 'You rest and I'll get you sorted out and more comfortable.'

Gloria's many years of experience caring for her children through various ailments helped her deal with the situation. She found a clean chamber pot and placed it on the bed beside Sylvia in case she was sick again. Then she cleared up the mess beside the bed while opening the window briefly to air the room. Once that was done, she brought a bowl of warm water,

soap, flannel and a towel and gently washed Sylvia's hands and face.

'There, that must feel better.' Gloria patted the older woman's hands dry with a soft towel. 'How are you now?'

'Stomach hurts.' Sylvia grimaced and laid her hands on her middle.

'Was it something you ate while you were in Norwich today?' Gloria asked.

Sylvia's forehead creased into a frown 'We had a meal while we were there. I had chicken.'

'It could 'ave been that if it weren't cooked properly,' Gloria said. 'What did Rosalind have?'

'Lamb…' Sylvia flapped her hand, screwing up her face. 'Don't want to talk about food.'

Gloria nodded. 'Fair enough. I'll fetch you a glass of water. You must take small sips of it to start with but it's important to keep drinking.'

Leaving Sylvia to rest, she went down to the kitchen thinking that since she'd come to live here, this was the first time she'd seen her hostess less than perfectly turned out. *There ain't no room for airs and graces when you're ill,* Gloria thought. Even Sylvia looked rough when she was poorly.

Saturday 16th December

Gloria woke with a start. Her thirty-two-year-old body felt stiff and achy, more like it belonged to someone twice her age. She stretched her arms out and wriggled her shoulders as she glanced over at the bed where she was glad to see Sylvia was

now dozing peacefully. The poor woman had been ill again twice more, so Gloria had thought it best to stay close by. She'd settled down to doze in an armchair by the fireplace, a blanket over her.

Hopefully the worst was over now, although after a nasty bout of sickness, it would take Sylvia a few days to regain her strength. She would need to rest and Gloria would see that she did.

Standing up, she quietly let herself out of the room to get washed and dressed before Sylvia woke up.

When Gloria returned to Sylvia's bedroom half an hour later with a tray, her hostess was awake, lying on her side.

'Good morning, 'ow are you?' Gloria put the tray down on the bedside cabinet.

'Weak, but a bit better. My stomach's not so sore.' Sylvia managed a wobbly smile. 'I saw you sleeping in the armchair. You stayed with me. Thank you.'

'I thought I should because if you needed me, I might not 'ave 'eard you in my room.' Gloria regarded Sylvia for a moment. 'You still look pale. Mind if I see 'ow 'ot you are?'

Sylvia shook her head and Gloria put her hand on the older woman's forehead.

'You're not as hot as you were last night. That's good. You'll need to take it easy for a while until you get your strength back. I've brought you a piece of dry toast to nibble on and more water. It's best to have plain things for a bit and give your stomach a chance to recover.'

'I don't fancy anything to eat right now, but thank you,' Sylvia said, struggling to sit up.

Gloria took the pillows from behind her, gave them a shaking to fluff them up and then propped them against the wooden headboard. Helping Sylvia ease herself back against

them, she told her, 'At least have some water. Remember, little sips to begin with.'

Gloria passed Sylvia the glass and watched over her while she took a few small mouthfuls, then handed it back.

'Thank you.'

'The toast is there for you for whenever you want it.' Gloria put the glass on the cabinet within reach of Sylvia. 'I'm going to light the fire in here, as I think you should stay in bed all day. If that's all right with you?'

Sylvia nodded. 'I won't be going any further than the bathroom today. I feel too weak. I appreciate your help, Gloria. Thank you.'

Gloria smiled at her, their eyes meeting. 'I'm glad to 'elp. You were very poorly last night.'

'I hope Rosalind's all right,' Sylvia said, a worried expression on her face.

'Should I telephone and find out?' Gloria offered.

'Please, if you wouldn't mind. Her number is in the notebook by the telephone.'

'She's a close friend of yours, ain't she?' Gloria adjusted the rumpled sheets and blankets, tucking them in around Sylvia to keep her warm.

'My only friend, actually.'

That didn't surprise Gloria. Sylvia was a prickly woman, her uppity attitude making her too picky over whom she socialised with, Rosalind being the only other person of sufficient social standing in the village. Sadly, that meant Sylvia missed out on being friends with a lot of lovely people, women like Hettie, Thea, Marianne and Prue.

'I didn't know anyone when I came 'ere,' Gloria said. 'But now I've got some lovely friends who I made goin' to The Mother's Day Club. It's a good place to get to know people. You ought to come along with me sometime.'

'To be honest, I'd never considered going.' Sylvia raised an eyebrow. 'I'm not an evacuee expectant mother, am I?'

'Well neither are Hettie, Prue or Thea but they go there to 'elp out, join in and 'ave fun.'

Sylvia nodded as she reached for the glass and took another small sip of water.

'I'll get the fire organised and be back shortly,' Gloria said. 'You rest.'

Downstairs, she had filled up a coal scuttle and was getting some newspaper and kindling ready in the scullery when Joyce arrived for her morning's work.

'Morning,' Joyce said, taking off her coat. 'What are you doing? It's a bit early to be lighting the fire in the sitting room, isn't it?'

'This is for a fire in Sylvia's bedroom. She's ill.'

'What's wrong?' Joyce looked concerned.

Gloria explained what had happened in the night. 'I thought she needed a fire up there to keep warm.'

'You shouldn't be lugging heavy coal buckets upstairs,' Joyce said. 'I'll see to the fire for Sylvia. You telephone Rosalind, find out if she's ill with the same thing.'

'All right, ta ducks. I'll do it straight away.'

It wasn't Rosalind who answered the telephone at the Grange, but Joan, her housekeeper, who Gloria knew from the WI.

'Hello Joan, it's Gloria 'ere, Sylvia's evacuee. I'm telephoning on Sylvia's behalf to check if Rosalind is well. Only Sylvia was taken ill overnight.'

'I'm sorry to hear that, but Rosalind's as right as nine pence.' Joan lowered her voice. 'She's had plenty to say about their shopping trip to Norwich yesterday.'

'Would you pass on a message to 'er that Sylvia is ill? She might want to visit.'

'I will,' Joan said. 'I hope Sylvia has a speedy recovery.'

'Thank you.' Gloria replaced the telephone receiver, thinking that if Rosalind hadn't been struck down, it was likely that Sylvia's upset stomach was because of something she ate. Rest, simple food and plenty of water would soon have her on the mend. Gloria would do whatever was needed.

CHAPTER 14

Wednesday 20th December

There was an air of industriousness at The Mother's Day Club this morning, Gloria thought, gazing around her. With just three days to go now until the Christmas party, the evacuee mothers had switched from their usual knitting or sewing as they chatted, to creating decorations. They'd set up a long trestle table around which the women worked, making paper chains out of strips of old newspaper, sticking the links together with flour and water glue.

At another table, others were cutting out triangles of newspaper to turn into bunting or making paper lanterns.

'Reuben's bringing the Christmas tree here first thing on Saturday morning,' Hettie said, coming over to Gloria. 'I think the best place to put it is over there.' She pointed to the corner to the left of the stage. 'It will be in full view, but not get in the way of any dancing.'

'What about some decorations for it?' Gloria asked.

'Don't worry, that's all sorted. The Girl Guides have been making Christmas decorations at their meetings for the past couple of weeks and have asked if they can decorate the tree for us,' Hettie explained.

'Good, we'll 'ave plenty to do on Saturday putting up the rest of the decorations and organising everything else.'

'And getting the food prepared. Friday's going to be hectic with all the baking I need to do, but I must admit I am thoroughly enjoying myself.' Hettie gave her friend a warm smile. 'I'm so pleased we came up with the idea for this.'

Gloria put her arm through Hettie's. 'You and me both. This party business 'as kept me busy. I've 'ad less time to dwell on things. We need to go through the party list this morning, check everything's in 'and. I 'ave worked out the order the entertainments will work best in...'

'Gloria!' Annie, who Hettie had helped with her knitting, called out. 'How long do you want this paper chain to be?'

'I'll just sort this out, and then we'll check through our plan. I won't be long.' Gloria said to Hettie and went over to where Annie was working. 'We need each one to reach across the width of the 'all with some extra to form a loop so it can 'ang down a bit. Let's see 'ow far you've got with yours.'

Gloria took one end of the paper chain, and Annie the other and they walked to opposite sides of the village hall, the chain links stretching out between them.

'It's not wide enough yet. It needs another couple of feet added on so it will 'ang down in a swathe,' Gloria said.

'I thought as much,' Annie agreed.

'You're doing a smashin' job.' Gloria helped Annie carry the paper chain back to the table. 'The 'all's goin' to look amazing decorated for our party.'

Gloria joined Hettie in the kitchen where she was preparing things for a tea break.

'Is everything all right with Annie?' Hettie asked as she put clean cups on a tray.

'Yes, she just needs to add a bit more. The paper chains might be made from newspaper but they'll still 'elp the place feel special for the party.' Gloria took a notebook and pencil out of her handbag. 'Here's the running order.' She turned to the correct page then laid it on the table in front of them. 'I've mixed up the acts to give us variety and thought we'd end it with a sing song so everyone can join in. I'm going to use Edwin's talent, getting him to play solo here.' She pointed to the list neatly written on the page. 'And he'll provide the main musical accompaniment to the sing song, along with Alf on the piano accordion.'

'That's a good idea. We need to make the most of Edwin's playing while he still lives here. You know he's waiting to get a place to train with the Friends Ambulance Unit and then he will be off, and for who knows how long.' Hettie sighed. 'Another of our young men to leave.'

Gloria nodded. 'I'd heard about that. The Christmas party will be a chance for him to 'ave some fun with people before he leaves. You'll miss 'im,' Gloria said, sympathetically.

Hettie nodded. 'It's lovely having him live with us at Rookery House, but it will be hard when he leaves. I'm so proud of him for standing up for what he believes in...' Hettie's voice wavered as tears filled her blue eyes. 'I know he'll do a wonderful job in the FAU.'

'The war won't last for ever, that's what I keep telling myself.' Gloria gave a half-hearted shrug. 'In the meantime, we must make the best of things...' She forced some brightness into her voice. 'Have we forgotten anything?' Gloria returned her focus to her list, turning the page in her notebook.

'I don't think so,' Hettie said.

'I've written down everything we've done so far and ticked

it off.' Gloria ran her finger down the column of items listed. 'We've got the 'all booked, the food sorted out – either being brought on the day or ingredients donated and you'll be using it in your baking on Friday. Reuben's delivering the Christmas tree on Saturday morning, and you've now said the Guides are decorating it.' Gloria made a note of that in the book. 'More decorations are being made out there.' She waved towards the door leading into the hall. 'We can put them up while the tree's being decorated. The food should arrive late Saturday morning and will be stored in here until it's time to set it out in the 'all after the entertainments. Is there anything else?'

Hettie shook her head. 'Everything's organised, and you've kept a track of things so well.' She tapped the notebook appreciatively. 'I've had promises to help with the clearing up afterwards from members of the WI. I think we're as well prepared as we can be.' Hettie smiled at Gloria. 'It's going to be a wonderful occasion.'

'I hope so. A few weeks ago, I wouldn't 'ave dreamed I'd be involved with organising something like this, but now look at us!' Gloria returned Hettie's smile. 'We make a good team.'

Hettie chuckled. 'We certainly do!'

~

Gloria opened her eyes and lay still, slowing coming back to consciousness. She hadn't intended to sleep, but after a busy morning at The Mother's Day Club, she had been tired, so came up to her room to have a lie down and rest. The next thing she knew, here she was waking up. The luxury of an afternoon nap was something she hadn't had with most of her other pregnancies, as she'd had young children to look after. But now she was here on her own it was possible and clearly needed.

She snuggled deeper under the covers, the patter of rain against the window making her want to remain warm and snuggly cocooned under the blankets and eiderdown. Her mind settled on this morning's Mother's Day Club, where the women had done a smashing job creating decorations. By the time they'd tidied up, ready to go home, there were enough paper chains, strings of bunting and paper lanterns to festoon the hall ceiling. They might have only been made from newspaper rather than coloured paper, but they would make the village hall look extraordinary and help lift the mood for their festive party.

Gloria glanced at the clock on the chest of drawers, which read a quarter to four. She must get up and go down to the kitchen, otherwise she wouldn't have enough of her allotted kitchen time to cook the piece of mutton she'd bought at the butchers that morning.

She swung her legs around and heaved herself up into a sitting position, then gasped as her baby jabbed a knee or elbow into her belly. 'It's all right!' Gloria stroked her hand over the soft, scarlet material of her dress, which was stretched over her rounded belly. Perhaps the baby had been asleep too and her getting up had disturbed it. 'I need to get a move on so we can have our tea!'

Downstairs, Gloria was sitting at the table chopping up carrots when Sylvia appeared. The arrival of her billeting host surprised Gloria. Sylvia rarely came into the kitchen while she was in there, unless, of course, she had something to complain about. What had she done now? Gloria wondered, slicing through a carrot. She couldn't think of anything. In fact, Sylvia had been almost friendly in the days since she'd

been ill. It had taken the older woman a while to recover, and Gloria had helped her as much as she would allow. Sylvia looked better today, back to normal with some colour in her cheeks.

'Good afternoon,' Sylvia said. 'Are you making your tea?'

'Yes, and don't worry, I'll be done and out of here by half-past five. I'm a bit later than usual startin' cos I fell asleep.'

'Oh, I've not come to hurry you along. Far from it.' Sylvia put her hands on the back of one of the kitchen chairs which was tucked under the table. 'I wanted to talk to you now that I'm better and thank you for your help when I was ill.' Her voice was sincere. 'You were so compassionate to me and went above and beyond what anyone could have expected. I appreciate what you did very much.'

'I could 'ardly ignore you being ill, could I? It wouldn't 'ave been right or kind.' Gloria's eyes met Sylvia's, who held her gaze for a few seconds before looking down at her hands, which gripped the top of the chair so tightly her knuckles had gone white.

Sylvia looked up again, biting her bottom lip. 'I have been thinking a lot while I recovered. After the way I've behaved towards you in my home, I didn't deserve your help, or your kindness. I'm not sure other people would have done the same for me.'

Was Sylvia referring to Rosalind? Gloria wondered. Although she had telephoned the Grange after Sylvia became ill, as far as Gloria knew, Rosalind had not paid her friend a visit to check on her or help her.

'You've given me a home here at Oak House.' Gloria put the chopped carrot into the saucepan of water with a plop.

'Yes, but I haven't been as welcoming as I could have been. I have given you all the necessary things required of a host, but to my shame, nothing more than that.' Sylvia's face

flushed. 'I misjudged you, Gloria. I was prejudiced and foolish. And I am truly sorry. Things must change here.'

Gloria's stomach lurched. 'You ain't asking me to leave, are you?'

Sylvia held up her hands. 'Absolutely not! I'm scrapping the ridiculous need for you to only use the kitchen at certain times. I want you to treat this as your *home,* and please, if you're willing, I'd like it if you joined me in the sitting room sometimes in the evenings. I would appreciate your company and the opportunity to get to know you better. And you can sing whenever you please.' Sylvia gave a hesitant smile. 'I hope you're happy to stay here and make this place into a proper home.'

Gloria studied Sylvia's face for a moment and could see the woman's words were genuine. 'Thank you! I'd like that very much. Can I make a suggestion?'

Sylvia nodded. 'Of course.'

'Why don't you come along to the party on Saturday? We went through the final arrangements this morning and it's coming together nicely. I know there ain't ever been a village Christmas party like it before, but there's a first time for everything. You'd be very welcome.'

Sylvia hesitated before answering. 'I'm not sure…'

'You don't 'ave to follow Rosalind. You should make your own mind up where…' Gloria halted. The words in her head had spilled out without her checking them first as she usually did when she was around Sylvia. 'I shouldn't 'ave…'

'No, you're right.' Sylvia pulled out the chair and sat down at the table opposite Gloria. 'I *do* only go to things that Rosalind goes to, and which she approves of. As I told you, she's my only friend in the village.'

Gloria pressed her lips together, wondering if what had just popped into her head would push things too far… but

sometimes you had to take a risk. 'Don't mind me askin', but 'as Rosalind been to see you or been in contact while you've been poorly? You know I telephoned to check if she was ill and tell her about you.'

Sylvia folded her arms. 'No, she hasn't.'

'Then I think it's time you widened your friendships. Rosalind might 'ave had good reason not to be in touch, but if I were you, I wouldn't let her rule my life anymore. You need to find your own way, Sylvia. Get out there and make new friends. There are a lot of lovely people in Great Plumstead, like Hettie and Prue. If you took the chance to get to know them, I'm sure you'd like them. Come to the Christmas party and start making more friends.'

Sylvia looked thoughtful as she considered what Gloria had suggested. 'Very well, I will. Thank you. Perhaps I could help. Is there something I can do?'

'I'm sure we'll be able to find you a job.' Gloria smiled at her host. 'We'd be glad of an extra pair of 'ands.'

Sylvia returned her smile. 'Then I'll be there.'

CHAPTER 15

Friday 22nd December

'Good King Wenceslas looked out on the feast of Stephen, when the snow lay round about, deep and crisp and even...'

Hettie looked around Rookery House's warm kitchen as she sang and thought how different today was. She'd spent many hectic days in the run-up to Christmases cooking food, but none had been filled with such jollity and joy as now.

Everyone was busy working hard preparing for tomorrow's party, but rather than the feverish pressure that had existed in the Hall's kitchen, here they were having fun. Each person was a volunteer who had given their time and skills for the village Christmas party.

'Are they ready to go in the oven?' Joan, fellow WI member and housekeeper from the Grange, asked as Hettie reached the end of the carol.

'Almost.' Hettie gave the sausage rolls she'd made a final glaze of egg wash. 'Are the others done?'

'Yes, I've just taken them out of the oven and they're cooling on the rack.' Joan, whose cheeks were rosy from the heat of the range, nodded her head towards the far side of the kitchen, where another table had been brought in to provide extra space. It was filling up with a variety of cooked foods, which gave off a mouth-watering aroma of smells as they cooled.

'These are ready.' Hettie passed Joan the filled baking tray. 'I've used up all the sausage meat from the butchers. We got four dozen sausage rolls out of it.'

'It was good of him to donate the meat, and he's coming to the party,' Joan said over her shoulder as she headed to the range.

'People have been so generous,' Hettie said. 'All the food shops in Great Plumstead have donated ingredients as well as the villagers who preferred to do that rather than cook themselves.'

'It's for a good cause and it sounds like most people from the village are going tomorrow.' Thea sat at the far end of the long kitchen table with Marianne, the pair of them peeling and slicing apples. 'We've almost finished these. Are you ready for them, Hettie?'

'Nearly. I'll get more pastry and start rolling out the cases for the apple tarts.' Hettie went to the pantry where she'd left the portions of pastry, that she had made earlier that morning, resting on the cool marble slab. Prue was in there, checking the jars of jam stacked on a shelf.

'Which sort of jam would be best in the Victoria sponges?' Prue asked. 'I've been trying to decide.'

'Plum jam is always nice. Or there's the blackberry and apple – that has a delicious fruitiness to it. Why not fill the cakes with different ones. That will give people a choice,' Hettie suggested.

Prue nodded, reaching for two jars. 'I'll use both then.'

Back in the kitchen, Hettie got to work rolling out the pastry into an even, thin layer. Then she used a cutter to cut out round pastry discs and placed them in the spaces in a metal baking tin, ready to be filled with slices of apple, a sprinkle of sugar and cinnamon. All the while she listened to the chat going on around her, which had now turned to the subject of the previous Christmas.

'I never thought last Christmas that I'd be living in the house I had dreamed about owning since I was a child,' Thea said.

'Or me living here after being evacuated out of London,' Marianne agreed. 'And soon to become a mother too!'

'Last Christmas, I ain't even 'eard of Norfolk,' Annie, who was washing up at the sink, admitted. 'And now look at me living in a village in the middle of the countryside!' She laughed.

'What about you, Hilda?' Prue asked.

Hilda, who'd impressed Hettie with her juggling skills at the auditions, was mixing up ingredients in a large bowl to make currant buns. She stopped stirring for a moment. 'I was 'elping my Dad on his market stall.'

'Were you juggling with the stock?' Hettie asked.

'Sometimes!' Hilda gave a shy smile. 'I never thought I'd ever be living out in the countryside, either.'

'The past year has brought changes for so many.' Joan picked up a tea towel and dried a clean baking tray, which Annie had washed. 'Hettie, your life has changed in a big way, too. Do you miss being Cook at the Hall?'

Hettie looked up from rolling out more pastry. 'No, not really. It was long days, hard work and a lot of responsibility. The time had come for me to stop and hand the job over to someone else. When Thea offered me the chance to move

here, it was perfect timing.' She smiled at Thea, their eyes meeting. 'I always expected to spend my retirement living on my own in a cottage with just a dog or cat for company, and now look at me!'

'What about your family?' Annie asked. 'I thought you were married. You're Mrs Brown, ain't you?'

'Oh, I've never been married, Annie. The *Mrs* is an honorary title that Cooks in Halls are given,' Hettie explained. 'I have got some family, but my two brothers live in Canada. Only my sister, Ada, still lives around here in the next village.'

Annie nodded. 'I see. I didn't know that about cooks being known as Mrs. Still, it's nice for you that your sister ain't far away.'

Hettie gave the young woman a smile. In theory, it *should* be nice to have a sister close by, but only if the sisters got on. Ada was a prickly character and she and Hettie weren't close. Although Hettie made the effort to keep in touch with her and went to visit regularly, especially as her sister had been widowed earlier in the year.

'What else needs doing, Hettie?' Prue asked, bringing Hettie's attention back to the work. 'I've sandwiched the sponges together with jam.'

'You'd better check the list,' Hettie said. 'I don't think there's much more to do.'

Prue held up the list. 'There are still the custard tarts to make. Shall I get started on the custard filling?'

'Yes, please.' Hettie put the last pastry disc into a baking tray and passed the trays down to Thea. 'If you add the apple, sugar and cinnamon then they can cook once there's space. How much longer do the sausage rolls need, Joan?'

Joan checked her watch. 'Another five minutes.'

Hettie nodded. 'The apple tarts should be ready by then.'

'This is like a military operation having to organise all the

cooking, getting the timings right so there's room in the oven and things are prepared in time,' Marianne said, putting pieces of apple into pastry cases. 'I would get in a terrible muddle if I was in charge. It's a good job you're keeping track of it all, Hettie.'

Hettie laughed. 'I've had years of practice getting timings right and organising what needs to be done, and when. Today is for fun. When it's finished, I won't have to do it all again tomorrow like I had to up at the Hall. And there was no singing as we worked there either – the butler wouldn't allow it!'

'Singing's 'elps the work go smoother,' Annie said. 'So let's 'ave another song. What's it to be?'

'*The Holly and the Ivy*,' Hettie suggested. 'I love that hymn.'

'All right then, on the count of three...' Annie said.

As one, they all sang the beautiful Christmas hymn Hettie had loved since she was small. Annie was right, Hettie thought. Singing helps with the work, and the happiness and joy too!

CHAPTER 16

Saturday 23rd December

Gloria stood, hands on her hips, in the middle of the village hall.

'Towards me a little, Edwin, that's it there!' She was supervising the hanging of paper chains across the width of the hall. Edwin and his sister Alice were working as a team, refusing to allow any of the expectant mothers from The Mother's Day Club to climb up on step ladders to reach the ceiling.

This morning, the hall was a hive of activity with the final preparations for that afternoon's party. In the corner to the left of the stage, Reuben was setting up the Christmas tree, which he'd cut on the estate and brought straight here. It filled the air with the fresh scent of pine. A group of Girl Guides waited nearby, ready to decorate it as soon as Reuben had finished positioning it in the galvanised pail of sand.

'On to the next paper chain,' Edwin said, climbing down his stepladder and moving it along the hall wall a few feet.

Annie and Sylvia stood waiting, holding a paper chain between them. Their job was to hand it up to Edwin and Alice, who'd also moved her ladder along on the opposite wall to her brother. The four of them worked well together and were making quick work of decorating the ceiling.

'Gloria, would you come and look at how we've set out the tables?' Prue asked, coming over to her. 'Hettie wants your opinion before we add the tablecloths.'

'Of course. Sylvia, can you take over here? Make sure the paper chains are put up evenly spaced out and level with each other. There's room for another three, by my reckoning. Then you and Annie can help Edwin and Alice put up the strings of bunting next. They need to loop along the sides of the hall in between where the paper chains are attached.'

Sylvia nodded. 'Certainly.'

Gloria gave her host a warm smile, delighted to see how well she was joining in and that she seemed to be enjoying herself.

'The hall's looking Christmassy,' Prue said as she and Gloria headed towards where a row of trestle tables had been set up alongside the entrance to the kitchen.

'It is!' Gloria beamed at Prue. 'I'm that excited and can't wait for two o'clock so we can open the doors and get the party underway.'

'What do you think?' Hettie stood behind the trestle tables. 'We've left room on this side so we can bring food out from the kitchen and set it out while leaving the front clear for people to serve themselves. Tea and cold drinks will be served from there.' She pointed to the far end. 'I think it's the best way to have it.'

'I agree,' Gloria said.

Hettie nodded. 'Good, I thought you would, but just wanted to check.'

'You're in charge of the food side of things, Hettie.' Gloria returned the older woman's smile. 'It's your area of expertise, not mine.'

Hettie chuckled. 'Another point of view is always worth having in case I'd overlooked something.'

'It's all coming together.' Gloria looked around them, delighted to see how the hall was being transformed from its usual functional space into a more festive, jolly-looking place perfect for a Christmas party.

'Where do you want these?' Thea approached, having just arrived, followed by Marianne and Lizzie, all carrying baskets packed with the food baked at Rookery House the day before.

'This way! We won't be putting the food out until halfway through the party.' Hettie gestured for them to go through to the kitchen. 'Put it on the table. I'll be in to sort it out in a moment. Prue, can you put the tablecloths on now, please?'

'Of course,' Prue said. 'Shall I add the arrangements of Christmas roses that I made?'

'Good idea.' Hettie bustled off to the kitchen.

'Let me help you with that,' Gloria said, as Prue took an ironed white tablecloth from a basket and shook it out. Gloria grabbed hold of one end and together she and Prue spread it over a table, smoothing it out, before repeating the process with more tablecloths on the other two tables. They'd just finished when the outside door opened, and two men walked in.

'It's Victor!' A look of surprise washed over Prue's face, followed by one of uncertainty.

Gloria's heart picked up its pace as instinct warned her that something was wrong.

'Who's in charge here?' The other man's voice was loud and pompous.

The hall fell silent, everyone stopping what they were doing to watch what was going on.

'That's me.' Gloria stepped forward.

'And me,' Hettie said, emerging from the kitchen. 'What can we do for you, Mr Platten?'

This must be Rosalind's husband, Gloria thought. He looked and sounded as stuck-up as his wife.

'We've come to inform you that we are requisitioning the village hall for an *emergency* meeting this afternoon. You must clear out and be gone in…' He pulled his watch out from his waist coat pocket. 'One hour. The hall must be vacated by noon.'

'Now look 'ere, we booked it, fair and square!' Gloria raised her chin, glaring at them, her hackles rising. 'You can't just come in 'ere and kick us out. We've got people coming 'ere this afternoon to enjoy themselves.'

'There's a war on and an essential emergency meeting arranged. This is the only venue that can accommodate it at such short notice.' Mr Platten looked down his nose at Gloria. 'Our need is *far* greater than yours. Mr Wilson, who's chair of the village hall committee,' he indicated Victor, who'd stood silently by Mr Platten until now, 'has the right to amend and cancel any bookings as needs must.'

'Is that right, Victor?' Hettie came over to stand by Gloria, pulling herself up to her full five feet, her blue eyes flashing with annoyance behind her glasses. 'Are you going to stop the people of Great Plumstead having their Christmas party?'

Victor licked his lips under his thin moustache, his cold, ice-blue eyes filled with arrogance. 'That's right. I have the authority. In a case such as this emergency meeting, there's no

alternative other than to cancel your booking. You have until noon to clear out.'

Mutterings of discontent filled the hall.

'Can't you find somewhere else, Victor?' Prue asked. 'We've put so much work and effort into the party over the past few weeks.' She threw her hands wide. 'There must be another place you can go or you could even meet here *after* the party.'

Victor narrowed his eyes, glaring at his wife. 'There isn't time! With a war on, the meeting takes precedence over a *party*. Arrangements have already been made. We'll return after noon and expect you all to be gone and there to be no traces of these ...' He looked around him at the decorations and Christmas tree, his lip curling in distaste, '*festivities* remaining.'

'But it's...' Gloria began.

Mr Platten held up a hand. 'You have until noon. Good day to you.'

With that, the pair of them turned and left, closing the door with a sharp clunk behind them.

A stunned silence held for a moment before the hall erupted into noise. Gloria stood speechless, her heart beating hard. She didn't want to accept what had just happened.

'Gloria, are you all right?' Hettie's voice was gentle.

She nodded. 'I can't believe they've just done that. They can't go back on a booking made in good faith, can they?'

'I'm afraid they can.' Prue's shoulders slumped. 'An emergency meeting, something for the war effort, takes precedence. There's nothing we can do. But if Victor knew about this beforehand and he didn't let on, I'll...'

'It makes no difference if he did or he didn't, Prue. The outcome is the same,' Hettie said firmly, laying a hand on Prue's arm. 'We still have to get out.'

'But all the work that's gone into it! Everyone was looking

forward to the party… It was supposed to make Christmas feel *better* for us all, not worse!' Gloria's eyes filled with hot tears. 'What are we going to do?'

Hettie put her arm through Gloria's and steered her over to some chairs. 'Sit down and we'll think about other options. Perhaps there's somewhere else we can go.'

'We need a place big enough, but there ain't anywhere else in the village,' Gloria stated flatly as Hettie sat down next to her.

'No one's house is big enough. A barn on a farm would be too cold even if we could find one empty.' Hettie fiddled with one of her grey curls, then patted it into place. 'There is a chance…'

'What?' Gloria asked.

'I need to ask. It's probably not going to work, but I think it's worth a try. Whatever happens, we must be out of here by noon.' Hettie stood up. 'I need to make a telephone call. Gloria and Prue, you must organise taking down all the decorations and be ready to leave.'

'We will,' Prue agreed. She held out her hand to help Gloria up. 'Come on, there's work to do and we haven't got long.'

Hettie hurried along the road from the village hall heading for Barker's grocers. Time was of the essence and if – and it was a big if – her idea paid off they needed to change plans as soon as possible.

Bursting in through the door of the shop, Hettie called to Grace Barker, who was working behind the counter serving a customer, 'Can I use your telephone, please? It's an emergency.'

'Of course. Please excuse me a moment while I help Hettie.

I'll be back directly,' Grace said to the customer. 'Whatever's happened?' she asked as she beckoned Hettie to follow her through to the back of the shop. 'Is someone hurt?'

'Nothing like that, but the Christmas party is in jeopardy. The hall's been requisitioned, and we've got to be out by noon!'

'Oh no! After all that effort. Here...' Grace indicated the telephone, which stood on a desk in the little office behind the shop. 'Make whatever call you need, Hettie. I hope you can fix it. Alf and I have been looking forward to this afternoon.'

'We all have.' Hettie took a deep breath, picked up the handset and waited for the operator to ask what number she required.

CHAPTER 17

'The ballroom at Great Plumstead Hall!' Gloria exclaimed gleefully, repeating what Hettie had just told them. She put her hand to her chest, a wide pillar-box red lipsticked smile lighting up her face.

'That's right.' Hettie looked at the others who'd gathered around to hear the news. 'Lady Campbell-Gryce was horrified to learn what's happened and offered us the use of the ballroom to hold the party, and help from her staff as well to get ready in time. Luckily the food her cook has made for our party hasn't been sent here yet, so that will be ready for us at the Hall. Her Ladyship is sending the chauffeur down to ferry people to the Hall, and Alf Barker will arrive with his van to transport the Christmas tree, decorations and food there, too. Our Christmas party *will* go ahead after all, but in much grander surroundings.'

Prue's eyes widened. 'How did you manage to fix that?'

'I simply asked if Lady Campbell-Gryce could help. I thought it was worth a try, and she came up with the generous offer. Alf and the chauffeur will be here soon, so are we ready

to move out?' Hettie saw that the paper chains and bunting had been taken down and the Girl Guides had removed the decorations from the tree.

'Just about,' Gloria said. 'But 'ow are we going to tell people the party's on at the Hall instead of 'ere?'

'Grace Barker is telephoning around those she can and asking each person to spread the news to their neighbours. You know how fast word spreads in the village. There won't be many who don't get to hear about it before two o'clock arrives. For any that haven't heard, we can pin a notice on the door telling them to go to the Hall instead.'

'Sounds like you've got it all worked out, Hettie. Thank you!' Thea said, putting her arm around Hettie's shoulders. 'Great Plumstead will have its first village Christmas party after all.'

~

Gloria stared at the impressive façade of Great Plumstead Hall from her front seat in the silver Rolls Royce. Built of golden honey-coloured stone, it glowed in the winter sunshine. 'Blimey! This is a step up from the village 'all, ain't it?'

The Campbell-Gryce's chauffeur glanced at her and smiled as he swung the car around the wide sweep of gravel with a crunching of tyres and brought it to a halt by the porticoed door. 'You'll have a lot more room in there for your party, that's for sure.'

Gloria turned around and beamed at Hettie, Prue, Sylvia and Annie who were sitting in the rear of the car, enjoying a luxurious lift here from the village hall.

'Do you like it?' Hettie asked.

'I do, it's smashing!'

Rather than wait for the chauffeur to come round and

open her door, Gloria clambered out and stood looking up at the hall as she waited for the others. It was far grander than she'd imagined. Their booking for the village hall might have been swept from under them, but they had landed on their feet with the offer to hold the Christmas party here instead.

The tooting of a horn heralded the arrival of Alf Barker's grocery van, which trundled across the gravel and came to a stop by the Rolls Royce. Gloria waved at Hilda and Thea, who sat in the front alongside Alf.

'Welcome!' a plummy voice called, attracting Gloria's attention. Lady Campbell-Gryce stood in the open doorway looking immaculately dressed. 'Do come in.'

'This way.' Hettie put her arm through Gloria's and led her towards the door. 'We've got a party to organise!'

After Hettie had introduced Gloria to her former employer, they went inside. Stepping into the entrance hall, Gloria had to stop herself from remarking at the size of it. The hallway, with its chequered black and white tiled floor and grand wooden staircase sweeping up to the next level, covered an area bigger than most houses. Even with a large, beautifully decorated Christmas tree standing at the far end, it had more space than in the village hall.

'After our telephone conversation, Hettie, I thought how best to organise things and decided it would be better if we served the food and drink in the dining room rather than have it in the ballroom.' Lady Campbell-Gryce walked across the hall, her shoes clicking on the tiled floor, and opened a double set of doors. 'We'll put extra seating in the entrance hall as well, so party goers can sit in there while they eat if the dining room is full, and it will give them more space to mingle. Staff, as you know…' Her Ladyship smiled at Hettie, 'are used to dealing with food in the dining room, so it will make it easier with the clearing up afterwards. I've instructed my staff to be

at your disposal, so please tell them what you need them to do.'

'Thank you,' Hettie said. 'That's a great help. We've got less time to get ready, so the more hands on deck, the better.'

'I understand you are in charge of the entertainments?' Lady Campbell-Gryce turned her attention to Gloria.

Gloria nodded. 'That's right.'

'Then you'll want to see the ballroom. Follow me.' Lady Campbell-Gryce crossed the hall to another set of double doors which lead to an even grander room, Gloria and Hettie following her.

This time Gloria couldn't stop a gasp escaping her lips as she followed her Ladyship into the ballroom. It was twice as long and double the width of the dining room, its high ceiling decorated with intricate carvings picked out in gold against the cream background. A roaring fire blazed in the large marble-surrounded fireplace, throwing out a welcoming warmth. Three floor to ceiling windows, swathed in crimson velvet drapes, looked out onto the terrace and gardens at the back of the house. It felt like a world away from the plain functional space of the village hall.

'I wondered perhaps if it would be best to use the far end near the grand piano as your stage area,' her Ladyship suggested. 'That will give you plenty of room for dancing.'

'This is smashing! We've got a lot more space 'ere than at the village 'all, and it's much lovelier.' Gloria's voice caught with emotion, and she blinked back tears. 'Thank you!'

Her Ladyship looked pleased. 'Can I leave you both to it? My butler, Stokes, is at your disposal. If you tell him what you need, and how to help, then he will organise it for you.'

'We've brought paper chains and bunting that we made at The Mother's Day Club,' Gloria said. 'But they might not be

suitable for putting up in 'ere as they're only made from newspaper!'

'Not at all. They will be splendid, I'm sure. There's a war on, so we must make best use of what we have. Please have them put up. I look forward to seeing it all later.' Lady Campbell-Gryce gave Gloria and Hettie a warm smile and left the ballroom.

'I can't believe we're 'aving our party 'ere!' Gloria grabbed hold of Hettie's arms and danced them both around. 'Am I dreaming?'

Hettie laughed. 'No, I can assure you it's all real and happening now. We'd better get a move on. Our guests are due here in an hour and a half and we've lots to do before then.'

By the time two o'clock came round, everything was ready. With help from the Hall staff working alongside those who had come from the village, they had arranged the ballroom for entertainments and dancing, while the dining room was well stocked with food for the hungry party goers.

Standing in the hallway by the closed front door, Gloria looked at everyone gathered round who'd helped today: Prue, Thea, Edwin, Alice, Marianne, Lizzie, Reuben, Sylvia, Alf, Annie and Hilda. 'Are we ready to declare Great Plumstead's first village Christmas party open?'

A chorus of 'Yes' echoed around the hall in reply.

Gloria looked at Hettie who stood opposite her by the door. 'Ready?'

'Whenever you are.' Hettie's blue eyes twinkled behind her round glasses.

Together, they pulled open the heavy door and were met by a loud cheer from the many villagers waiting outside.

'Welcome to the first Great Plumstead Christmas party!'

Gloria declared triumphantly, then stood to the side and gestured for the party goers to come in.

Hettie looked around the ballroom, delighted by the number of villagers of all ages who had come to the party – from the recently arrived evacuee expectant mothers to people who'd lived their entire lives in Great Plumstead. It was gratifying to see them enjoying themselves, laughing and clapping along to the slapstick tap-dancing routine being performed by three members of the Girl Guides at one end of the ballroom. Gloria, who stood to the side of the makeshift stage area, was in her element and was compering the entertainments magnificently.

This was the last act before the communal sing song rounded off the entertainments. After that, it would be time for the food, so Hettie decided to check everything was ready. She slipped out of the ballroom and across the hallway into the quietness of the dining room.

They had set the food out on the long, cloth-covered dining table, and there was plenty of it. Those who'd promised to make something had brought it with them, and Lady Campbell-Gryce had supplied more from the Hall's kitchen. Combined with Hettie's baking from the day before, it was to be quite a feast and smelled deliciously mouth-watering. Hettie made her way along the table, checking everything was beautifully presented. It all looked wonderful.

'Hello Mrs Brown. I hope you like what I've made for the party,' a soft voice said from the doorway.

Hettie turned and recognised Mrs Shepherd, the lady who had replaced her as the Hall's Cook. She'd seen her in church on Sundays but hadn't yet met her properly.

Mrs Shepherd stepped towards Hettie and held out her hand. 'I'm pleased to meet you.'

Hettie shook the younger woman's hand. 'And you, too. And please, call me Hettie.'

'I'm Dorothy.'

'Come and show me what you've made.' Hettie beckoned the younger woman over to the table.

'I wasn't sure what food you already had organised, so I made a variety of things.' Dorothy stood by Hettie and pointed out various dishes. 'There are mini cheese and chive scones, scotch eggs, fruit turnovers – with apple or plum filling, parkin, rock cakes and a selection of sandwiches. All things that are easy to eat with fingers. I hope that's all right with you.' She hooked her short bobbed brown hair behind her ear.

'Definitely!' Hettie's eyes met Dorothy's as she smiled at her. 'It all looks delicious, and I like the variety. It complements the rest of the food.'

A look of relief passed over Dorothy's face. 'I've been so worried about what to make. I have heard so much about you, and what a marvellous cook you are. You are quite an act to follow, Hettie!'

'I was Cook here for a long time, but I know for certain that you wouldn't have got the job unless you were an excellent cook yourself. Her Ladyship told me you came highly recommended.' Hettie put her hand on the younger woman's arm. 'Remember, every cook does things her *own* way. As long as the food tastes good, that's what matters. I'm looking forward to trying what you've made.'

'Why not try something now?' Dorothy suggested.

'All right.' Hettie selected a mini cheese scone and took a bite, chewing slowly as the flavours filled her mouth: strong, tangy cheese, complemented by the oniony chives in the lightest of crumbly scone. 'This is delicious.'

Dorothy sighed in relief. 'I'm glad you think so. Your praise means a lot to me.'

'You have nothing to worry about, Dorothy. Your cooking skills are much to be admired.' Hettie paused, listening to the sound of singing coming from the ballroom. 'How about joining in the sing song before the food is served?'

'I'd like that.'

Hettie slipped her arm through Dorothy's and the pair of them walked through the hallway to the ballroom where a rousing rendition of *Daisy Bell* was being sung with great gusto by the party goers, accompanied by Edwin on the grand piano and Alf on his piano accordion.

As she sang along, Hettie mused how fitting it was that she was standing here beside Dorothy, whose timing of making the Christmas cake had been the seed for this event. If Hettie hadn't dropped her list into Barker's grocers that morning a few weeks back when the order for the Hall's Christmas cake ingredients was being put together, would this party have ever taken place? The answer was probably not. She would never have felt that lurch of her stomach, the feeling that her life had shifted but that not all of her had caught up with the momentous change.

Hettie was grateful that fate had taken her to Barker's at the right moment, which had led to such a lovely event for so many. It was strange how life twisted and turned, how chance meetings and remarks could make things happen. Now wasn't the time for such deep considerations though, so Hettie took another deep breath and sang on with all her heart.

CHAPTER 18

Sunday 24th December – Christmas Eve

Gloria was glad of a quiet time after the exciting day yesterday. It had been an emotional one ranging from the joy of decorating the village hall for the Christmas party, to the plunging depths of despair after the shocking news that they were being thrown out for a meeting. The rescue by Hettie and Lady Campbell-Gryce had resulted in a magnificent, joyous party at the Hall which had filled Gloria with happiness.

Gloria had spent this morning working companionably alongside Sylvia in the kitchen as they prepared for their Christmas dinner tomorrow. The fat cockerel bought from the butcher was ready in the larder, and they had brought vegetables in from the garden ready to peel in the morning. Then, after a simple meal of soup together at midday, they'd decorated the Christmas tree in the sitting room.

Now a lie down or even an afternoon nap was all Gloria

wanted. Lying on her comfortable double bed, with the eiderdown thrown over her to keep warm, she was enjoying a well-earned rest. Had she been at home in London, this would have been impossible. On a normal Christmas Eve there would be so much more to do amidst her children's excitement.

This Christmas was different in so many ways. Yesterday's party, along with the run-up to it with all the planning and organisation beforehand, had gone some way to filling the gaping hole left by not being at home with her children or husband this year. Gloria wasn't the only one whom the party had helped. The cheerful faces of all who'd attended had been testament to the value of holding Great Plumstead's first Christmas party. The call for there to be another one next year by many party goers had been a welcome validation for what they'd done. Whether or not it would happen again, it was too soon to tell. Who knew where they would be in a year's time? Gloria's eyes grew heavy thinking about it all, and rather than fight the wave of sleep tugging at her, she let herself drift away.

Someone was knocking… and kept on knocking.

'Gloria!' Sylvia's voice called.

Gloria struggled up from the warm, fuzzy depths of sleep and opened her eyes. Her bedroom was in semi-darkness as the daylight outside was fading on the short winter's day.

'Gloria,' Sylvia called again. 'Can I come in?'

'Yes,' she mumbled. How long had she been asleep? she wondered.

Her bedroom door opened, and Sylvia peered around it. 'Did I wake you?'

Gloria pulled herself up into a sitting position. 'What's the matter? What time is it?'

'Almost four o'clock and you've got a visitor. A man!' The corners of Sylvia's mouth twitched. 'He *says* he's your husband.'

'Charlie! Charlie's 'ere!' Gloria put a hand to her face.

'He's very tall, with brown curly hair, a beard and twinkly...'

'Green eyes, and a great bear of a fella!' Gloria finished for her. 'I can't believe it. What's he doin' 'ere?'

Sylvia gave Gloria a wry smile. 'He has come to visit his wife, of course! Shall I say you'll be down in a few minutes? We're having some tea while we wait. He's looking forward to seeing you.'

Gloria's eyes flooded with tears. 'Tell 'im I'll be down directly.'

As Sylvia left the room, Gloria leaned back against the bed's headboard, her heart galloping inside her chest. Her Charlie was *here*, downstairs! He'd come to see her, and here she was lying in bed with her hair a mess and her dress crumpled. Gloria didn't want his first sight of his wife since September to be a tangle-haired, sleep-fuzzy woman. She needed to make herself presentable and fast.

Gloria swung her legs down and heaved herself out of bed. A quick face wash and teeth clean, a slick of her pillar-box red lipstick, redo her hair, change into her best dress and then she'd be ready.

Ten minutes later, Gloria made her way downstairs, wearing her favourite emerald-green dress and her white peep-toed high-heeled shoes Her stomach fluttered at the sound of Charlie's deep voice coming from the sitting room and the sight of his kitbag propped up against the front door. She paused outside the closed sitting room door for a moment

as her emotions threatened to spill over. Steady on, Gloria, told herself firmly, you don't want his first glimpse of you to be a tearful one. She lifted her chin and smiled. Charlie's arrival here was smashing and filled her with joy. She didn't want to spoil it by weeping, even if her tears were happy ones. Gloria opened the door and went in, but seeing Charlie was her undoing. Despite her best intentions, her tears of happiness spilled over.

'Glorious!' Charlie leapt to his feet, crossed the room and swept her up in his arms and then swung her around, before returning her to the floor and kissing her soundly on the lips.

'You look wonderful,' he said, looking down at her, his own eyes glistening. He wiped away a tear running down her cheek with his thumb. 'It's so good to see you!' Charlie pulled her close and held her tight.

Gloria closed her eyes and leaned her head against Charlie's chest where she inhaled the salty smell of the sea on his thick sailor's jumper.

'I'll leave you two to have some time together,' Sylvia said.

Gloria opened her eyes and smiled at the older woman. 'He's definitely my Charlie.'

Sylvia chuckled. 'I can see that and you're most welcome to stay here, Charlie. I don't want to hear any more talk of you needing to find a room to lodge in.'

'Thank you,' Charlie said. 'I appreciate that.'

'Thank you for these.' Sylvia held up a box tied with a red ribbon. 'I've never had chocolates from New York before. It will be a new experience for me and such a treat.'

Left alone, Charlie led Gloria over to an armchair, sat down and pulled her onto his lap. 'How are you, Glorious?'

'All the better for seein' you. I can 'ardly believe you're 'ere.'

'You have me for two whole days. I need to leave on Wednesday morning to be back, ready to sail on Thursday.

Until then, we've got the chance to spend Christmas together.' His green eyes held Gloria's.

She nodded and took one of his big hands in hers, entwining their fingers. 'We'll make the most of every single second.'

'How's this little one?' Charlie laid his free hand on Gloria's swollen belly, laughing as the baby responded with a sharp kick.

'Good and it's a fine dancer in the middle of the night sometimes. I can't wait to meet 'im or 'er next year and have a child to cluck over again. I miss our children I…' Her voice wavered.

'And they miss their ma, too. They told me so and send you lots of love and hugs.'

Gloria frowned. 'What do you mean, *they told* you so?'

'I've been to Devon.' Charlie grinned. 'I went to see the children first so I could check they're 'appy for you. And they are. They ain't 'alf grown as well.'

She stared at her husband for a few moments, tears filling her eyes again. 'You've seen them?'

'Yes. I left them last night to come 'ere. They're fine, Glorious, 'onestly. The two sisters they live with treat them like their grandchildren. They couldn't 'ave wished for a better billet. Our children are in safe hands there, I promise you. I've got letters, drawings and presents for you from them in my kit bag.'

Tears ran down Gloria's cheeks as she smiled at her darling husband. 'Hearing that and knowin' you've visited them and checked they are well and 'appy for yourself… it means the world to me. Thank you.'

'I know you worry about 'em and miss 'em.' Charlie took her in his arms, and she leaned against him and let out a deep, heartfelt sigh.

'What's that for?'

'Because I'm 'appy and relaxed and 'ave got the best Christmas present ever.'

Charlie laughed, the deep sonorous sound resonating through his chest. 'So have I. Happy Christmas Glorious!'

CHAPTER 19

Monday 25th December – Christmas Day

Hettie loved singing and especially Christmas carols. Since she'd first learned the tunes and words as a child, they'd been part and parcel of each festive season. Now she only had to hear the introductory notes of a carol, and it filled her with a festive glow. This Christmas afternoon, Hettie was sharing the joy of singing the age-old songs with people who'd become her family. Prue and Alice had arrived here a short while ago, leaving Victor at home as he still refused to see Edwin, even at Christmas. Both Prue and Alice were wholeheartedly joining in along with everyone else at Rookery House as Edwin played the piano.

The combination of carols, the crackle from the roaring fire under the mantlepiece draped with holly and ivy, the pine-scented Christmas tree festooned with glass baubles reflecting the firelight, all combined with good company, made Hettie's heart swell. This time last year, she had been

exhausted after a marathon cooking session making a Christmas meal for both the servants and the Campbell-Gryces. She wouldn't have had any energy left to sing or play the parlour games that they had planned for later, after tea. This year was different, and Hettie was enjoying herself. She caught Thea's eye, and they smiled affectionately at each other.

They were halfway through *Silent Night* when Reuben's dog, Bess, barked from the kitchen, warning them that someone had arrived. The visitor might have knocked on the back door, but it would have had been impossible to hear over the singing.

'That must be Gloria.' Hettie slipped out as the others carried on.

Hettie was greeted by Bess as she went into the kitchen. The dog came bounding over and then rushed to the back door, giving another brief bark, before sitting quietly waiting to see who'd come to visit.

'Merry Christmas!' Hettie said as she opened the door. It surprised her to see that Gloria wasn't on her own.

'Merry Christmas!' Gloria beamed at her. 'I 'ope you don't mind, but I've brought my husband with me. Charlie, this is my dear friend, Hettie.'

He stepped forward and held out his hand. 'I'm pleased to meet you, Hettie. Thank you for helping my Glorious... Gloria. She's told me 'ow you've supported her since she got 'ere and especially in the past few weeks. I appreciate it.'

'It's good to meet you, too, Charlie.' Hettie shook his large hand. 'It's been a pleasure getting to know Gloria. Come on in. We're having a sing song so your talent will be welcome, Gloria.'

'You should 'ear Charlie,' Gloria said as she took off her coat. 'He's got a lovely deep baritone.'

'When did you arrive?' Hettie asked, taking Charlie's overcoat and hanging it up on a peg with Gloria's.

'Yesterday. I wanted it to be a surprise.' He smiled at his wife, who was glowing.

'It was that all right. And he bought me this dress from New York.' Gloria twirled round, the skirt of her new silk, peacock-blue dress swirling outwards. 'But by far the best thing is 'aving Charlie with me for a while. The best Christmas present I could *ever* wish for.' Gloria put her arm through Charlie's and gave him a loving smile, which he returned, before throwing his arm around her and hugging her to him.

'I'm delighted for you both,' Hettie said, thinking how wonderful it was to see her friend so happy. 'Come on through and I'll introduce you to everyone.'

Gloria was right, Hettie thought, when they started to sing once more after introductions had been made — Charlie had a fine baritone which along with Gloria's superb voice, was a fabulous addition to the swell of singing mingling in harmony, filling the sitting room with music. They'd moved on from carols to popular songs, and the jaunty, uplifting words and tune of *You are my Sunshine* sent a shiver of delight dancing down Hettie's spine.

~

'Do you think this will be enough?' Prue asked, arranging the slices of bread that she'd buttered in an attractive arrangement on the plate.

'If we run out, we can always cut and butter some more.' Hettie placed the final mince pie on top of a pyramid of pies and stepped back to survey the kitchen table where she, Prue and Thea had been preparing the Christmas Day tea. 'I'm not

sure how hungry anyone is after our enormous meal earlier, but we need to have something.'

'There's plenty to choose from.' Thea took blue and white plates from the dresser and stacked them at one end of the table.

Hettie nodded. 'Everyone can help themselves to what they want. I think that's everything.' Her eyes scanned over the food, ticking off each item she'd planned – the bread and butter, cold meats, chutneys, pickled onions and pickled red cabbage, and mince pies. 'We need the Christmas cake. I nearly forgot.'

'I'll fetch it,' Thea said, heading to the pantry. 'I'm looking forward to having a slice.'

'Let's hope it's turned out well,' Hettie said when Thea returned a few moments later with the cake, which had been stored in the pantry maturing since Hettie had made it back in November. She'd fed it occasionally with a couple of spoonfuls of brandy, so it should now be rich and moist. And she'd decorated it with white icing the week before, thinking that it might be a long time until she'd be able to bake another Christmas cake like this.

'Your Christmas cakes are always delicious, Hettie,' Prue said. 'Even though I use your recipe, mine never taste as good as yours!'

'This will be the last of its kind for a while, with rationing coming in,' Hettie said, thoughtfully. 'But whatever happens, I'll do my best as always.'

'I'm sure you will,' said Thea.

Hettie smiled. 'Right, I'll cut some slices and then we'll be ready to call the others in for their tea.' She plunged the knife into the cake but halted as a memory flashed into her mind of the morning in Barker's grocery shop in early December.

'Are you all right?' Thea asked, a concerned look on her face.

Hettie nodded. 'Yes. Cutting into the cake just reminded me of how I felt when I heard that the Campbell-Gryce's new cook hadn't yet made the cakes at the Hall. How much it unsettled me and prompted me to do something about it.'

Thea put her hand on Hettie's arm, her eyes dancing with warmth. 'I'm pleased you did. You've turned a Christmas that was strange and difficult for many, into something joyful and memorable.'

'The Christmas party was a triumph!' Prue said.

'I'm so glad I had that shake-up in Barker's,' Hettie told them in a heartfelt voice. 'It has made my first Christmas here at Rookery House that much more special.' She smiled at her two dear friends. 'Merry Christmas to us all!'

Dear Reader,

I hope you enjoyed reading *A Wartime Christmas at Rookery House.* It was a delight to write and a chance to spend time with Hettie and Gloria, getting to know them and their backgrounds better. They will of course be returning in more Rookery House books in the future!

I love to hear from readers – it is one of the greatest joys of being a writer – so do please get in touch. You can contact me through my website www.rosiehendry.com or via my Facebook page Rosie Hendry Books, Twitter @hendry_rosie or follow me on Instagram @rosiehendryauthor. Subscribing to my newsletter is the best way to keep up with all my latest book news – you can do this on my website.

If you have time and would like to share your thoughts about this book, do please leave a star rating or review. I appreciate each one and it's wonderful to hear what you think of the story. It helps me with my writing knowing what readers like and encourages new readers to try my books. Thank you!

With my warmest wishes,

Rosie

IF YOU ENJOYED A WARTIME CHRISTMAS AT ROOKERY HOUSE...

It would be wonderful if you could spare a few minutes to leave a star rating, or write a review, at the retailer where you bought this book.

Reviews don't need to be long – a sentence or two is absolutely fine. They make a huge difference to authors, helping us know what readers think of our books and what they particularly enjoy. Reviews also help other readers discover new books to try for themselves.

You might also tell family and friends you think would enjoy this book.

Thank you!

Read on for the beginning of
A Wartime Welcome at Rookery House
an uplifting family saga that celebrates friendship and community in wartime Britain.

England, October 1940

When VAD nurse **Evie** narrowly avoids being killed in an air raid during the London Blitz, it propels her to make a life-changing decision to break free of her troubled and unhappy life. She escapes to the Norfolk countryside to start afresh, with a job at the newly opened Great Plumstead Hall hospital, and a wonderful new home at Rookery House.

CHAPTER ONE

London, October 1940

Genevieve Hamilton-Jones hurried out of the hospital and headed towards the nearest bus stop. It was half past six and not long before tonight's blackout time when the city would be plunged into darkness. She was later leaving her shift than usual as there'd been several admissions to the ward this afternoon. Now, with her feet throbbing after being on them for hours, all she wanted was to get home before the air-raid siren went off, as it had every night since the Blitz started last month. Night after night, the bombers had returned to pound London with high explosives and incendiary bombs. It was a wonder there was anything left standing, she thought.

Looking over her shoulder, Genevieve spotted a red double-decker approaching and luckily it had her route number on the front. She picked up her pace, running the last few yards along the pavement, reaching the stop as the bus pulled up at the kerb with a choking blast of exhaust fumes.

Climbing on board, she made her way to an empty seat next to a young woman on the lower deck.

'Just made it!' Genevieve smiled at the woman as she stowed her small, brown leather suitcase under the seat before sitting down.

The woman returned her smile. 'Are you going somewhere?'

Genevieve frowned. 'I beg your pardon.'

'Your suitcase.' The woman pointed to where Genevieve had put her case, as the bus pulled out into the traffic with a noisy rev of its engine. 'Sorry, I'm being nosy, only I'm off tomorrow myself. I've got to pack my suitcase when I get home. I'm that excited I can hardly wait!' Her brown eyes danced with happiness as she looked at Genevieve.

'No, I'm not going anywhere apart from home. I carry my uniform in the case, I always change out of it before I leave for home.'

Genevieve knew it wasn't usual to do that – none of the other nurses did – but in her case, it was wise to do so. She couldn't risk being seen wearing it out of the hospital.

'Are you in one of the services?' the woman asked.

Genevieve shook her head. 'No, I'm a nurse. I've just finished my shift.'

'I'll be going into uniform myself tomorrow. I can't wait to wear it and I will be so proud to be seen in it. Don't you want to wear your nurse's uniform out of the hospital – I've seen other nurses wearing theirs?'

'I prefer not to,' Genevieve said matter of factly. She didn't want to explain and was relieved that at that moment the conductor appeared, and they each bought a ticket.

'What are you going to do?' Genevieve asked once the conductor had moved on.

'I'm joining the WAAF!' The woman beamed. 'Today was

my last day at my boring office job. I'm so looking forward to getting away and doing something more exciting instead. I'm reporting for my basic training tomorrow, and once that's over I don't know what I'll do, depends on what they think I'd be best at.' She spoke quickly, her excitement bubbling over. 'I fancy being a driver – I've always wanted to learn to drive.'

'Good luck with it, I hope you get your wish, it's important to do what you enjoy.' Genevieve understood the woman's enthusiasm for her new career, and the joy that came from doing what your heart desired. It had taken her so long and much careful planning to become a nurse and now it was absolutely the best thing in her life. It was her secret and she loved it.

'Thanks! John, he's my fiancé, is already in the RAF – he works on planes, keeping them fit to fly. He's as pleased as punch that I'll be a WAAF. We might get lucky and be stationed in the same place.' The woman paused as she opened her wine-red handbag, which was resting on her lap, and took out a photograph, holding it for Genevieve to see. 'This is him.'

Genevieve looked at the photograph of a smiling man dressed in RAF uniform. 'He looks very nice.'

'Oh, he is! He's lovely, I'm very lucky.' The woman gently traced her fiancé's face with the tip of her finger before putting the photograph back in her handbag. 'Have you got a chap in the services?'

Before Genevieve could reply, the air-raid siren suddenly began its eerie wail over the London rooftops and was met by groans from several of the other passengers sitting nearby.

'Can't they leave us alone for one bleedin' night?' an elderly man moaned, loudly. His comment was greeted by nods and sounds of agreement from other passengers.

'The bombers are early tonight!' the woman said as the bus slowed and pulled over to the side of the road. 'Nightly air raids are something I will *definitely* not miss. I'm hoping to be sent somewhere where I can get a whole night's sleep in my bed and not have to traipse out to an air-raid shelter.'

'Everybody out!' the conductor shouted from the back of the bus as it came to a juddering halt. 'Make your way to the nearest underground station. As quick as you can – if you please!'

The passengers stood up and filed off the bus and Genevieve followed along with the woman. Most of them turned left and hurried down the street, and she was about to do the same when someone grabbed her arm.

'It'll be quicker to go through there,' the woman said, pointing to the opening of an alleyway between two buildings a little further along the street from where the bus had stopped. 'I live not far away from here and know this area like the back of my hand.' She looked up at the sky which had faded from blue to an opaque grey as dusk fell, frowning as the familiar droning of planes' engines grew louder. 'Come on, those bombers aren't far off, we need to hurry.'

'Lead the way.' Genevieve followed the woman into the shadowy alley which cut through to the street running parallel to the one where the bus had stopped. She'd only gone a few yards in when she suddenly realised that she'd left her suitcase on the bus. She halted. 'I need to go back – I've left my case. I need it, it's got my uniform in…'

The woman stopped and turned to look back at her. 'Go on then, but you'd better be quick. I'll save you a space to sit in the underground if you like. I'll see you below in a little bit, don't be long – the bombers are coming!'

'I'll be as fast as I can.' Genevieve ran back along the alley,

out onto the street and returned to where the red double-decker was parked. The bus conductor and driver were about to leave and head for shelter themselves. 'I've left my suitcase on the bus – can I get it, please? It's got my nurse's uniform inside it, and I need it for work.'

'Go on then, hurry up!' The conductor rolled his eyes.

'Thank you.' She gave him a quick smile and climbed aboard, quickly retrieved her case from under the seat and had just stepped out of the bus onto the pavement when a whistling scream filled the air, growing louder by the second.

'Get down!' the conductor roared, grabbing hold of Genevieve's arm, yanking her to the ground as he went down beside her, followed by the driver close by.

Landing on the hard pavement with a thud, Genevieve was about to protest at his rough manhandling when there was a loud bang as a bomb exploded nearby. Instinctively ducking her head, she squeezed her eyes shut and covered her ears with her hands as she lay on the ground. Genevieve was aware of a wave of turbulence and falling debris. Dirt and dust pattered down, and an acrid smell of cordite filled the air. She knew that smell from other raids – it was the stench of bombs.

'You all right?' The bus conductor's voice was gruff beside her.

Genevieve opened her eyes, brushing her hands over her dusty face. 'I think so.' She sat up and looked at the conductor and driver, both of whose dark uniforms were now covered in grey dust. 'Where's the bomb? Where did it land?' She peered around her and miraculously apart from another layer of dust and dirt on the London street, there didn't appear to be much damage.

'Must have landed in that alleyway,' the driver said,

scrambling to his feet. 'Lucky it did – if it had fallen out here in the street, it would have been a whole different story. Come on, we need to get to a shelter before any more land here.' He looked up, grimacing at the sight of bombers passing over, high up above the city, dark silhouettes against the fading sky.

The alleyway! Genevieve had been there only moments before and had left the young woman there. Had she reached the end and the safety of the street on the other side before the bomb hit?

Genevieve staggered to her feet, her legs struggling to keep her upright as her bones seemed to have turned to rubber. 'I need to go and see... she might be injured.'

'Who?' the conductor asked.

'The woman who I sat next to on the bus. She knew the alley was a shortcut to the underground, we were both going that way but then I remembered I'd forgotten my suitcase.' She glanced down at her case which lay abandoned on the pavement, the brown leather now coated with a film of dust like she was herself.

'We'll go and look – you stay here.' The conductor glanced at the driver who nodded in agreement.

'But...' Genevieve protested.

'Stay there!' the driver's voice brooked no argument.

She did as they asked, watching as they walked the short distance to the alleyway and went in. Her stomach knotted as she waited for their return. Trying to distract herself, Genevieve looked around and noticed a handbag lying on the pavement a few yards further along the street. She hurried over, picked it up and brushing off some of the covering of gritty dirt, saw it was wine-red coloured – like the one the woman had. Could it be hers? She undid the clasp and opened it – inside, along with a purse, powder compact and lipstick,

was the photograph of the RAF fiancé Genevieve had seen earlier. There was no doubt that it belonged to the woman from the bus. It must have been blown out onto the street in the blast, she thought, in which case its owner must be in the alleyway, probably injured and needing first aid.

Genevieve hurried towards the entrance to the alley and met the conductor and driver coming out.

'Is she there? I found her handbag.' She held up the bag.

'No one's in there, just some rubble from the bomb blast,' the conductor said. 'And we checked the street at the other end. She's not there either.'

Genevieve frowned. 'But her handbag's here, it was blown out.'

'Oy! You should be in a shelter!' a loud voice shouted.

She turned to see an air-raid warden hurrying towards them, his face scowling under his steel helmet.

'There was a woman in the alley where the bomb fell. This is her bag, the bomb blast must have blown it out,' Genevieve quickly explained.

'But she's not there now,' the driver added. 'No sign of her.'

The air-raid warden frowned. 'Wait there.'

He hurried into the alleyway and returned a few moments later. 'You sure she was there, ain't gone out the other end?'

'We checked,' the conductor said. 'She's vanished.'

The air-raid warden nodded, his face solemn. 'Must have been a direct hit then.' He sighed. 'Nothing left of her…'

Genevieve stared at him, feeling as if a bucket of icy water had been thrown at her. 'You mean she's *completely gone*… just like that?'

The warden nodded. 'It happens sometimes – there's no body left. I'm sorry for your loss.'

'I didn't really know her, I just sat next to her on the bus. You'd better take this.' She held out the handbag to him. 'It will

have her details in, her name…' Her voice cracked as she suddenly realised she didn't even know the woman's name.

'I'll see to it so that her family are informed,' the warden said kindly, taking the bag. 'Now get to a shelter, all of you, as quick as you can.'

Genevieve couldn't recall how she'd got to the underground station. She must have retrieved her suitcase from where she'd dropped it when the conductor dragged her to the ground. Now sitting on the floor, her case beside her, she leaned back against the cold, tiled wall of the platform and stared around her at all the people settling down for the night. Many were well prepared for a long stay having brought blankets and food parcels with them – no doubt having fled down here often during the past few weeks. Most of them were civilians but there were a few people in uniform too.

Genevieve took some slow, steady breaths to try to calm her pounding heart, her body shivering with shock from what had happened. Sitting here in this stuffy atmosphere that smelled of mouldy bread wasn't helping, but it was safer down here than outside in the streets. A dull crump from above echoed through the platform sending a shower of dust raining down from the ceiling. The raid was still on, and it might be many hours yet before the all-clear sounded.

A sob welled up inside Genevieve and she squeezed her hands into tight fists to try to get a firm grip on her emotions. It was hard to comprehend how the young woman, who'd been so full of excitement and joy at the prospect of her new life, had been snuffed out in an instant. Gone… just like that. With nothing left of her for her family and fiancé to bury. The

only thing that had survived the bomb was her handbag which had been thrown clear in the blast.

That could have been Genevieve's fate too. If she hadn't left her suitcase on the bus and gone back for it, then she'd have been there in the alley when that bomb had hit. A moment's forgetfulness leaving her case behind had saved her life. It hadn't been a conscious decision, just simply forgetting it was under her seat in the hurry to get off the bus. That small action had made all the difference between life and death.

Genevieve closed her eyes, wrapping her arms around her body, hugging herself tightly to quell her shaking. Anyone's life could be extinguished in a moment in this war; you didn't need to be a soldier off fighting on the front line in a foreign land to be killed. It was a sobering thought, and after what she'd just witnessed it felt like a wake-up call. *There but for the grace of God go I*, as the saying went. And but for her leaving her suitcase on the bus, Genevieve's life would probably have ended today. It was as if she'd been given another chance, another opportunity to live her life, but this time the way she wanted to. She should grab it with both hands, squeezing out every last drop of enjoyment and doing something worthwhile.

Up to now, her life had largely been one dominated by others – twenty-two years of being told what to do by other people, their choices mapping out most of how she lived. Genevieve might now have a job that she loved, but it had to be carried out in secrecy and with stealth, for fear of what might happen if the truth was discovered. She was living a half-life. Did she want that to carry on?

Her stomach tightly knotted at the thought of what her future might hold. What would her life be after the war ended? Did she want it to return to how it had been before? The answer was an emphatic, no. Life was precious and

should not be wasted living in such a way – what she'd witnessed today had shown her that. So where *did* her future lie?

A woman started singing further down the platform, a sweet lilting song and others joined in too. Genevieve opened her eyes and looked along the crowded platform, tears welling up as the notes filled the air, bringing with them a sense of hopefulness and joy despite the circumstances that had driven the people to shelter below ground.

She needed more joy in her life, she realised, to embrace the whole of it with as much enthusiasm as the young woman on the bus had done. But that was impossible if Genevieve continued to live as she had been doing. She had to make a *change*, she needed to escape – but how? And did she even dare?

The answer suddenly came to her. She could pretend that she had been in that alley when the bomb had landed and had suffered the same fate as the young woman. Genevieve Hamilton-Jones could have ceased to exist, disappearing with the detonation of a high explosive bomb, leaving nothing but her handbag to show that she'd been there. There would be no body to identify her: just her handbag with its identity card in, the key to her flat and her purse. She could walk away, start again and no one would know. She could live as Evie Jones, the name she used at the hospital to protect her real identity and keep her secret safe.

The idea of escaping but with no one knowing that she had was exhilarating. The possibility of tasting complete freedom filled her with joy, gave her a sense of lightness. For the first time in her life, she could be in charge of her destiny – she could pursue her dreams without fear of reprisal or punishment.

It would be a lie, though, breaking the law even, a voice in

her head reminded her. But the alternative of more years of the same filled her with dread. She couldn't, she wouldn't, go on living like this any more – today had shown her that life was simply far too precious to waste. But did she have the courage to break away?

CHAPTER TWO

Norfolk – one week later

Thea Thornton turned the van off the road, passing between the two gate houses and onto the long drive leading down to Great Plumstead Hall. She was on Women's Voluntary Service duty, transporting equipment needed for establishing the Hall in its new role as a Red Cross Military Hospital for convalescent servicemen.

She had swapped her usual WVS uniform dress for a more practical pair of the service's green overalls, replacing the service's felt hat with a red and white polka dot scarf tied around her dark brown bobbed, curly hair, with the bow on top. She might not look so smart, but this outfit was far more suitable for hauling boxes around like a removal man. Today's work made a change from driving the WVS canteen which was a regular job that Thea did each week, and with the hospital due to open in a few days' time, they needed all the help they could get.

A brisk, cold wind sent golden leaves spiralling down to the ground as she drove through the avenue of mature beech trees lining the drive, and the lowering grey clouds were threatening rain. Thea hoped it would hold off until they'd got the van emptied of its load.

Approaching the Hall, which was built of honey-coloured stone, she drove across the wide sweep of gravel that lay in front of the house and pulled up outside the porticoed front door, her delivery not having to go around the back as normal ones would. Now the Hall was being converted into a hospital, things were altering here just as they were in the village. War had brought so many changes to Great Plumstead and not all of them for the worse, Thea thought. It had shaken things up, bringing new people to the village starting with the evacuee expectant mothers' arrival last September – and that in her opinion was a good thing.

Switching off the engine, she got out and went around to the back of the van and was opening the doors ready to begin the task of unloading when the familiar figure of her older brother Reuben came out of the front door ready to help. At fifty-one-years-old, eight years older than herself, his brown hair was threaded with silver, giving him a distinguished look, which suited him, Thea thought.

'Hello.' Thea greeted him with a warm smile. 'How are things coming along?'

'The hospital beds and other furniture arrived this morning,' Reuben said, reaching into the van and taking hold of some boxes. 'It's beginning to look like a hospital, but there's still a lot of work to do before it's up and running.'

Reuben normally worked on Great Plumstead Hall's estate, usually on the farms, but for the past week he'd been brought in to help with the many preparations needed – from taking paintings off the walls, to constructing protective wooden

casings around marble pillars in rooms that were to be used as wards. The wear and tear of using the building as a hospital would be much greater than that of living in it as a home. The owners, Lord and Lady Campbell-Gryce, wanted to protect their home and belongings as much as possible.

Thea picked up a couple of boxes and followed Reuben towards the Hall.

'This lot has to be piled up in the hallway until they can be unpacked. Matron's strict orders,' Reuben informed her as they went inside. He carefully put his boxes down on one side of the wide hallway on the chequered black and white tiled floor.

Thea placed her boxes beside his and hearing voices coming from one of the rooms leading off the hall, went to the door and looked inside.

'That was the dining room and is now being turned into a ward,' Reuben said, coming to stand beside her.

Inside, a portly woman in a nurse's uniform with a starched white veil on her head, and a prickly air of authority about her, was ordering several young nurses around as they made up the beds.

'That's Matron Reed,' Reuben whispered, turning his head towards Thea. 'Best keep clear of her! Come on, those boxes won't unload themselves.'

It took nearly fifteen minutes to transfer all the boxes from the van into the hall. Some were heavier than others, and from reading the label on each one to see what was inside, Thea saw that their contents ranged from medical supplies to recreation items to keep the patients occupied. All of it essential equipment for the running of the hospital and the successful convalescence of the patients, both physically and mentally.

'That lot's going to take a while to unpack and sort out,' Thea said placing her final box down and standing back to

survey the large pile of boxes in the hallway. 'Setting up a hospital from scratch is no quick task.'

'You're absolutely right about that!' A plummy voice said from behind Thea.

She turned around and saw the poised figure of Lady Campbell-Gryce approaching across the hall, a notebook in her hand. As always, her Ladyship was immaculately turned out. Her short wavy brown hair carefully styled, and her silk dress, one of Marianne's designs Thea noticed, was creaseless.

'Good afternoon, Miss Thornton.' Lady Campbell-Gryce greeted her. 'Thank you so much for helping us by bringing the stores. And yes, there's certainly a lot to be done if we are to be ready for our first intake of patients next week. Reuben has been marvellous making the adaptations to the rooms for us.' She gave Reuben an appreciative smile. 'Although it seems odd to see my dining room being turned into a ward.'

Lady Campbell-Gryce glanced in the doorway of the newly created ward, where Matron Reed spotted her and nodded her head in acknowledgement. Her Ladyship returned Matron's nod, and then turned to face Thea. 'But it's all coming together and I'm sure it will be absolutely fine. There is one problem though, which I'm hoping you might be able to help me with, or perhaps know someone else who can.'

'What's that?' Thea asked.

'We've unexpectedly been allocated another VAD nurse. She's arriving next week but, unfortunately, we don't have a billet for her. Some of our nurses are billeted here, in the old servants' rooms, and others are lodging with Rosalind Platten at The Grange in the village. You've probably heard that Rosalind's taken on the voluntary role of Quartermaster of our hospital, and has provided billets for some of the nurses as well – but sadly she doesn't have room for another one. Is

there any chance that you could billet the new nurse at Rookery House?'

Thea considered for a moment. There was of course the room that Anna – a German refugee – had recently vacated having gone to teach at a boarding school. Anna hoped to come back to Rookery House in the holidays, but for the rest of the time it would stand empty... with a nurse needing accommodation, it would be wrong of her not to offer it.

'Yes, I could. Which day should I expect her?'

'On Monday, ready to start work here on Tuesday.' Lady Campbell-Gryce flicked through her notebook, turning over pages until she found what she was looking for. 'Her name is Evie Jones. I can find out what time she's due to arrive and let you know.' She reached out and touched Thea's arm. 'Thank you for your help, both today and with lodgings, it's very much appreciated. Right, I need a word with Matron.' And with a nod of her head, Lady Campbell-Gryce went into the ward.

'Looks like you've got yourself another lodger then. Bet you didn't expect that when you agreed to ferry supplies to the hospital did you?' Reuben chuckled.

Thea turned to her brother, her gaze meeting his. 'No, but it's the right thing to do. Think where else she could have ended up, perhaps even lodging at Prue's and having to live with the dreadful Victor!' She knew her sister Prue would have been welcoming, but certainly not her unpleasant husband.

Reuben grimaced. 'Then you have saved this Evie Jones from a nasty experience.'

CHAPTER THREE

Prue Wilson checked her list and was relieved to see that there was just one more stop to make. It had been a long, tiring and very trying afternoon and she was feeling all of her thirty-nine years. She was both frustrated and disappointed to discover the lack of empathy that some villagers still had for others, not caring for those who'd faced worse troubles than any that had fallen upon the residents of Great Plumstead so far in this war.

She'd hoped that after having the evacuee mothers arrive last September, who'd successfully settled into village life, more villagers would have softened their attitudes to helping strangers. But there were still some hard-nosed individuals who'd never have agreed to what Prue asked of them if she didn't have the weight of the law on her side as local billeting officer.

Mounting her bicycle, she headed for her sister Thea's home at Rookery House, where she wouldn't have to battle to get what she needed.

'You're just in time for a cuppa.' Hettie gave a welcoming smile as Prue went into the cosy kitchen of Rookery House. 'Thea's just got back and is upstairs getting changed, then we're going to have some fresh-baked scones if you'd like to join us.'

'Oh, that sounds wonderful, thank you.' Prue smiled at the older woman whom she'd known all her life. Hettie had been a good friend of Prue's mother and as good as any aunt to her. She'd worked as cook at Great Plumstead Hall until her retirement last year and anything she baked was always delicious. Tea and one of Hettie's scones would be a most welcome antidote to Prue's difficult afternoon.

'Sit yourself down, you look like you could do with it. What's happened?' Hettie asked putting another cup on the table and pouring out a cup of tea from the large brown teapot which was covered with a colourful knitted tea-cosy.

Prue pulled out a chair at the scrubbed wooden kitchen table and sat down. 'It's been one of those days.' She sighed, smoothing down her ash-blonde hair which was beginning to come loose from its roll at the nape of her neck. 'There are some people in this village who never cease to amaze me. Being billeting officer is *not* one of my favourite roles.'

'Are more evacuees expected then?' Hettie's blue eyes were concerned behind her round glasses.

'Yes, mothers and children who've been bombed out of their London homes. Can you imagine it… your home gone just like that? And with it happening to so many people now, there's a desperate shortage of alternative accommodation for anyone to move into in London.' Prue added some milk from the jug to her tea and stirred it in with a teaspoon. 'That's even if you wanted to stay there with your children with all the

bombing going on. If it was me, I'd want to get my children to safety, go as far away from there as I could.'

Hettie passed Prue a plate with a freshly baked scone covered with home-made butter and jam on top. 'Have you got enough billets organised?'

'Thank you. I'm not sure, it depends how many evacuees we're sent. It's always better to have too many billets available than not enough. I'm hoping that Thea will agree to have some.' Prue took a bite of scone enjoying the delicious combination of butter, raspberry jam and Hettie's fine baking.

'Have some what?' Thea asked coming into the kitchen. 'What good works have you been up to today, Prue?' She teased, her blue eyes twinkling.

'Some evacuees,' Prue said. 'I'm here in my role as village billeting officer. I've been told to expect some mothers and children from London any day now and was hoping you'd be able to give a home to some.'

Thea sat down at the table opposite Prue and poured herself a cup of tea from the teapot, then added some milk. 'Well, I would have, but I'm afraid I don't have the room any more.'

Hettie frowned. 'What about Anna's room? She's not using it now that she's away, and when she comes back in the school holidays, we can set up a temporary bedroom for her in the dining room.'

'If you'd asked me this morning, Prue, then I'd have said yes, but I've already promised the room to somebody else,' Thea explained. 'I've been asked to billet one of the nurses from the hospital and agreed to do it. I can't go back on my word.'

'Fair enough.' Prue nodded. 'As billeting officer, I heartily applaud you doing your bit for whoever you take in.' She gave

her sister an approving smile. 'A nurse for the hospital is just as important as an evacuee mother and children.'

'Who asked you?' Hettie asked.

'Lady Campbell-Gryce when I was delivering equipment to the Hall. All the other nurses are billeted either in the old servants' rooms at the Hall or at the Grange with Rosalind as she's the new Quartermaster. They're one bed short for the new nurse who's arriving on Monday – so her Ladyship asked me.' Thea took a sip of tea. 'Evie Jones is her name.'

Hettie nodded, her curly grey hair bobbing around her head. 'Well, it will be good to have her here, I miss Anna and like having a full house.'

'How's Anna getting on in her new job?' Prue asked.

'Very well,' Thea said. 'She's enjoying it and happy to be teaching again. After all she went through being imprisoned in Holloway and then on the Isle of Man, she deserves to enjoy her life and be doing something she loves.'

'I'm glad to hear she's doing well.' Prue knew what a difficult time it had been for Thea after German-born Anna had been arrested and imprisoned for being an enemy alien, despite being a Jewish refugee from Nazi oppression. Her sister had tirelessly campaigned to get Anna released and had finally succeeded but only after Anna had endured months of imprisonment.

'I wonder what this Evie will be like,' Hettie pondered. 'I hope she'll fit in nicely with us.'

'I'm sure Evie will soon settle and fit in well.' Thea smiled at Hettie reassuringly. 'So will you be having some more evacuees?' Thea directed her question at Prue.

'Of course, we've got two spare rooms with Edwin and Jack no longer at home.' A dart of anxiety for her sons jabbed Prue's heart as both of her sons were off doing their bit for the war: Jack in the Royal Engineers stationed in the North of

England, and Edwin working for the Friends Ambulance Unit in London and in the thick of the Blitz. They were officially her *step*-sons, but she loved them as much as if she'd given birth to them, thinking and worrying about them both every day.

'And what does Victor say about that?' Hettie asked, her eyebrows raised behind her glasses.

Prue tapped her fingers on the side of her teacup, her gaze meeting the older woman's. 'He doesn't know yet, and no doubt he'll complain about it, but he can't stop me having them. He'll just have to like it or lump it!'

Thea and Hettie glanced at each other and laughed.

'Good for you.' Thea reached across the table and laid her hand on Prue's arm. 'You don't want to take any nonsense from him.'

'Don't worry, I won't be.' Prue's eyes met Thea's, a silent message passing between them.

HEAR MORE FROM ROSIE

Want to keep up to date with Rosie's latest releases?

Sign up to receive her monthly newsletter at her website.
www.rosiehendry.com

Subscribers get Rosie's newsletter delivered to their inbox and are always the first to know about the latest books, as well as getting exclusive behind the scenes news, plus reader competitions.

You can unsubscribe at any time and your email will never be shared with anyone else.

ACKNOWLEDGMENTS

Thank you to my wonder editor, Catriona Robb, cover designer, Andrew Brown and proof reader, Isobel, who all helped me bring the book together.

A big thank you to all the readers and bloggers who read and review my books, and keep in touch.

My dear writing friends are a great support and I appreciate their friendship, company, wise words and listening ears. A huge thank you especially to Pam Brooks, Victoria Connelly, Elaine Everest, Fiona Ford, Jean Fullerton, Jenni Keer, Lizzie Lamb, Clare Marchant, Heidi-Jo Swain, Claire Wade and Ian Wilfred.

Finally, thank you to David, who listens and supports me with all I do.

A sweet romance set on the gorgeous Scottish island of Orkney where family secrets unfold and second chances for love beckon...

At a career crossroads, twenty-something Laura Sinclair returns to Orkney to celebrate her grandmother, Ishbel's, seventieth birthday. Laura's visit becomes far more complicated than she'd anticipated when her plans to avoid her former love, Matt, fail disastrously as she runs into him on her first day back!

Turning seventy isn't going to stop strong-willed Ishbel Sinclair from taking chances in life, or love. Leaving the island on a secret, surprise visit to meet an old flame, her trip back-fires with a completely unexpected turn of events.

As Laura waits to find out which direction her career will take, can she face up to her rekindled feelings for Matt? And will Ishbel find the love that slipped through her fingers once before?

An uplifting island romance that will warm your heart and show you that it's never too late for a second chance at love.

ALSO BY ROSIE HENDRY

East End Angels novels

East End Angels

Secrets of the East End Angels

Christmas with the East End Angels

Victory for the East End Angels

Rookery House novels

The Mother's Day Club

The Mother's Day Victory

A Wartime Welcome at Rookery House

Rookery House novella

A Wartime Christmas at Rookery House

Standalone novel

Secrets and Promises

Standalone novellas

A Home from Home

Love on a Scottish Island

Rosie Hendry lived and worked in the USA before settling back in her home county of Norfolk, England, where she lives in a village by the sea with her family. She likes walking in nature, reading (of course) and when she has the time, even some dressmaking!

Rosie writes stories from the heart that are inspired by historical records, where gems of social history are often to be found. Her interest in the WWII era was sparked by her father's many tales of growing up at that time.

Rosie is the winner of the 2022 Romantic Novelists' Association (RNA) award for historical romantic sagas, with *The Mother's Day Club,* the first of her series set during wartime at Rookery House. Her novels set in the London Blitz, the *East End Angels* series, have been described as 'Historical fiction at its very best!'.

To find out more visit **www.rosiehendry.com**

Printed in Great Britain
by Amazon

13491234R00084

Lightning Source UK Ltd.
Milton Keynes UK
UKHW050201031220
374498UK00007BC/828

9 781916 115699